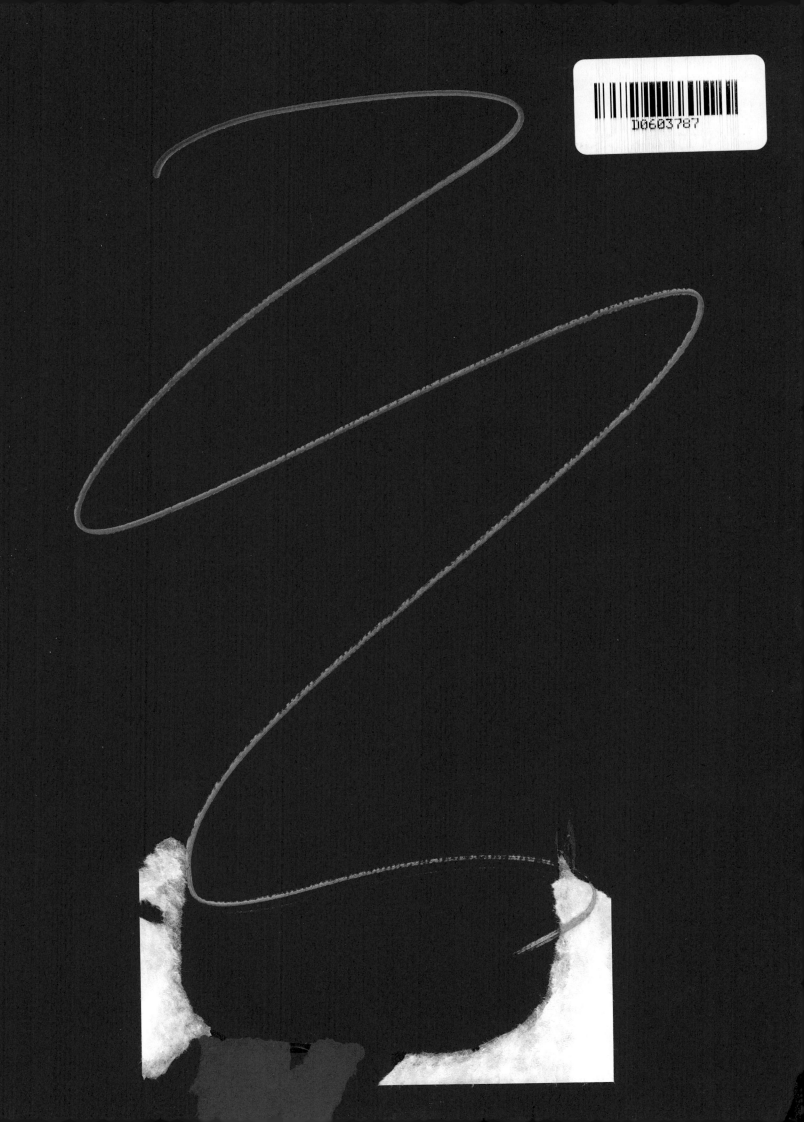

SHERLOCK HOLMES IN AMERICA

Sherlock Holmes Analyzes a Perfect Stranger

By JOHN T. McCUTCHEON

SHERLOCK HOLMES——"*Ah, a stranger whom I've never seen before.*"

"*How do you do, sir——I observe that you are in the coal trust; also that you have just had a narrow escape; that you have no children; that you were in a great hurry this morning; that you have been writing, and that you shaved with your left hand this morning. Are you going away on the afternoon or the evening train?*"

"*Why, this is simply marvelous, Mr. Holmes. Everything you've said is true. How in the world did you find out all these things about a man you've never heard of before?*"

"*By a very simple process of deduction. I can tell by your hands that you are in a trust, and I know it was the coal trust by the hungry way you looked at my purse there on the table, and by the fact that you glanced apprehensively around you as if expecting some one to hit you with a club. I knew that you had just had a narrow escape, by the fact that three bricks grazed you, and the brick dust is still on your coat. You have no children, for if you had you would have some consideration for poor people who have children. I knew that you expected to take a journey, because I understand the grand jury is in session. I also knew that you had shaved with your left hand because your face is cut, and there is ink on your right forefinger, showing that you were writing out an order to whoop the price of coal while shaving with your left. You were in a hurry, because you had time to have only one shoe polished. It's all very simple.*"

BILL BLACKBEARD

SHERLOCK HOLMES IN AMERICA

FOREWORD BY DEAN DICKENSHEET

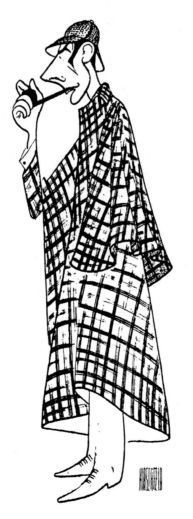

HARRY N. ABRAMS, INC., PUBLISHERS, NEW YORK

Half-title page: detail from a Hearst, and Alexander Film Corporation, advertisement in *Moving Picture World*, November 19, 1921.

Frontispiece: cartoon by John T. McCutcheon from the Chicago *Record-Herald* for January 16, 1903.

Title page: Al Hirschfeld's caricature of Paxton Whitehead as Holmes in *The Crucifer of Blood*, as published in the New York *Times*, January 5, 1979.

Copyright page: detail of a panel of *School Days* Sunday comic strip, by Clare Victor Dwiggins, November 19, 1909.

Contents page: Frederic Dorr Steele drawing for a San Francisco *Bulletin* Holmes-series advertisement, April 2, 1925.

Page facing foreword: detail of a sketch by Lee Conrey illustrating an article, "Sherlock Holmes: A Strange Figure in the Land of Ghosts," as seen in the San Francisco *Chronicle*, February 3, 1929.

Page 11: a sketch by Guy Hungerford that appeared in the book review column of *Judge* magazine for October 1, 1927.

Project Director: Margaret Kaplan
Editor: Donn Teal
Designer: Judith Michael

LIBRARY OF CONGRESS CATALOGING IN PUBLICATION DATA

Blackbeard, Bill. Sherlock Holmes in America.
1. Doyle, Arthur Conan, Sir, 1859-1930.—Characters—Sherlock Holmes.
2. Holmes, Sherlock (Fictitious character). I. Title.
PR4624.B5   823'.8   79-1133
ISBN 0-8109-1609-6

CONTENTS

Steele 1925

THE AMERICAN PROFILE OF SHERLOCK HOLMES
by Dean Dickensheet

There is no question that Sherlock Holmes is British, both by birth and residence, and—until his encounter with Professor Moriarty at Reichenbach Falls—by publication as well. True, *The Sign of the Four* had been commissioned, and first published, by *Lippincott's Magazine* of Philadelphia in February, 1890, but that periodical, though technically American, was then essentially trans-Atlantic in tone and much of its content.

A major change occurred, however, with the advent of the post-Reichenbach Holmes. Not in the sense of the notorious observation made by a Cornish boatman to Doyle that, after Reichenbach, Holmes "was never the same man again," but in the publishing of the narratives themselves. The British *Strand* appearances continued as before, of course, with the splendid and copious illustrations of Sidney Paget and his successors, but the *force majeure* behind the reappearance of Holmes in the stories that later made up *The Return of Sherlock Holmes* was so thoroughly American that one can appropriately visualize a team of exuberant Yankee editors, headed by P. F. Collier of *Collier's Weekly* himself, drawing Holmes up with a lavish financial rope, hand over hand, from the dread chasm below the Swiss falls.

There had, of course, been an obvious American thread in Watson's accounts of his famed mentor at all times, as early as the introduction of the classic duo in *A Study in Scarlet.* But now, in the stories of *The Return* and later, it grew even stronger—so much so that, four decades later, a Sherlockian who was also a multi-termed President of the United States theorized that Holmes had been reared in America. And Holmes's own dreams of a reuniting of Britain and America, as expressed in "The Noble Bachelor," demonstrate a firm link of interest on the part of the detective himself. But there is no doubt that Doyle's keen awareness that American money had in large part brought about the resurrection of Holmes (in the ensuing series of short stories, at least) led to the increased use of character origins and experiences, and references, which reflected his sense of a broad reading public to the west of Dingle Bay.

Certainly Americans returned the Doylean concern manyfold, in stunning illustrations and delightful parodies and pastiches, as well as in film and stage adaptations of the Sacred Writings that are among the best ever produced. Disputes still rage on the relative merits of the British illustrators—Paget predominating—and the American—principally Frederic Dorr Steele. In two fields of Holmesiana, however, the Americans have outpaced the British almost from the beginning: humorous writing and comic and journalistic art. Whether the reason for this lay in the greater irreverence of the "colonial" or in the need for continual attention to the vast American public thirst for the Master Detective in any form, the development of Sherlock Holmes as a figure frequently and variably accessible in popular art approximations was far more rapid in the States than in Britain. Curiously, however, America produced no equivalent of the direct imitations of Holmes in mass circulation periodicals that England encountered in the long-lived "Sexton Blake" series, begun by Harry Blythe in 1893; or that Germany (and other countries by means of translations) endured in the endless "Sherlock Holmes/Weltdetectiv" run of dime novels launched there in 1907. Perhaps the pre-existing abundance of cheap detective fiction in America, from Nick Carter to Old Sleuth (an abundance lacking in England and on the Continent), filled the mass reader's need for "more" of the Sherlockian excitement and fun.

In the same turn-of-the-century period when the United Kingdom had prominently enjoyed only *Punch* editor R.C. Lehman's short series about "Picklock Holes" and a year of weekly, anonymously authored episodes of "Chubb-lock Homes" in *Comic Cuts*, the Americans had relished numerous long and short works in both magazine and book form by Doyle's widely read stateside friend John Kendrick Bangs, as well as the beginning in the popular press of several decades of Gus Mager's comic strips, *Sherlocko the Monk* and *Hawkshaw the Detective*. In more isolated, single appearances, Holmes was burlesqued generally by the second string of British authors, such as Robert Barr and Frank Richardson (although Kenneth Grahame is the marked exception here, in his touching on the canon in *The Wind in the Willows*), while in America such major writers as Mark Twain and Bret Harte took on Holmes in grand style at some length.

Later, while burlesques and cartoon usages of Holmes subsided from even their relatively mild Edwardian peak in Britain, they flourished in the United States, notably in the famed cartoons of H.T. Webster (both a nationally renowned comic-strip artist and a founder of Philadelphia's Sherlockian group, the Sons of the Copper Beeches) and in such an amusing, long-lived post-Mager strip as Jim Wallace's *Dinky Dinkerton*. At the same time, spoofs of Holmes routinely proliferated in the comic-strip worlds of Mickey Mouse, Popeye, Rip Kirby, Little Orphan Annie, Superman, and many other well-known characters. American editorial cartoonists, too, were prone to use the Baker Street sage as a standard symbol of investigation, whether criminal, political, or scientific. Here, presidents, governors, mayors, and senators, as well as law-enforcement officers, donned deerstalkers and picked up magnifying lenses.

Finally, in the field of dramatic adaptation, America not only provided (albeit in the form of two British actors) the most popular latterday physical symbols of Holmes and Watson (in Basil Rathbone and Nigel Bruce), but acclaimed on the boards what is inarguably the finest and most enduring of Sherlockian plays, William Gillette's *Sherlock Holmes* of 1899—which made its brilliant star the nationally approved likeness of Holmes for forty years before Rathbone's ascension. The American association of Gillette with Holmes was one of the great artistic phenomena of the time: it led to a thirty-three-year stage tenure for the author-star, the formation of several foreign companies and tours, two films and two radio adaptations (with Gillette starring in one of each), and the near-eclipse of Gillette's career as a general actor and playwright. Steele's use of Gillette as the model for his striking and classic *Collier's* illustrations greatly increased the popular association of the actor with the character, while local newspaper artists throughout the country took the arrival of the play in their cities as a challenge to their own ability to depict the detective—as Gillette. The play itself has hardly survived Gillette's own death in 1937, as was proved by its highly successful revivals in London and New York on virtually its 75th anniversary.

The present volume is an extensive selection of these many American tributes, both fore- and back-handed, to Sherlock Holmes in the popular periodical press—not that of the land of his birth, but that of the land which has subsumed him most wholly to itself. Diverse and far-ranging as this collection is, it can never be comprehensive. As witness to which—check your local newsdealer.

DEALINGS WITH THE FIRM OF CALABASH, DEERSTALKER, AND LENS
The Image of Sherlock Holmes in Popular Art and Literature
by Bill Blackbeard

Almost four decades ago the late Anthony Boucher, one of America's best-known Sherlockians, published a brilliant satirical novel called *Rocket to the Morgue.* The 1942 detective novel dealt opinionatedly with the science-fiction writing fraternity—from an admiring presentation of Edmond Hamilton, doyen of American science fiction writers, to a near-definitive excoriation of L. Ron Hubbard, founder of Scientology. Its lovingly developed focus, however, was on the writings of one H. Fowler Foulkes, a Boucher creation closely modeled on A. Conan Doyle, and specifically on Foulkes's series of novels and stories about Dr. Garth Derringer, a fabulously gifted scientist, based in turn on Doyle's second-best-known series character, Professor George Challenger of *The Lost World* and "When the Earth Screamed." Boucher chose Doyle's Professor Challenger as a model for the world-famed fictional hero of his novel because of the book's science fiction orientation, but he left his reader in little doubt about the actual Doyle character he had in mind when he wrote such details about his Dr. Derringer as the following:

Leland Stanford University still receives letters begging scientific advice and addressed to:

Garth Derringer, Ph.D.
Department of Physics,

and whimsical scholars delight in visiting the Foulkes Memorial Library of that University to confound each other with variorum readings from the earlier texts.

The story is told of a seismographic expedition which attained after arduous months the supposedly unattainable upper reaches of the Kulopangu. The chief of the Ngutlumbi was entranced by the elaborate apparatus set up to record earthquake shocks. He inspected it from all angles and at last inquired, confident of the answer, "Dokka Derinja, him make?"

It is clear in these passages that Boucher is thinking of the actual worldwide fame and popularity long accorded Doyle's Sherlock Holmes but never granted his own preferred Professor Challenger, despite the latter's consistent appeal for those lucky few who manage to discover him. An actual, similarly isolated African native of forty years ago might very well have spoken knowingly, not of Challenger, of course, but of "Schlokka Hums," after looking at a picture of the detective in full regalia, much as he would have beamed with awareness at images of Charlie Chaplin, Tarzan, or Mickey Mouse. Or as an Eskimo or a Tibetan, or a New Yorker, exercising different pronunciations, might have done. But it would have been the physical *image* which would have evoked the response, from memories based almost entirely on cinematic experience. The suggestion in Boucher's novel that an abstract, nonphysical characteristic of Derringer, the man's inventiveness, would have sparked an unsophisticated native's attribution of a complex machine to the doctor, is not likely. If Derringer had indeed shared the worldwide fame of Holmes, his recognition in the far corners of it would have had to have been in terms of a personal physical image of some virtually unique sort, something so individual, fundamental, and visually linked in the memory with a once-new and exhilarating entertainment experience that it would never be forgotten. King Kong is such an image, or magna-image, if you like. The Shadow and Superman, though limited in international range by poor cinematic representation, loom as large. Others, as mentioned above, would obviously be Mickey Mouse, Charlie Chaplin, and Tarzan. And Sherlock Holmes.

Almost alone among these famed images, that of Holmes possesses a curious ambiguity, for it exists in two distinct forms. One of these is the ascetic, pale, lean, hawk-nosed Englishman in smoking jacket, with a straight pipe, who represents Holmes immediately to his cognoscenti audience but means little to the general public unless the Holmes name is attached as an identifying label. The other is a basically faceless image which features a magnifying glass, a meerschaum calabash pipe, and a deerstalker cap (with or without a plaid cape to match the deerstalker) and instantly communicates *Sherlock Holmes!* to anyone on sight. Those close to the Holmes canon much prefer the former image and use it in their texts and publications about the detective (sometimes deigning to incorporate the deerstalker), but, like everyone else, they respond with immediate recognition when they see the latter. (The calabash or the lens may be omitted from this holy trinity in a given representation without losing the impact of identity, or even the two together, but *never* the deerstalker, which in itself is sometimes used to designate Holmes.) In order to understand how this odd imaginal split occurred, and to examine what bearing it may have on the present and future popularity of Sherlock Holmes, we must look into the nature of popular images, how they emerge, how they are appropriated by the general public, and what their effect seems to be on the various arts that give them birth.

Of the several factors involved in the lasting popularity of any narrative work of art, whether in prose fiction, poetry, cinema, comic strip, or drama, the primary one is arguably the appeal of the physical images of the characters to a broad spectrum of readers. A character's attitudes and ideas, or mannerisms of speech and thought (granting such exceptions as Mr. F.'s Aunt, Mr. Dooley, and certain characters of Shakespeare), seem not to have as much to do with his or her memorability (and by extension the memorability of the narrative work involved) as does his or her visual image.

In cinema and drama, this visual image, coupled with personal magnetism, is often called star quality and is crucial to the success of any production. While there are many instances in both arts of given actors bringing vivid life to uninspired characters in dull scripts, there are almost no instances of well-written or well-directed parts opening memorable careers to lackluster actors. (Obviously I am not referring to film and stage actors as critics perceive them, but as the paying public does.) Since in film and drama the variety of available images is effectively limited (with all due credit to the make-up work done on various Masseys and Chaneys) to the available stock of competent actors, it is clear that writers and directors must shape their character concepts to fit these actors, and most in fact do so.

In the case of the comic strip, easily the most malleable of the graphic narrative arts, the artist limns his figures on paper exactly as he visualizes them. Thus his imagination, within the limits of his competence, impinges immediately upon that of his audience with no intervening verbal formulations or limitations of human physiognomy to blunt or alter the impact desired. (A similar freedom, obviously, but one considerably curtailed by individual cell costs and extant animation techniques, exists for the storyboard artists working in animated cartoons.) Physical image here, as in film and drama, is clearly central to the whole narrative function.

(I have not included the curious position of radio or recorded spoken drama in this brief discussion of the major narrative arts, since no production in either form has ever enjoyed or can enjoy longevity as a continually popular work unaided by visual images. The *Shadow* and *Lone Ranger* radio dramas of the 1930s and later are, of course, still widely if obscurely rebroadcast, but this is only because of the hearty life maintained in the popular imagination by the powerful visual images of the two heroes. The purely auditory impact of The Shadow's laugh or the Lone Ranger's "Hi yo, Silver, h'away!" could not have served alone to insure lasting popularity for these shows, as we can readily observe from the failure of the equally potent sound cues created for such once-famed radio drama series as *Chandu the Magician, Renfrew of the Mounted,* or *The Inner Sanctum* to sustain public interest after their initial release. Since no concurrent and independently successful visual images of these latter, studio-created shows existed to link them into the popular memory, they faded from mass awareness as soon as they left the air.)

It is less so, certainly, in prose and poetry. But here as well the popular appeal of cleanly limned images has left its mark. Printed narrative fiction has frequently been augmented by book and magazine illustrations, executed in many mediums. This illumination of text, as it were, reached a peak between 1800 and 1910, then declined precipitately as book publishers reduced expenses by eliminating the once-numerous illustrations, leaving them to the popular fiction magazines and newspapers. The reading public, needless to say, was never consulted about this abolition of book illustration; it was simply told that it had become "old-fashioned," or "juvenile," and the editors and publishers who began by cutting out art for economic reasons came in time to believe this themselves. What was lost, of course, was the once-vital imaginal link of book fiction with its audience, except for books specifically designed for children under twelve, and as a result very few works of fiction published primarily in book form after 1920 are recalled by the general reader with the kind of immediate and pleasurable visual association that brings such earlier books to mind as *Huckleberry Finn, Notre Dame, Don Quixote, Treasure Island, The Three Musketeers, David Copperfield, The War of the Worlds, Vanity Fair, Oliver Twist, Trilby, Tarzan,* and many others, including of course the Sherlock Holmes titles. (In fact, the very demand by latterday readers for the retention of illustrations in many of these classics led publishers and academics to perceive these works as thus self-evidently children's books, so that they were often relegated to the juvenile ghettos of bookstores and libraries between World War I and the 1960s.) It is worthy of note in this context that Charles Dickens, indisputably the most gifted writer of hallucinatively visual prose of his time, or since, chose to work closely with selected illustrators in nearly all of his novels to assure that his readers would literally *see* his characters as he did. Often he asked an illustrator to submit dozens of sketches of each character, from which he would pick the images he felt most closely suited his own fiercely visualized concept. He had, in short, managed to anticipate the then-unknown freedom of the comic strip artist in sending an immediate and concretely graphic visual image to his reader.

Images, a hundred years ago, clearly not only sold books. They also made the most imaginative titles into universally recollectable and constantly re-printed classics in a way that has not been possible since. It is of course true that the less graphically imaginative writers of the period, the Eliots, Hardys, Merediths, and their kin, eschewed all illustrations where possible, and gener-ally wrote in such a restrained way that even the most independently imagina-tive illustrator would have found little in their works to build on in terms of physically memorable characters. The public, as expected by these authors, found their characters very much like actual people, but they also found them just as forgettable as most actual people. There has never been, as we know, much lasting popular market for these writers, assigned student sales aside. Evidently, the nineteenth-century alliance between popular image and the public hunger for larger-than-life, heroically proportioned figures was not a casual one.

Before returning to our primary theme of the effect of derived graphic images on the popularity and longevity of the Sherlock Holmes stories, it may be of further interest to touch on the nature of the general reader of fiction, sharply reduced though his or her ranks may be today in an age of switch-on visual entertainment.

Why *does* the typical reader respond so readily and enthusiastically to hard-edged, specific graphic renditions of the figures he finds memorable in fiction: the Long John Silvers, Count Foscos, Pickwicks, Draculas, d'Artagnans, Daisy Millers, and others? The answer seems, sadly, to lie in the limitations of the average reader himself. Vivid personal imagination is clearly not the forte of this general reader, any more than it is that of the general audience for any widely popular narrative art. The average reader does, certainly, enjoy some occasional kindling of his imagination by a genuinely provocative writer, which is why a Faulkner novel or its equivalent appears on the best-seller lists from time to time; but today's typical page-turner generally simply fills in the faces of the stock characters in the generally flat and hackneyed works he reads with those of friends, relatives, actors, or political personalities (as he also does, it should be added, in his occasional encounters with the works of genuinely imaginative contemporary writers), unless he reads the novels after seeing films adapted from them, in which case, of course, the recalled visages of the actors involved do very nicely for him. He finds nothing wrong with this—he is, after all, only turning to prose to pick up inside information or to find story content which he rightly feels other entertainment media will not or cannot bring him because of censorship and the relative brevity of narrative time in spoken drama—and he typically recalls what he has read in conveniently communicable terms of "this guy who runs the film studio," "this nosy cop," "this sexy waitress," or the like, only rarely using the actual names of the characters involved. (The names of popular series heroes, like Mike Hammer, are an obvious exception.) Thus, whether vaguely or superbly conceived by authors, their characters are only vaguely retained by the reader—until *seen* in the later film version. A concretely rendered graphic image with a label is needed for reader recollection in contemporary fiction as strongly as it was needed in the past.

With the reading public's turn in recent decades to mass paperback novels with their categorically keyed covers, and the disappearance of illustrated fiction magazines (aside from a handful of genre publications), the only remaining mass sources of graphic character images are the comics and the movies (including the cinema adjunct of television). Although the comics recycle the still-famed fictional images of The Shadow and Tarzan from time to time, it is the film studios which have done the most over the past fifty years to keep the great literary images, including that of Sherlock Holmes, alive and thriving in the popular mind. It is usually a recalled cinema image, rekindled by a current paperback cover daub that resembles it, which entices the contemporary reader to purchase an original narrative in reprint. Having enjoyed Holmes in a movie, he feels he may like him in a book. With luck, he may pick up a Conan Doyle story, rather than one of the many pastiches of the canon which presently crowd the newsstands, and join the thousands of readers who still devour the entire Holmes *oeuvre* from beginning to end. Good enough. The image as vital link in fictional survival continues. But the Curious Matter of the Dual Holmes Image—the one of Holmes himself that is logically derived from the works, and to which few react, and the one made up of the three not uncommon artifacts which everyone recognizes on sight—remains to be analyzed. The game is afoot, and shall be pursued.

Among the popular images of narrative fiction, a handful are what we might term magna-images. These are the almost universally recognized figures of such internationally popular characters as Mickey Mouse, Tarzan, Popeye, and Sherlock Holmes. Almost alone among such figures, Holmes and Tarzan share common origins in prose fiction, rather than in the comic strip or film. Yet the ape man's basic, simple image has not altered in the popular mind since its first definitive framing on a magazine cover in 1914 and its initial, imitative film delineation by Elmo Lincoln; that of Holmes, as we have observed, has evolved markedly since the earliest crude drawings of the detective were prepared by Conan Doyle's father for the first book edition of *A Study in Scarlet* in 1888. Since the real popularity of Sherlock Holmes did not begin until the short stories first appeared in the *Strand* magazine in 1891, strikingly illustrated by Sidney Paget, the first *Study in Scarlet* illustrations (dropped in later editions) fortunately had little effect in framing a popular image of Holmes. The Paget illustrations, of course, did.

Hired by mistake (the *Strand* editors thought they were buying the services of Paget's better-known brother, Walter, then famed for his dark, savage illustrations of H. Rider Haggard's *King Solomon's Mines* in 1887), Sidney Paget swiftly became the definitive Holmes illustrator of the 1890s, both in England and America. For many aficionados, he was *always* the definitive illustrator. In Paget's work, readers first glimpsed the hawklike visage so long associated with Holmes, the dressing gown, and the pipe. These were the relatively singular elements which then set Holmes apart from other popular figures in contemporary fiction, and they were promptly utilized by parodists and political cartoonists of the day in limning Holmesian images for their own purposes. Holmes was becoming a household word even in 1891, the *Strand* stories were appearing for months on end, and journalistic artists seeking for a quick "handle" on the new character seized on the lean profile, pipe, and gown as tags of identity the sophisticated public would know at once.

Away from his Baker Street digs, however, Holmes was much less striking, being depicted by Paget as sharing the bowler hat and dark, formal clothing commonly worn in the City in that period. Paget did veer briefly from this cobblestone array of uniform bowlers although readers and the cartoonists then paid little attention, when he introduced the famed deerstalker cap in his drawings for the fourth Holmes story in *The Strand,* "The Boscombe Valley Mystery," where Doyle's text called it a "close-fitting cloth cap." Obviously donned by Holmes for countryside and travel activity, it reappeared in the thirteenth story, the adventure of "Silver Blaze," where Doyle termed it an "earflapped travelling cap," and where Paget once again drew it as a deerstalker. Omitted in the illustrations for the novel *The Hound of the Baskervilles,* the deerstalker resurfaced in the Paget art for no fewer than five of the first six stories in *The Return of Sherlock Holmes,* which began in *The Strand* in 1903, although it was not mentioned specifically by Doyle in any of them. As of that date, a basic part of what was to become the popular image of Holmes was established for good. Winifred Paget, the artist's daughter, wrote in a letter to the English *Picture Post* of December 16, 1950, that he himself often wore a deerstalker. "I imagine," she continued, "that he chose this type of hat for himself as being suitable and comfortable for tramping around the countryside, which fact possibly inspired him to depict Holmes wearing a deerstalker on similar occasions." She concluded on a sad note by mentioning that Paget's own deerstalker, which survived him by many years, eventually succumbed to moths and was consigned by his wife "to the dustbin." *O tempora, O deerstalker Pagetica!*

In America, these later Paget illustrations did not appear, since *The Return* was purchased for publication by *Collier's Weekly,* where the stories were lavishly illustrated by an outstanding American artist, Frederic Dorr Steele. Steele sensibly emulated Paget in maintaining the early dressing gown and pipe image, and included the deerstalker prominently in several of his interior and cover drawings. But Steele modified the saturnine Paget image of Holmes, limning a much more circumspectly handsome Holmes, and one based to a great extent on the stage appearance of the footlight Holmes already made famous in America by the gifted actor and dramatist William Gillette. The Steele Holmes was very much to the American taste of the time, and the young artist became the preferred illustrator in the United States for all the subsequent Holmes stories. Although he was often replaced by other artists in various American magazines printing the current Holmes tales, he was never supplanted in the favor of the increasingly vocal Holmes fans. Over the years, Steele eventually rendered his inimitable drawings for no fewer than fifty-four of the fifty-six short stories and all four of the novels. This was a role Paget unfortunately could not equal in England, because he died in 1908.

Despite the reader popularity enjoyed by Steele, his magazine illustrations rarely attained the permanence of book publication, and as a result it was the actor, playwright, and novelist Gillette, continually in the public eye, who came to personify the popular image of Holmes in America during the first quarter of this century. Although at least one other actor of at least equal charm and dramatic imagination, John Barrymore, appeared prominently in the role of Holmes in a 1922 film titled *Sherlock Holmes,* Gillette's omnipotence as Everyman's Holmes remained unshaken through his last theatrical tour in 1929–33. (His only serious competition came from a noted English actor, Eille Norwood, who made forty-five two-reel silent films as Holmes, and two features, between 1921 and 1923. Norwood had a keen Sherlockian face and demeanor, but there is little evidence in newspapers of the time that his British-made series had any considerable American circulation, or that popular cartoon and parody portrayals of Holmes in this country veered even briefly toward a Norwood image of the detective.)

Gillette made only one very early film as Holmes, in 1916, based on his own play, *Sherlock Holmes.* Inept distribution and promotion plus poor photography, printing, and editing sped it to quick oblivion. With no effective record of his performance to survive him, Gillette's hold on the general imagination as the real, right Holmes understandably died with him—died, actually, with his last curtain call. A new generation found itself in turn galvanized by Basil Rathbone's marvelously evocative performance as Holmes in the 1939 *Hound of the Baskervilles.* For them, Rathbone promptly "became" Holmes, as Gillette had done for their fathers and grandfathers.

A number of other actors, of course, played Holmes in both English and American films over the past fifty years, including a marked variety of performers in the big-budget productions of recent years. During this time, Holmes was featured in two nationally distributed comic strips, in a number of comic book adaptions, and was portrayed by many magazine and book-jacket artists who quickly eclipsed the public memory of Steele's largely unreprinted illustrations. The resulting dazzle of varied Holmesian faces seen by the public during a half-century in which the popular images of Tarzan, Mickey Mouse, The Shadow, Superman, King Kong, and similar household figures, all controlled by owners concerned with imaginal quality and consistency, remained virtually unchanged, left the mass audience with no common facial perception of Holmes at all. Recently, artists have tended to settle for a hawkish profile, which lends a certain quasi-uniformity to book-cover and magazine artwork, but the film studios still seem to feel that virtually anyone, from Peter Sellers to Rod Steiger, can perform as Holmes, so long as they retain the vital trappings. And, of course, it is these trappings which have, in lieu of a fixed, whole physical image of Holmes familiar to the broad public, become themselves the popular Holmesian image.

We have traced the early origins of the deerstalker in Sidney Paget's illustrations, where it was picked up by a plethora of later artists (and was, of course, used by Gillette in his recurrent tours of the play). The magnifying glass as a popularly perceived Holmesian instrument and symbol dates even further back—to the first Holmes novel, in fact. Here, in the third chapter of *A Study in Scarlet,* we read how Holmes "whipped a tapemeasure and a large, round magnifying glass from his pocket" to examine with minute care the wall on which someone has written "RACHE" in blood. In the first illustration of this scene, drawn by D. H. Friston for the initial appearance of *Study* in *Beeton's Christmas Annual* for 1887, we see Holmes gazing intently through his glass at the scarlet word on the wall: a classic image which has been reprinted literally hundreds of times in articles and studies on Holmes and Doyle. The closely applied lens is a highly pictorial device, understandably pounced upon and exaggerated by parodying cartoonists in a thousand subsequent drawings. Interestingly, the magnifying glass is rarely used in serious Holmes adaptations or pastiches, since its introduction for more than the briefest and most vital bit of business generally strikes readers or audiences as comic—a reaction to which Doyle may have become sensitive fairly early, since there is little notable use of a lens in the canon after *A Study in Scarlet.* But the visually elegant glass, often depicted focusing a beam of light or enlarging some foreground object, holds its status, when combined with a deerstalker and a calabash pipe, as a touchstone that evokes Holmes at once.

The meerschaum calabash, alone of the three parts of the basic Holmes image, cannot be accounted for canonically. Holmes's pipe rarely was called more than "a pipe" or "his pipe," and the earlier illustrators, including Paget, drew a plain, straight pipe without ornamentation in accord with the text.

Steele, however, gave his Holmes a curved pipe on the 1904 *Collier's* cover for "The Adventure of the Three Students" (although he drew him with a straight pipe on other covers of the same period), and repeated it in a close-up profile on the cover of the special "Sherlock Holmes Number" of *Collier's* for August 15, 1908. Meanwhile, Doyle had personally approved of Holmes smoking a meerschaum calabash in the London production of Gillette's *Sherlock Holmes* play in 1901, and Doyle himself bestowed a calabash on his own footlight Holmes when *The Speckled Band* opened at London's Adelphi Theatre in 1910. It is little wonder that the calabash eventually found its way into the popular imagery of Holmes, even though not directly anticipated at any point in the printed text of the stories or in the illustrations of the first two decades, or that millions of readers now "see" Holmes smoking a calabash in their minds' eyes when they read Doyle's casual references to Holmes "taking up his pipe."

Thus the origins of the Trinity. Its acceptance by now as the graphic quintessence of Holmes is universal in the United States and much of the rest of the world, even in the upper reaches of the Kulopangu. Don a deerstalker, clench a calabash in your teeth (and a calabash calls for a humdinger of a clench), display a magnifying glass in one hand, and take a stroll down Piccadilly (or Main Street). The number of times you will hear "bonkers" or "loopy" in various shouted or whispered contexts from young passersby as they fix fascinated eyes on you (their elders remaining largely mute, through prudent circumspection) will be exceeded only by the satisfying number of times you will hear "Sherlock Holmes! He thinks he's Sherlock Holmes!" You may well make the press if you persist, and the captions under the photographs will, without fail, also talk about "Sherlock Holmes." The alienist in police employ will want to know how long you have believed you were Sherlock Holmes, and you will be called "the nut who dressed up like Sherlock Holmes" by your neighbors for many years to come. All *that,* promptly and without special solicitation, from simply combining three separately unprovocative pieces of period apparel and taking a walk. (Admittedly, even a deerstalker alone will get you head-turns in most of the United States, while a calabash is also uncommon enough in the streets to fetch glances, but worn or carried *singly* they will not normally lead to a questioning of your rationality, although the matter of your sartorial good sense is something else again.)

What the present collection seeks to do, among other rather unusual things —such as bringing together a large number of rare, worthwhile, and long-sought items of American Sherlockiana, introducing many long-unseen Holmes illustrations, comics, advertisements, play and film reviews, and re-printing long-desired stories by John Kendrick Bangs and others, plus commentary and poetry by Christopher Morley, Vincent Starrett, *et al.*—is to demonstrate the impact of this popular Sherlockian image on the American mass media in its several forms, and the continual restrengthening of the image through its recurrent use in these media. This the editor thinks it does soundly *in extenso,* providing a great deal of superlative entertainment and many unexpected surprises along the way. It is hoped the reader will agree, and will feel he is indeed, in the presence of this Sherlockian abundance, "a child again on Christmas morning"—to quote Booth Tarkington.

STORY ILLUSTRATIONS

The following fifty-odd pages provide a representative cross section—in black-and-white and color—of American illustrations of Arthur Conan Doyle's Sherlock Holmes stories in the popular press from 1891 to 1949, with the emphasis (as always in this volume) on both the little-known and the famed but rarely seen.

The earliest American illustrations of the Holmes canon appeared between 1891 and 1892, solely in newspapers subscribing to the S. S. McClure syndication of The Adventures of Sherlock Holmes in the United States. Published concurrently with the Sidney Paget drawings in the London Strand magazine, none of the very commercial sketches below and on the following page can compare with the British. Reprinted here are all those that ran in the Chicago daily Inter Ocean. The various artists involved, drawing anonymously or signed cryptically as "C.," "B.," "W.B.," and "Drake," were members of an illustrating company of the time which contracted to supply drawings for the syndicated stories; their identities are otherwise unknown. (For an engaging discussion of some of these drawings, see Walter Klinefelter's Sherlock Holmes in Portrait and Profile, Syracuse University Press, 1963, pp. 37–43.)

"A SCANDAL IN BOHEMIA"

July 11, 1891

I SAW IT AS SHE HALF DREW IT OUT.

"I AM THE KING."

"THE RED-HEADED LEAGUE"

August 8, 1891

"A CASE OF IDENTITY"

September 5, 1891

HE REACHED FOR THE HUNTING CROP.

"WHY DID YOU COME TO CONSULT ME IN SUCH A HURRY?"

"THE FIVE ORANGE PIPS"

November 7, 1891

"THIS IS THE ENVELOPE."

"DEATH!" SAID HE.

"THE MAN WITH THE TWISTED LIP"

December 6, 1891

"AND WHAT AM I CHARGED WITH?"

AND THEN VANISHED.

17

"THE ADVENTURE OF THE NOBLE BACHELOR"

March 13, 1892

"YOU'RE ANGRY, ROBERT!"

LORD ROBERT ST. SIMON.

"THE ADVENTURE OF THE BERYL CORONET"

PART I

April 17, 1892

"YOU THIEF!"

SHE PLACED HER HAND OVER HIS HEAD.

PART II

April 24, 1892

"NOW, WHAT DO YOU THINK WOULD HAPPEN,
IF I DID IT, MR. HOLDER?"

"THE ADVENTURE OF THE COPPER BEECHES" PART I

June 12, 1892

OPENED A POCKET-BOOK AND TOOK OUT A NOTE.

PART II

June 19, 1892

MR. RUNCASTLE DROVE ME IN HIS DOG-CART
TO THE COPPER BEECHES.

"I'LL THROW YOU TO THE MASTIFF."

"YOU THIEVES, SPIES AND THIEVES."

18

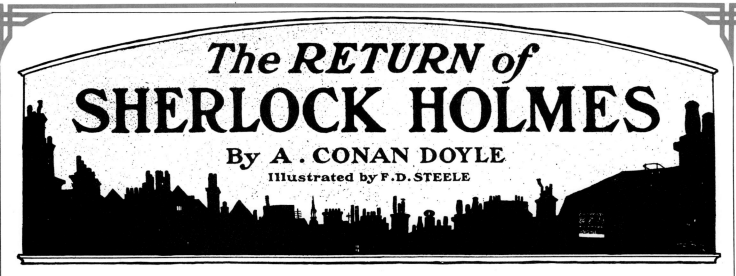

The RETURN of SHERLOCK HOLMES

By A. CONAN DOYLE
Illustrated by F. D. STEELE

I.—THE ADVENTURE OF THE EMPTY HOUSE

September 26, 1903

WITH A SNARL HE TURNED UPON HIS HEEL.

SHERLOCK HOLMES STOOD SMILING AT ME OVER MY STUDY TABLE.

"MY COLLECTION OF M'S IS A FINE ONE."

COLONEL MORAN SPRANG FORWARD WITH A SNARL OF RAGE.

The first of Frederic Dorr Steele's inimitable Holmes illustrations appeared in the issue of Collier's *for September 26, 1903, when that magazine began printing* The Return of Sherlock Holmes. *(The cover he rendered for that issue can be found on the first color page following page 32.) All of Steele's drawings for Collier's 1903-5 series appear in the next pages, with their dates of publication.*

The RETURN of
SHERLOCK HOLMES
By A. CONAN DOYLE
Illustrated by F.D. STEELE

II.—THE ADVENTURE OF THE NORWOOD BUILDER

October 31, 1903

"I ARREST YOU FOR THE WILFUL MURDER OF MR. JONAS OLDACRE."

A MASS OF DOCUMENTS, WHICH WE WENT OVER TOGETHER.

IT WAS MORE THAN A STAIN. IT WAS THE WELL-MARKED PRINT OF A THUMB.

THERE WAS A SORT OF SULKY DEFIANCE IN HER EYES.

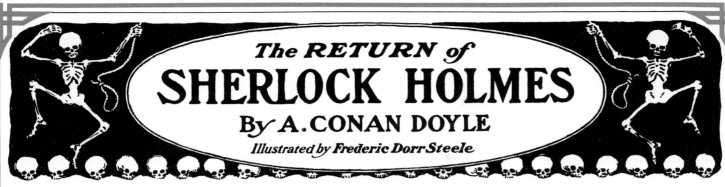

The RETURN of SHERLOCK HOLMES
By A. CONAN DOYLE
Illustrated by Frederic Dorr Steele

III.—THE ADVENTURE OF THE DANCING MEN

Christmas 1903

"WHAT DO YOU MAKE OF THESE?"

OUR FIRST ATTENTION WAS GIVEN TO THE BODY OF THE UNFORTUNATE SQUIRE.

THE COMPOSURE OF DESPAIR.

"WELL, GENTLEMEN, YOU HAVE THE DROP ON ME THIS TIME."

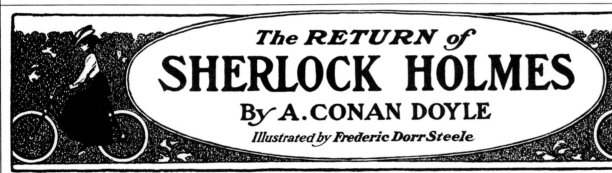

The RETURN of SHERLOCK HOLMES
By A. CONAN DOYLE
Illustrated by Frederic Dorr Steele

THE ADVENTURE OF THE SOLITARY CYCLIST

December 26, 1903

MISS VIOLET SMITH, TEACHER OF MUSIC.

"IT WAS A STRAIGHT LEFT AGAINST A SLOGGING RUFFIAN."

The RETURN of
SHERLOCK HOLMES
By A. CONAN DOYLE
Illustrated by Frederic Dorr Steele

THE ADVENTURE OF THE PRIORY SCHOOL

January 30, 1904

"I CAN NOT IMAGINE HOW I CAME TO BE SO WEAK."

THE DUKE AND HIS SECRETARY.

"YOU INFERNAL SPIES!" THE MAN CRIED.

The RETURN of
SHERLOCK HOLMES
By A. CONAN DOYLE
Illustrated by Frederic Dorr Steele

THE ADVENTURE OF BLACK PETER

February 27, 1904

WE WATCHED HIM.....HE RETURNED WITH A LARGE BOOK.

"THEN HOW DO YOU ACCOUNT FOR THAT?"

THE THIRD APPLICANT WAS A MAN OF REMARKABLE APPEARANCE.

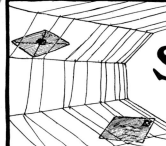

The *RETURN* of
SHERLOCK HOLMES
By A. CONAN DOYLE
Illustrated by *Frederic Dorr Steele*

THE ADVENTURE OF CHARLES AUGUSTUS MILVERTON

March 26, 1904

THERE WAS SOMETHING OF
MR. PICKWICK'S BENEVOLENCE IN HIS LOOKS.

"YOU COULDN'T COME ANY OTHER TIME—EH?"

SHERLOCK HOLMES IN DISGUISE.

The *RETURN* of
SHERLOCK HOLMES
By A. CONAN DOYLE
Illustrated by *Frederic Dorr Steele*

THE ADVENTURE OF THE SIX NAPOLEONS

April 30, 1904

HOLMES HAD JUST COMPLETED HIS EXAMINATION
WHEN THE DOOR OPENED.

HE PICKED UP HIS HUNTING-CROP
AND STRUCK NAPOLEON.

HE CARRIED A LARGE
OLD-FASHIONED CARPETBAG.

The RETURN of SHERLOCK HOLMES
By A. CONAN DOYLE
Illustrated by Frederic Dorr Steele

THE ADVENTURE OF THE THREE STUDENTS

September 24, 1904

"I TRUST, MR. HOLMES, THAT YOU CAN SPARE ME A FEW HOURS."

BANNISTER EXPLAINS.

The RETURN of SHERLOCK HOLMES
By A. CONAN DOYLE
Illustrated by Frederic Dorr Steele

THE ADVENTURE OF THE GOLDEN PINCE-NEZ

October 29, 1904

THE PROFESSOR WAS SEATED BY THE FIRE.

"NOW, MY DEAR HOPKINS, DRAW UP AND WARM YOUR TOES."

"YES, SIR, IT IS A CRUSHING BLOW," SAID THE OLD MAN.

The RETURN of
SHERLOCK HOLMES
By A. CONAN DOYLE
Illustrated by Frederic Dorr Steele

THE ADVENTURE OF THE MISSING THREE-QUARTER

November 26, 1904

WE LOOKED UP TO FIND A QUEER LITTLE OLD MAN,
JERKING AND TWITCHING IN THE DOORWAY.

DR. LESLIE ARMSTRONG.

The RETURN of
SHERLOCK HOLMES
By A. CONAN DOYLE
Illustrated by Frederic Dorr Steele

THE ADVENTURE OF THE ABBEY GRANGE

December 31, 1904

THE LADY LAY BACK EXHAUSTED UPON A COUCH
ENVELOPED IN A LOOSE DRESSING-GOWN
OF BLUE AND SILVER.

SHERLOCK HOLMES EXAMINES THE GLASSES.

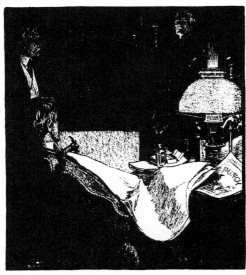

HE STOOD WITH CLENCHED HANDS AND HEAVING BREAST.

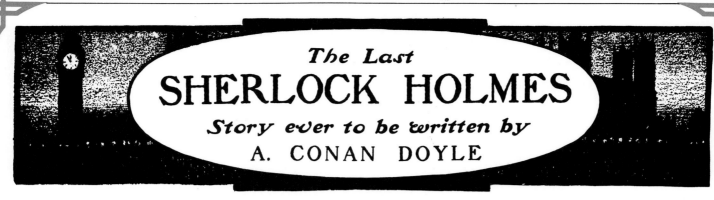

The Last
SHERLOCK HOLMES
Story ever to be written by
A. CONAN DOYLE

THE ADVENTURE OF THE SECOND STAIN

January 28, 1905

SHE SEATED HERSELF WITH HER BACK TO THE WINDOW.

"THERE *IS* A SECOND STAIN!"

"MADAM, I HAVE BEEN COMMISSIONED TO RECOVER THIS IMMENSELY IMPORTANT PAPER."

August 20, 1905

"THE ADVENTURE OF THE BLUE CARBUNCLE"

THE BIRD GAVE A GULP.

August 27, 1905

"THE ADVENTURE OF THE ENGINEER'S THUMB"

A WOMAN BENT OVER ME...A CANDLE IN HER RIGHT HAND.

In 1905, when the current Holmes series of tales closed in Collier's, various newspapers in America began to reprint the stories, generally illustrating them with the work of staff artists. The Sunday Portland Oregonian drawings on this page are typical of the earliest productions of this kind, and are by Dan Smith, an illustrator of some note. The Return heading appeared as early as April, and is probably by Smith. The heading did not mean, however, that all stories used were from that collection of Holmes.

More such newspaper art follows on the subsequent pages, with dates and identities of the artists given where known.

September 17, 1905

"THE ADVENTURE OF THE COPPER BEECHES"

"IT WAS MY COIL OF HAIR."

October 22, 1905

"THE STOCKBROKER'S CLERK"

"MY BOY, MY BOY, YOU ARE MUCH TOO GOOD TO BE A CLERK AT MAWSON'S."

October 10 and 17, 1907
H. B. Eddy for
**"THE SIGN
OF THE FOUR"**
in the San Francisco Call

WITH THREE LONG HOPS I WAS ON HIM.

*This and the succeeding
illustrations are for the
Portland* Oregonian *unless
otherwise designated.*

May 14, 1911
G. A. Dowling for
**"THE ADVENTURE OF
THE DEVIL'S FOOT"**

HOLMES SPRANG TO HIS FEET, ALL ENERGY IN AN INSTANT.

HOLMES PACED WITH LIGHT, SWIFT STEPS ABOUT THE ROOM.

May 21, 1911
"THE DEVIL'S FOOT"
(continued)

STERNDALE SPRANG TO HIS FEET.
"I BELIEVE YOU ARE THE DEVIL HIMSELF!" HE CRIED.

BESIDE IT, SAT THE DEAD MAN, LEANING BACK IN HIS CHAIR.

July 9, 1911
G. A. Dowling for

"THE ADVENTURE OF THE EMPTY HOUSE"

THEN, CROUCHING DOWN,
HE RESTED THE END OF THE
BARREL UPON THE LEDGE OF THE OPEN WINDOW.

THE UNFORTUNATE YOUNG MAN WAS FOUND LYING NEAR THE TABLE.

"HE ALWAYS KEPT SO FAR
FROM ME THAT I COULD NOT
CLEARLY SEE HIS FACE."

July 23, 1911
Anonymous for

"THE ADVENTURE OF THE SOLITARY CYCLIST"

"NO, SHE'S YOUR WIDOW."

July 30, 1911
G. A. Dowling for

"THE ADVENTURE OF BLACK PETER"

THE NEXT INSTANT HOLMES AND THE SEAMAN
WERE ROLLING ON THE GROUND TOGETHER.

HE WAS PINNED LIKE A BEETLE ON A CARD.

August 27, 1911
Anonymous for
"THE ADVENTURE OF THE SIX NAPOLEONS"

FINALLY, HE PICKED UP HIS HUNTING CROP AND STRUCK NAPOLEON A SHARP BLOW ON THE TOP OF THE HEAD.

BUT BEFORE WE COULD MOVE, THE MAN HAD EMERGED *AGAIN*.

September 3, 1911
Anonymous for
"THE RESIDENT PATIENT"

IT WAS A DREADFUL SIGHT THAT MET US AS WE ENTERED THE BEDROOM DOOR.

HE WAS SITTING BOLT UPRIGHT IN HIS CHAIR, STARING AT ME WITH A PERFECTLY BLANK AND RIGID FACE.

September 10, 1911
Anonymous for
"THE CROOKED MAN"

HIS FEET TILTED OVER THE SIDE OF AN ARM CHAIR, AND HIS HEAD UPON THE GROUND.

"MY GOD! ARE YOU IN THE POLICE YOURSELF?"

September 24, 1911
Milton Werschkul for
"THE STOCKBROKER'S CLERK"

SUCCEEDED AFTER A MOST
DESPERATE RESISTANCE
IN ARRESTING HIM.

OUR YOUNG COMPANION LOOKED AT ME WITH
A TWINKLE IN HIS EYE.

February 11, 1912
H. B. Eddy for
"SILVER BLAZE"

*in the Boston
Sunday* American

"TEN MINUTES' TALK WITH
YOU, SIR," SAID HOLMES, IN THE SWEETEST OF VOICES.

The remainder of the art on this page is by Eddy for
"THE SIGN OF THE FOUR"

in the Sunday American, *April 21 (first two) and 28, 1912*

"IF YOUR FRIEND," SHE SAID, "WOULD BE GOOD ENOUGH TO STAY,
HE MIGHT BE OF INESTIMABLE SERVICE TO ME."

NOT ONLY HIS FEATURES,
BUT ALL HIS LIMBS WERE
TWISTED AND TURNED IN A
MOST FANTASTIC FASHION.

"LOR' BLESS YOU, SIR, HE IS THAT FORWARD HE GETS
ALMOST TOO MUCH FOR ME TO MANAGE."

IT WAS AT THE WINDOW.

November 24, 1912
Lee Conrey for

"IN THE SINGULAR EXPERIENCE OF MR. SCOTT ECCLES"

(also known as "The Adventure of Wisteria Lodge")
in the Seattle
Post-Intelligencer

December 1 and 8, 1912
Lee Conrey for

"SCOTT ECCLES"

(continued)

HE HELD UP THE CANDLE BEFORE AN EXTRAORDINARY OBJECT WHICH STOOD AT THE BACK OF THE DRESSER.

"HE CREPT UP BEHIND ME JUST AS I HAD FINISHED THE NOTE."

January 25, 1914
Lee Conrey for

"THE ADVENTURE OF THE DYING DETECTIVE"

in the Portland Oregonian

Reproduced on the next eleven color pages are the covers drawn by Frederic Dorr Steele for the 1903–5 Collier's *issues publishing the thirteen stories of what became* The Return of Sherlock Holmes. *For two stories, the adventures of "The Dancing Men" and "The Six Napoleons" (Christmas 1903 and April 30, 1904),* Collier's *did not use a Holmes cover.*

IN THIS NUMBER—"THE RETURN OF SHERLOCK HOLMES"

Beginning a New Series of Detective Stories by A. CONAN DOYLE

Collier's

Household Number for October

DRAWN BY FREDERIC DORR STEELE

VOL XXXI NO 26   SEPTEMBER 26 1903   PRICE 10 CENTS

Collier's

Household Number for November

Sherlock Holmes

In this Number Solves
The Mystery of

The

Norwood Builder

VOL XXXII NO 5   OCTOBER 31 1903   FRICE 10 CENTS

Collier's

Household Number for January

Steele 03

VOL XXXII NO 13   DECEMBER 26 1903   PRICE 10 CENTS

Collier's

Household Number for February

Collier's

Household Number for April

VOL XXXII NO 26   MARCH 26 1904   PRICE 10 CENTS

A Sherlock Holmes Story in This Number

Collier's

Household Number for October

"The Adventure of the Three Students"

VOL. XXXIII NO. 26   SEPTEMBER 24 1904   PRICE 10 CENTS

Collier's
Household Number for November

THE
ADVENTURE
of the
GOLDEN
PINCE-NEZ

VOLUME XXXIV NO 5   OCTOBER 29   PRICE 10 CENTS

A Sherlock Holmes Story in This Number

Collier's

Household Number for December

THE ADVENTURE
of the
MISSING THREE-QUARTER

VOL XXXIV No 9   NOVEMBER 26   PRICE 10 CENTS

Collier's

Household Number for January

THE ADVENTURE
of the
ABBEY GRANGE

Vol XXXIV No 14   DECEMBER 31 1904   PRICE 10 CENTS

"THE COST OF TAKING PORT ARTHUR." — See page 20

Collier's

THE NATIONAL WEEKLY

The
Last Adventure
of
Sherlock Holmes

in this number

Vol XXXIV No 18   JANUARY 28 1905   PRICE 10 CENTS

For August 15, 1908, Collier's *devoted most of a "Special Issue" to Arthur Conan Doyle and Sherlock Holmes, featuring a new Holmes story, "The Singular Experience of Mr. J. Scott Eccles" (it would be published in Doyle's 1917 collection,* His Last Bow, *as "The Adventure of Wisteria Lodge," and is also known as "The Tiger of San Pedro"). Again, Frederic Dorr Steele did the cover, reproduced above, accompanying it with six interior illustrations; all are on this page and the next.*

Our client sat up with staring eyes.

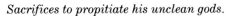

Sacrifices to propitiate his unclean gods.

The queer thing in the kitchen.

The light from the window streamed across the shrubbery.

"They had gagged me, and Murillo twisted my arm round."

The crime was ascribed to Nihilism, and the murderers were never arrested.

¶ *"Fancy anyone having the heart to hurt him," Ferguson muttered as he glanced at the angry red pucker on his baby's throat. All this time Holmes was staring intently at the window across the room.*

After World War I, though color illustrations for Holmes stories were commonplace in American magazines, covers devoted to the detective (in the manner of the Steele classics for Collier's) were fewer, owing to the rage for women subjects on covers of most of the slick paper fiction magazines of the period. Typical of interior Holmes illustrations, however, are these two by W. T. Benda for "The Adventure of the Sussex Vampire," from Hearst's International for January 1924.

¶ *Mrs. Ferguson kneeling by the cot gave no answer to her husband's reproaches save to gaze at him with a wild despairing look in her eyes.*

¶ *Something was moving along the passage, something dark and crouching; then suddenly it emerged into the light and I saw that it was he.*

¶ *I dare say it was twenty seconds or so that I lay paralyzed and watched its face. Then it vanished and I lay cold and shivering till morning.*

Steele continued to be the popular Holmes illustrator despite the work of Benda and others. The drawings on this page and the next are for "The Adventure of the Creeping Man"; they ran in Hearst's International for March 1923.

¶ The hall door slowly opened and against the lamp-lit background Holmes and Watson saw the tall figure of Professor Presbury. As he stood outlined in the doorway he was erect but leaned forward with dangling arms.

¶ "Hardly enough, Mr. Holmes!" the old man cried in a high screaming voice.

¶ With his dressing-gown flapping on each side of him he looked like some huge bat glued against . . . the moonlit wall.

The *Adventure* of the Retired Colourman

HOLMES sprang at him like a tiger, and twisted his face toward the floor.

The Famous Detective Solves the Mystery of the Young Doctor Who Played with Another Man's Wife

HOLMES' eyelids drooped so lazily that he might almost have been asleep.

HE tore up one of his wife's photographs in my presence. "I never wish to see her damned face again!" he shrieked.

I was slipping through the pantry window in the early dawn when I felt a hand inside my collar.

"THE LIFE OF SIR ARTHUR CONAN DOYLE," BY JOHN DICKSON CARR

To illustrate this biografy of Conan Doyle, J. Allen St. John has chosen to picture the author's famous brain child, Sherlock Holmes, shadowed by the faithful Dr. Watson, as they roam a London street within sight of Big Ben and a familiar hansom cab. The book, published by Harper & Brothers, is reviewed in this issue.

J. Allen St. John, the popular illustrator for the Edgar Rice Burroughs Tarzan, Mars, and Venus series of novels, among others, did this little-known rendering of Holmes and Watson for the cover of the Chicago Tribune "Books" section for February 13, 1949, as commissioned by book editor Vincent Starrett.

Four of the wilder covers for the plagiarized German pastiches of the Holmes stories (first published in 1907), as rendered by Spanish artists for the Spanish-language translation of the series. Printed in American "nickle thriller" format, dozens of these sensational titles are still kept in print by Mexican publishers and are widely sold to Spanish-speaking Americans in the Southwest today.

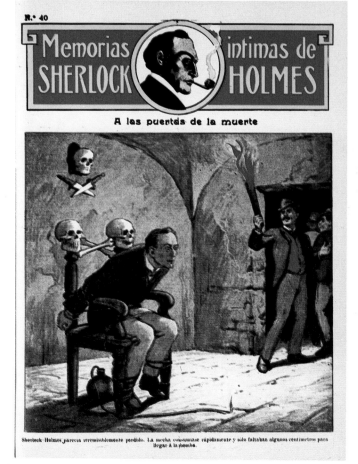

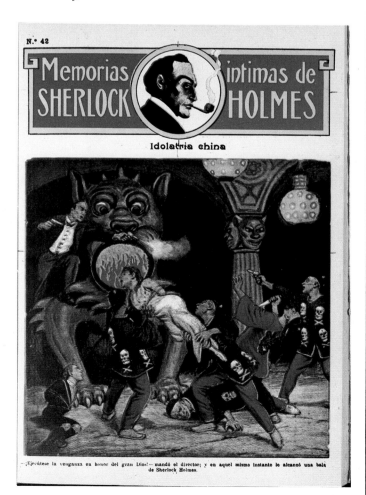

A remarkable drawing of Sherlock Holmes by Lee Conrey, as published in the Seattle Post-Intelligencer for January 4, 1914, illustrating "The Dying Detective."

Illustrated from Chicago Sunday Tribune   *August 20, 1911*

October 29, 1911

November 5, 1911

November 12, 1911

**"THE MAN
WITH THE
TWISTED LIP"**

"HOLMES," I WHISPERED, "WHAT ON EARTH ARE YOU DOING IN THIS DEN?"

OUR FOOTFALLS RANG OUT CRISPLY.

**"THE ADVENTURE OF
THE BLUE CARBUNCLE"**   *November 19, 1911*

This page and the next include a number of reproductions of covers, and interior illustrations, from a series of tabloid sections, published weekly and each devoted wholly to a Holmes story, that ran in the Seattle Post-Intelligencer from August 1911 through March 1912. Two staff artists, "Cargs" and E. S. Morris, illustrated.

IT WAS INDEED THE
UNFORTUNATE BUTLER.

*Above and left:
January 28, 1912*

**"THE MUSGRAVE
RITUAL"**

WE WENT DOWN
A WINDING STONE
STAIR.

MEMOIRS of
SHERLOCK HOLMES
By A. CONAN DOYLE
Illustrated by E. S. Morris

THE
REIGATE
PUZZLE

February 4, 1912

March 3, 1912

MEMOIRS of
SHERLOCK HOLMES
By A. CONAN DOYLE
Illustrated by E. S. Morris

THE
NAVAL
TREATY

March 10, 1912

MEMOIRS of
SHERLOCK HOLMES
By A. CONAN DOYLE
Illustrated by E. S. Morris

THE
FINAL
PROBLEM

The Adventure of the Speckled Band

The Doyle Holmes stories continued to be illustrated.... Here are a set of drawings—beautifully done by John Alan Maxwell—for The Golden Book magazine of December 1930.

A YOUNG LADY HAS ARRIVED IN A CONSIDERABLE STATE OF EXCITEMENT.

"THE VERY HORROR OF MY SITUATION LIES IN THE FACT THAT MY FEARS ARE SO VAGUE."

"YOU WILL EXCUSE ME FOR A FEW MINUTES WHILE I SATISFY MYSELF AS TO THIS FLOOR."

DRAMATIC, CINEMATIC, AND RADIO REVIEWS AND ADVERTISEMENTS

Onscreen and on-the-air representations of Sherlock Holmes aside for the moment, the onstage presentation (not counting vaudeville, burlesque, and musical comedy) of the detective was for decades limited essentially to two plays: Doyle's The Speckled Band, based on his short story, and American William Gillette's Sherlock Holmes, based in part on a Doyle play. The Gillette production, generally featuring the stunning bravura performance of its author and star, was much the more successful of the two in the United States and was performed in virtually every major city in the country at least once, in recurrent tours. (It reached Europe by 1901, and was especially admired in Denmark and Sweden; in Great Britain, H. A. Saintsbury became famous in Gillette's role and would star in a 1916 filming of Doyle's The Valley of Fear.) The play all but vanished from the boards following the author's death in 1937—one rare revival was by the Birmingham Repertory Theatre in England in 1952, Alfred Burke as Holmes—until a major Broadway revival in 1974. Accordingly, a great part of the material in the following pages will depict and describe the Gillette work and its author.

The section opens, however, with an amusing and almost forgotten Holmesian oddity of the theater: the performance of noted prizefighter James J. Corbett as Holmes in a brief Chicago production that opened on December 30, 1903. The Chicago Examiner review of the play is reprinted here (the byline, "Forrest Arden," was an Examiner house name for staff reviewers), together with the Great Northern Theatre ad for the show, also from the Examiner. The "Raffles" character also played by Corbett was, of course, the gentleman-burglar invented by Doyle's brother-in-law, E. W. Hornung.

James J. Corbett as "Raffles" Baffles New "Sherlock Holmes"

By Forrest Arden

It's a good thing that William Gillette is in town this week. He is thereby afforded the chance of a lifetime to step around to the Great Northern Theater and see how Sherlock Holmes should be played. Also, he might learn some things about playing Raffles if he has any ambitions that way, James J. Corbett being the gentlemanly instructor.

Mr. Corbett plays Raffles in his new piece, "The Burglar and the Lady," which Langdon McCormick built up by mingling the well-known attributes of Doyle's "Sherlock Holmes" with E. W. Hornung's "Raffles." Both characters are in the play, which opens up a new line of thought for ambitious playwrights. For instance, a judicious mixture of "Uncle Tom's Cabin" and "Rip Van Winkle" might make a dramatic cocktail that would be worth while and something great might result from the shaking up of "Hamlet" and "Othello" in the same bag.

Inasmuch as the former champion pugilist of the world plays Raffles, it is an easy guess that Sherlock Holmes gets the worst of it in every act and that "the burglar" finally gets "the lady." In this newest dramatic uplift, however, Mr. Corbett proceeds along new lines. Instead of foiling the other fellow with a right cross to the jaw and a left hook to the solar plexus, which have been the stand-bys of the forty-foot-ring drama in the past, the actor uses nothing more persuasive than a

pair of large 44-caliber revolvers when he wants to indicate that it is time for the curtain to fall. In nearly every instance Sherlock Holmes ends the act by gazing thoughtfully into the revolvers and reaching for the chandelier. This is a distinct advance over the corkscrew punch that has

GREAT NORTHERN

STARTING MATINEE TO-DAY

Special Matinee New Year's Day
Usual Mats. Wed. and Sat.

MITTENTHAL BROS. AMUSEMENT CO.
—PRESENT—

James J. Corbett
as "RAFFLES" in
The Burglar and the Lady

By LANGDON McCORMICK
Introducing the two Greatest Stage
Heroes of Modern Times
Raffles and Sherlock Holmes

Next Week—ARIZONA

dominated most of Mr. Corbett's artistic efforts in the past.

The "big scene" of the play comes in the second act when Raffles demonstrates how easily a bank safe is robbed by the scientific burglar of to-day. No rough work

with drills and gunpowder and wet blankets—that is all done away with now. When his trusty assistant has gained entrance to the bank and neatly snapped a pair of handcuffs on the faithful but trusting watchman, Raffles produces an electric drill from his kit bag. Donning a pair of rubber gloves, he attaches a plug on the end of a long wire leading from the drill to an incandescent lamp socket in the wall. The current is turned on, there are a number of blinding blue flashes—and presto, the chilled steel around the combination melts and runs like cheese, the combination falls into Raffles' hands and the door swings open. Tremendous applause greets this deft bit of real realism, showing the quick appreciation the public gives to progress in all lines.

To add to the interest of the bank-robbing scene it is performed in the presence of the bank cashier, who has come to the place to rob the safe himself and is detected by Raffles and his faithful assistant. Trembling and scared, he is compelled to sit in a chair and watch the exciting scene and when Raffles has drawn the redhot combination from its place in the door he drops it into the cashier's lap. What for? How simple! To burn his fingers so Sherlock Holmes will suspect the cashier of the robbery, of course. It is deduction backward, you see. Also the faithful assistant dons a "lame shoe" so the tracks in the dust will look like those of a lame man—

another great thought for the young idea in the gallery.

Having counted out the money and sent the limping assistant away with it, Raffles thoughtfully telephones for the police—as he is in disguise as a detective all this time. Sherlock Holmes arrives on the patrol wagon. Evidently "Sher" slept in the dormitory up-stairs with the reserves. He suspects Danvers, the detective (who is Raffles all the time, mind you), and places him under arrest at the muzzle of a long and shining gun.

But that doesn't bother Raffles. Oh, dear no. He lights a cigar with all the sang froid of the real Sherlock Holmes in the other play, gets ready to go with the policemen and asks Sherlock to assist him on with his overcoat. The great detective grudgingly holds the coat. Raffles slips his hands into the sleeves, then into the pockets and the next instant—zowie! Up he comes with two guns, one out of each outside pocket, trained on Holmes and the policemen. With a laugh of scorn he calmly backs off, R 3, and the curtain descends on the discomfited officers. Great? Well, it would make Charles E. Blaney blink, all right.

The love interest is not as well sustained as the title of the piece would indicate, but "the lady" is there good and strong in nearly every act. Norma Gray, who wins the somewhat tarnished heart of the burglar, is played by Mary Fermier, for many years leading woman with Joseph Murphy in his string of Erin-go-braghs. Dore Davidson, who plays the faithful assistant to the burglar, is also a well-known actor. Arthur V. Johnson plays Sherlock Holmes in a most determined manner, and Lily Sinclair Murray does very well in a pathetic bit of character work.

On October 24, 1910, Charles Frohman's introduction of Doyle's play The Speckled Band to American audiences opened in Boston to a rave review (only a bit shortened here) in the Boston American, reproduced on the following page. And Frohman's production of Sherlock Holmes, starring William Gillette, was due to open a week later at the producer's Hollis Street Theatre, as two ads from the American indicate, above. The Speckled Band used a live snake as the "band," just as Doyle had done in the play's first London performances. A stage photograph of three of the Boston Band's principal characters appears below, as it was published in the New York Evening Journal for November 29.

Irene Fenwick as Enid Stoner, Ivo Dawson as Dr. Watson, and H. H. McCollum as Ali,
in a scene from The Speckled Band, *at the Garrick Theatre.*

"SPECKLED BAND" THRILLS

Presented by a Splendid Cast, Including a Real Live Poisonous Snake

By Nicholas Young

Who said melodrama was dead? It was a foul slander. The throbbing drama had everything its own way at the Boston Theatre last evening—there was nothing else in sight, as you discovered in Charles Frohman's little nerve loosening palpitation that moved into town yesterday.

The opening of Mr. Frohman's producing season in Boston was done in full view of Sir Arthur Conan Doyle's "The Speckled Band," which caught the big audience where its best emotions were stored. It was another case of Sherlock Holmes to the rescue, and there was nothing quiet about the operation. It was no place for a man with a weak heart.

Few, if any, detective stories have equalled in thrilling intensity the Sherlock Holmes stories, and in "The Speckled Band" Sir Arthur dipped his pen deep into bright red ink. It was exhilarating, too, to follow the weird, cruel career of Dr. Grimesby Rylott, who plied a murderous game upon his own stepdaughters with a well trained serpent of the deadly poisonous variety.

Sherlock Holmes Is Welcome

The cunning of Rylott and his weird brutality made Holmes a welcome figure in the case. The timid man in the audience would have trusted no other detector of crime in a problem like this. It was no boy's work to face Rylott, as he was played by Edwin Stevens, who wore the whiskers of a philanthropist, but who didn't live up to the reputation of his beard.

Mr. Stevens easily made Rylott the dominating character in the play. By exceedingly intelligent acting he completely submerged his own marked personalities in the fiendish task laid out for him by the playwright. . . .

"The Speckled Band" brought one positive treat in Miss Irene Fenwick, a young English actress, who spread a delicious charm over the entire evening. Miss Fenwick's first appearance in Boston brought its own reward—both to the young woman herself and the audience. . . .

In Charles Millward you had a Holmes that met every requirement. The popular tradition of Holmes among theatregoers naturally follows a straight road to the Gillette idea, and Mr. Millward approached that idea with exceptionally good taste. He was a Holmes you could believe in, made so by a discriminating knowledge of character making. Mr. Millward was direct and forceful. . . .

If you like melodrama in large doses "The Speckled Band" will hold your attention. The audience last evening met it more than half way and gave it a stirring welcome. The introduction of a real snake in the third act was a bit of midway realism that sprinkled a few chills through the house. It was a well trained snake, too, for he played his part with a fine sense of proportion.

"The Speckled Band" is a strong play, admirably acted, and offers new proof that melodrama is on the market again.

A nervous artist's impressions at the new, creepy detective play.

From "The SPECKLED BAND"

DR. RYLOTT (LYN HARDING) in an uncanny frolic with his snake the "SPECKLED BAND", by which later he proposes to murder his step-daughter ENID STONER.

PHOTO BY MOFFETT

HOLMES (CLIFFE)

DR. RYLOTT warns SHERLOCK (H. COOPER) to cease his investigation of the mysteries at STOKE MORAN.

WITH THE IRISH PLAYERS

MOFFETT PHOTO

MISS EITHNE MAGEE

MISS KATHLEEN DRAGO

PHOTO BY MOFFETT

ENID STONER (MISS RENEE KELLEY), DR. WATSON (DAVID PROCTOR) and SHERLOCK HOLMES, listening to the weird music which heralds the coming of the "SPECKLED BAND" to the young woman's bed-chamber.

The Chicago Daily Tribune *for February 4, 1914, reviewed a production there of* The Speckled Band, *with Lyn Harding as the wicked Dr. Rylott. H. Cooper Cliffe was Holmes; David Proctor, Watson; and Renee Kelly, Enid Stoner. Said critic Percy Hammond of the* Tribune: *"There is wind outside the manor, and green lights illumine the dusk face of an Indian sehtinel as he stands guard at the casement....Above the lady's couch is a useless ventilator from which hangs a useless bell cord. Through this aperture the reptile will crawl and descend via the cord to the bed beneath, there to insert the virulent fang....You hear an outlandish melody played somewhere in the distance upon a mellow flute, calling the viper to duty....You hold your breath and fasten your eyes on the ventilator." Above is a montage of photos of the Chicago* Speckled Band *production. Note, at top center, Dr. Rylott tempting the "band" out of its wicker cage!*

PITYING THE POOR CRIMINALS

By Percy Hammond

WILLIAM GILLETTE AS "SHERLOCK HOLMES"

With what a vast compassion may we view the pitiful struggles of the intrepid and cunning propagandists of Evil as they seek a little triumph in Mr. Gillette's "Sherlock Holmes"! They scheme and they are courageous; they confront great perils and plan great campaigns of crime, only to be foiled in a well selected word and action or two by the sepulchral and eery agent of Good.

As Sisyphus doth roll, ever frustrate, the stone, so do these picturesque scoundrels compound their deeds of depredation, engage in a seemingly successful execution of them, and then at the instant of fruition have them terminate in discomfiture and discomfort.

*   *   *

These sympathetic reflections in favor of iniquity and those who perpetrate it were inspired by Mr. Gillette's return Monday night to the Blackstone in that agitating agent of entertainment distilled from the stories of A. Conan Doyle. Mr. Gillette, as the instrument of justice, was so infinite in his clairvoyance, so certain in his operations to circumvent wrong, that his adversaries, no matter how pernicious, evoked the sentiment of pity.

For instance, in the scene where the placid Sherlock invaded the Stepney gas chamber, an awful place to invade, with seemingly no hope to emerge alive, my suspense was all in behalf of the conspirators. They didn't stand a chance. Calm, immaculate, imperturbable, unarmed (save for a shot or two of cocaine), Mr. Gillette entered this grim and sinister rendezvous, noiselessly noisy. Against him was the Napoleon of misdemeanor, old Prof. Moriarty, with a malevolent troupe of banditti whose favorite sport was assassination. There he was, as I knew, anemic, probably full of dope, a skinny and somewhat adult knight, crusading for an affected heroine who was imprisoned in an adjacent dungeon. Yet I could feel more alarm for his opponents than for him or for her.

*   *   *

They were a chatty lot, these miscreants,

Chicago Daily Tribune *critic Percy Hammond here reviews the famed William Gillette as Holmes on January 12, 1916, in one of the many continuing revivals the playwright-actor did of his 1899* Sherlock Holmes. *(The reader will note that the famed cigar did not stay lit on opening night.) Above: Clare V. Briggs, noted by several generations for his marvelous comic studies of American domestic life in such newspaper series as "When a Feller Needs a Friend" and "Mr. and Mrs.," shines in an early drama-page portrayal of Gillette as Holmes for the Chicago* Sunday Tribune *of February 12, 1914. Below: This unusual pictorial advertisement—regrettably a bit mutilated—ran in the New York* World *for October 24, 1915; in its implied warning of "final performances" it was a bit premature!*

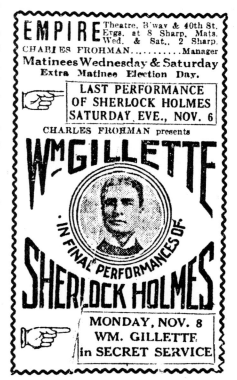

influenced, as I seem to be, by the insistent rhetoric of the main person of the drama. They talked and talked, crouching now and then, but not springing as they should have sprung. This tardiness was fatal. Mr. Gillette, interrupting a well balanced sentence by one of his opponents, smashed the dim lamp and, with the heroine in his arms, made a contemptuous exit. It was his plan to leave his lighted cigar upon a window sill, indicating thus that there was his means of egress, while really he departed through a side door. Last evening the lighted cigar did not work, but at that his escape was graceful, Gillettesque, and inevitable.

*   *   *

In his impersonation of Sherlock Holmes Mr. Gillette adds a new paradox to histrionics. He makes the character of the detective sententiously loquacious! That is to say that he speaks at length, and as he speaks at length you may see and hear the parentheses, the commas, and the semicolons separating and arranging the divisions of his sentences. But at the same time his quizzical remarks appear to have a brevity, an acid, staccato quality quite in keeping with your idea of a supernatural sleuth.

*   *   *

At any rate it is a bully show. Some one in back of me last evening described it with superiority as a good play for the Food and Drink set. It is more than that. It is a shrewd, tricky, conscienceless, and entertaining exhibit composed for the purpose of refreshing and amusing that numerous and not at all unintelligent class who do not care to ask "why?" in the theater. If Prof. Moriarty seeks to murder Sherlock Holmes in circumstances entirely foolish, uncharacteristic, and unnecessary, since Sherlock is to be much better and more safely assassinated later, it does not bother them. It does not bother me. And I am glad to know that Mr. Gillette appreciates in these performances of his the value of some nice, shivery, melodramatic music as an accompaniment to the tuneful proceedings upon the stage.

William Gillette Returns

And Sherlock Holmes Makes His Last Bow in the Flesh—A Memorable Event

By Edwin C. Hill

The Gay Nineties with us again—all mixed up in laughter and tears with Nineteen Twenty-nine—middle age renewing its irresponsible youth—Sherlock Holmes and Grover Whalen—Prof. Moriarty and Nicholas Murray Butler—the brutal Craigin in the Stepney Gas Chamber, and Dan Frohman sitting in a proscenium box—those wicked Larrabees, Jim and Madge—Winthrop Ames and Margaret Anglin and David Belasco and Charles Dana Gibson and Father Duffy—all commingled and confused in a lovely fog of sentiment. William Gillette returned to the stage. Sherlock Holmes making his last bow in the flesh.

That was the priceless drama enacted last night in the New Amsterdam Theater when Mr. Gillette came back after an absence of eight years to foil the wicked and rescue the virtuous. The play itself meant little. Probably the audience of last night could have dispensed with every single character except for the old Master of Acting. Probably the audience would have been as well pleased if he had walked alone through a few of the scenes, favoring us with those flowing and inimitable gestures of his hands and those crackling dry ironicisms that a whole generation has known. It was not the old play that counted—it was the old master himself.

If too many years have not come crowding upon your shoulders perhaps you do remember the first act—toward the end—where the Larrabees are trying to extort from Alice Faulkner the papers—those indispensable papers of melodrama. And perhaps you remember when poor Alice is about to be tortured the tall, slim, cool competent figure that makes his way into the Larrabee apartment—just in time. You never heard such a storm of applause as quaked the walls of the New Amsterdam last night when Mr. Gillette made his unforgettable entrance. Sherlock was on the job. There was no more need for worry. Sherlock had aged some, but Sherlock at seventy-four was as much a match for the blackest rascals of London as Sherlock ever was at forty-four.

Throughout the play the applause was like the firing of heavy guns. In the big scene of the play, when Holmes, at bay in the gas chamber, gets his cigar well alight, puts Alice behind him, smashes the lamp with a chair and is lost in the darkness

while his cigar glows from the table top, you would have thought the house was coming down. It was that way to the end at every important and significant climax. At other times the breathless silence that is accorded only to the great of the theater.

It is not likely that any old favorite of the public ever returned to meet a greater degree of admiration and respect. Youth in the house looked on and admired the courage that does not know how to quit. Older folks who had seen a younger Gillette—a Gillette with maybe a brisker

By 1929, Gillette had become a theatrical legend, and when he once more revived Sherlock Holmes *he was greeted everywhere with reviews and public response that echoed the sentiment of critic Edwin C. Hill's remarks, reprinted here from the New York* Sun *for November 26. As Hill put it, "It was not the old play that mattered—it was the old master himself." The portrait sketch above, by Manuel Qatael, is from the* Sun *of November 25. On December 13,* Life *magazine published the Ralph Barton caricature below.*

*YESTERDAY AND TODAY—
TAKE YOUR CHOICE.
William Gillette in the revival of "Sherlock Holmes" at the New Amsterdam, and Betty Starbuck in "Heads Up!" at the Alvin.*

step and perhaps a firmer voice—felt their hearts warmed in a way they could scarcely explain to themselves. Very largely the audience was made up of folk that are approaching or have passed the meridian of life—men and women who had seen Mr. Gillette thirty years ago, in his first appearance in "Sherlock Holmes"—or of others that witnessed the revivals of 1907 and 1909. They were renewing their youth. The fountain had not quite run dry.

At the very outset of the performance, before the curtain was raised upon the classic melodrama, Dr. Nicholas Murray Butler, president of Columbia University, appeared upon the stage and said a few words—just enough to set the key of the evening. He explained what an occasion of sentiment Mr. Gillette's return was, and requested the audience to remain after the last curtain while a tribute was being paid to Mr. Gillette. Not ten people left the crowded theater after the last darkening of the stage, and when the lights came on again Prof. William Lyon Phelps of Yale appeared before the footlights holding in his hands a book of letters—a book of embossed green leather covers, whose pages were made up of letters from a hundred men and women of note, all congratulating Mr. Gillette upon his return to the stage and especially upon his return in the play he himself has always liked best. Calvin Coolidge wrote from Northampton. Booth Tarkington said that he would rather see Mr. Gillette in Sherlock again than be a child on Christmas morning. Sir A. Conan Doyle, Sherlock's creator, wrote to say that his Sherlock was a wan and shadowy creature compared to the vivid, flesh-and-blood character that Mr. Gillette had given to the world. Dr. Henry Van Dyke wrote from Princeton, and there were letters from John Philip Sousa and Daniel Frohman and Francis Wilson and many, many more.

While Prof. Phelps spoke, Mr. Gillette stood by, keeping himself well under control, but perilously near the breaking point as any one could see. And when Mr. Phelps ceased and it came his time to talk a little, he made a delightful speech whose words counted not at all. It was the tone of his voice, the pride and appreciation in it, and the look in his eye that counted. It was nearly midnight before the house was cleared. . . .

"SHERLOCK HOLMES" BIDS FAREWELL TO US MODERNS

Few of the Older Generation Can Forget Their Thrill When They First Saw Gillette, Now on His Last Tour, in His Characterization of the Great Detective

By Walter Prichard Eaton

William Gillette is trouping again. The actor whose face and figure, whose voice and manner, gave the entire English-speaking world their mental image of Sherlock Holmes 30 years ago, is saying his farewell to our stage, and in this same character of Sherlock Holmes.

In a season when detective fiction, detective plays and "crime" melodramas seem to be the most popular fare, Gillette brings his daddy of the mall to light again, gets out the old silk dressing gown, fills the old pipe, composes his long, Yankee features into a sardonic mask and shows a new generation of Americans what manner of playwright and actor he was, before he retires permanently to his castle by the Connecticut. New Haven saw him first, Boston this week, then his own city of Hartford, and then Philadelphia, Baltimore and so on around through the Middle West before he finally doffs his make-up forever in New York city next May....

His first appearance in New York, at the age of 22, was at the Park Theatre, in "The Gilded Age," in 1877. He played the Foreman of the Jury, and spoke two lines, "We have," and "Not guilty." His first success as an actor came in Boston, at the old Museum, in Gilbert's "Broken Hearts." His first effort as a playwright was "The Professor," produced at the Madison Square Theatre, New York, on June 1, 1881, in which he played the title part.

Handsome Young Man

Gillette has always been a somewhat aloof though not unfriendly man, with a large share of that New England reticence which is, of course, his birth-right. In those youthful days he must have been rather extraordinarily handsome, to judge by his early pictures, but even his good looks were reticent. His was not the startling beauty—there is really no other word for it—of Harry Montague, who helped to found and named the Lambs Club, nor the dashing good looks of Maurice Barrymore, whom Gillette chose first for the hero of "Secret Service."...

Sherlock Holmes lighting the cigar that plays such a vital part in the thrilling climax to the Gas House Scene.

In 1886, at the Madison Square Theatre, Gillette produced an original play, "Held by the Enemy," one of the first Civil War dramas worth attention. Other adaptations followed, including one of Rider Haggard's "She" and Mrs Ward's best seller, "Robert Ellsmere," a book now quite forgotten, but in its day the talk of the town.

"Secret Service"

By the '90s Gillette was 35. He had written or adapted many plays, and meanwhile had constantly practiced his art as an actor.

And then Gillette wrote a play which was both popular and important, "Secret Service." It was first acted in Philadelphia, in 1895, with Maurice Barrymore, the handsome and witty father of Ethel and John, as the hero, and it was but a very moderate success. Barrymore was a splendid romantic actor, but he was not keyed to the style in which Gillette was working here. At the Garrick Theatre, New York, later the cradle of the Theatre Guild, in October, 1896, Gillette brought the play to Broadway, himself now playing

Capt Thorne, the Union spy, and its success was enormous. The next year he took the production to London and repeated his triumph.

Turns to Sherlock Holmes

After adapting a light comedy from the French, Gillette next turned to the reigning literary sensation of the day, or, at any rate, a sensation sharing the throne with Kipling—the Sherlock Holmes stories. Obviously the hero of those tales was cut to his measure as an actor and the public would be curious to see him in the part. On the opening night of the drama at the Garrick Theatre in New York, Nov. 6, 1899, Gillette made a characteristic curtain speech.

This little speech, which drips with the dry ironic wit of the author, a wit which he never permitted, alas! to stray very prominently into his plays, even his comedies, shows clearly enough that there was at least a faint burlesque element in "Sherlock Holmes." In piling up the improbable situations, the dangers and excitements, Gillette was indulging in a sly

Above and on the following page is the main body of a lengthy illustrated nostalgic piece on Gillette by Walter Prichard Eaton from the Boston Globe *for November 17, 1929. It salutes the actor's lifetime role as Holmes.*

laugh at the public. But, curiously enough, he also was indulging in a sly laugh at the critics and "highbrows." . . .

WILLIAM GILLETTE
Actor and Author, Today

The "Fade-out"

Gillette believed, and no doubt believes still, that the theatre is a commercial undertaking and exists to entertain people. He has said so many times. So with all the technical skill of a Pinero in ordering his incidents and with a technique of acting as modern and naturalistic as the critics could desire, he wrote and produced this preposterous play, made the thousands who sat before it in the theatre shiver with excitement, carried it to England and there repeated its success and accumulated another fortune for himself and his manager—as who should say—"That for your Ibsen!"

As a craftsman Gillette presented this play with every ounce of ability he could muster—which is a great deal. But as a man he stood above it and smiled at it and at the theatre where it flourished and at the public which flocked to it. As a man William Gillette always has suggested an intelligence bigger than the plays he has written.

In "Sherlock Holmes" he popularized, if he did not invent, the "fade-out," letting his stage slowly darken before the curtain came down. The device undoubtedly conspired to end each act with a touch of dream quality, and softened the shock of the absurdities.

He also made use of a device first successfully employed in America by James A. Herne—the quiet ending to an act instead of the traditional slam-bang climax and quick curtain dropped on the tableau.

In one act Holmes' office boy, Billie (an invention of Gillette's, not of Doyle's), has gone on a dangerous mission. Meanwhile there has been great excitement on the stage. But at last Sherlock sits alone in silence, smoking—and Billie dashes in, with clothes torn, but successful on his errand. Gillette took the pipe out of his mouth, contemplated the disheveled youth, mentally sized up, as the audience knew, the dangers the lad must have fought, and then drawled lazily: "Billie, you are a good boy."

"Yes, sir," said Billie. And on that little scene the lights dimmed out.

This was part of Gillette's technique of suggestive under-statement, and also his shrewd method of leaving you, the audience, after tickling you with exciting but wildly improbable incidents, a final memory of something quiet and natural and true. A marvelous showman, Will Gillette!

Hopelessly Identified

What he looked like in the role anybody knows who has even seen a picture of Sherlock Holmes, because after he had once played the part not even the artists could ever imagine Sherlock Holmes looking like anything but Gillette, and so delineated him. Character and player were as hopelessly identified together as were Rip Van Winkle and Joe Jefferson.

After three years as Holmes, Gillette acted for a season in the title role of Barrie's "The Admirable Crichton," again a part admirably adapted to his ideal of imperturbable, calm force and dry, sardonic humor. In 1905 he acted in London and America in his own play, "Clarice," wherein he tried, without conspicuous success, to achieve emotion through character rather than incident. Later he adapted and played Bernstein's "Samson," played in "Dear Brutus," in Clare Kummer's "A Successful Calamity," in a play

With his pipe going full blast Sherlock Holmes could solve any problem.

of his own, "The Dream Maker," in 1921, in which he tried vainly to go back to his melodramatic formula, and in a revival of "Diplomacy." . . .

But the plays he wrote after "Clarice" did not fit in the new age. Something had come into playwriting which escaped him. Perhaps it was something he had laughed

GILLETTE AS SHERLOCK
Drawn from Life by Frederic Dorr Steele

at. Perhaps the theatre had gained a higher standard of "amusement" than prevailed when exciting situation for its own sake was enough to make success. At any rate, Gillette in later years had to act in the plays of others to keep afloat on the modern current, and at length he chose rather the retirement of his estate in Connecticut, on the bank of the river not far from its mouth. . . .

Part of Theatrical History

But be that as it may, all of us who can remember the '90s recall with gratitude the thrilling evenings, or the merry evenings, his plays then gave us, the revelations he made to us of new possibilities of illusion from naturalness, and the potent spell of his own icily calm but strangely dynamic acting. Younger ones among us can remember him, perhaps, as Crichton, sardonically sitting by that pot of stew, or as the tall, black figure in "A Successful Calamity" or the wistful father with his dream child in "Dear Brutus."

But nobody who ever saw him as Sherlock Holmes will think of him first in any role but that. The impersonation was one of those rare and unforgettable marriages between a player and his part which occur but seldom in a generation, and are always enshrined in theatrical history. If we have any respect at all for our traditions, any affection for our artists, William Gillette's farewell tour of our stage this Winter ought to be a happy climax to his long and brilliant career.

MACE GREENLEAF AS
SHERLOCK HOLMES

The "final" Gillette tour continued, the praises never ceasing to ring for the aging actor. An advertisement (below) for Seattle's Metropolitan theater, displaying Booth Tarkington's oft-repeated praise of Gillette, appeared in the city's Post-Intelligencer for February 21, 1932. On February 27, the paper's critic Everhardt Armstrong announced that "'Sherlock Holmes' is all the more enjoyable because in the revival it has been subjected to no ill-advised retouching. It is a play frankly of its period, a play that takes us back to the London of four-wheelers and the ceremonious manners of a less nervous age than ours. Mr. Gillette, still jaunty in his long overcoat and cap, gives a performance remarkable for its polish. Watching him, you rub your eyes. Can it be possible that this gifted actor made his debut as long ago as 1875?"

Other actors have starred in the Gillette-scripted Holmes in the course of the play's history. Typical of these, perhaps, was Mace Greenleaf, shown at left as he was sketched in the Los Angeles Examiner for October 8, 1906. Otheman Stevens, who reviewed the Los Angeles production for the Examiner, had this to say of the actor: "Mace Greenleaf succeeded in making Holmes what he should be, intensively repressed in action, a quiet egotist who justifies his self-esteem—one who, despite his profession of thief-catcher, maintains the pose of a gentleman…"

An important new production of Sherlock Holmes, on Broadway, would be mounted almost forty years after Gillette's death. But, earlier, a musical interpretation of "A Scandal in Bohemia," from The Adventures of Sherlock Holmes, would premiere in Boston as Baker Street; its New York opening was on February 16, 1965. With a book by Jerome Coopersmith and music and lyrics by Marian Grudeff and Raymond Jessel, the musical starred Fritz Weaver as Holmes, Inga Swenson as Irene Adler, Peter Sallis as Watson, and Martin Gabel as Moriarty. MGM would produce the original-cast recording. Opposite: Weaver, Swenson, and Gabel as they appeared in Baker Street.

Further, nonmusical, recordings of Holmes stories include Caedmon's Basil Rathbone discs and Decca's "Doctor Watson Meets Sherlock Holmes and The Final Problem" (dramatized by John Keir Cross), with Sir John Gielgud as Holmes, Ralph Richardson as Watson, and Orson Welles as Moriarty.

For the Christian Science Monitor of November 18, 1974, John Beaufort reviewed the major revival in New York of William Gillette's Sherlock Holmes that year. He told how "Fog of the kind that Dickens described as 'a London particular' seeps out from the stage of the Broadhurst Theater as the curtain rises.…The wail of violins and the moan of cellos have briefly set the mood of Victorian mystery." Beaufort found that "the performance keeps faith with the author's high-style melodramatics" and that "the British cast delivers the florid dialogue with the kind of serious make-believe which is a tribute to the players' art." He praised the "meticulous precision of Mr. Wood's aquiline-featured detective." In the Toronto Globe and Mail for January 11, 1975, an entertaining and informative commentary not merely on the new production and its origins but on the play's history appeared—with an amusing simulation of turn-of-the-century British newspaper headlines. Only slightly abridged, the article follows, on pages 66 and 67, with, topmost, a meditative John Wood as he appeared in the play.

Photograph by Martha Swope

PRESUMED DEATH OF MR. SHERLOCK HOLMES

Tragic Occurrence as the Detective Plunges from Precipitous Ledge

PROF. MORIARTY ALSO PERISHES

Unprecedented Efforts at Revival Successful in Manhattan Melodrama

From Our Own Correspondent Mr. Herbert Whittaker. New York

Because I was involved, in a humble way, with the astonishing events, I have agreed to set down the true facts behind the return of Holmes to unprecedented power and popularity in the English-speaking world. You could call it, in all proper respect, The Case of the Third Coming.

It is well-known to Mr. Sherlock Holmes' many friends that he had been resurrected following a dastardly attempt on his life by the late Arthur Conan Doyle. I refer to the unfortunate affair at the Reichenbach Falls, when Doyle, admittedly jealous, caused both Holmes and his great enemy, Professor Moriarty, to plunge to their deaths.

I do not have to remind my readers that six or seven years later, Holmes defied Doyle and nature by returning to life in pursuit of the Hound of the Baskervilles. Doyle accepted defeat, offering no explanation (as if one were possible) and Holmes continued his unprecedented career until his retirement to a small Sussex farm in 1903.

Friends and admirers of the illustrious detective were not astonished perhaps when an obituary, reported as that of Mr. Sherlock Holmes, president of the South Sussex Apiarist Society, appeared in the Strand Magazine, generally accounted a reputable periodical, in the December, 1948, issue.

There was admittedly a strong belief at that time that Holmes had been done to death by the public which pretended such respect. But by 1948, radio television and even ballet had taken over Holmes from the theatre, where he had made his first appearance (in effigy, I need not add) as early as 1894 when impersonated by an obscure Glaswegian actor named John Webb.

The infamous Doyle encouraged such

theatricalities, although notably not gifted as a dramatist. While pretending "grave doubts about putting Holmes on the stage," he secretly sent a five-act drama, first to Sir Herbert Beerbohm Tree, and later (when that was rejected) to the American impresario Charles Frohman. Of that, I shall have more to say later.

But by 1948, Holmes had been impersonated, and even guyed, by such thespians as Basil Rathbone, John Barrymore, Eille Norwood, Clive Brook (very un-Holmesian), Raymond Massey, Arthur Wontner (the most Holmesian), to be followed by Peter Cushing, Stewart Granger and Robert Stephens, star of the controversial Private Lives of Sherlock Holmes.

If the Strand obituary was not entirely to be trusted, one could not avoid the impression that Holmes had died a victim of mass impersonation.

Yet in New York last week, I was astonished to see that hawk-like face dominating the crime and mystery sections of Brentano's, Scribner's and Doubleday, all illustrious booksellers along Fifth Avenue! And, just as surely as that profile rules these emporiums, Sherlock Holmes is also declared box office champion of the Broadway stage in a revival by no less a distinguished body than the Royal Shakespeare Company.

So successful has this drama, Sherlock Holmes, been in New York (as it was in London earlier), that every American actor who can muster a modest British accent is now being auditioned by the importers . . . to replace the English actors when American Equity declares their stay ended. "Sherlock Holmes is alive and back and living in Manhattan!" as the billboards like to say.

How did all this all come about?

I propose, as a fortunate bystander, to relate the true facts behind this Third Coming of Sherlock Holmes, but I shall take the liberty of calling it, instead, The Case of the Missing Melodrama.

I happened to be staying overnight with an old friend, Ronald Brydon. . . . He had driven me to Oxford to see 'Tis Pity She's a Whore, and we were to return to London on the morrow.

It was late when we returned. . . . As we sat down over a drink in the book-lined room, I knew that something was troubling my friend.

Brydon has had a remarkable career since his days of study at Trinity College, University of Toronto. He became a most distinguished colleague as drama critic for The Observer, then, called to an even more precarious trade, became literary manager, or dramaturge, of the Royal Shakespeare Company. . . .

"I have been reading old melodramas," he began. And I understood the reason for his gloom. "I feel that the RSC must venture into Victorian melodrama next but the old texts are all so dreadful, mere scenarios for stage effects. But it is a period we have not explored. Nor has anybody else."

I showed no signs that I knew what he was thinking. My friend was referring to the great rivalry, for popularity and subsidy, between the RSC and the National Theatre of Great Britain, with the arch-actor Sir Laurence Olivier at its helm and, far more sinister, another former critic, Kenneth Tynan, as a power behind the throne.

In his anxiety to discover a Victorian melodrama suitable for revival and again outwit Olivier and Tynan, my old friend had overlooked one salient fact.

No all the most successful Victorian melodramas were of British origin! Hadn't the United States developed a lively trade in melodrama by the last quarter of the Victorian era? I asked.

The name of William Gillette's great success, Sherlock Holmes, came up. A dear old friend of mine, Roberta Beatty, whom Brydon had not met, had toured in it as a very young actress when Gillette revived it for the last time.

I recalled her story of the moment when the great impersonator of Holmes, by then in his seventies, had whipped off the wig of his disguise one night and with it had come the old actor's own Holmes wig. He stood bald, save for the metal band which clamped his sideburns on. But such was the power of Gillette over his audience, recounted Miss Beatty, that not a single soul dared laugh as Gillette recovered his missing hair-piece, donned it and proceeded to bring the scene to its accustomed climax.

I glanced across at my friend. In his eyes was a strange gleam of inspiration. I coul see there the glimpse of future triumph over the proud Sir Laurence, the cynical Tynan and the whole fabric of Britain's vaunted National Theatre! He spoke:

"And we have just the perfect actor to play Holmes!" he cried. "His name is John Wood. I shall write to the Gillette estate tomorrow!"

Which I presume he did, for not long after, after I had returned to these shores, my friend wrote of the success of the enterprise born that night. It transpired that what Gillette had played, with such acclaim (in London as in America) was Doyle's original script, heavily re-written by the American actor to suit his own purposes. This even included a romantic involvement for Holmes as "a happy ending."

Sure enough, at New York's Broadhurst Theatre last week, that same John Wood took Miss Mel Martin, as Alice Faulkner, in his arms for the final curtain. But up until that moment, Wood had been as hawkily positive, as magnificently self-sufficient, as omnipresent as a true impersonator of Sherlock Holmes must be.

"The Broadway audience sits," I wrote to my dear friend Brydon the following night, "entranced by the goings-on at the rented home of the treacherous Larrabees, at 221B Baker Street (with young Sean Clarke playing the role of Billy, which young Charlie Chaplin had opposite Gillette in 1905) in the Stepney gas chamber, Moriarty's stronghold and Dr. Watson's consulting-room, with fog swirling about the London streets in between.

"Never" I wagered, "has the Broadway audience heard so much plot-making, seen so little characterization or enjoyed itself so hugely as they did in welcoming the return, once again, of the thrice-immortal Holmes." . . .

...Further stage interpretations of Holmes would follow—most significantly (for the late 1970s), Paul Giovanni's The Crucifer of Blood. *A caricature by Al Hirschfeld of Paxton Whitehead as the detective (see title page) appeared in the New York* Times *for January 5, 1979.*

Scenes from New York playwright Paul Oakley's projected Hound of the Baskervilles *were read at the annual dinner of the Adventuresses of Sherlock Holmes on January 9, 1981, in New York. (The Adventuresses' organization was founded in 1967 by women at Albertus Magnus College in New Haven, Connecticut, in protest against the exclusively male Baker Street Irregulars. Since 1974, their dinner, as well as the annual meeting and dinner of the Irregulars, has taken place on the Friday nearest January 6, a date agreed upon by Sherlockians as Holmes's birthday.) The final act of Oakley's new* Hound *ends on an uncanonical note. Holmes suggests, "Now my dear Watson, I think we can call the constabulary to have all this taken care of. We must return to London, and turn our thoughts into more pleasant channels. I have a box tomorrow night for* Les Huguenots. *Have you heard the De Reszkes?" His friend counters with: "Buffalo Bill's Wild West entertainment also opens tomorrow. I don't suppose, Holmes, you'd be willing to forego the opera just this once in favor of Sitting Bull?" Holmes (at curtain): "Oh, really, Watson."*

FARNUM, GILLETTE, GISH AND YOUNG ON SCREEN

By the Photoplay Editor

A good many weeks after its release date, "Sherlock Holmes," the Essanay film introducing William Gillette to the screen, reached Philadelphia yesterday at the Princess. Possibly the delay has been a matter of waiting till the censors got through with dear old innocent Sherlock and his needle, but perhaps it has simply proved too "static" a film for many of the exhibitors.

At any rate, H. S. Sheldon's screen version follows the stage play of Mr. Gillette's altogether too closely. Act by act we watch the parlor of the Larrabees, the Moriarty's cellar, Holmes's study, the Stepney gas chamber and Doctor Watson's consulting room. As a result the action is slower than it should be and the connection of the various parts and people of the plot isn't so very clear or interesting. However, we have Mr. Gillette on the screen and that aquiline profile can still raise a thrill.

* * *

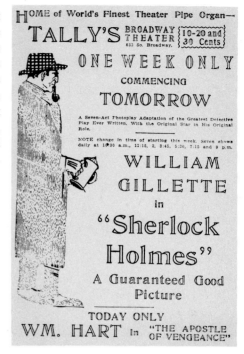

William Gillette, seen opposite in a still from the 1916 film made from his Sherlock Holmes, *was not the first motion-picture Sherlock. The earliest Holmes film had been produced in 1903:* Sherlock Holmes Baffled; *the first actor to do a Holmes series was a Dane, Viggo Larsen, in 1908–9; a French Holmes was film actor Georges Treville, in 1912 and 1916; Ferdinand Bonn, a German playwright-actor, had been a 1914 Holmes for Vitascope;* A Study in Scarlet *was filmed in England in 1914, with James Bragington as the detective—these among many other Holmes films and Holmes actors. Not many American newspapers printed formal reviews of motion pictures as early as 1916, so that a broad spectrum of critical reaction to Gillette's film that year is not accessible. As a sample, one review is reprinted above that ran in the Philadelphia* Evening Ledger *on September 12. At right is an advertisement for the movie that ran in the Los Angeles* Times *for June 25. The film—essentially the play translated to the screen, and the only visual record of Gillette's performance at the height of his talents as Holmes—is not known to exist today.*

An engaging caricature of Holmes composed entirely of swirling pipe smoke enhances a January 27, 1917, Moving Picture World *trade-journal announcement (above) of the American release of a British Holmes feature of 1916. The film was produced by Samuelson Film Mfg. Co., Ltd., and starred Henry A. Saintsbury as Holmes, with Arthur M. Cullin as Watson.*

In its December 3, 1921, issue, Moving Picture World *announced American distribution of the first sizable British venture into Sherlock Holmes film production—the fifteen-title Alexander Film series starring Eille Norwood as the great detective. At the top of the next page: A follow-up advertisement for the series, in the same trade journal for December 24, featured (unlike the earlier ad) a companion for Holmes—Hubert Willis as the series' Watson. All two-reelers, the titles included these stories, from various Doyle collections: "The Beryl Coronet," "The Man with the Twisted Lip," "The Resident Patient," "The Dying Detective," "The Devil's Foot," "A Case of Identity," "A Scandal in Bohemia," "The Noble Bachelor" (a good choice, for Sherlockians generally consider this to be Doyle's best "American" Holmes story), "The Yellow Face," "The Red-Headed League," "The Copper Beeches," "The Empty House," "The Tiger of San Pedro" (an alternate title for "The Adventure of Wisteria Lodge"), "The Priory School," and "The Solitary Cyclist." The second Alexander Film series of Eille Norwood as Holmes, released in 1922, included "The Adventure of the Norwood Builder"! Both series were produced by Stoll Picture Productions in England.*

The John Barrymore Sherlock Holmes, *of 1922, was believed, like the Gillette film, to have been lost. Quite recently it has, fortunately, surfaced—to the delectation of film fans and Sherlockians alike. Below is a review (only slightly abbreviated here) of the film from the San Francisco* Chronicle *for November 21. On September 26, the Philadelphia* Evening Ledger *had said of Barrymore's Holmes: "The part of the great detective gives Barrymore no great emotional acting opportunities, but those who believe he cannot satisfy the part should go and be undeceived. He is just as Gillette was before him, cool, calculating and resourceful, the kind of a hero to send shivers up one's spine, and then thaw them out with a laugh or a sigh of satisfaction. Barrymore plays the part as if he enjoyed it more than anything he ever did."*

Opposite and on the succeeding pages: a stunning still from the Barrymore film and three advertisements—the first as printed in the Portland Oregonian *for October 28, 1922, the second from the* Oregonian *for October 27, and the third from the San Francisco* Examiner *for November 25.*

BARRYMORE IS SEEN IN FINE MYSTERY PLAY

**Sherlock Holmes' Many
Thrilling Adventures Given
at Imperial Theater**

CROWDS DELIGHTED

**Star's Art Is Paramount,
Though There Is
Strong Cast**

By George C. Warren

Albert Parker has transferred to the screen something of the elements of mystery, power and fascination that Conan Doyle's great deductor, Sherlock Holmes, holds for readers and which William Gil-

lette put so well on the speaking stage. It is the Gillette play, amplified a bit with explanatory notes in the form of scenes showing the early history of Alice Faulkner and her sister Rose and the causes that led Holmes to take up his life work of trapping the slimy Moriarty, that is at the Imperial Theater and is holding attention there of large audiences.

Barrymore Is Star

John Barrymore is the star of the production, although in acting values Gustave von Seyffertitz follows closely in his footsteps in the favor of the audiences. It is a great performance Von Seyffertitz gives of the poisonous spider who is head of the London crime world.

But Barrymore's wonderful art is paramount after all and dwarfs everything else

in the picture. His classic profile seems a bit blurred, however; the chin is taking on a strength it has not had before, and the lower jaw seems to have grown heavier than formerly, all of which goes to making a stronger face for the admirable Jack. . . .

The story of [Holmes's] rescue of the girl and his capture of Moriarty is one of breathless interest.

All the thrills of melodrama are in the picture plus the touch of mystery and the added glow of romance.

The cast is a remarkable one aside from Barrymore and Von Seyffertitz. Carol Dempster is the Alice, and a sweet-faced one; Hedda Hopper and Anders Randolph play the evil Larrabees; Roland Young is the Dr. Watson, and others are William H. Powell, Robert Schable, Percival Knight, Reginald Denny, David Torrence and Louis Walhesm.

72

John Barrymore

America's foremost actor brings to the screen the greatest dramatic role of all time.

in

SHERLOCK HOLMES

Directed by Albert Parker. Adapted from William Gillette's stage play founded on Sir Conan Doyle's stories

Don't miss it when it comes!

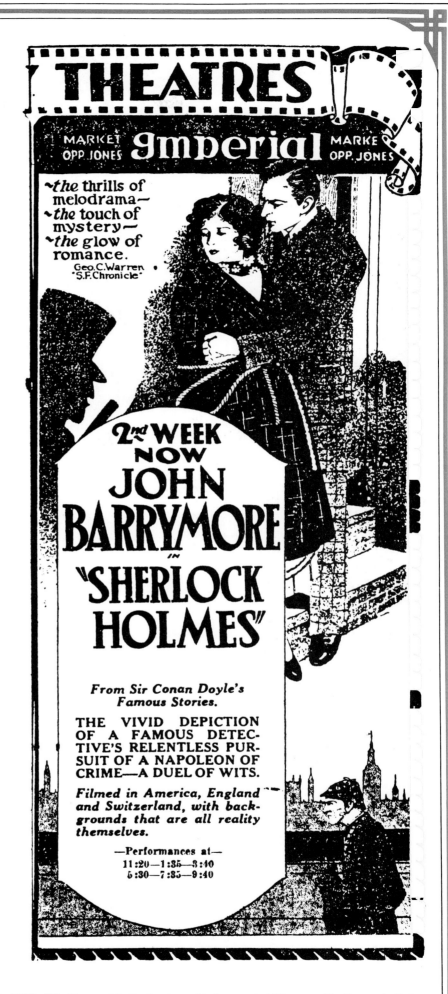

Barrymore was by no means the sole movie Holmes of the 1920s. Eille Norwood, in England, would of course hold the record for the most—forty-seven—Holmes films, all made between 1921 and 1923, though only two were feature-length motion pictures. American actor Carlyle Blackwell would be the last silent-film Holmes—in Germany's Der Hund von Baskerville, *in 1929.*

Below, left, is a rare advertisement for Eille Norwood's Hound of the Baskervilles, as it appeared in the San Francisco Examiner for December 4, 1921.

Film spoofs of Sherlock Holmes would be many, in the 1920s (as well as in the 1930s and 1940s). In July 1922, Los Angeles's Loew's State theater offered a Metro film, Sherlock Brown, "A Rapid-Fire Comedy Drama," starring Bert Lytell. Less than a year later, the Seattle Post-Intelligencer (January 7, 1923) carried a movie announcement for Doris May in Up and At 'Em; above is a detail of the ad. On July 4, 1924, the same newspaper printed the advertisement, below, for the famed Buster Keaton (mustachioed!) Sherlock Jr.

"Quick, Watson, the needle!" It's our old friend, Sherlock Holmes, doing a comeback. Clive Brook plays him in the picture at Granada. But where's the fore-and-aft-cap? Sketch by Korburg.

At the twenties' end, British actor Clive Brook became the screen's first talking Holmes in The Return of Sherlock Holmes; *the ad, above left, is from the* San Francisco Examiner *of December 6, 1929. The film was set in that year rather than in the late nineteenth century—and note the comment on the updating in a caption under Korburg's sketch of Brook from the October 20* San Francisco Call-Bulletin *at top right. Brook would remain the screen's principal new incarnation of Holmes for the next few years; in 1930, he and William Powell, celebrated for his Philo Vance performances in screen adaptations of the S. S. Van Dine books, would "meet" in a skit in Paramount's multi-star vehicle* Paramount on Parade.

Brook's second film as the Great Detective was Sherlock Holmes, *of 1932, with Reginald Owen as Watson. Filmed once more against a contemporary background, the picture's plot likewise had little to do with Gillette's play of the same name—or with anything in the original Doyle canon. Below, left, is an advertisement that ran in the* San Francisco Chronicle *for November 18. The second ad for Brook's* Sherlock Holmes, *an unusual one, was seen in the Portland* Oregonian *for April 8, 1933. The* Oregonian *revealed: "The story tells of the reign of terror that Moriarty intends to institute in London and to carry out his threat he imports the most dangerous criminals from every part of the globe. First, he intends to get rid of Holmes and Gore-King, the latter at the head of Scotland Yard. A plot whereby Holmes will become the unsuspecting slayer of Gore-King fails, even though the master criminal has engineered it. Then starts the final series of events that lead to the capture of Moriarty. This is not done, however, until Moriarty has had his inning against Holmes by holding his sweetheart captive and causing the detective no end of trouble."*

The first sound adaptation of Doyle's The Speckled Band (1930) starred Raymond Massey, and was released in America by its English producers in early 1932. On January 13, a Philadelphia Evening Ledger review told: "With a good Sherlock and a good villain the picture measures up as first rate entertainment. Raymond Massey…is the astute detective, illustrating all of the competence and not too much of the complacency of the character. Lyn Harding, also a Shakespearean actor…is the excellent villain." Above, from the film, are Harding (left) and Massey. The advertisement for the film is from the Ledger for January 12.

In his autobiography, A Hundred Different Lives (Boston: Little, Brown, 1979, pp. 113–14), Massey had this to say about the film: "The film-makers would have nothing to do with the calabash pipe…Mrs. Hudson and the enchanting disorder of Baker Street, the violin and the hypodermic needle. Instead Holmes was given a magnificent suite with glass flowers and modern art furniture, typists, secretaries, dictaphones…" The film also featured Athole Stewart and Angela Baddeley.

Opposite page: Britisher Arthur Wontner made the greatest number of sound films—five—as Holmes before Basil Rathbone took on the mantle. Michael Pointer, in The Sherlock Holmes File (New York: Clarkson N. Potter, Inc., 1976, p. 47), has complimented Wontner highly: "It is hard to write about Arthur Wontner's portrayals of Holmes without an excess of superlatives. After a string of Holmeses of assorted shapes and styles…his appearance in The Sleeping Cardinal in 1931 tended to make enthusiasts lightheaded in their response." Pointer describes Wontner as a "gentler, mellower Holmes…but a character of great intellectual strength." Like those of Clive Brook, the Wontner films were contemporary in setting, as were all but the first two Rathbone movies that would follow—underscoring the fact that it was usually the popularly perceived image of Holmes that brought viewers to these films, not a fond familiarity with the original texts.

The publicity still for the Wontner film The Missing Rembrandt provides a glimpse of the actor's Watson, Inspector Lestrade, and Mrs. Hudson. The advertisement, and indeed the review, of The Triumph of Sherlock Holmes—both from the Philadelphia Evening Ledger for August 23, 1935, the year of the film's American release—reflect the low-key, though appreciative, American reception of the Wontner Holmes.

CARLO RAVELLI · THE AGENT · INSPECTOR LESTRADE · DR. WATSON · MRS. HUDSON · SHERLOCK HOLMES · LADY VIOLET · CLAUDE · THE BARON

"The MISSING REMBRANDT"
Sherlock Holmes Thriller
with ARTHUR WONTNER
— A First Division Release —

SHERLOCK HOLMES IS REVIVED IN FILM ON EUROPA SCREEN

Arthur Wontner Plays Lead in British Mystery "THE TRIUMPH OF SHERLOCK HOLMES" —Europa

Produced by Julius Hagen for Gaumont-British. Directed by Leslie S. Hiscott. From the Conan Doyle novel, "The Valley of Fear."

THE CAST

Sherlock Holmes ...... Arthur Wontner
Dr. Watson .... Ian Fleming
Prof. Moriarty........... Lyn Harding
John Douglas .... Leslie Perrins
Ettie Douglas .... Jane Carr
Inspector Lestrade ... Charles Mortimer

If Sherlock Holmes could view his glorification in "The Triumph of Sherlock Holmes" at the Europa, his verdict would be "Element'ry, my dear Watson, element'ry."

There's no toying with supersmooth villains in this opus. Prof. Moriarty waves

threatening arms and grimaces horribly— and meets his death with a satisfying "clunk" in the castle moat. Inspector Lestrade grasps all the more obvious clues in film-police style. Holmes himself steers straight through the tangled evidence. He reaches the solution almost as soon as the

the Cool EUROPA
Market Above 16th
STARTS TODAY!
Sir Arthur Conan Doyle's
Master Sleuth Solves His
Greatest Case!
"The TRIUMPH of SHERLOCK HOLMES"
ARTHUR WONTNER
LYN HARDING

audience, with never a wrinkle on his brow to indicate the great brain at work. Dr. Watson really steals the show with his unerring grasp on the wrong solution, and shy determination to be in the front row.

The result is perhaps the most delightful sort of relaxation. This "Triumph" is one

in which the audience can take part, and one in which a reader of Conan Doyle, whatever his present sophistication, can feel again the early fascination exerted by Sherlock Holmes. The production is also "element'ry."

Holmes has retired, but a juicy murder in the neighborhood, and a plea for help from Inspector Lestrade, bring him to the scene of the crime. Prof. Moriarty, his pet enemy, has engineered the plot and is drawn from his lair to rescue a subordinate villain. Holmes, by an interest in setting-up exercises and floor plans of the castle, assembles an unwilling cast for the denouement.

Arthur Wontner looks the part of Holmes, even to the long-waisted dressing gown. His pipe, however, will inconvenience Americans. It teams up with the unfamiliar British accent and spoils some of the dialogue. Moriarty finds a perfect combination of physical strength and half-mad facial expression in Lyn Harding. Ian Fleming does a splendid job, in a role whose limits are not so clearly defined, as the dapper Dr. Watson.

Basil Rathbone, in the artfully and faithfully produced Hound of the Baskervilles, released as a major film by Twentieth Century-Fox, burst like a bombshell on the popular audience's awareness in 1939. He is seen, opposite, with his cohort, Nigel Bruce, in a still from the film. For most American moviegoers, little remembering by then the ill-distributed Wontner and Massey pictures, and quite forgetful of the Brook films of the early thirties, seeing Rathbone and Bruce on the screen was like discovering Sherlock Holmes and his assistant for the first time. The importance of the film may readily be judged by its announcement, left, which filled the top ten inches of a twelve-inch double-feature ad in the San Francisco Chronicle for March 30.

With Eileen Creelman's review, the New York Sun used the portrait sketch of Rathbone by Manuel Qatael, at lower left, on March 25. Creelman called the film "tense, frequently and not too obviously relieved with humor, and enacted by a cast that makes characters out of figures in a mystery melodrama. Basil Rathbone, lean, nervous and looking exactly like any description of the brilliant Mr. Holmes, is in top form as the super-detective....A shrewd bit of casting has put Nigel Bruce in the role of the pompous slow-witted doctor. The pair...should certainly be seen in other Conan Doyle tales....Some grand eerie photography heightens the suspense, giving the moor a distinct personality of its own." Ms. Creelman felt that Fox had "avoided two pitfalls, playing the melodrama in either the Metro-Goldwyn-Mayer flip and casual manner, or in the Warner breathless-paced pace....The picture is far from old-fashioned, but it tells the yarn in much the same spirit as it was written." The cast included Richard Greene as Sir Henry Baskerville, Wendy Barrie as Beryl Stapleton, Lionel Atwill as James Mortimer, John Carradine as Barryman, and Beryl Mercer as Mrs. Mortimer.

Another early drawing of Rathbone as Holmes, at lower right, is by Feg Murray for his King Features syndicated "Seein' Stars" for March 25.

SOMETHING TELLS ME THAT THIS DOESN'T AGREE WITH ME

BRITISHER
BASIL RATHBONE
HAD TO LEARN TO SMOKE A PIPE FOR HIS ROLE OF SHERLOCK HOLMES IN "THE HOUND OF THE BASKERVILLES". (HE HAD POSED FOR PUBLICITY PICTURES WITH A PIPE IN HIS MOUTH MANY TIMES—BUT NEVER ACTUALLY SMOKED ONE.)

Illustrating the growth of the use of Holmes's image for burlesque in films of the late 1930s and beyond is a cut, below at left, of Robert Woolsey (of the once-famed Wheeler and Woolsey comedy team) in Holmesian costume for the film The Nitwits, *1936, seen as it appeared in the Los Angeles* Times *for April 7. To the right of Woolsey: Lou Costello, of the Abbott and Costello team, in a 1951 Holmesian burlesque,* Abbott and Costello Meet the Invisible Man *(H. G. Wells's character bedeviled the two stars); the picture appeared in a publicity release in the San Francisco* Chronicle. *The* Oakland Tribune *for January 29, 1943, ran the advertisement for* Who Done It?—*in which the "wiser" of the two comedians used the Holmes hat and pipe, Costello assuming the guise of a Watson. At bottom left is a desperate-looking Errol Flynn in a deerstalker (from the film* Footsteps in the Dark*), as seen in the Oakland* Post-Inquirer *on April 9, 1941. At far right: A Charlie-McCarthy-as-Sherlock-Holmes silver-plated spoon was offered by* Chase & Sanborn *in 1936 to anyone who sent the company ten cents plus a Chase & Sanborn coffee label. Below the spoon is a still from* Charlie McCarthy, Detective *as it appeared in the San Francisco* News *on February 10, 1940; Mortimer Snerd and ventriloquist Edgar Bergen look on.*

From the collection of Jerry Margolin; photo courtesy April DeSalvo

The Holmes screen legend would not—will not—die. Peter Cushing (1959), Christopher Lee (1962), and John Neville (1965) would play later Holmeses, among other actors. The 1970s, especially, would witness a great return of interest in the Doyle detective. Holmes, played by Nicol Williamson, would meet Sigmund Freud in the film adaptation of Nicholas Meyer's 1976 novel, The Seven-Per-Cent Solution. *Christopher Plummer, opposite, as Holmes would battle Jack the Ripper in Avco Embassy Pictures' 1978 film* Murder by Decree. *And...of course, there has been television; and though a thorough survey would be impossible, suffice it to say that TV had its first Sherlock Holmes series—broadcast live by the BBC—as early as 1951.*

SHERLOCK HOLMES IN RADIO DRAMAS

Noted Detective Character to Be Portrayed

SERIES STARTS TONIGHT

Bringing to life Sherlock Holmes, the great character detective created by the late Sir Arthur Conan Doyle, and his inseparable companion Dr. Watson, a new series of radio dramas entitled "The Adventures of Sherlock Holmes" will be introduced to The Oregonian station's listeners tonight between 9 and 9:30 o'clock under the sponsorship of G. Washington Coffee.

Tonight's episode will be "The Musgrave Ritual" with Richard Gordon and Leigh Lovell, and Joe Bell as narrator. While hunting a buried treasure at the old Musgrave manor Sherlock Holmes discovers the body of a man. In the course of events he solves the murder mystery and also uncovers the treasure.

Sherlock Holmes emerged on radio in late 1930, at virtually the same time popular dramatic broadcasting had spread from coast to coast. (Broadcasting in the 1920s had tended toward music, sports, news, and instructional shows.) Sponsored by G. Washington Coffee—one of their 1934 ads (San Francisco Examiner, *May 28) appears, right—this first national radio Holmes show was announced with typical radio-page fanfare; above is the announcement that appeared in the Portland* Oregonian *for January 5, 1931. The paper would describe later, on October 12, the national Holmes radio craze: "A release from New York tells of something new in radio—a Sherlock Holmes party. Guests are invited in for bridge or backgammon, and when the creepy tones of the opening music of the Holmes program float out of the loudspeaker, the lights are turned out. There's something about darkness that makes the drama acutely real. When the last notes fade away the lights are switched on and the palpitating nerves of the audience are quieted with a cup of ————* (*Holmes himself couldn't guess what.)"*

On the opposite page are some Oregonian *illustrations and commentary for its local first Holmes radio year.*

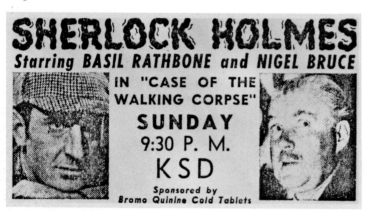

At left are some later radio advertisements for Holmes programs—with a by-then-famous duo as principal characters. Topmost: from the St. Louis Post-Dispatch for November 2, 1941; bottom left: a Petri Wine ad in the San Francisco Chronicle, early 1943; and bottom right: a WOR Petri Wine ad from the San Francisco Daily News for October 4 of the same year.

Opposite page, bottom: actor Kevin McCarthy "at work" as Holmes in one of the 1980 presentations of the CBS Radio Mystery Theater, created by Hyman Brown. The program was aired by more than 250 stations and by Armed Forces Radio.

With "The Adventure of the Speckled Band," which inaugurated the earlier series, Sherlock Holmes will return to the air tonight at 8:15 o'clock, and will broadcast through The Oregonian at the same hour every Monday night from now on. After tonight, instead of giving a separate adventure each time, the producers will select longer stories and present them as serials of varying length. The first of these will be "The Hound of the Baskervilles." The cast is the same as last year—Richard Gordon as Sherlock Holmes, Leigh Lovell as Dr. Watson and Edith Meiser, who is adapting the stories for the radio, in the leading feminine roles.

Above and right: William Moyes's Oregonian *column, "Behind the Mike," comments on the September 14 program for 1931 and provides a sketch of the show's Holmes (the artist's name is unclear). At far right: the cartoon, with Moyes's December 21 comment, reflects the continuing popularity of the Holmes program.*

Not until 1935 would the legendary William Gillette CBS radio broadcast as Holmes be heard. Announcements of it told how the night of its presentation, November 18, would mark the sixtieth anniversary of Gillette's first appearance on the stage and the thirty-sixth of his first appearance as Holmes.

By the late 1930s, Rathbone and Bruce would dominate not only the movies but the airwaves as the Holmes/Watson team.

SHERLOCK HOLMES—RICHARD GORDON

BEHIND THE MIKE
WITH WILLIAM MOYES.

Lots of Christmas stuff on the air tonight. S. Claus, Harry von Tilzer, A. P. Sloan and Sherlock Holmes all with one idea in mind—to make sure you have a merry Christmas. Mr. Claus will drop in via Death Valley at 5:30. A washing machine company will stir up a program of Yuletide music by the Hamilton male chorus of Chicago at 6. Messrs. von Tilzer and General Motors Sloan will radiate holiday cheer at 6:30. Real Folks (appearing for the last time under that title) will have a Christmas tree celebration. Sherlock Holmes and Dr. Watson will halt in their pursuit of criminals to give Dickens' Christmas carol. All over KGW.

THE HOLMES IMAGE
IN ADVERTISING

The popular Holmes image has been a godsend to advertisers, since it compels instant and sympathetic audience recognition without the need to pay a cent to any trademark or copyright holder—so long as the name "Sherlock Holmes" itself is avoided. In this early ad by Collier's, however, the words were used instead—without the image. Doyle's famed "dancing men" cipher (from the adventure of the same name published in The Strand *for December 1903 and in* Collier's Weekly *of December 5 that year) is used here amusingly as part of what seems to have been a mass-advertising campaign to get new readers for the then-still-new magazine; this ad was printed in the Chicago* Record-Herald *for December 17, and others similar to it appeared.*

The first of the several "dancing men" messages of the original Doyle adventure has been included, here, above the advertisement.

On the following page is the Sherlockian-story text of a Collier's advertisement by the Columbus (Ohio) Recording Lock Company that appeared in the October 29, 1904, issue. For our purposes here, the art (a small duplication of a Frederic Dorr Steele Holmes) has been removed; the art also included a photograph of the inside face of the lock of the safe that was being advertised. An earlier "Sherlockian" advertisement by the same safe company—without story—had been placed with Collier's *in its September 24 issue.*

Opposite, at bottom of the page: again, a Holmesian ad sans image of the detective. Collier's *ran this advertisement for a "Sherlock Holmes" card game in its November 26 issue, quoting the Boston* Herald *and New York* World *in the ad. Said the* World: *"Sherlock Holmes is the liveliest of all the games which have become popular fads. The game is laughter and excitement from beginning to end, and while light in its nature, is becoming as much of a rage as Ping-Pong in its prime." The game was made by Parker Brothers, of Salem, Massachusetts, New York, and London, "the makers of Pit, Squire, Bid, Flinch..." The price of the game—available from "Department Stores, Stationery and Sporting Goods Dealers everywhere," said the ad—was "fifty cents; gold edge, seventy-five cents."*

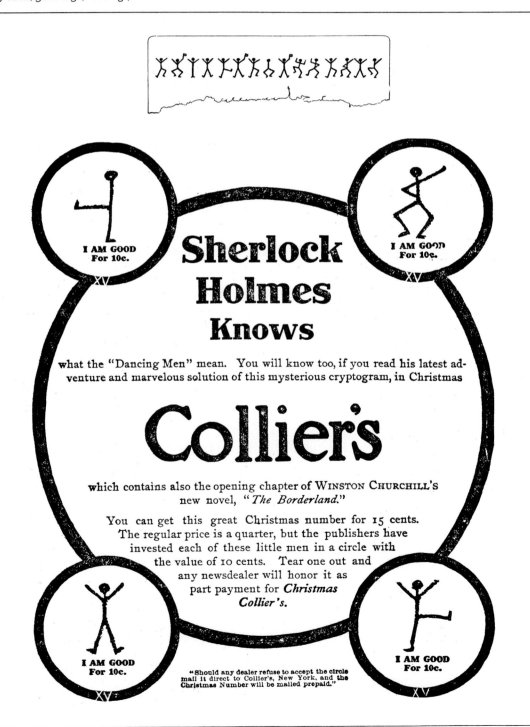

Sherlock Holmes
AND THE
SLEEPLESS WATCHMAN

"My Dear Watson," said Sherlock Holmes suddenly; this was in our lodgings in Baker street shortly before I was married. I had been nursing my old wound and plunging at intervals into a new treatise on Phloroglucin-Vanillin tests with preserved milk while Holmes pored over what appeared to be a bronze door plate with a small clock set in the face of it. "What do you make of this?" at the same time handing the plate to me. I knew the great man's methods and looked the plate over carefully, applying them, when Holmes interrupted me.

"A simple thing," said he, "and yet at the same time one which, when it is universally used, will, I'll wager, put Lestrade, stupid as he is, on a par with the best of us." He paused for a moment, as was sometimes his habit, and then continued. "Watson," he said, "the man who does not prevent a crime when he can, encourages it, and I tell you frankly that this piece of mechanism will do more to prevent crime than you and I and all Scotland Yard combined. Do you follow me now while I point out

what it does, you will yourself note the value of it no doubt. In the first place every time a key is inserted in the lock it prints a record. It tells if the bolt was locked or unlocked, and what is more, my dear Watson, it records the exact time of each operation and tells who is the operator.

"You can readily imagine how quickly the burglary of Eckstein's diamond shop in the Strand would have been discovered if this had been used. It instantly detects a duplicate as well as a skeleton key.

"It also gives a record of the time and watchman who tries your door, and that, Watson, without his key in any way operating the bolt.

"It tells you if your shop or warehouse was properly locked at night and by whom.

"It tells you who opened your door in the morning and at what time.

"It tells if the place was entered between closing and opening time and by whom. You will remember the League of Red-Headed Men. No doubt, it would have saved our hard-headed friend a lot

had he had it at the time. These, Watson, are but a few of the things that this most remarkable lock does and as I said before, this information is worth a good deal to anyone, be he merchant, shopkeeper, or banker, and it is information that you can absolutely secure in no other way.

"It's a watchman that is always alert, that is unerringly correct and that you cannot bribe or tamper with in any way. Rather remarkable, don't you think, Watson, this sleepless one?"

Don't you think that this lock which will tell *you* if your door has been locked or unlocked and who was the operator; that will tell you if the watchman tries *your* door and the time that he does it; that tells you what time *your* store or office was opened and closed, would be of value to *you*? It will cost you a cent a day for such a record. Can *you* afford to be without it? "The Sleepless Watchman" is the title of our book which tells all about it and which we will be pleased to send you upon request. Columbus Recording Lock Company, Box 743, Columbus, Ohio.

The New Game,
"Sherlock Holmes"

Not an advertisement precisely, this striking drawing of Holmes was done by Eliot Keen for a puzzle contest introduced by the New York Herald on Sunday, June 3, 1906, and again illustrates the freedom with which some publications of those days felt they could make routine use of the Holmes name and figure. In the drawing various clues to a description of the burglarizer of the household were hopefully evident to the keen-minded boy or girl; fifty successful children were to be given nickel badges and would become "detectives of the Sherlock Holmes Amateur Agency."

The advertisement below (a detail of the full-page ad) promoted the Hearst Daily Georgian and Sunday American of Atlanta in a companion newspaper, the Chicago Evening American for November 11, 1915. Here we have Holmes as unmistakably as he has ever been rendered, exerting full reader impact without any actionable copyright violation—simply because, unlike such initially graphic popular images as Superman or Mickey Mouse, there was no protected pictorial concept of the detective.

Truth Has Nothing to Conceal!

The Circulation of The Atlanta Georgian and Hearst's Sunday American Is Open to the Minutest Inspection—Success Welcomes Investigation

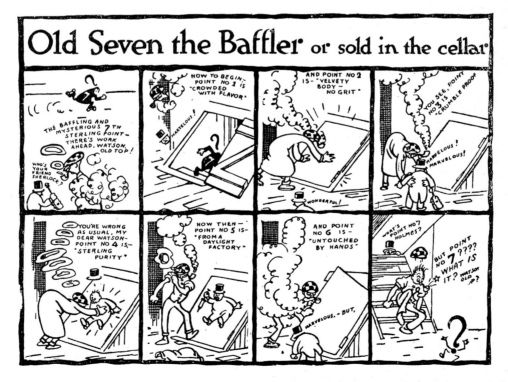

The above examples from a very amusing series of newspaper ads for Sterling Chewing Gum appeared across the country in 1915 (these are from the New York Evening Journal for October 21 and 16). Only the two ads reprinted here—the second without its lower, gum detail—featured "The Wizard of Baker Street"; earlier and later ads simply emphasized the "Old Seven the Baffler" character alone. The artist is unfortunately unidentified, although his style would indicate that this was probably the work of Al Frueh, a noted strip cartoonist of the period.

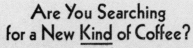

The Serene Tobacco ad is from 1919 (Chicago Tribune); the Folger's Coffee ad, promoting a comedy detective radio show called Black and Blue, is from 1931 (Oakland Tribune); the pulp magazine ad, "Look Men!" is from the mid-thirties, and ran for years. The two O. Soglow ads, for Tydol Gasoline (August 14, 1935) and for the Hotel Taft (May 5, 1936), were drawn locally for the New York Sun; the Taft ad, small and local, must have escaped Doyle notice.

These two soap "story" advertisements ran in newspapers across the nation on May 30, 1937, and September 10, 1939. "The Mystery of the Stolen Soap," for Rinso, at left, had Sherlockian symbolism only in its opening panel, as did Oxydol's "The Great Washing Machine Mystery," below. The advertising agency artists are unidentified.

Below: The engaging use of Marge Henderson's Little Lulu as a Sherlockian figure (plus a "Watson" bizarrely garbed in similar gear) promoted Kleenex Tissues in hundreds of U.S. Sunday comics sections on May 11, 1947.

Elementary

—my dear Watson!

MORE MEN WEAR BOND CLOTHES THAN ANY OTHER CLOTHES in AMERICA

We solve the diaper dilemma of 1943

At left: detail from an ad by Bond Clothes that appeared in the San Francisco Examiner for September 16, 1943. Above: a "cuddly" detail from an ad by Famous-Barr Company; limited to St. Louis, it ran in the Post-Dispatch for September 21, 1943. The Carnation Quick Wheat ad appeared in the Seattle Post-Intelligencer for January 26, 1944. The deerstalker, calabash, and magnifying glass are a detail from Union Oil Company of California's national advertisement as seen in the San Francisco Chronicle for June 24, 1944. At bottom left: detail of a nationally distributed Phillips 66 ad as seen in the St. Louis Post-Dispatch on July 21, 1944. (By 1944, Phillips 66 apparently felt that using the term "a Sherlock Holmes," without an accompanying direct portrayal of the detective, was secure from charges of copyright violation—probably on the grounds that the term had entered the language as a synonym for "detective.") At bottom right: detail of the House of P. Y. Chong ad in the Honolulu Advertiser, March 14, 1946.

HOW TO FIND OIL

THE MAN WHO CAME TO BREAKFAST

ONE MOMENT, YOUNG MAN, JUST WHAT IS THIS WE HAVE HERE?

IT'S CARNATION QUICK WHEAT, MISTER ---- YOU'RE WELCOME TO TRY SOME WITH ME!

IT LOOKS LIKE YOU'VE MADE A DISCOVERY THAT PLEASES YOU!

INDEED, INDEED! IN ALL MY TRAVELS I'VE NEVER TASTED A FINER HOT CEREAL!

Carnation *Quick* Wheat is enriched with 50% more Vitamin B₁ than the whole grain from which it's made! Naturally rich in Niacin and Iron. And you'll really enjoy the distinctive wheat flavor of this new, improved whole wheat cereal!

VITAMIN B₁ ENRICHED

CARNATION QUICK WHEAT

A hot breakfast in 4 minutes

I'm a terrible SHERLOCK HOLMES

Phillips 66

PLEASE HELP ME!

SHERLOCK HOLMES SAY: HOW P. Y. MAKE SO WONDERFUL CHARCOAL BLOIL STEAK IS STILL BIG MYSTELY TO ME!

Opposite page: A Holmesian Basil Rathbone graces a Chesterfield Cigarettes ad that ran in the American Weekly for October 26, 1946.

A "Holmes" inspects, for Sunshine Krispy Crackers; the ad was seen in This Week magazine for April 11, 1948. Below: detail of a nationally distributed advertisement for Imperial, Hiram Walker's Blended Whiskey, from the Reno Evening Gazette for May 3, 1950; a verse above the men continued, in another panel: "...for whiskey with the mellow taste that we old-timers knew—just tell the man you want Imperial!"

A "Holmes" and a "Watson" do some cavorting in a cartoon story-type advertisement for Winston Cigarettes. The ad appeared in newspapers nationally, on or about May 9, 1957. The strip is by an unidentified advertising agency artist.

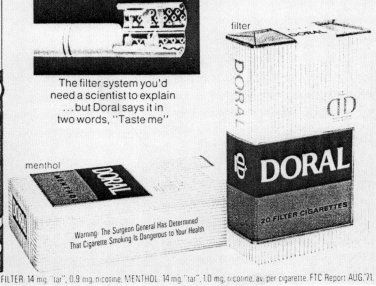

In 1971, Doral Cigarettes used this "Holmes and Watson" cartoon strip nationally in many magazines. The advertising agency artist, who favors a smiling Holmes, is unidentified.

PSEUDO-SHERLOCKIAN STORIES AND BURLESQUES: I

The spoofing of Doyle's Sherlock Holmes adventures became, quite early on, a pastime of many American writers. The following burlesque of Holmes by William B. Kahn appeared in The Smart Set *magazine for October 1905. Little seems to be known of the author; his name is not prominent on the* Smart Set's *contents page before or after, nor—despite the title—were there any other adventures of Oilock Combs in the magazine or, apparently, elsewhere. In 1964 the work appeared under separate covers in a limited edition—222 copies: copies 1 through 221, plus 221b—published by the Beaune Press as* An Adventure of Oilock Combs.

The Succored Beauty

By William B. Kahn

ONE night, as I was returning from a case of acute indigestion—it was immediately after my divorce and I was obliged to return to the practice of my profession in order to support myself—it chanced that my way homeward lay through Fakir street. As I reached the house where Combs and I had spent so many hours together, where I had composed so many of his adventures, an irresistible longing seized me to go once more upstairs and grasp my friend by the hand, for, if the truth must be told, Combs and I had had a tiff. I really did not like the way in which he had procured evidence for my wife when she sought the separation, and I took the liberty of telling Combs so, but he had said to me: "My dear fellow, it is my business, is it not?" and though I knew he was not acting properly I was forced to be placated. However, the incident left a little breach between us which I determined on this night to bridge.

As I entered the room I saw Combs nervously drinking a glass of soda water. Since I succeeded in breaking him of the morphine habit he had been slyly looking about for some other stimulant and at last he had found it. I sighed to see him thus employed.

"Good evening, Combs," said I, extending my hand.

"Hello, Spotson," cried he, ignoring my proffered digits. "You are well, I see. It really is too bad, though, that you have no servant again. You seem to have quite some trouble with your help." And he chuckled as he sipped the soda water.

Familiar as I was with my friend's powers, this extraordinary exhibition of them really startled me.

"Why, Oilock," said I, calling him, in my excitement, by his prænomen, "how did you know it?"

"Perfectly obvious, Spotson, perfectly obvious. Merely observation," answered Combs as he took out his harmonica and began playing a tune thereon.

"But how?" persisted I.

"Well, if you really wish to know," he replied, as he ceased playing, "I suppose I will be obliged to tell you. I see you have a small piece of court plaster upon the index finger of your left hand. Naturally, a cut. But the plaster is so small that the cut must be very minute. 'What could have done it?' I ask myself. The obvious response is a tack, a pin or a needle. On a chance I eliminate the tack proposition. I take another chance and

eliminate the pin. Therefore, it must have been the needle. 'Why a needle?' query I of myself. And glancing at your coat I see the answer. There you have five buttons, four of which are hanging on rather loosely while the fifth one is tightly sewn to the cloth. It had recently been sewn. The connection is now clear. You punctured your finger with the needle while sewing on the button. But," he continued musingly and speaking, it seemed, more to himself than to me, "I never saw nor heard of the man who would sew unless he was compelled to. Spotson always keeps a servant; why did she not sew the button on for him? The reply is childishly easy: his servant left him."

I followed his explanation with rapt attention. My friend's powers were, I was happy to see, as marvelous as they were when I lived with him.

"Wonderful, Combs, wonderful," I cried.

"Merely observation," he replied. "Some day I think that I shall write a monograph on the subject of buttons. It is a very interesting subject and the book ought to sell well. But, hello, what is this?"

The sound of a cab halting before the door caused Combs's remark. Even as he spoke there was a pull at the bell, then the sound of hasty footsteps on the stairs. A sharp knock sounded upon the door. Combs dropped into his armchair, stuck out his legs in his familiar way and then said: "Come in."

The door opened and there entered, in great perturbation, a young lady, twenty-three years of age, having on a blue tailor-made suit, patent-leather shoes and a hat with a black pompon ornamenting it. She wore some other things, but these were all that I noticed. Not so Combs. I could see by the penetrating glance he threw at her that her secret was already known to that astute mind.

"Thank heaven," she cried, turning to me, "that I have found you in!"

"Are you ill, madam?" I began; but suddenly realizing that I was not in my office but in Combs's consultation room, I drew myself up stiffly and said: "That is Mr. Combs."

The young lady turned to him. Then, lifting her handkerchief to her beautiful eyes she burst into tears as she said: "Help me, help me, Mr. Combs."

The great man did not reply. An answer to such a remark he would have regarded as too trivial. The lady took down her handkerchief and, after glancing dubiously at me, said to Mr. Combs: "Can I see you privately?"

Once, and once only did I ever before or, indeed, since, see such a look of rage on Combs's face. That was when Professor O'Flaherty and he had that altercation in Switzerland. (See "Memoirs of Oilock Combs." Arper & Co. $1.50.)

"Madam," said he in frigid tones, "whatever you desire to say to me you may say before Dr. Spotson. How under the sun, woman," he cried, losing control of himself for a moment, "would the public know of my adventures if he were not here to write them?"

I threw Combs a grateful look while he reached for the soda water. The visitor was momentarily crushed. At last, however, she recovered her equanimity.

"Well, then," she said, "I will tell you my story."

"Pray, begin," said Combs rather testily.

"My name is Ysabelle, Duchess of Swabia," the visitor commenced.

"One moment, please," interrupted Combs. "Spotson, kindly look up that name in my index."

I took down the book referred to, in which Combs had made thousands of notes of people and events of interest, and found between "Yponomeutidæ" and "yttrium" the following item, which I read aloud:

"Ysabelle, Duchess of Swabia; Countess of Steinheimbach; Countess of Riesendorf, etc., etc. Born at Schloss Ochsenfuss, February 29, 1876. Her mother was the Duchess Olga, of Zwiefelfeld and her father was Hugo, Duke of Kaffeeküchen. At three years of age she could say 'ha, ha!' in German, French, English, Italian and Spanish. Between the ages of five and fifteen she was instructed by Professor Grosskopf, the eminent philosopher of the University of Kleinplatz. By sixteen her wisdom teeth had all appeared. A very remarkable woman!"

As I read this last sentence, the duchess again burst into tears.

"Pray, pray, compose yourself, duchess," said Combs, taking a pipe from the table and filling it with some tobacco which he absent-mindedly took from my coat-pocket.

The duchess succeeded in calming herself. Then, rising majestically and gazing at Combs with those wonderful eyes which had played havoc with so many royal hearts, she said, in solemn tones:

"I am lost!"

The manner in which she made this statement as well as the declaration itself seemed to make a deep impression upon Combs. Without uttering one word he sat there for fully four minutes. The way in which he puffed nervously at the pipe showed me that he was thinking. Suddenly, with an exclamation of delight, he dashed out of the room and down the stairs, leaving the amazed duchess and myself in his apartments. But not for long. In forty-three seconds he was again in the room and, dropping into his chair thoroughly exhausted, he triumphantly cried:

"I have it!"

Never had I seen my friend wear such a look of victory. The achievement which merited such an expression upon his countenance must have been remarkable. By and bye he recovered from his fatigue. Then he spoke.

"Madam," he said, "I have the answer."

The duchess sobbed in ecstasy.

Combs continued:

"The moment that you said you were lost," he began, "an idea came to me. You must have noticed, Spotson, how preoccupied I seemed before. Well, that is the sign of an idea coming to me. Before it had time to vanish I dashed down the steps, into the vestibule, looked at the number of this house and jotted it down. Madam," he cried, drawing out a book and looking at one of the pages, "madam, you are saved! You are no longer lost! This is No. 62 Fakir street. You are found!"

During this entire recital the duchess had not said a word. When Combs had finished she stood for a moment as if she did not understand and then, realizing the fact that she was rescued, she wept once more.

"My savior," she cried as she prepared to leave the room, "how can I ever thank you?" And she pressed into Combs's outstretched hand a large gold-mesh, diamond-studded purse.

The door closed, the carriage rolled away and the Duchess of Swabia was gone.

"Spotson," said Combs to me, "don't forget to write this one down. It has a duchess in it and will sell well to cooks and chambermaids. By the way, I wonder what she gave me."

He opened the purse and there, neatly folded, lay two hundred pounds in bills.

"Bah!" cried Combs contemptuously, "how ungrateful these royal personages always are."

© 1954 Los Angeles Times

Oilock Combs, at the end of the story above, is a disgusted and frustrated grand sleuth. No less disgusted—and footsore, as well—is this "Holmes" by artist Bruce Russell, which accompanied Walter Wilson's "Lying Down to Think It Over" column in the Los Angeles Times *at a much later date: May 5, 1954. (The seated gentleman is brother Mycroft Holmes.)*

SHERLOCK HOLMES UMPIRES BASEBALL

Gives an Exhibition of the Scientific Method of Rendering Decisions

ABUNCH of old-time fans were sitting in the rear of a downtown cigar stand the other day, talking over the good old times of the past, when baseball was the real goods and everybody would turn out to witness an exhibition of the national sport, without too much regard to the quality of the article.

The discussion finally wandered into the umpire line, when one old-timer, that looked like a reproduction of the character of the fat man portrayed by Gibson in his famous cartoon, "Three Strikes and Out," broke into the conversational game.

"Did any of you ever hear of the time Sherlock Holmes umpired a baseball game?"

No one had, and so he continued:

"I was playing on a nine in a small town in Iowa one summer and was mixed up in a way in the first and only exhibition ever given by Sherlock Holmes of the correct way to umpire.

"We were playing a series of games with another town about thirty miles distant, and the feeling between the two teams and their following was at a high pitch. Hardly a game passed without ending in a free-for-all fight or mobbing the umpire.

"There were two twins playing on our team that looked so much alike that even the players that worked with them every day were unable to tell them apart, except by looking at their feet. One of the twins had a very slight deformity to his right foot, so slight that it would never be noticed by a casual observer.

"In order to keep the records straight on the batting order we named one of the twins 'Leftfoot' and the other 'Rightfoot.'

"'Rightfoot' had been batting like a fiend ever since the opening of the season, while 'Leftfoot' was somewhat weak with the stick, but the best fielder on the team. 'Leftfoot' played center field and 'Rightfoot' covered the right garden.

"Whenever it looked as if we were in a pinch it was the custom to ring in 'Rightfoot' in place of 'Leftfoot' occasionally to even up matters. He was always good in a pinch, and many a time had won the game by taking the place of 'Leftfoot' at the bat.

"We called our team the Knockers and the other bunch with which we were playing the series answered to the name of the Pickle Eaters.

"The Pickle Eaters had grown suspicious that we were working a smooth game on the batting order and were getting very particular about the selection of an umpire.

"We had a game scheduled at home one Sunday afternoon and were looking for a large bunch of trouble when the Pickle Eaters entered a protest against the regular umpire acting and refused to start the game until some one else was selected.

"Just as the controversy had reached the stage when it looked as if it would be necessary to dish back the money to the crowd, a tall, cadaverous-looking man, leading a dog that looked like a cross between a bloodhound and an Irish setter, stepped from the bleachers and volunteered to take charge of the ceremonies.

"Without even waiting for an answer the tall stranger walked out to the position back of the pitcher's box and called the game. The assurance of the man won the

Hardly a game passed without ending in a free-for-all fight or mobbing the umpire.

point, and both teams went into the game without further argument.

"Talk about science in umpiring a ball game, that guy certainly had everything skinned that ever came over the pike. He could outrun any man on either team and was always at the spot when it looked as if the decision would be close. There was no disputing his decision, because he was always in the proper position to hand out the right dope.

Umpire Was Real Goods

"It was in the last inning that the real sensational decision of the game occurred, which marked the stranger as the greatest exponent of the baseball umpiring art and assisted in revealing his identity.

"We were up for the last crack at the ball, with the Pickle Eaters two runs in the lead. There were two out and all of the bases full when the scorer called 'Leftfoot' to the bat. It was a tight hole and the captain decided to take a chance on ringing in 'Rightfoot.' He gave the signal and the chief willow swisher went to the plate. He swatted the first one that came over squarely on the nose and landed it over the center field fence, and went trailing around the bases, bringing in all of the men ahead of him.

"Almost as soon as 'Rightfoot' landed on the ball the head guy of the Pickle Eaters was out with the big protest, claiming that it was the wrong man up. The lanky one listened to his tale of woe and was at the bench to meet 'Rightfoot' when he wandered in from his little canter. Before the startled player had time to draw his breath the umpire had grabbed his foot with one hand and sliced a piece off the heel of his shoe with a sharp knife that he was carrying in the other hand. He performed a similar operation on 'Leftfoot' and then started for the outfield like a shot.

Has the Clews

"When he reached the spot where 'Rightfoot' was accustomed to stand in the right garden he went down on his knees and examined the ground for several minutes with a microscope, then made for the center pasture, where he repeated the performance. Without saying a word he rushed back to the bleachers' stand, where his dog was fastened, and after releasing the queer-looking animal rubbed the piece of leather that he had clipped from 'Rightfoot's' shoe over his nose and ordered the dog to 'go find him.' The hound went around the bases at a modest canter, almost perfectly imitating the gait of 'Rightfoot,' and wound up at the players' bench by taking a firm hold on the surplus bottom of 'Rightfoot's' trousers.

" ' "Rightfoot" out for batting out of his turn,' shouted the umpire. 'Side out and the Pickle Eaters win.'

"Not even a protest was entered to the decision. It was all done so quick and in such an amazing manner that no one thought of disputing the decision.

"The players gathered in a crowd to discuss the strange proceedings, but when they looked for the stranger both he and the dog had disappeared. No one had noticed them leave the grounds, and just how he got away is a mystery that is still being discussed by the old-timers back in the little village.

"We were asking each other who the man could possibly be when the town constable came forward and volunteered the information that the erstwhile umpire was Sherlock Holmes, who had been investigating a strange murder case in an adjoining hamlet."

Examined the ground for several minutes with a microscope.

"Sherlock Holmes Umpires Baseball" was published in the news columns of the Seattle Post-Intelligencer *for Sunday, February 25, 1906. It carried no byline but was illustrated by staff artist John "Dok" Hager, who drew the daily comic strip* Dippy Duck *for the paper and later did* Waddles *for the* Christian Science Monitor.

Raffles Holmes. The Redemption Of Young Billington Rand.

By John Kendrick Bangs

another Inferno

"JENKINS," said Raffles Holmes, lighting his pipe and throwing himself down upon my couch, "don't you sometimes pine for those good old days of Jack Sheppard and Dick Turpin? Hang it all! I'm getting blisteringly tired of the modern refinements in crime and yearn for the period when the highwayman met you on the road and made you stand and deliver at the point of the pistol."

"Indeed I don't," I ejaculated. "I'm not chicken-livered, Raffles, but I'm mighty glad my lines are cast in less strenuous scenes. When a book agent comes in here, for example, and holds me up for $19 a volume for a set of Kipling in words of one syllable, illustrated by his aunt and every volume autographed by his uncle's step-sister, it's a game of wits between us as to whether I will buy or not buy, and if he gets away with my signature to a contract it's because he has legitimately outwitted me. But your ancient Turpin overcame you by brutal force; you hadn't a run for your money from the moment he got his eye on you, and no percentage of the swag was ever returned to you, as in the case of the Double Cross Edition of Kipling, in which you get back at least 50 cents' worth of paper and print for every $19 you give up."

"That is merely the commercial way of looking at it," protested Holmes. "You reckon up the situation on a basis of mere dollars, strike a balance and charge the thing to profit and loss. But the romance of it all, the element of the picturesque, the delicious, tingling sense of adventure which was inseparable from a road experience with a commanding personality like Turpin—these things are all lost in your prosaic book-agent methods of our day. No man writing his memoirs for the enlightenment of posterity would ever dream of setting down upon paper the story of how a book agent robbed him of $200, but

the chap who has been held up in the dark recesses of a forest on a foggy night by a Jack Sheppard and made to give up as little as sixpence would always find breathless and eager listeners to or readers of the tale he had to tell."

"Well, old man," said I, "I'm satisfied with the prosaic methods of the gas companies, the book agents and the riggers of the stock market. Give me Wall street and the Gas Trust and you take Dick Turpin and all his crew. But what has set your mind to working on the Dick Turpin end of it, anyhow? Thinking of going in for that sort of thing yourself?"

"M-m-m—yes," replied Holmes hesitatingly, "I am. Not that I pine to become one of the Broom Squires myself, but because I—well, I may be forced into it."

"Take my advice, Raffles," I interrupted, earnestly. "Let firearms and highways alone. There's too much battle, murder and sudden death in loaded guns and a surplus of publicity in street work."

"You mustn't take me so literally, Jenkins," he retorted. "I'm not going to follow precisely in the steps of Turpin, but a holdup on the public highway seems to be the only way out of a problem which I have been employed to solve. Do you know young Billington Rand?"

"By sight," said I, with a laugh. "And by reputation. You're not going to hold him up, are you?" I added contemptuously.

"Why not?" said Holmes.

"It's like breaking into an empty house in search of antique furniture," I explained. "Common report has it that Billington Rand has already been skinned by about every skinning agency in town. He's posted at all his clubs. Every gambler in town, professional as well as social, has his I. O. U.'s for bridge, poker and faro debts. Everybody knows it except those fatuous people down in the Kenesaw National Bank, where he's employed, and the Fidelity Company, that's on his bond. He wouldn't last five minutes in either place if his uncle wasn't a director in both concerns."

"I see that you have a pretty fair idea of Billington Rand's financial condition," said Holmes.

"It's rather common talk in the clubs, so why shouldn't I?" I put in. "Holding him up would be at most an act of petit larceny if you would measure a crime by what you get out of it. It's a great shame, though, for at heart Rand is one of the best fellows in the world. He's a man who has all the modern false notions of what a fellow ought to do to keep up what he calls his end. He plays cards and sustains ruinous losses because he thinks he won't be considered a good fellow if he stays out. He plays bridge with ladies and pays up when he loses and doesn't collect when he wins. Win or lose, he's doomed to be on the wrong side of the market just because of those very qualities that make him a lovable person—kind to everybody but himself and weak as dishwater. For heaven's sake, Raffles, if the poor devil has anything left don't take it from him."

"Your sympathy for Rand does you credit," said Holmes. "But I have just as much of that as you have, and that is why at half-past 5 o'clock tomorrow afternoon I'm going to hold him up, in the public eye, and incontinently rob him of $25,000."

"Twenty-five thousand dollars? Billington Rand?" I gasped.

"Twenty-five thousand dollars, Billington Rand," repeated Holmes, firmly. "If you don't believe it come along and see. He doesn't know you, does he?"

"Not from Adam," said I.

"Very good—then you'll be safe as a church. Meet me in the Fifth Avenue Hotel lobby at 5 tomorrow afternoon and I'll show you as pretty a holdup as you ever dreamed of," said Holmes.

"But—I can't take part in a criminal proceeding like that, Holmes," I protested.

"You won't have to—even if it were a criminal proceeding, which it is not," he returned. "Nobody outside of you and me will know anything about it but Rand himself, and the chances that he will peach are less than a millionth part of a half per cent. Anyhow, all you need be is a witness."

There was a long and uneasy silence. I was far from liking the job, but, after all, so far Holmes had not led me into any difficulties of a serious nature, and, knowing him as I had come to know him, I had a hearty belief that any wrong he did was temporary only and sure to be rectified in the long run.

"I've a decent motive in all this, Jenkins," he resumed in a few moments. "Don't forget that. This holdup is going to result in a reformation that will be for the good of everybody, so don't have any scruples on that score."

"All right, Raffles," said I. "You've always played straight with me so far, and I don't doubt your word—only I do hate the highway end of it."

"Tut, Jenkins!" he ejaculated with a laugh, giving me a whack on the shoulders that nearly toppled me over into the fireplace. "Don't be a rabbit. The thing will be as easy as cutting calvesfoot jelly with a razor."

Thus did I permit myself to be persuaded, and the next afternoon at 5 Holmes and I met in the lobby of the Fifth Avenue Hotel.

"Come on," he said, after the first salutations were over. "Rand will be at the Thirty-second street subway at quarter after 5, and it's important that we should catch him before he gets to Fifth avenue."

"I'm glad it's to be on a side street," I remarked, my heart beating rapidly with excitement over the work in hand, for the more I thought of the venture the less I liked it.

"Oh, I don't know that it will be," said Holmes carelessly. "I may pull it off in the corridors of the Waldorf."

The pumps in my heart reversed their action and for a moment I feared I should drop with dismay.

"In the Wald—?" I began.

"Shut up, Jenkins!" said Holmes, imperatively. "This is no time for protests. We're in for it now and there's no drawing back."

Ten minutes later we stood at the intersection of Thirty-third street and Fifth avenue. Holmes' eyes flashed and his whole nervous system quivered as with the joy of the chase.

"Keep your eyes open, Jenkins, and you'll see a pretty sight," he whispered, "for here comes our man."

Sure enough, there was Billington Rand on the other side of the street, walking along nervously and clutching an oblong package, wrapped in brown paper, firmly in his right hand.

"Now for it," said Holmes, and we crossed the street, scarcely reaching the opposite curb before Rand was upon us. Rand eyed us closely and shied off to one side as Holmes blocked his progress.

"I'll trouble you for that package, Mr. Rand," said Holmes quietly.

The man's face went white and he caught his breath.

"Who the devil are you?" he demanded angrily.

"That has nothing to do with the case," retorted Holmes. "I want that package or—"

"Get out of my way!" cried Rand, with a justifiable show of resentment. "Or I'll call an officer."

"Will you?" said Holmes, quietly. "Will you call an officer and so make known to the authorities that you are in possession of $25,000 worth of securities that belong to other people, and which are supposed at this moment to be safely locked up in the vaults of the Kenesaw National Bank along with other collateral?"

Rand staggered back against the newel post of a brownstone stoop, and stood there gazing wildly into Holmes' face.

"Of course, if you prefer having the facts made known in that way," Holmes continued, coolly, "you have the option. I am not going to use physical force to persuade you to hand the package over to me, but you are a greater fool than I take you for if you choose that alternative. To use an expressive modern phrase, you will be caught with the goods on, Mr. Billington Rand, and unless you have a far better explanation of how those securities happen to be in your possession at this moment than I think you have, there is no power on earth can keep you from landing in State's prison."

The unfortunate victim of Holmes' adventure fairly gasped in his combined rage and fright. Twice he attempted to speak, but only inarticulate sounds issued from his lips.

"You are, of course, very much disturbed at the moment," Holmes went on, "and I am really very sorry if anything I have done has disarranged any honorable enterprise in which you have embarked. I don't wish to hurry you into a snap decision, which you may repent later, only either the police or I must have that package within an hour. It is for you to say which of us is to get it. Suppose we run over to the Waldorf and discuss the matter calmly over a bottle of Glengarry? Possibly I can convince you that it will be for your own good to do precisely as I tell you and very much to your disadvantage to do otherwise."

Rand, stupefied by this sudden intrusion upon his secret by an utter stranger, lost what little fight there was left in him, and at least seemed to assent to Holmes' proposition. The latter linked arms with him, and in a few minutes we walked into the famous hostelry just as if we were three friends bent only upon having a pleasant chat over a cafe table.

"What'll you have, Mr. Rand?" asked Holmes, suavely. "I'm elected for the Glengarry special, with a little carbonic on the side."

"Same," said Rand, laconically.

"Sandwich with it?" asked Holmes. "You'd better."

"Oh, I can't eat anything," began Rand. "I—"

"Bring us some sandwiches, waiter," said Holmes. "Two Glengarry specials, a syphon of carbonic and—Jenkins, what's yours?"

The calmness and the cheek of the fellow.

"I'm not in on this at all," I retorted, angered by Holmes' betrayal of my name. "And I want Mr. Rand to understand—"

"Oh, tut!" ejaculated Holmes. "He knows that. Mr. Rand, my friend, Jenkins has no connection with this enterprise of mine, and he's done his level best to dissuade me from holding you up so summarilly. All he's along for is to write the thing up for—"

"The newspapers?" cried Rand, now thoroughly frightened.

"No," laughed Holmes. "Nothing so useful—the magazines."

Holmes winked at me as he spoke and I gathered that there was method in his apparent madness.

"That's one of the points you want to consider, though, Mr. Rand," he said, leaning upon the table with his elbows. "Think of the newspapers tomorrow morning if you call the police rather than hand that package over to me. It'll be a big sensation for Wall street and upper Fifth avenue, to say nothing of what the fellows will make of the story for the rest of the hoi polloi. The newsboys will be yelling extras all over town, printed in great red letters. 'A Club Man Held Up in Broad Daylight for $25,000 in Securities That Didn't Belong to Him. Billington Rand Has Something to Explain. Where Did He Get It?'"

"For heaven's sake, man! Don't!" pleaded the unfortunate Billington. "God! I never thought of that."

"Of course you didn't think of that," said Holmes. "That's why I'm telling you about it now. You don't dispute my facts, do you?"

"No, I—" Rand began.

"Of course not," said Holmes. "You might as well dispute the existence of the Flatiron building. If you don't want tomorrow's papers to be full of this thing you'll hand that package over to me."

"But," protested Rand, "I'm only taking them up to—to a—er—to a broker." Here he gathered himself together and spoke with greater assurance. "I am delivering them, sir, to a broker on behalf of one of our depositors who—"

"Who has been speculating with what little money he had left, has lost his margins and is now forced into an act of crime to protect his speculation," said Holmes. "The broker is the notorious William C. Gallagher, who runs an uptown bucket shop for speculative ladies to lose their pin money and bridge winnings in, and your depositor's name is Billington Rand, Esq.—otherwise yourself."

"How do you know this?" gasped Rand.

"Oh, maybe I read it on the ticker," laughed Holmes, "or, what is more likely, possibly I overheard Gallagher recommending you to dip into the bank's collateral to save your investment at Green's Chop House night before last."

"You were at Green's Chop House night before last?" cried Rand.

"In the booth adjoining your own, and I heard every word you said," said Holmes.

"Well, I don't see why I should give the stuff to you, anyhow," growled Rand.

"Chiefly because I happen to be long on information which would be of interest, not only to the police, but to the president and board of directors of the Kenesaw National Bank," said Holmes. "It will be a simple matter for me to telephone Mr. Horace Hawtry, the president of your institution, and put him wise to this transaction of yours and Gallagher's, and that is the second thing I shall do immediately you have decided not to part with that package."

"The second thing?" Rand whimpered. "What will you do first?"

"Communicate with the first policeman we meet when we leave here," said Holmes. "But take your time, Mr. Rand—take your time. Don't let me hurry you into a decision. Try a little of this Glengarry, and we'll drink hearty to a sensible decision."

"I—I'll put them back in the vaults tomorrow," pleaded Rand.

"Can't trust you, my boy," said Holmes. "Not with a persuasive crook like old Bucketshop Gallagher on your trail They're safer with me."

Rand's answer was a muttered oath as he tossed the package across the table and started to leave us.

"One word more, Mr. Rand," said Holmes, detaining him. "Don't do anything rash. There's a lot of good fellowship between criminals, and I'll stand by you all right. So far nobody at the bank knows you took these things, and even when they turn up missing if you go about your work as if nothing had happened, while you may be suspected, nobody can prove that you got the goods."

Rand's face brightened at this remark.

"By Jove!—that's true enough," said he. "Except Gallagher," he added, his face falling.

"Pah! for Gallagher," cried Holmes, snapping his fingers contemptuously. "If he as much as peeped we could put him in jail, and if he sells you out you tell him for me that I'll land him in Sing Sing for a term of years. He led you into this—"

"He certainly did," moaned Rand.

"And he's got to get you out," said Holmes. "Now, good-bye, old man. The worst that can happen to you is a few judgments instead of penal servitude for eight or ten years, unless you are foolish enough to try another turn of this sort, and then you may not happen on a good-natured highwayman to get you out of your trouble. By the way, what is the combination of the big safe in the outer office of the Kenesaw National?"

"One-eight-nine-seven," said Rand.

"Thanks," said Holmes, jotting it down coolly in his memorandum book. "That's a good thing to know."

THAT night shortly before midnight Holmes left me. "I've got to finish this job," said he. "The most ticklish part of the business is yet to come."

"Great Scott, Holmes!" I cried. "Isn't the thing done?"

"No, of course not," he replied. "I've got to bust open the Kenesaw safe."

"Now, my dear Raffles," I began, "why aren't you satisfied with what you've done already? Why must you—"

"Shut up, Jenkins!" he interrupted with a laugh. "If you knew what I was going to do you wouldn't kick—that is, unless you've turned crook, too."

"Not I," said I, indignantly.

"You don't expect me to keep these bonds, do you?" he asked.

"But what are you going to do with them?" I replied.

"Put 'em back in the Kenesaw Bank, so that they'll be found there tomorrow morning. As sure as I don't Billington Rand is doomed," said Holmes. "It's a tough job, but I've been paid a thousand dollars by his family to find out what he's up to, and, by thunder, after following his trail for three weeks I've got such a liking for the boy that I'm going to save him, if it can be done, and if there's any Raffles left in me such a simple proposition as cracking a bank and putting the stuff back where it belongs, in a safe, of which I have the combination, isn't going to stand in my way. Don't fret, old man, it's as good as done. Good night."

And Raffles Holmes was off. I passed a feverish night, but at 5 o'clock the following morning a telephone message set all my misgivings at rest.

"Hello, Jenkins," came Raffles' voice over the wire.

"Hello," I replied.

"Just rang you up to let you know that it's all right. The stuff's replaced. Easiest job ever—like opening oysters. Pleasant dreams to you," he said, and, click, the connection was broken.

Two weeks later Billington Rand resigned from the Kenesaw Bank and went West, where he is now leading the simple life on a sheep ranch. His resignation was accepted with regret, and the board of directors, as a special mark of their liking, voted him a gift of $2500 for faithful services.

"And the best part of it was," said Holmes, when he told me of the young man's good fortune, "that his accounts were as straight as a string."

Many of John Kendrick Bangs's classic burlesques and parodies of the Holmes stories were serialized nationally in American newspapers. Typical in art and layout is the preceding narrative; it is from Bangs's "Raffles Holmes" series, and was published in the Sunday Portland Oregonian for March 4, 1906. The collection, one of the rarest and most avidly sought-after of the Bangs books, was printed as R. Holmes & Co. by Harper & Brothers, New York, the same year.

POTTED · NOVELS

BEING A SERIES OF CANNED LITERATURE SELECTED FROM AMONG THE WORLD'S QUICKEST SELLERS PUT UP IN SLICES FOR HURRIED READERS · · EDITED BY JOHN KENDRICK BANGS

A PRAGMATIC ENIGMA

A CHAPTER FROM "THE FAILURES OF SHERLOCK HOLMES" BY A. CONAN WATSON, M.D.

IT WAS a drizzly morning in November. Holmes and I had just arrived at Boston, where he was to lecture that night on "The Relation of Cigar Stumps to Crime" before the Browning club of the Back Bay, and he was playfully indulging in some deductive pranks at my expense.

"You are a doctor by profession, with a slight leaning toward literature," he observed, rolling up a small pill for his opium pipe and placing it in the bowl. "You have just come on a long journey over the ocean and have finished up with a five hour trip on the New York, New Haven, and Hartford railroad. You were brushed off by a colored porter and rewarded him with a sixpence taken from your right-hand vest pocket before you left the train. You came from the station in a cab, accompanied by a very handsome and famous Englishman; ate a lunch of baked beans and brown bread, opening with a Martini cocktail; and you are now wondering which one of the Boston newspapers pays the highest rates for press notices."

"It is the thing that we see the most clearly that we perceive the more quickly, my dear Watson."

"Marvelous! Marvelous!" I cried. "How on earth do you know all this?"—for it was every bit of it true.

"It is the thing that we see the most clearly that we perceive the more quickly, my dear Watson," he replied, with a deprecatory gesture. "To begin with, I know you are a doctor because I have been a patient of yours for many years. That you have an inclination toward literature is shown by the fact that the nails on the fingers of your right hand are broken off short by persistent banging on the keys of a typewriting machine, which you carry with you wherever you go and with which you keep me awake every night, whether we are at a hotel or traveling on a sleeping car. If this were not enough to prove it I can clinch the fact by calling your attention to the other fact that I pay you a salary to write me up and can produce signed receipts on demand."

"Wonderful," said I; "but how did you know I had come on a long journey, partly by sea and partly by rail on a road which you specify?"

"It is simplicity itself," returned Holmes wearily. "I crossed on the steamer with you. As for the railroad, the soot that still remains in your ears and mottles your nose is identical with that which decorates my own features. Having got mine on the New Haven and Hartford, I deduce that you got yours there also. As for the colored porter, they have only colored porters on those trains for the reason that they show the effects of dust and soot less than white porters would. That he brushed you off is shown by the streaks of gray on your white vest where his brush left its marks. Over your vest pocket is the mark of your thumb, showing that you reached into that point for the only bit of coin you possessed, a sixpence."

"You are a marvel," I murmured. "And the cab?"

"The top of your beaver hat is ruffled the wrong way, where you rubbed it on the curtain roller as you entered the cab," said

Holmes. "The handsome and famous Englishman who accompanied you is obvious. I am he, and am therefore sure of my deduction."

"But the lunch, Holmes, the lunch, with the beans and the cocktail," I cried.

"Can you deny them?" he demanded.

"No, I cannot," I replied, for to tell the truth his statement of the items was absolutely correct. "But how, how, my dear fellow, can you have deduced a bean? That's what stumps me."

Holmes laughed.

"You are not observant, my dear Watson," he said. "How could I help knowing when I paid the bill?"

"A distinguished man—who does not wish it known that he is calling—a Harvard professor."

In proof he tossed me the luncheon check, and there it was, itemized in full.

"Aha!" I cried, "but how do you know that I am wondering which one of the Boston papers pays the best rates for press notices?"

"That," said he, "is merely a guess, my dear Watson. I don't know it, but I do know you."

And this was the man they said was losing his powers!

At this moment there came a timid knock on our door.

"A would-be client," said Holmes. "The timidity of his knock shows that he is not a reporter. If it were the chamber maid, knowing that there were gentlemen in the room, she would have entered without knocking. He is a distinguished man, who does not wish it known that he is calling, for if it were otherwise he would have been announced on the telephone from the office—a Harvard professor, I take it, for no other kind of living creature in Boston would admit that there was anything he did not know, and therefore no other kind of Bostonian would seek my assistance. Come in."

The door opened and a rather distinguished looking old gentleman, carrying a suit case and an umbrella, entered.

"Good morning, professor," said Holmes, rising and holding out his right hand in genial fashion and taking his visitor's hat with his left. "How are things out at Cambridge this morning?"

"Marvelous! Marvelous!" ejaculated the visitor, infringing somewhat on my copyright; in fact, taking the very words out of my mouth. "How did you know I was a professor at Harvard?"

"By the matriculation mark on your forefinger," said Holmes, "and also by the way in which you carry your umbrella, which you hold as if it were a pointer with which you were about to demonstrate something on a chart, for the benefit of a number of football players taking a four years' course in life at an institution of learning. Moreover, your address is pasted in your hat, which I have just taken from you and placed on the table. You have come to me for assistance, and your entanglement is purely intellectual, not spiritual. You have not committed a crime, nor are you the victim of one—I can tell that by looking at your eyes, which are red, not from weeping, but from reading and writing. The tear ducts have not been used for years. Hence I judge that you have written a book, and after having published it, you suddenly discover that you don't know what it means yourself, and inasmuch as the critics over the country are beginning to ask you to explain it you are in a most embarrassing position. You must either keep silent, which is a great trial to a college professor, especially a Harvard professor, or you must acknowledge that you cannot explain—a dreadful alternative. In that bag you have the original manuscript of the book, which you desire to leave with me in order that I may read it and if possible detect the thought, tell you what it is, and thus rid you of your dilemma."

"You are a wonderful man, Mr. Holmes," began our visitor, "but if you will let me"——

"One moment, please," said Holmes, eying the other closely. "Let us deduce next, if possible, just who you are. First let us admit that you are the author of a recently published book which nobody understands. Now, what is that book? It cannot be 'Six Months,' by Helenor Quinn,* for you are a gentleman, and no gentleman would have written a book of that character. Moreover, everybody knows just what that book means. The book we are after is one that cannot be understood without the assistance of a master like myself. Who writes such books? You may safely assert that the only books that nobody can understand these days are written by one James—Henry James. So far so good. But you are not Henry James, for Henry James is now in London translating his former works into Esperanto. Now, a man cannot be in London and in Boston at one and the same time. What is the inevitable conclusion? You must be some other James!"

The hand of our visitor trembled slightly as the marvelous deductive powers of Holmes unfolded themselves.

"Mummarvellulous!" he stammered.

"Now, what James can you be if you are not Henry?" said Holmes, "and what book have you written that defies the interpretation of the ordinary mind hitherto fed on the classic output of Hall Caine, Laura Jean Libbey and Gertrude Atherton? A search of the six best sellers fails to reveal the answer. Therefore the work is not fiction. I do not recall seeing it on the table of the reading room downstairs, and it is not likely, then, to be statistical. It was not handed me to read in the barber shop while having my hair cut and my chin manicured, from which I deduce that it is not humor. It is likely, then, that it is a volume either of history or philosophy. Now, in this country today people are too busy taking care of the large consignments of history in the making that come every day from Washington in the form of newspaper dispatches to devote any time to the history that was made in the past, and it is therefore not at all

---

*Doubtless a cautious reference to Elinor Glyn, a British novelist whose candid *Three Weeks* had shocked readers in 1907—B.B.

probable that you would go to the expense of publishing a book dealing with it. What, then, must we conclude? To me it is clear that you are therefore a man named James who has written a book on philosophy which nobody understands but yourself, and even you"——

"Say no more!" cried our visitor, rising and walking excitedly about the room. "You are the most amazingly astonishing bit of stupefying dumfounderment that I have ever stared at!"

"In short," continued Holmes, pointing his finger sternly at the other, "you are the man that wrote that airy trifle called 'Pragmatism.'"

There was a silence for a moment and then the professor spoke up.

"I do not understand it at all," he said.

"What, pragmatism?" asked Holmes with a chuckle.

"No, you," returned the professor coldly.

"Oh, it's all simple enough," said Holmes. "You were pointed out to me in the dining room at luncheon time by the head waiter, and, besides, your name is painted on the end of your suit case. How could your identity escape me?"

"Nevertheless," said the professor with a puzzled look on his face, "granted that you could deduce all these things as to my name, vocation and so on, what could have given you the idea that I do not myself know what I meant when I wrote my book? Can you explain that?"

"That, my dear professor, is the simplest of my deductions," said Holmes. "I have read the book."

Here the great man threw himself back in his chair and closed his eyes, and I, realizing that I was about to be a witness of a memorable adventure, retired to an escritoire over by the window to take down in shorthand what Holmes said. The professor, on the other hand, was walking nervously up and down the room.

"Well," said he, "even if you have read it, what does that prove?"

"I will tell you," said Holmes, going into one of his trances. "I read it first as a man should read a book, from first page to last, and when I got through I could not for the life of me detect your drift. A second reading in the same way left me more mystified than before, so I decided to read it backward. Inverted it was somewhat clarified but not convincing, so I tried to read it standing on my head, skipping alternate pages as I read forward and taking in the omitted ones on the return trip. The only result of this was a nervous headache. But my blood was up. I vowed to detect your thought if it cost me my life. Removing the covers of the book, I cut the pages up into slips, each the size of a playing card, pasted these upon four packs of cards, shuffled them three times, cut them twice, dealt them to three imaginary friends seated about a circular table and played an equally imaginary game of muggins with them, at the end of which I placed the four packs one on top of the other, shuffled them twice again and sat down to read the pages in the resulting sequence. Still the meaning of pragmatism eluded me."

There was a prolonged pause, interrupted only by the heavy breathing of the professor.

"Go on," he said hoarsely.

"Well," said Holmes, "as a last resort I sent the book to a young friend of mine who runs a printing shop and had him set the whole thing in type, which I afterward pied [scrambled], sweeping up the remains in a barrel, and then drawing them out letter by letter, arranging them in the order in which they came. Of the result I drew galley proofs, and would you believe it, professor, when I again proceeded to read your words the

thing meant even less than it did before. From all of which I deduce that you did not know what pragmatism was, for if you had known the chances are you would have told us. Eh?"

I awaited the answer, looking out of the window, for the demolition of another man is not a pleasant thing to witness, even though it involves a triumph for one of our most respected and profitable heroes. Strange to say, the answer did not come, and on turning to see the reason why I observed to my astonishment that Holmes and I were alone, and, what was worse, our visitor had vanished with both our suit cases and overcoats as well.

Holmes, opening his eyes at the same moment, took in the situation as soon as I did and sprang immediately to the 'phone, but even as he took down the receiver the instrument rang of itself.

"Hello," said he, impatiently.

"Is this Mr. Holmes?" came a voice.

"Yes," replied the detective, irritably. "Hurry up and get off the wire. I want to call the police. I've been robbed."

"Yes, I know," said the voice. "I'm the thief, Mr. Holmes. I wanted to tell you not to worry. Your stuff will be returned to you as soon as we have had it photographed for the illustration of an article in tonight's Boston Gazoozle. It will be on the newsstands in about an hour. Better read it; it's a corker: and much obliged to you for the material."

"Mummarvellulous!"

"Well, I'll be blanked!" cried Holmes, the phone receiver dropping from his nerveless fingers. "I fear, my dear Watson, that, in the language of this abominable country, I've been stung!"

TWO hours later the streets of Boston were ringing with the cries of newsboys selling copies of the 5 o'clock extra of the Evening Gazoozle, containing a most offensive article, with the following headlines:

DO DETECTIVES DETECT?
A Gazoozle Reporter, Disguised as a Harvard Professor,
Calls on Sherlock Holmes, Esq.,
And Gets Away with Two Suit Cases
Full of the Great Detective's Personal Effects,
While Dr. Watson's Hero
Tells What He Does Not Know About
PRAGMATISM

Rarest of all Bangs book titles is Potted Fiction *(New York: Doubleday, Page, & Co., 1908), which includes the marvelous Holmes burlesque reprinted above, very much as it appeared in the* Sunday San Francisco Call, *May 31, 1908. Unlike the preceding Raffles Holmes story, the illustrations of "A Pragmatic Enigma" are illegibly signed with initials that look like EMD or EWD.*

The Recrudescence of Sherlock Holmes

BY WEX JONES

FOR five years Holmes had sat motionless in his big armchair, his eyes as blank as cantaloupes.

"All the great criminals are dead," he remarked.

"Yes," I replied, "there's not a decent criminal left," thinking regretfully of the strange case of Mr. T. Rott Rubbish, the Adventure of the Purple Freckle, and the Odd Happening in the Deserted Icebox.

The boy handed Holmes a telegram. As the great sleuth read the few words his eyes lit up. He trembled like a hound on the scent. He passed me the telegram.

> "West Upper Tooting.
> "Pinky Pink may I call on you hinky dink.
> > "DOODLEBUG DINGBAT.
>
> "Collect."

"What do you make of it, Watson?"

"It comes from West Upper Tooting and you will have to pay for it."

"Good, very good. You're improving, my dear Watson," said Holmes. "Lend me sixpence, will you. Thank you. You see you were wrong. Never jump at conclusions—you've paid for the telegram yourself. The message indicates no crime, but possesses an element of the grotesque. I can see, of course, that it was sent by some one whose name is not Doodlebug Dingbat, who writes with a soft pencil and takes me for an escaped lunatic.

"Come, Watson, we will go to West Upper Tooting and find this fellow."

Arrived in West Upper Tooting, Holmes looked quickly around, suddenly fell upon his knees and examined the pavement with a powerful microscope.

"There's some one in that house, Watson," said Holmes, pointing to a large boarding-house.

I could see several persons at the window, so I was aware that Holmes was right again. Ignoring the open door, Holmes smashed in a window and leaped into the room.

A fat man with side whiskers looked up in some amazement.

"You are not Doodlebug Dingbat," said Holmes in an icy voice.

"No," replied the man, "are you?"

Holmes was right again.

"I notice you have a watch, suffer from toothache, that you use a safety razor, and that something disagreed with you. I could tell you more, but that's enough," concluded Holmes.

The fat man glared. "I have a watch chain, but no watch," he said. "My teeth are all false, though one of them is broken. I have never used a safety razor; I was thrown out of an automobile on my face two days ago. As for something disagreeing with me, you are right. One of the other boarders disagreed with me; hence this black eye. You've got one right, Holmes; with perseverance you may become a detective some day."

Holmes gasped. "Who are you?" he asked.

"Hawkshaw the Detective," replied the stranger, tearing off his false whiskers.

"And the telegram?" said Holmes.

"Just to see how much of a chump you could be," responded Hawkshaw.

Holmes turned and beat me unmercifully. It's hard to be the friend of a hero.

Wex Jones, a staff writer for the Hearst chain of newspapers, turned out a number of Sherlockian spoofs as humorous filler for the editorial pages of those papers. "The Recrudescence of Sherlock Holmes," above, is typical; it appeared in the San Francisco Examiner on August 22, 1908. The drawings were by Hearst staff cartoonist H. B. Martin. In an April 1909 Holmes parody, "Curlock Holmes Is Foiled in Washington"—which brought the detective with Watson to America at President Theodore Roosevelt's request—Jones had changed Holmes's given name. Apparently the American representatives of the Doyle copyrights had raised some difficulty over the use of the correct name by Jones. The "Washington" story, a weak piece not included here, had Lestrade (spelled "Lestrange") on his way to America for lack of work and posited that Holmes was paid a dollar a word for everything Watson turned out (a wry comment on Doyle's alleged earnings).

Dr. Watson Gets Peevish

WONDERFUL!

I SEE THAT YOU ARE FOND OF EGGS BOILED A MINUTE AND A HALF!

Hamorlin—

By James J. Montague

"LOOK here, Holmes," I said, "you're getting all to the bad. A few years ago when a man came in here you'd look at him a few minutes through narrowing eyes and say:

"'Aha! I see that you are a Scotch Presbyterian, that your wife is a suffragette, that you are fond of eggs boiled a minute and a half and served sunnyside up on graham toast, that you have a yellow tortoise-shell cat whose name is Lionel and who prefers his cream a trifle turned, that your tailor is a Welshman with a spavin on his right hock, and that when you were twenty-one years old you proposed to and were rejected by a bar maid named Mary Tupper Albaugh.' Why don't you do that any more?"

Holmes merely grunted.

"And," I continued, "when a man was found dead in the House of Commons you would deduce from his watch that he was a watchman, from his waistcoat that he was a relative of T. L. Woodruff, and from the fact that he was a play censor that he had probably been murdered by Bernard Shaw. Then you would find Shaw by the fire in the eye of an actor he had been rehearsing three weeks previous, track him to his lodgings, and turn the whole matter over to Scotland Yard. Now you let some country detective do the whole work. What's the matter with you, anyway?"

"My dear Watson," said Holmes, smiling slightly, "did you ever see a man under an automobile using all his hands and all his brains to get it to go?"

"Often," I replied.

"Did you ever see him stay under the machine after it had started?"

"No, of course not."

"Well, when I was doing the stunts that you have been telling of I was fixing the machine. Now it is started, and I'm getting pretty well paid as the chauffeur. See!"

I saw.

H. B. Martin did a more elaborate drawing for the James J. Montague burlesque at left; it comes from the Chicago Sunday Examiner for August 30, 1908. Here again, as in the week-earlier Wex Jones "Recrudescence" story, Holmes's name is used without indication that he is meant to be any other than the Holmes, suggesting that the Hearst staffers presumed that fictional use of Holmes as a character was unprotected in the United States— possibly because of their awareness of the public domain status of Doyle's A Study in Scarlet and other stories. If so, Doyle representatives must have swiftly disabused them of this idea, as the aforementioned "Curlock Holmes Is Foiled in Washington" of 1909 indicates.

Ballade of Baker Street

By CAROLYN WELLS

I'VE followed many a devious way,
  I've traveled fast and traveled far;
Beyond the night, across the day,
  By many a mountain, lake, and scar.
  'Neath ilex, palm, and deodar
I've viewed the homes of Fame's *élite*;
  Ah, why does frowning Fortune bar
Those hallowed rooms in Baker Street?

THERE'S Carlyle's house (you have to pay),
  Houses of Shakespeare, Poe, Legare;
There's Landor's at Fiesole,
  And Some One's Villa at Dinard.
  Nero's and Borgias' houses jar,
Though Baedekers their charms repeat;
  They should note with a double star
Those hallowed rooms in Baker Street.

MY EAGER quest I would not stay
  For jeweled house of Alnaschar,
Diogenes' quaint tub of gray—
  Historic Bough of old Omar—
  Peterhof of the Russian Czar—
These were to me no special treat,
  Could I but reach, by cab or car,
Those hallowed rooms in Baker Street.

L'ENVOI

SHERLOCK! My fondest wishes are
  That on a day I yet may greet,
Haply in some far avatar,
  Those hallowed rooms in Baker Street.

Above: a reprint of Carolyn Wells's classic "Ballade of Baker Street"—exactly as it appeared in the August 15, 1908, special Sherlock Holmes issue of Collier's.

Sure Way to Catch Every Criminal. Ha! Ha!

Sherlock Holmes, "Raffles," Arsene Lupin, M. Lecocq, Carolyn Wells and Other Infallible Detectives Test the New Scientific "SPEAKING LIKENESS" Discovery.

THE International Society of Infallible Detectives had assembled in their luxurious offices on Fakir street, this time to hold an indignation meeting.

"Utterly absurd," declared President Sherlock Holmes; "the Bertillon system is sufficiently unnecessary, but this Portrait Parle is a thousand times worse."

"What is it?" asked the Thinking Machine,* querulously, "what is a Portrait Parle?"

"Don't you know any French?" asked M. Lecocq,* superciliously; "it is a—a portrait that tells."

"It's a speaking likeness," broke in Raffles,* and Holmes exclaimed: "Speaking likeness! It's a screaming absurdity!"

"It's a roaring farce," contributed Arsene Lupin* to the general opinion, and Luther Trant* remarked thoughtfully: "It's a thundering shame!"

"But what is it?" whined the Thinking Machine; "do somebody tell me!"

"Well," said Raffles, who was ever polite to the pettish old man, "it's a way of describing criminals so you can always recognize 'em. It's a special description of each feature, a record of each measurement and a detailed account of any peculiarities the subject may possess."

"Perfectly absurd!" ranted Holmes; "as if those weren't the very things I deduce from abstract clews. The very deductions that I have built my fame upon! Show me the clews, and I describe the Portrait Parle myself!"

"Marvelous, Holmes! Marvelous!" said Dr. Watson, but a trifle mechanically, as he was absorbed in an intricate testing experiment, and had his head in a rubber bag.

"I think it's a great thing," declared M. Lupin, "if I had had such a help in my younger days, I should now be even more celebrated than I am."

"Nonsense, Lupin," said Holmes, with a slight trace of saturninity in his tone, "only a defective detective needs such a help. To my mind this Portrait Parle takes away all my chance for spectacular exploits; it leaves me no room for marvelous deduction."

"And incidentally leaves me without an appropriate comment," said Watson, who had recovered his head.

"Detecting isn't what it used to be," complained M. Lecocq; "why, even the climate has changed, and that 'light snow,' so indispensable in footprint work, now rarely falls at the right moment."

"But one doesn't need footprints with finger and thumb prints," observed Luther Trant.

"No," grunted the Thinking Machine, "and with this new Portrait Parle one doesn't need a detective instinct at all."

"Of course not," assented Holmes, bitterly, "one might as well see the omelette and then deduce broken eggs."

"Marvelous, Holmes, marvelous," breathed Watson, sadly, half fearing he said the words for the last time.

At that juncture the telephone rang and the Chief of Police wished speech with the society.

Being nearest the instrument, Arsene Lupin answered.

"Here's luck, fellows," he said, after hearing the message. "The Chief wants us to hunt up a hidden criminal, and he is sending us his Portrait Parle."

Various sniffs, sneers and snorts greeted this information, but with true detective taciturnity they awaited the arrival of the new labor-saving device. A messenger arrived with a box, which Watson placed on the table.

The members of the society gathered round and stood agape, agog and agley, while President Holmes lifted the cover.

They saw what seemed to be a collection of hastily gathered junk. There was an old lantern, a gimlet, an iron hook, and a hatchet. Then in a small box was a scarab, or Egyptian beetle. In another box was an apple and a carrot, and wrapped in a sheet of butcher's paper, was an uncooked mutton chop. In a caterer's box was a tempting looking pie.

Raffles looked at the pie appropriatively, but, after all, he was only a dilettante detective. The others, being the real thing, scorned to think of food, save for the Thinking Machine, who greatly desired to munch the apple.

President Holmes folded his arms and put on a look that was saturnine to his very finger tips. "What do you hear the portrait say, gentlemen?" he asked.

---

* Several well-known turn-of-the-century fictional detectives and/or rogues were: the Thinking Machine (actual name, Professor Augustus S. F. X. Van Duzen), created by Jacques Futrelle (1875–1912) in the novel *The Chase of the Golden Plate* (1906) and featured in some twenty-odd successive short stories; Monsieur Lecocq (no first name is ever cited), created by Emile Gaboriau (1832–1873) in the novel *L'Affaire Lerouge* 1866 and featured in four subsequent novels; Raffles (full name, A. J. Raffles), created by E. W. Hornung (1866–1921), brother-in-law of Arthur Conan Doyle, in the short-story collection *The Amateur Cracksman* 1899 and featured in three subsequent books (the Raffles series was later carried on by Barry Perowne in nine titles); Arsène Lupin, created by Maurice Leblanc (1864–1941) in the novel *Arsène Lupin* (1907) and featured in subsequent works; and Luther Trant, created by Edwin Balmer (1883–1959) and William MacHarg (1872–1951) in the short-story anthology *The Achievements of Luther Trant* (the only collection: 1910).—B.B.

M. Lupin thrust his hand among his frogged lapels and said, oracularly:

"It is a great scheme. Behold, we construct our man at once. He is an archaeologist, we learn from the scarab."

"And a butcher, we learn from the cutlet," broke in M. Lecocq, who was ever the jealous rival of his compatriot.

"He is a pastry cook," suggested Raffles, still eyeing the pie, which was a meringue.

"A farmer," declared the Thinking Machine, with his eyes wandering from the apple to the carrot.

"A carpenter, more likely," said Arsene Lupin; "see the gimlet, the hatchet and that big iron hook."

replied, for each was intent on puzzling out the meaning of the Portrait Parle.

"The hatchet indicates that it is buried," mused Holmes, "and the lantern will be useful in digging."

"We don't have to dig at night," said Raffles. "I think the mutton chop and pie indicate dinner time."

"Well, anyway, we're to dig," persisted Holmes, and Lupin said solemnly, "Of course; why, that beetle is the clew as the Gold Bug was. It's a case of buried treasure. The Hook, of course, is a locality, a peninsula or rocky coast."

"And the apple indicates the Garden of Eden, I suppose," jeered Arsene Lupin, "it's too far away, I won't go there."

"I think it's a great thing," declared M. Lupin.

"And the lantern?" asked Holmes, looking aquiline for a change.

"That proves the farmer," whined the Thinking Machine, insistently.

"Not at all," said Holmes, "it proves we are to look for an honest man."

Watson declaimed a few well chosen words, and then Raffles said, airily: "But we're to look for a criminal. The lantern merely means it's a light matter, after all."

"Does the carrot imply we are donkeys?" demanded M. Lecocq, who was quick to catch an implication. But no one

"You're all too literal," said the Thinking Machine, peevishly, "these things are merely imaginative suggestions. The apple is remindful of Paris and Helen, and so, I reason, the criminal we're to search for is a beautiful woman."

"Then let us *cherchez la femme* at once," cried Raffles, who was ever a gallant.

"We'll never accomplish anything working together," said Holmes, at last. "All celebrated detectives must celebrate alone. Go your ways, my friends; remember the Portrait Parle, and return to-morrow night with the criminal it represents."

Glad to pursue their favorite and well known methods, the

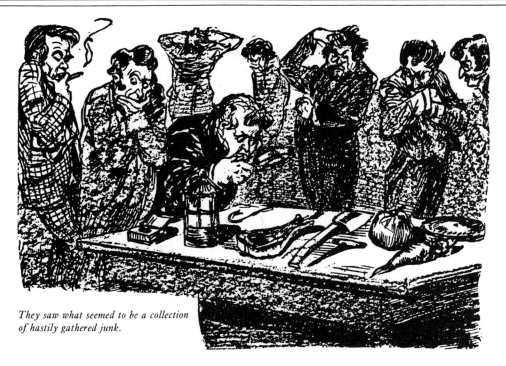

They saw what seemed to be a collection of hastily gathered junk.

infallible detectives broke up the meeting and disappeared.

Back to the Fakir street rooms they trooped the next night, each triumphantly leading a criminal of his own selection, and each secure in a true detective complacency that his was the right man.

A messenger arrived with a box, which Watson placed on the table.

M. Lupin had arrested a prominent archaelogist, the Thinking Machine brought a blustering, well-to-do farmer, and Raffles brought a dapper French pastry cook. Each had his quarry, and as the meeting convened President Holmes prepared to hear and pass judgment on the various claims from his own infallible viewpoint.

The telephone bell rang.

"Is this Mr. Holmes?" asked the Chief of Police.

"Yes," said Holmes, asininely—I mean aquilinely.

"Well, we have found the criminal we wanted, so you may call off your search."

"Indeed," said Holmes. "May I ask you to bring him over here and compare him with the Portrait Parle which you sent me?"

"I will bring him at once," replied the urbane and obliging Chief.

The members of the International Society of Infallible Detectives sat in grim gloom until the Chief arrived, leading an abject looking criminal, whom they scanned with interest. He was assuredly not a scientific man, nor was he apparently a farmer; nor yet, to all appearances, a carpenter or a pastry cook.

"I fear," began President Holmes, in a sarcastic monotone, "we do not entirely understand the fluent language of your Portrait Parle."

"No?" said the Chief of Police, in surprise; "why, my dear sir, you've only to look at this man to see that he is perfectly photographed by the Portrait Parle I sent you. Observe his features! Is he not lantern-jawed, beetle-browed, gimlet-eyed, apple-cheeked and hatchet-faced? Has he not a hook nose, mutton chop whiskers, carroty hair and a pie mouth? Are you all so dense you cannot understand such a speaking description?"

"Enough, Chief," said Holmes, with a wave of his long, white hand; "enough; your Portrait Parle is a chatterbox!"

The Chief arrived, leading an abject-looking criminal.

LATEST—DESICCATED DETECTIVE STORIES, BOILED TO THE BONE

By A. Conning Goil

DON'T be deceived into spending $1.18 net and waste golden hours staying up nights to be harrowed! Read these ten-minute tales of canned crime and condensed duplicity and be thrilled while you wait for your car! Study the powdered processes of the great girl detective, Shirley Combs, and stay with her while she elucidates the mystery of an evaporated vanishing. You can do it while the coffee is coming to a boil!

No. 1—The Finger Print Failure

It was misting great drops as I noiselessly inserted my night key into the door of our Faker Street apartment, a beastly day, in fact, and I was heartily glad to find Shirley Combs in. I called a greeting from the vestibule.

"How could you tell I was there?" she asked banteringly; "by the light?"

"No," I replied, not without pride, "I could hear you playing the ukelele."

"You are improving, Marietta, decidedly you are improving," she said, half to herself, as she mixed a coca-cola from a demijohn and a siphon standing on a table at her elbow. "What did you find new at the American store?"

I started. "Why-ah—how did you know?"

"You are smoking, are you not?" queried the svelte sleuth I have learned to dote on and admire. I glanced at my hand. I was, in fact, smoking. "Well," she explained, "one whiff from your cigarette was enough to inform me that you were experimenting with that new San Joaquin valley tobacco from America. Where had you come in contact with it? Of course, as soon as the possibility of growing it had been demonstrated and news of the experiment had been published in the Porterville Herald, my clipping bureau had at once apprised me, but I knew that the English public had only one means of becoming acquainted with it and that was at the American Store. Besides, had I been deceived in the odor the bulkiness of your side pocket could denote only a huge pennant such as is given away with the new smokes and I saw at once you had been spoofed with the same silly old bait."

I had not finished my long gasp of astonishment when a low sibilant whistle sounded in the room. It was the speaking tube from the street door. Shirley picked up the tube, worked the catch, and promptly spoke into the opening: "Come right up, M'sieu Roquette."

I must have looked my utter amazement, for Shirley said: "You were going to ask how I could recognize a person by his whistle in the tube. It is true I have never made the acquaintance of M. le Prefect of the Paris police, but I could tell from his photograph, which of course I have, that his upper left bicuspid and lower right incisor are missing. My specialized knowledge of the laws of formation of sound in the human throat and the effects produced upon that sound by the conformation of the mouth enabled me to project in my brain an auditory impression of his voice. Simple, is it not?"

During the conversation which ensued between M. Roquette and Shirley Combs, she kept up a gentle, plaintive strumming on her ukelele, intermittently sipping coca-cola, as she leaned back in her chair, through a swivel-jointed straw made especially for the noted female apprehender of miscreants. I mention this straw, with its universal joint, merely to give the reader an idea of the many-sidedness of Shirley Combs. The soft, pleading melody which she evoked from the strings of the Hawaiian instrument produced a wonderful calming effect upon the plainly distraught nerves of the Gallic police chief, and by the time he had reached

MY POSITION IS IN DANGER

the end of his narrative he was gesticulating in a perfectly normal manner. Let me paraphrase his story:

"Chu Chu the Locomotive has vanished into thin air, and still he continues his daylight depredations. He has disappeared absolutely. There are no secret hiding places in a circus tent, are there? And yet he got away with the entire receipts of one performance of Scarnum and Scaley's circus only three days ago.

"The loss was discovered before the grand parade around the big ring had started. The tent was pitched in an open field, and anyone leaving it could have been seen for several minutes, no

PIECES OF SKIN

TAL THE DIP

I WAS GLAD TO FIND SHIRLEY COMBS IN

matter what direction he took. No one left the tent—my detectives, who were on the lookout, assure me of that. We searched everyone, both in the audience and among the performers and employees. Chu Chu's finger prints were found in several places on the safe; it could have been no one else—the Bertillon system is never at fault. No Chu Chu to be found among all that crowd—I was there—you see, these outrages have put France in an uproar—my position is in danger—I was on the spot and personally looked into all the faces there."

"Faces?" broke in Shirley, "you should have looked at their hands. But never mind, go on."

"Then we began to look for the money. It could not have been taken away. My men—I did not trust even the circus hands—pitchforked over all the hay, examined the stomachs of all the large animals with electric lights—we even cut open the big python because he would not uncurl enough so that we might determine by means of the light the nature of a huge lump about the middle of his length. It was a pig, of course. Then we searched all the 10,000 persons present. THE MONEY COULD NOT BE FOUND."

"Did you look in the safe again?" queried Shirley and then quickly added; "but never mind, go on."

"That is all."

"Very well, then, if you wish to leave the case entirely in my hands, I will tell you who your man is a week from tonight. By the way, I suppose you recognized among the crowd at the circus some men with records?"

"Indeed, but yes," volleyed the Frenchman, "there was Arson the Fire, Dago the Red—but I will send you all their names and a report on each tomorrow. Dieu t'enriche, Miss Combs, God bless you. So much I have heard of you I feel sure that you will be successful. I shall sleep."

"One thing more," said Shirley. "You might ascertain if any of those men who were present and who were known to the police seemed to be in mourning."

"You are strange, mam'selle—but very well; you shall have it."

As soon as M. Roquette had left the room, Shirley changed from her comfortable Turkish trousers to her modified Bulgarian ecru eponge with the mackerel blue sash and the Nell rose guimpe, and a saucy little late-asparagus Poiret hat with marabout edging and stick-up of hard winter wheat.

"You will have to show a little speed," she said to me, "if we intend to get to that cubist exhibit at all."

"But surely," I remonstrated, "this case is of so great importance—"

"Tut! tut!" she cut me short. And so, of course, we went, and Shirley and I spent the afternoon leaning over the railing deciphering titles in the hope of finding some clue to the picture itself. Here Shirley's marvelous powers of deduction were given full play, but that is not germane to my story.

The next afternoon Shirley looked up from the reports she was reading which, true to his word, the prefect of Paris police had sent, and phoned to Scotland Yard. Upon getting in communication with the chief, she said:

"This is Shirley Combs. You will find that Amos Ward, represented as a cousin of Tal the Dip, was buried in the churchyard at Holcombe-under-the-Hedge about a month ago. Kindly have the body exhumed, and let me know what you find about the external appearance. Goodbye."

The next day, when the chief of Scotland Yard called up Shirley, I listened in on the extension in the bedroom, but only in time to hear Shirley say: "Ah, I thought so," and then she hung up the phone.

Shirley Combs at once sent a message to M. Roquette. It was this: "Arrest Tal the Dip. He has the goods."

"And now," Shirley said to me when we had settled down to our books and chocolates once more, "I suppose you want to know how I discovered that Tal the Dip was the man. I don't know myself: it was womanly intuition, I guess. At any rate, this is what happened: Chu Chu the Locomotive did not disappear; he died. From the report I learned that Tal the Dip was always a close associate of Chu Chu. He had skinned the hand of his friend and put the skin upon a glove which he took care to wear when cracking cribs.

"Naturally, as Chu Chu's finger prints were the only ones to be found near the job, attention was diverted from our friend Tal the Dip, who snapped Chu Chu's fingers, as it were, under the noses of the French police. That is all. Simple, is it not?"

NEXT WEEK: A Double-Voiced Detective Story. Maybe.

The foregoing early distaff Holmes burlesque, presenting one Shirley Combs, appeared in the Los Angeles Sunday Tribune *for April 27, 1913, and may itself be by a woman, as the byline suggests. The illustrator is Herman Roeg.*

THE MORNING SMILE

Wex Jones, Editor

OUR DOUBLE-BARRELED DETECTIVE STORY

Story written by Gilbert K. Chestyton. Solution by Con'em Boyle.

I. The Mystery of the Grange.

THE GRANGE was a lonely house, surrounded by a moat. For the benefit of American readers I may say that moats are not a cereal, although one appears in this serial. [This lightens the tragedy a bit.]

In the Grange live, or rather lived, for some of 'em are dead, Sir Edward Plantagenet, Miss Ermentrude Plantagenet, Bill Plantagenet, a butler and two maidservants.

On the morning of the 15th the butler found everybody in the house had been murdered. Everybody but the butler himself, of course; otherwise he couldn't have discovered 'em. The butler hurriedly unlocked the door and rushed out to inform the police.

II. The Solution.

Elementary, my dear Watson.

As the dead persons had all been murdered, it is clear one of them couldn't have slain the others and then committed suicide.

Even if this theory had been tenable, no person in a murderous mood would pass over a butler. Everybody hates a butler, and he would have been the first victim.

Commonplace, my dear Watson. You have an exaggerated idea of my powers.

Since the door was locked, the butler killed all the victims himself.

No, no, Watson; never mind sending for the police. No butler would murder himself out of a situation. He killed these people in his sleep, and is therefore not to blame. We must help him to get another job, possibly in a family we do not like. Elementary, my dear Watson.

OUR DOUBLE-BARRELED DETECTIVE STORY

The Shot in the Dark. Story by Rudyard Tippling. Solution by W. J. Spurns.

SPLURGE lay on his face, just as he had fallen by the sideboard.

He was clad in pajamas.

A look of unspeakable terror was on his face. There was blood on the floor, and a chair had been overturned showing there had been a struggle.

Not a person in the house had witnessed the tragedy. James Harkins, the butler, said that during the night he had heard Mr. Splurge shout something, he wasn't sure what, but distinguished the word "bite." He thought Mr. Splurge was talking in his sleep and paid no more attention to it.

The Solution.

Elementary, my dear Watson.

The gas, as you see, was not burning. This affair must then have happened in the dark.

Harkins' testimony is of the utmost importance, taken in conjunction with the spot where the body lies. "Bite"— what does that suggest to you? Nothing? My dear Watson, you should get a tenant—nobody home, nobody home.

What bite would a man dread so that he would cry aloud in the night? Snake-bite, of course. Snakes, my dear Watson. And a man who sees snakes in the night—what does he do?

I will reconstruct the scene for you. Splurge thinks he sees snakes. He goes to the dining room in the dark. Just as he is reaching to the sideboard for a drink he barks his shins on a chair. Everybody does that in the dark. Tut, tut, Watson; elementary. You should read my monograph on "Shins in Their Relation to Furniture."

The chair is overturned and some drops of blood fall to the carpet. Splurge falls over the chair and is too weak to get up.

SPLURGE ISN'T DEAD! And when you visit him in your professional capacity, my dear Dr. Watson, I should recommend the application of ammonia.

Tut, tut. Watson; elementary.

Note by Dr. Watson—I have called this adventure "The Shot in the Dark," although poor Mr. Splurge didn't get the shot he was after.

OUR DOUBLE-BARRELED DETECTIVE STORY

The Mystery of the Clock That Wouldn't Strike.

Story by G. Bernard Whiskers.

(Solution by Con'em Doyle.)

THERE was no doubt about it. In fact, there was no reason why there should be any doubt about it.

The clock did not strike.

And yet the lovely Countess of Crumpsall carried it about with her.

Wex Jones returns to our attention in a prolonged series of parodies from between 1914 and 1916 and most of them starring one Timelock Foams; a cross section of the series is given here, including the first and last examples. Calendar dates for the stories are not particularly relevant, since the various Hearst papers (for which they were written as part of Jones's weekly newspaper burlesque column) ran them interchangeably, altering the Jones date to suit their own timetables and space.

Even a duller mind than mine could scent a deep mystery here.

Why prize a clock that did not bell the hours? Why be seen with such a clock in public?

Ah, why indeed?

* * *

Elementary, my dear Potson; elementary.

The clock was on the lady's stocking. See my monograph on "Silk Stockings in Their Relations to Crime and Colds in the Head."

But the author is a chump, Potson, as you have doubtless observed. No? Where are your brains, Potson, such as they are?

The clock must have been striking to attract attention!

TIMELOCK FOAMS, THE CRIMINAL'S TERROR

The Adventure of the Two-Faced Clock.

"POTSON," said Foams, "a murder may be committed this afternoon in that room across the street."

"Let us prevent it, then," I responded.

"Potson," said Foams, "you're an awful boob. If I prevented the murder, as I could easily do by shooting the victim myself, there would be no mystery for me to solve. Surely even your so-called brain can grasp that fact."

Foams was right, as usual.

"But how will you know if the murder has been committed?" I asked.

"By a clock, my dear Potson."

"How—" I began.

"Elementary, Potson, elementary. A clock, as you doubtless know, has a face. I have hung a clock on the wall of that room. Needless to say, if a hideous crime is committed before the clock, its face will turn pale. I shall thus know by examining the clock if the murder has been committed."

"But a man's face is pale when he's run down," said I, "and presumably this is the case with a clock also."

"Nonsense, Potson. The case of a clock has nothing to do with its face."

* * *

That evening we forced our way into the room.

Foams looked eagerly for the clock.

It had been turned with its face to the wall.

"Potson," said Foams, "this is Moriarity's work. We shall never know now whether murder has been done or not."

TIMELOCK FOAMS, THE GREAT DETECTIVE

The Mystery of the Alarm Clock That Didn't Alarm.

"POTSON, you chump!"

The voice seemed to come from a long way off. . . .

"Potson, I say. Get up, you chump!"

The voice sounded as if I were dreaming, but I knew from the use of the word "chump" that the speaker was Foams.

I awoke at last.

As Foams saw my eyes open, he said, "Look at the time, you chump, that is if the cold molasses you call your brains can absorb such a simple impression."

Foams, I deduced, was peeved. I looked at the clock. It was 11:30; a bright, sunny morning.

"I see it's 11:30, Foams," said I, yawning and stretching myself.

"And I was to have delivered the stolen crown jewels to the Prince of Ruritania at 10:15," ejaculated Foams.

"Well," said I, "why didn't you?"

The great detective appeared agitated. He bent and straightened the massive brass rail of the bed in his nervous fingers. After a long pause he spoke. "I didn't deliver them," he said, "because I did not awake in time. Why didn't you call me, Potson, you chump?"

"I was asleep, too."

"You're too stupid to be allowed to sleep, my dear Potson."

"But I set the alarm clock for 9:30, Foams," I responded.

"This must be Moriarity's work, Potson. That alarm clock didn't go off."

I jumped out of bed and ran to the alarm clock. The hand of the alarm pointed to 9:30 as I had placed it the night before, and the alarm itself was run down.

I looked at the bell. That was all right, too.

Here was a mystery indeed.

"Foams," I called.

The great detective paid no attention to me.

Evidently the alarm had sounded all right at 9:30, and never before had it failed to awaken Foams, whose hearing was as sharp as a rabbit's.

"Foams." Again I addressed the great detective, and again he failed to answer me.

Foams finally sat down.

"Potson," he said, "for the first time in my life I am baffled."

"What's this?" I asked, as I pulled a piece of cotton batting from his ear.

"Moriarity!" cried Foams. "He wouldn't do anything so crude as to bust the alarm. He put this cotton in my ears when I was asleep."

"Then I solved this mystery," said I.

"Tut, tut, Potson, you chump," answered the great detective. "Accident, that's all. No brain work."

"Anyway I got results," I answered, and for once the great detective had nothing to say.

TIMELOCK FOAMS, THE GREAT DETECTIVE

He Solves the Famous Mystery of the Goldfish Globe.

"WHAT does the pint of cold molasses you call your brain make of that, Potson?" said Foams to me one morning as we breakfasted lightly on poached tea and toasted eggs.

Foams pointed to a small aquarium globe which stood in the window of our modest room in Bakingpowder street. Usually the water in the globe was clear and three goldfish were to be seen flashing around in its crystal depths.

But now the water was whipped into such foam that nothing could be seen through its whiteness.

"Perhaps the cat is attacking the goldfish," I suggested.

"Tut, tut, Potson. Your suggestion is unusually stupid, even for you. Cats hate water more than that.

"Maybe the goldfish have gone crazy," I said.

"My dear Potson," said Foams, "I fear you are hopeless. Even a mad goldfish would not have strength enough to thrash the water like that.

"Simple, my dear Potson. In the first place, the rumpus is caused by a fish, as nothing else could live in the water. It is caused by a fish bigger than the goldfish, which are too weak, and yet a fish not too big to fit into the globe. It is caused by a fish which is laboring under some aimless excitement, as there would be no reason for a fish to toss away its own supply of water. *That disturbance, Potson, is caused by a pickled herring.*"

Foams went over and emptied out the water. In the globe was a fish, but *it was not a pickled herring.*

For once Foams was wrong. The fuss had been kicked up by a soused mackerel.

TIMELOCK FOAMS, THE GREAT DETECTIVE

The Mystery of the Missing Shell.

"SHELL missing."

The words in black type were printed clear across the top of the newspaper. I showed the page to Foams.

"Now, my dear Potson," said he, "tell me what impression those words make on the mass of scrambled eggs you are pleased to call your brain?"

"Some battleship"—I began.

"Tut, tut, Potson, most of the shells a battleship fires are missing something or other. Stimulate your brain-pan of cold molasses and simulate thinking."

"An oyster on the half"—

"Nonsense, Potson. Your head resembles the trenches insofar as it's full of mud. An oyster on the half shell would be too common an object to get space on the front page. Try to stir the solid chunk of bone you call your head."

"A scrambled"—

"Stop, Potson, my dear fellow. I know you are going to say 'egg,' but don't do it. The shell is missing from almost every scrambled egg, and there would be no mystery about such a case. I fear, Potson, that you are what some persons call very thick."

"A peanut"—

"Pish, Potson. likewise tush! A peanut is too insignificant to attract attention."

I confess I became a little peevish. If my mind does not act so quickly as Foams's there is no necessity to constantly remind me of the fact.

"All right," said I. "Solve the blamed thing yourself."

"Absurdly simple, my dear Potson," rejoined Foams. "An easy process of elimination tells me that a snail had lost its shell. Now a snail rushing along without its shell would be a strange sight, and would attract a lot of attention. Simple, Potson, if you use what you are pleased to call your intellect."

Probably Foams was right.

TIMELOCK FOAMS, THE GREAT DETECTIVE

The Adventures of the Moving Picture House.

"POTSON, my dear chump," said Foams one evening, as we sat in our modest Faker street diggings, "things have been rather dull lately. What do you say to a moving picture show?"

I was astonished to hear Foams propose this, for the only recreation I had ever known him to seek was an occasional concert when Kubelik played.

Personally, I prefer the movies to any other form of recreation, but as Foams thought them unintellectual I had not ventured to go frequently. So now I answered, "Righto, Foams, I'm with you."

Once in the moving picture house I settled down to enjoy myself.

A funny little blighter, with a small, black mustache and trotters that curl up at the ends, was on the screen, and his extraordinary antics almost made me bally well smile. Of course, it would be bally bad form to laugh, you know, so you may guess how surprised I was when a loud guffaw from Foams broke the silence.

I had never, in all our years of crime detecting, seen Foams smile, much less laugh. While wondering over this, Foams suddenly arose and said, "Come, Potson, let us get out of this." The slope-shouldered blighter was just about to push a fat woman into a lake, but there was no resisting Foams, and I had to leave before the splash.

"Potson," hissed Foams when we got outside, "this is Moriarity's work. He was acting that part on the screen. I see his object. He thought he would make me laugh so much that I would be in a weakened condition on leaving the penny-odeon and he would then find me an easy prey. Let us get home at once."

Maybe Foams was right, but I wish I could have seen that fat woman flop into the lake.

TIMELOCK FOAMS, THE GREAT DETECTIVE

The Mystery of the Railway Station Sandwich.

WE had twenty minutes to wait for the train which was to take us to Little Stoke Pogis by the Pond, whither the great detective had been summoned to investigate the mysterious murders which had set that town all agog.

"Potson, my dear chump," said Foams, "you had better get a bite to eat while we are waiting for the train. There will be dangerous work ahead of us when we reach Little Stoke Pogis by the Pond, and there will be no time to think of food."

I spoke to the tall, languid goddess in black and ordered two ham sandwiches.

"Two?" said Foams.

"Yes, one for you," I replied. "As a medical man I insist upon your eating something. You haven't had a real meal in ten days, and if you become interested in this Little Stoke Pogis case you won't eat until it's finished, so I insist upon your eating one of these sandwiches I have just ordered."

"My dear Potson," said Foams. "In addition to being a chump you are a tyrant."

The goddess in black placed the sandwiches on the counter, and I saw Foams stiffen all over like a pointer on the scent of birds.

"Potson," he hissed, "do you notice anything about those sandwiches?"

"No," said I, after studying them for several minutes, "they look just like two good ham sandwiches to me."

" 'Good!' " Foams fairly ground out the word through clenched teeth. " 'Good!' "

"Yes," said I; "see, there's a nice thick piece of ham in each."

" 'A nice thick piece of ham in each,' " continued Foams. "And do you notice that the bread is fresh? Did you ever see fresh bread in a railway sandwich before?"

When reminded of it thus I had to confess that such a thing was absolutely unknown.

"This is Moriarity's work," said Foams. "He expected we would wait to eat such good sandwiches and thus miss the train to Little Stoke Pogis, his confederates there escaping in the meanwhile. But he didn't reckon with the intellect of

Timelock Foams. I saw through his plan. We do not eat the sandwiches and we catch the train."

But we found the train had gone while Foams was deducing.

TIMELOCK FOAMS, THE GREAT DETECTIVE

The Adventure of the Two-Dollar Bill.

AS Foams and I sat in our modest diggings in Faker street, I reflected that our finances were at a low ebb. My little pension did not go very far, and although Foams had won much fame by solving the Mystery of the Speckled Bantam's Egg, and the Strange Case of the Duke's Bunion, we had not profited in a pecuniary way.

Foams sat in his big chair, alternately playing his own compositions on his violin and shooting himself full of hop. I had to go out for some cigarettes, and lest I should be tempted to spend any of our slight bankroll I left the two-dollar bill on the table.

"I'll be back in a moment," I told Foams.

"Potson," answered the great detective, "you are a chump. Before you go, however, hand me the needle."

I went down to the little tobacconists at our door, bought my cigarettes and hastened back.

"Heavens, Foams, where's the two-dollar bill?" I exclaimed, as I instantly noted it had vanished from the table.

Foams laid down his fiddle.

"Moriarity's work," he said. "The arch-criminal thinks the loss of that bill will cause our starvation, and without my intellect on the side of the law he would have no serious opposition."

"But, Foams," I interrupted, "you were here all the time."

"It only shows the devilish cunning of the fellow, Potson. Moriarity is the greatest criminal in history."

"I wasn't gone a minute," I said.

"Potson," said Foams, "your mind, as you must admit yourself, is not fitted to cope with such intellects." And the detective took another shot of hop.

Later that evening I went out to visit some old army friends. On the way I passed Lyric Hall and idly noted posters announcing "Nijeffsky, the Great Lithuanian Violinist; tickets $2."

Just as I was passing on I was surprised to see Foams hurry up to the box office and purchase a ticket, which he paid for with a single bill.

I wonder . . .

TIMELOCK FOAMS, THE GREAT DETECTIVE

The Adventure of the Locked Door.

WE were returning from Sussex, where we had been engaged in solving the famous case known as the Icebox Murders, and were walking down Faker street, close to our modest diggings.

"Potson," said Foams, "you have the key?"

I felt in my pockets. "No, I haven't the key," I replied.

"Of all the chumps, my dear Potson," said Foams, "you romp away with the biscuit."

"Why, you said you'd take the key when we were going out."

"Potson, you are an ass," replied Foams.

"But"—

"I was merely trying to test your powers of observation, my dear Potson. I did say I would take the key." Here Foams felt in his pocket and his face seemed to turn a shade paler than usual.

"Potson!" he exclaimed. "My pocket has been picked!"

"What have you lost?" I asked.

"Nothing but the key," replied the great detective.

"Are you sure you picked it up from the table?" I asked.

"Don't be a chump, Potson. This is Moriarity's work. He foresaw that we should be unable to get into our diggings, and that I should catch cold in the night air."

We were now at our modest abode and as we mounted the steps the door opened and Mrs. Muggins greeted us. "I was watching for you, Mr. Foams," she said. "I found your key on the table in your room and knew you wouldn't be able to get in."

* * *

"The cunning of that arch-criminal, Moriarity," said Foams, as he settled himself on the lounge with his fiddle. "He evidently hurried back with the key to allay any suspicion."

I wonder if Moriarity really did all that or if Foams just forgot the key.

TIMELOCK FOAMS, THE GREAT DETECTIVE

The Mystery of the Strange Noise.

OF course, as a medical man, I knew Foams would appear a little "queer" to the layman.

In our modest diggings in Faker street I had closely studied the great detective, and I knew that anyone with an intellect like his must be supernormal.

But lately I had been somewhat worried. Foams had purchased a costume which at first I took to be a disguise of some kind. As we had been out on a number of cases, Foams had every opportunity to don the mysterious togs, but I had never seen him wearing them.

Then Foams had bought a large, full length mirror, which he had placed in his own room. This at first I guessed was to help him judge the effect of his disguises, and I did not pay much attention to it. Indeed when I mentioned the matter, the great detective's only reply had been, "Potson, you are a chump."

Lately, however, Foams had taken to locking himself up in his room, and he was not studying a case, because I could hear strange mutterings and could hear him moving about and stamping his feet.

Of course I never ventured to question Foams. The great detective's only reply to questions he did not invite was, "Potson, you are a chump."

One afternoon Foams had, as usual, locked himself in his room, and I could hear indistinct mutterings. Suddenly there came the most awful groaning, then a dull sickening thud, a few faint moans and all was still.

"He's dead," I cried, and burst in the door.

There on the floor lay the great detective. He had on black tights and a sword lay beside him.

"He's dead," I sobbed. "This is Moriarity's work."

Foams rose to a sitting posture.

"Potson," said he, "you are a chump"— How I rejoiced to hear those words. "Can't you see I am rehearsing Hamlet?"

Watson, Once Epaminondas, Joins Deteckative Gubb

By Ellis Parker Butler

THE celebrated Philo Gubb, paper-hanger and detective, full graduate of the Rising Sun Detective Bureau's Correspondence School of Detecting, and artistic interior decorator, reclined on his open folding bed, a bottle of milk in one hand, a sugared bun in the other. The great elucidator of hidden crime was attired in pajamas and bathrobe, and he was eating the bun according to the Fletcher system, in which he was a staunch believer. Half erect against his pillow, he inserted a part of the bun in his mouth, bit off a portion and masticated it thoroughly. When the portion of bun was thoroughly masticated, Mr. Gubb's large and virile Adam's apple glided upward, hesitated and glided downward again, with all the precision of some sort of mechanical jigger. After each portion of bun Mr. Gubb took a small amount of milk into his mouth, masticated it thirty times and swallowed that. In his regular and systematic manner he proceeded with his frugal breakfast.

The great detective was allowing himself this luxury of a breakfast in bed because he had worked late the night before. Mrs. Sarah Quimby, a widow, having received an offer of marriage from a gentleman named Orpheus Butts, had set the wedding day, and having set it, had decided that it was only right that her house should be entirely repapered before the ceremony. Mrs. Quimby was a woman of somewhat keen perceptions, and she reasoned in somewhat this manner: When a man marries for the love of a woman, that woman invariably prepares for the ceremony by attiring herself in entirely new garments. Too sensible to fool herself, Mrs. Quimby admitted to herself that Orpheus Butts was marrying her for love of her house and not for love of herself. Therefore it was proper that the house should be attired in entirely new garments for the wedding ceremony, and therefore she had called in Mr. Gubb—wall-paper being, in a way, the garments of a house.

The wedding day being set, it was necessary that the papering be done in some haste in order that Mrs. Quimby might have time to give the house its proper wedding lingerie (or, to speak plainly, new window curtains and so forth and to clean up the mess paper-hangers always leave). For this reason Mr. Gubb had worked late the night before to finish the job. It had been midnight when he turned up his straight-edge, pasting table, remainders of wall paper, paste pall, brush and so on, and had left the house. Mr. Orpheus Butts, being an unemotional and weary suitor, had gone home about 10 o'clock, and Mrs. Quimby had gone to bed about 11 o'clock, leaving her maid—Susan Dickelmeyer—to close the house after Mr. Gubb left.

Susan Dickelmeyer had waited in the kitchen, and when Mr. Gubb was ready to leave, he had to poke Susan with the end of the long handle of his paste brush several times before she stretched and groaned, "Oh, Lord! Is it time to get up already?" and finally awakened sufficiently to let Mr. Gubb out and lock the door behind him.

Because of this late work Mr. Gubb was taking an hour of relaxation in bed. He was about half through the bun and a quarter through the bottle of milk when some one tapped on his door. Mr. Gubb hurriedly slid his feet to the floor and sat keenly erect on the edge of his bed, the milk bottle in one hand and the bun in the other. Something in the quality of the sound of the tapping made Mr. Gubb think it was the announcement of a lady's coming. The tapping had not been that of a horny-knuckled man; it was a dulled sound, such as might have been made by a lady's hand encased in a glove.

With exceeding care Mr. Gubb set the milk bottle under the bed and put the bun under the pillow. With extreme caution lest he made any telltale noises, he removed his temporary attire and began drawing on his garments, keeping one nervous eye on the door, for he could not recall whether he had turned the key or not. He was half-clad when the tapping on the door came again.

"In just one part of a moment of time, please!" he said. "I ain't quite completely dressed into my garments yet, but I will be immediately soon."

The tapping ceased, and in a few minutes Mr. Gubb was fully attired. He even paused to give his hair a few strokes of the brush, and then he went to the door. The key had been turned after all, and Mr. Gubb unlocked the door and opened it. Instead of a woman he saw a fat boy, the fattest boy he had ever seen in his life. The boy was so fat that his clothes bulged everywhere; the buttons of his coat seemed to hold him in precariously, and between the buttons, his coat gasped and bound him into great rings of adiposity like automobile tires. His wrists were like fat knees and his hands like puffs of flesh, and the fat, thick fingers explained why his tapping had been muffled. His cheeks bulged as if pumped up with a bicycle pump and crowded his eyes almost out of sight. Even his forehead was fat. He breathed heavily, like a grampus, but he smiled and smiled and smiled! Unutterable good-nature beamed from his face—crass, indestructible, idiotic good-nature. He stood, a heavy canvas telescope traveling-bag at his feet, and grinned at Mr. Gubb.

"Hello, Uncle Philo," he said.

The voice was a surprise. It was a thin, weak treble, diluted to a whisper and ending in a wheeze. It was as if a hippopotamus spoke, and its voice was the voice of a short-winded canary bird. Mr. Gubb stood and stared.

"Don't you know me, Uncle Philo?" wheezed the fat boy squeakily. "I'm Epaminondas, but you don't have to call me that. You can call me Eppy for short. Papa calls me Eppy. Everybody calls me Eppy for short."

And still Mr. Gubb stood staring. It was first necessary for him to accustom himself to the idea that anything as fat as this fat boy could be. That in itself was hard to believe. Then it was necessary to force himself to believe that his sister could have a child as fat as this fat boy. Then it was necessary to convince himself that this boy was that boy. It was all hard to believe, but the boy seemed to be so sure he was Epaminondas and a nephew that slowly Mr. Gubb began to take some stock in the idea. Before the massively cheerful certitude of the boy Mr. Gubb was forced to believe. No doubt this was Epaminondas.

Mr. Gubb had never seen Epaminondas before. He had not seen his sister—once a teacher of Greek in the Darlingport High School—since she had married Otis Smits, one of Darlingport's fair-to-middling tailors; but there was really no reason to doubt that this fat boy was Epaminondas Smits. The boy said so himself.

"I'm quite pleased to see you looking so well," said Mr. Gubb. "I presume you have come down to Riverbank for a spell of visit?"

The fat boy grinned engagingly and wheezed.

"Papa said I should bring all my things," he squeaked; "so I brought them. Papa said if you wanted me to sleep on a cot I'd better tell you to let me sleep on the floor, so I'd be safer. Papa says it isn't safe for me to sleep on a cot—when the cot broke one of its legs it might run into my lung and give me consumption."

Mr. Gubb cocked his birdlike head and studied Epaminondas.

"You aim to remain staying past over night or more?" he asked. Epaminondas nodded his head. It did not nod far, because his chin hit the roll of fat above his collar; but it was an indubitable affirmative.

"I'm going to stay all the time," he squeaked. "Papa says I'm too stupid to be a tailor. Papa says a tailor has to have at least a little sense; so papa said: 'Ach, Himmel! you'll never be a tailor; go down and let your Uncle Philo make a detective out of you!' So I've come to be a detective."

He wheezed awhile after this long speech and then added:

"I haven't anything to do now; you can begin teaching me right away. Papa says—"

Mr. Gubb interrupted Epaminondas by opening the door wider and standing aside, and Epaminondas bent down—turning almost purple in the face—and raising his canvas telescope, brought it inside the room. He dropped it the instant it was over the doorsill. This exertion had almost exhausted him.

Mr. Gubb had been thinking, not rapidly but deeply. He did not want Epaminondas, and he did not need him, but it was quite evident he had him. Fate, so often mysterious, had given him Epaminondas. Here Epaminondas was. A feeling of tardy and regretful affection for his long-neglected sister surged over Philo Gubb. He remembered her now as she had been when a little girl, dainty in a frilled white dress and blue sash, lisping prettily as she walked beside Philo, holding his hand, looking up at him with pride in his protective bigness. He saw her—still visualizing her as the baby girl in a blue sash and fluffy skirts—trying to do something with Epaminondas, trying to make something of him. A surge of brotherly tenderness swept over Philo. To take Epaminondas and try to make something out of him was little enough to do for a dear sister so long neglected.

Epaminondas had removed his hat, and after trying the edge of the folding bed and deciding it was too frail to hold a youth of his weight, had seated himself in the arm chair before Philo Gubb's desk.

"I'm ready to begin to be a detective right away, Uncle Philo," he reminded the great detective. Mr. Gubb stood with one hand on the highest point of the folding bed and looked Epaminondas straight in the eye.

"The deteckative business ain't learned into a few minutes, Epaminondas," he said severely. "Personally myself I had to devote up long periods of time to studying into the twelve complete lessons of the Rising Sun Deteckative Bureau's Correspondence School of Deteckating, before I started to begin to think I knowed almost nothing whatever about it. It's going to take a long period of time to learn you even the first beginnings!"

"I don't care," piped Epaminondas. "I've got more time than almost anybody has."

"You're so much bigger, you ought to have," said Mr. Gubb, not meaning a joke, but that if Epaminondas was as stupid as his size indicated, he would be a slow learner. "If you was smaller sized, I could have you help out when I'm working onto the decorating and paper-hanging ends of my lines of work, but you ain't and you can't. But you ought to be assisting to help me in some form of shape or manner whilst learning to be a deteckative. A deteckative apprentice ought to be a help, just the same as what a paper-hanger apprentice is."

"Yes, Uncle Philo," wheezed Epaminondas.

"So I ain't so badly sorry that you've come," said Mr. Gubb, "because for a long period of time I've been hampered up in my deteckative career in one kind of way. Have you ever heard of the great deteckative Sherlock Holmes?"

"Yes, Uncle Philo," wheezed Epaminondas.

"Then I don't need to explain out to you," said Mr. Gubb, "that Sherlock Holmes wouldn't have solved out hardly none of his cases if he hadn't Watson to hand him the needle when he needed it, and to be surprised full of amazement at 'most anything Mr. Holmes said to him. Ain't that so?"

"Yes, Uncle Philo," squeaked Epaminondas.

"So I'm going to begin to start you in for a Watson," said Mr. Gubb. "To do deteckating in A1 first-class manner every deteckative ought to have a Watson. I don't much care to like your name of Epaminondas, anyway, and I ain't particular fond of Eppy for short, so from now on forth your name will start to be Watson."

"All right, Uncle Philo," said Epaminondas.

"And when I say anything like, 'And so you see, Watson, this wisp of straw tells me Jonas Hook committed the murder,' you'll say 'Marvelous!'"

"Yes, Uncle Philo," said Epaminondas, "and what else do I say?"

"Well, for the present and until the future," said Mr. Gubb, "you don't need to trouble to say anything else but that. 'Marvelous' is a good enough thing for a Watson to say, and he can't repeat it over hardly too much." He hesitated, and then continued: "Up to the present moment of time, Watson," he said, "I ain't started to begin to use hypodermic morphine into my arm, so I'm not fixed and provided with no hypodermic morphine needle. The only needle I've got into my regular possession is that one sticking into my pincushion on my desk, and I use it to repair up the rips and tears I get into my clothing garments. So for the present and until the future when I say, 'The needle, Watson!' you can hand me that sewing needle."

"Yes, Uncle Philo," said Epaminondas, obediently, "but—"

"But what, Watson?" asked Mr. Gubb.

"But I'll have to do only the best I can," said Epaminondas. "One reason papa always got so mad at me was because I couldn't pick up a needle—my fingers are so fat."

Mr. Gubb saw the truth of this. Fingers as fat as Epaminondas' would have trouble in picking up any article as small and as elusive as a needle. It would be like an ordinary person trying to pick up a needle while wearing driving gloves.

"You needn't have no sort of worry about that, Watson," said Mr. Gubb. "As soon as I can spare a few moments of time I'll secure the purchase of a horseshoe magnet for you to pick up the needle with."

"Marvelous!" said Epaminondas. Mr. Gubb looked at the cheerful fat face doubtfully. There was, however, no sign of ridicule there.

"That ain't hardly the proper occasional place to say it," he said, "but I guess you've got the inkling of the idea. Here is lesson one of the Rising Sun Deteckative Bureau's Correspondence School of Deteckating's lessons, and when you ain't Watsoning you can study up into it. Just now I ain't got a deteckating job onto my hands, so whilst you study I'll go ahead and clean out my paste pail."

Epaminondas settled back in his chair and opened the small pamphlet, and Mr. Gubb began the cleansing work he had indicated. They were so engaged when a new tapping sounded on the door, and Mr. Gubb went to learn who thus disturbed them. The disturber was Mrs. Sarah Quimby.

"Gubb," she said the moment he opened the door, "some devil has robbed me!"

It seemed fairly evident from the lady's appearance that she had discovered the robbery after its occurrence and not while it was taking place. If she had discovered the robber in the act, she would probably have come dragging him by one foot in a more or less mangled condition, or in case the robber was a veritable giant, she would have shown by her attire and injuries that a frightful struggle had taken place. Mrs. Quimby was not the sort of woman to be robbed without a struggle unless it was done on the sly. She was a square-jawed, square-shouldered and square-toed woman, and when she folded her arms she looked dangerous. Perhaps one reason was that for ten years, earlier in her life and before she sought retirement and obscurity in Riverbank, she had been known as Maggie the Kid, champion female boxer of the U.S.A., willing to meet all comers of her own age and weight. As Mrs. Quimby she had been able to conceal her past, but she could not conceal her looks—they stuck out and hit you. She looked dangerous.

As Mrs. Quimby stood at the door, she held a square parcel in her good right hand. This she thrust at Mr. Gubb, and he took it and held it while she related the tale of the burglary.

"And you want I should detect out the robber and send him or her, as the case may be, to jail in prison?" said Mr. Gubb when she had finished her story.

"Jail! Prison!" exclaimed Mrs. Quimby with scorn. "Jail and prison for the devil that robs me! No, Mr. Gubb! You find out who robbed me and leave the rest to me. Don't talk to me about jail and prison. You find the murdering malefactor, and I'll take care of him!"

She opened one hand, palm upward, and slowly closed the fingers, at the same time showing her teeth like a wolf. A shudder ran up and down Mr. Gubb's back. Somehow, Mrs. Quimby's pretty little action seemed to suggest a slow and horrible but irresistible death.

"Yes, ma'am," said Mr. Gubb, and satisfied that the case was now in good hands, Mrs. Quimby departed. "Watson," said Mr. Gubb, "quick! the needle!"

"Yes! Uncle Philo," squeaked Epaminondas, and after several unsuccessful attempts he managed to grasp the sewing needle in his fat fingers. He handed it to Mr. Gubb. Mr. Gubb ran the point through the sleeve of his coat and returned the needle to the pincushion.

The story of the robbery was a simple one, but one full of mystery. Mrs. Quimby had had in a japanned-tin cash box $44 in bills and some odd cents in change. As was her custom she had placed the cash box in a drawer of the sideboard in her dining-room. She distinctly remembered placing it there soon after dinner because she had opened it to take out a dime to give Susan Dickelmeyer to pay the milk boy for an extra measure of cream, because Mr. Orpheus Butts had remained for dinner, and as Mr. Butts used a lot of cream on his baked apple Mrs. Quimby felt she would need an extra measure. The cream was only 5 cents a measure, but Mrs. Quimby owed the boy 5 cents

in addition. This made 10 cents. Mr. Butts remarked, "You oughtn't to keep money around like that," and Mrs. Quimby had said, "If I can't keep money in my own house, locked in a box and locked in a drawer, where can I keep it?"

Now the money was gone. It must have been taken after midnight, Mrs. Quimby said, because Mr. Gubb had worked there until midnight. Asked whom she suspected, Mrs. Quimby had said, "Everybody!" Alone with Epaminondas in his office bedroom Mr. Gubb now confronted the mystery, and it was his task to solve it. With the fat nephew standing behind him and wheezing with excitement Mr. Gubb undid the square parcel and discovered it to be the japanned-tin cash box. The lid had

"Watson," he said, "this here case amazes you, don't it?"

been roughly wrenched open, breaking the lock and bending the edge. With some difficulty Mr. Gubb opened the lid and looked inside. Mrs. Quimby had said the only clews she had been able to find were inside the box. They were there. They were a coat button of a peculiar watery drab and a broken knife blade. A wisp of black thread hung in the eyes of the button—thread of about the size known as No. 8 black cotton. The knife blade was the blade of a pocket knife and was thick and strong, evidently from a pocket knife of unusual size and strength. Mr. Gubb looked at them carefully.

"Watson," he said, "this here case amazes you, don't it? You wonder how I'm going to start out to begin to find out who stole the money, don't you? With these three clews I'll have no difficult trouble finding the thief. In about half an hour we'd ought to know about who stole the money."

He paused and waited.

"Well, why don't you say it?" he asked.

"Say what?" asked Epaminondas.

"Why don't you say what I told you to say?"

"Oh!" said Epaminondas. "Marvelous!"

"Well may you say so, Watson," said Mr. Gubb, "for you don't yet understand the methods of deteckative work. Now, here, Watson, is a button—a commonly ordinary button, most probably dropped by the thief from off of his clothing garments. Where would you find a button like this one is?"

Epaminondas stared at the button stupidly for a moment while

Mr. Gubb looked at it through a magnifying glass. Suddenly Epaminondas' face brightened.

"On your coat, Uncle Philo!" he exclaimed squeakily.

With a start Mr. Gubb looked at his own coat buttons. They were exactly like the clew button Mrs. Quimby had put in the cash box. Not only so, but where there should have been five buttons on Mr. Gubbs' coat there were but four. Where the fifth button should have been dangled a bit of black thread of the size known as No. 8 black cotton. With an uneasy feeling Mr. Gubb picked up the knife blade. A week or more earlier, while at work, Mr. Gubb had tried to pry open a paint can with his knife and the blade had snapped off. He had slipped the broken blade into his overall pocket. Now he reached into his trousers pocket for his knife, opened the broken stump of blade and fitted the clew portion to it. It fitted exactly!

"Marvelous!"

"Now don't say that no more until I make a remark," said Mr. Gubb peevishly. "Quite many times things can accidentally happen that don't prove nothing at all whatever. Anybody that's anywhere can drop off buttons and knife blades with no meaning whatsoever at all."

He was rather cross about it, it seemed to Epaminondas.

"Will you tell me when to say it?—to say 'Marvelous'?" the fat boy asked.

"Say it when it is time to say it," said Mr. Gubb sharply, and he drew the cash box toward him and began examining it through the magnifying glass. "Ah, Watson!" he exclaimed, "a clew!"

"Marvelous!" said Epaminondas, but without much enthusiasm.

"You may very well say that exclamation, Watson," said Mr. Gubb. "For what, Watson, do I find the discovery of onto this tin cash box? Finger prints! And, Watson, science tells us there ain't no two fingers into the whole entire world makes the same identical prints."

"Marvelous!" said Epaminondas, hoping it was the right time to say it.

"Indeed it most certainly is," said Mr. Gubb. "But for these finger prints, Watson, somebody might pretend to say I was the thief of Mrs. Quimby's cash money, for I was the last person into the dining room except Susan Dickelmeyer. But here, Watson, we have the proof."

"Marvelous!" squealed Epaminondas, now sure he was right in saying it.

Using the magnifying glass Mr. Gubb began carefully tracing on a white sheet of paper a replica of the lines of the finger prints on the cash box. As his pen drew the lines Mr. Gubb bit gently on the end of his tongue, thus assisting the work of art. Epaminondas watched breathlessly. He felt he was seeing one of the marvels of detective science performed before his eyes.

"There!" said Mr. Gubb, completing his task. "There, Watson, you see the finger and thumb prints of the thief that criminally stole Mrs. Quimby's cash money. Beyond this, deteckative science can't go no further. Finger prints can't lie. Whomsoever it was made those finger prints is the criminal thief, and—"

"Marvelous!" said Epaminondas.

Mr. Gubb paid no attention to the exclamation. His eyes were glued to a spot in the corner of the sheet of paper where his ink-stained thumb had left an impression. The impression of Mr. Gubb's thumb and the impression of the thumb that had left a mark on the cash box were exactly alike in every particular!

Slowly Mr. Gubb turned the sheet of paper to see the finger mark on the other side. It was the exact duplicate of the finger impression on the cash box!

"Marv—" Epaminondas began.

"Stop that!" snapped Mr. Gubb. Epaminondas stopped it.

The position in which Mr. Gubb had placed himself was a most serious one. Confronted by such evidence as he had before him, he would, had the evidence pointed to any other man, have declared instantly that he had found the criminal. He arose, and with his hands clasped behind him he walked up and down the floor with long, nervous strides. Epaminondas watched him, breathing heavily.

"Stop that! Stop wheezing in that manner of way!" cried Mr. Gubb. "Can't you see I'm into a serious predicament, without a fat wheezer awheezing at me?" Suddenly he drew himself together. "Watson," he said in a calmer tone, "this here is a most certainly serious case."

It did not seem an auspicious opening for "Marvelous!" and Epaminondas did not know what else to say; so he said nothing. He grinned.

"Every clew into this case," said Mr. Gubb, "points out that I am the criminal malefactor what stole Mrs. Quimby's cash money away from her. Also furthermore," he added, "I've got into my pants pocket right now bills and change of more than $50, and a woman with a jaw like Mrs. Quimby has got wouldn't hesitate to identify it as her currency cash. It is a serious kind of matter, Watson. There ain't nothing whatsoever into the Rising Sun Deteckative Bureau's Correspondence School of Deteckating's twelve complete lessons that tells a deteckative what to do when the clews say the deteckative is the criminal thief.

"I'm into a serious kettle of predicament, Watson!"

"Marv—" Epaminondas began, and then saw that it was no time to say it.

"If this here theft case," continued Mr. Gubb, "was one that would be tried out into the courts, I wouldn't be afraid of nothing whatsoever. No judge would jail a deteckative like what I am. But Mrs. Sarah Quimby ain't going to trifle with no jury judge by no manner of means. As soon as she finds out to whom the clews point at, Watson, she's going to tear the victim limb from limb, and—"

There was a heavy knock at the door, and Mrs. Quimby entered. It was evident she was madder than ever.

"Well," she snapped. "What's what? What you found out?"

Mr. Gubb swallowed twice before he could speak.

"Into the deteckative business and profession, Mrs. Quimby," he said falteringly, "things can't be hurriedly rushed. Up to the present moment of time I have only so far as yet examined the clews you fetched here. They point quite immediately direct at one individual person—"

"Man or woman?" asked Mrs. Quimby sharply.

"A—a male man," said Mr. Gubb reluctantly.

"Oh!" cried Mrs. Quimby with intense anger, slapping her fists together in a way that would have destroyed any ordinary knuckles. "I knew it! Just wait until the proof is complete, Philo Gubb! I'll male man him—"

Mr. Gubb dared not look the lady in the eye. The watery drab button was in his fingers, and he turned it over and over nervously. As his downcast eyes noticed what his fingers held, he slipped the button hurriedly into his vest pocket.

"Be—before proceeding to start beginning the revenge," he faltered, "deteckative procedure demands the requirements that the deteckative into charge of the case had ought to disguise himself up and—and detect that way to a more or less extent."

"I want to be sure! I want to be sure," explained Mrs. Quimby. "When I think what I'm going to do to the man when I am sure, I don't want to turn myself loose on him until I am sure! You go right on, Mr. Gubb, and go on quick. That's all I say! Work quick. The longer I wait, the madder I get, and I don't want to commit absolute murder, which I am liable to if I get madder and madder much longer."

"Yes'm," said Mr. Gubb. "I think I'll get into disguise No. 18B, East Indian Snake-Charmer, which cost me $18.40 out of the Rising Sun Deteckative Bureau's supply catalogue, and—"

"Get into anything you want to," said Mrs. Quimby, "but I'll be back here at 4 o'clock and when I do come back I want to know what's what!"

With this Mrs. Quimby left the place, and Mr. Gubb turned to Epaminondas.

"Watson, the needle!" he said, and Epaminondas turned flatly and, after several attempts, clasped the sewing needle in his fat fingers and handed it to Philo Gubb. The detective ran it through his coatsleeve and replaced it in the pincushion. "And now, Watson," he said, "just kindly be so good as to help to assist me into this disguise."

Disguise No. 18B was one of the most ornate in Mr. Gubb's collection. There was a violently purple turban and a robe of screaming red. To complete the effect Mr. Gubb removed his shoes and stockings and covered his feet and legs, arms, hands and face with brown grease paint and slung on his arm a small grass basket containing a stuffed cotton snake. Thus prepared, he left the room and proceeded to the home of Mrs. Quimby, leaving Epamonindas in charge of the office-bedroom.

Time passed. Epaminondas, after testing the folding bed, put a pillow on the floor and indulged in sleep. He awoke, ate what remained of Mr. Gubb's sugared bun and drank the milk remaining in the bottle, and slept again. Again he awoke and seemed greatly refreshed and fatter than before. His brain seemed amazingly clear, as it always did for perhaps five minutes after a good nap. For a minute or two he sat in the desk chair thinking deeply. His Uncle Philo was in trouble! Clews over which his Uncle Philo seemed to have no control were the cause of all the trouble.

Epaminondas turned the chair toward the desk. With the side of his forefinger he scraped the broken knife blade to the edge of the desk and into his fat palm. His eyes fell on a rat-hole in the corner of the room. Wheezing loudly, he walked to the corner and bent down and dropped the knife blade down the rat-hole. He returned to the desk, and with his handkerchief carefully wiped the entire surface of the japanned-tin cash box. Then, with a happy wheeze he dropped to the floor again and went to sleep.

Shortly before 4 o'clock Philo Gubb returned to his room. He was a discouraged detective. Not a clew had he found to turn aside the rude hand of a logic that pointed to himself as the thief. At 4 o'clock Mrs. Quimby would return with blood in her eye, and he would be forced to report that, so far, the evidence pointed to himself. Then, as Noah and the late Mr. Louis Fourteen of France remarked, the deluge! but it would be a deluge of blood. Mr. Gubb put his bare browned foot on Epaminondas and pushed him. Epaminondas sat up, and Mr. Gubb removed the scarlet robe and drew on his trousers and vest.

"Uncle Philo," Epaminondas wheezed in his thin treble, "the clews are gone."

"Gone!" exclaimed Philo Gubb, his drawn face brightening.

"Uh-huh," said Epaminondas. "They're all gone. I wiped them off the tin box and lost the knife-blade."

For a moment Mr. Gubb's eyes glowed with joy.

"Why, in that case of circumstances," he exclaimed, "there don't nothing point to me in no manner of way! I ain't no more indicated at than what nobody is. You shouldn't ought to tamper with no clews, whatsoever, Watson, under no manner of circumstances, but—but into this particular case I'll forgive—forgi—"

His voice hesitated and died away, for his fingers were feeling in his vest pocket, and they touched the watery drab button. And then the door opened violently, and Mrs. Quimby entered.

"Well?" she asked harshly.

"Madam—Mrs. Quimby—ma'am," said Mr. Gubb slowly and reluctantly, "into this case I am obligated to be obliged to beg to report that the only remaining clew points into the direction of one male gentleman not heretofore guilty of any crime whatsoever."

"Well," said Mrs. Quimby with remarkable calmness.

"The fatal button clew which I have into my hand points out the indication that P. Gubb, paper-hanger and decorator, whilst paper-hanging and decorating into your house and home must have thefted the $44 and odd cents, which P. Gubb, deteckative, is ready here and now to return back to you. While P. Gubb, paper-hanger and decorator, refuses to confess he done it, P. Gubb, deteckative, so begs to report."

"Marv—" Epaminondas began. Mr. Gubb cast a glance at him, and Epaminondas subsided.

Mrs. Quimby did not leap into Philo Gubb with hands like cat's claws; nor did she instantly attack him with the hard fists of Maggie the Kid, champion female boxer of the U.S.A.

"Well!" she exclaimed mockingly. "I declare I never was so relieved in all my life! I made up my mind that nobody took that money but Orpheus Butts, and I declare it made me rousing mad to think the man I was going to marry would bust into

"Just wait until the proof is complete, Philo Gubb! I'll male man him."

my cash-box and rob me when the orange blossoms was all but upon my brow! My, my! what a relief to know you stole it yourself. I'm that happy I don't know what to do!"

"I'm prepared to return back the forty-four dollars—" Mr. Gubb began, but Mrs. Quimby waved a careless hand.

"Oh, tut! How you talk!" she laughed. "Keep it! I'd give twice that to have my feelings relieved the way you have relieved them. I don't harbor ill will, Mr. Gubb. The best of us might be tempted when money is left around like that. If an old rounder like me hasn't sense enough to put her money in a safe place when paper-hangers or plumbers or such are around the house, she ought to lose it. I can make allowance for human nature, Mr. Gubb, but if a bridegroom has the meanness to rob his blushing bride—! Mr. Gubb," she added seriously, "Susan Dickelmeyer has confessed she stole the money—and that she stole a button and a knife-blade from you and left them on the sideboard where the cash-box was, so as to throw suspicion on you."

It is not too much to say that it was enough for Mr. Gubb also. He bowed low when the happy Mrs. Quimby left the room. Then he turned to Epaminondas. The glad light in Philo Gubb's birdlike eyes seemed to call for some remark.

"Marvelous!" said Epaminondas.

"Into the deteckative profession," said Mr. Gubb, "there is quite a considerable much that is more marvelous than some folks imagine to think, Watson."

"Yes, Uncle Philo."

With the careless air of a great but successful detective who has one success after another and thinks little of them, Mr. Gubb walked to the wall and took down his workday coat. From a spool of No. 8 black cotton on his dresser he unreeled about a yard of thread and snapped it off. From his vest pocket he took the watery drab coat-button. Seating himself on the edge of the folding-bed, he turned to Epaminondas.

"The needle, Watson!" he said, in the calm, unexcited tone of a bachelor about to sew on a button.

Ellis Parker Butler's Philo Gubb, Correspondence School Detective *(Houghton Mifflin Co., 1918) has long been regarded by detective fiction buffs and collectors as an amusing minor classic in the small enclave of humorous detective fiction. With its fine Rea Irvin illustrations, in a variety of styles, it has also become a much-sought rare book. What has not generally been known, however, is that Butler originally penned a Holmes-oriented chapter for the volume and included it in the McClure newspaper serialization of the work as Chapter VIII. For whatever reason (most likely it was length—the printed book runs to 352 pages), Butler dropped the chapter from the published work, leaving it forgotten in the yellowing pages of a few dozen newspapers—until now, as reprinted in the several foregoing pages. The illustrations for the story, as serialized, were done by Thornton Fisher, a comic-strip artist of the period.*

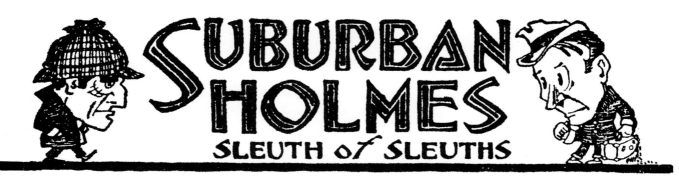

THE GREAT POWDER PUFF MYSTERY

(One of the Adventures of Mr. Suburban Holmes, Great Deducter.)

By Slippery Elm.

SPUDS GIMLET sneered evilly and pointed an accusing finger at his cowering victim.

Percival Giglamps stood silent, while icy drops of perspiration bedewed his alabaster forehead.

Gwendolyn Corncob, beautiful and only daughter of Silas Corncob, the great banker, sobbed softly while great tears suffused her lovely eyes.

Banker Corncob himself stood by, his glance tinged with scorn as it rested upon Percival, turning to admiration as it shifted to Spuds Gimlet. The scene was the marble steps of Banker Corncob's haughty mansion atop Nob Hill, whence he was wont to gaze out upon the Golden Gate, where the sun so often threw upon the waters a golden glow which had pleasant effects upon the aged banker.

All the while this information has been supplied to the shrewd reader, Spuds Gimlet continued to point his accusing finger.

"So, Percival," he said at last, "you are a crook."

A shudder wracked the slight frame of beautiful Gwendolyn, and she cast a beseeching glance toward Spuds and her father, and then looked reproachfully at Percival, whose aristocratic lineage and fine education should have kept him in the straight and narrow path.

"Believe me, kid, I never done it," exclaimed Percival.

"I was sure of it," exclaimed Gwendolyn.

"That's what they all say," sneered Spuds, who, as the reader may have discovered, was right there when a sneerer was wanted.

"I have always suspected Percival," Spuds continued. "I have my eye on Gwendolyn myself because with the fame that I am winning in my profession, I have thought that perhaps some day I might —she might—"

Spuds broke off in confusion, blushing becomingly, while Banker Corncob gave him a glance of mingled happiness and gratitude.

"The minute Gwendolyn reported to the police station that she had been robbed, I knew it must be Percival. I went to the place she described in Golden Gate Park, where she missed her treasure. There on the lawn I found bits of blue silk floss, evidently slipped off while she was embroidering—You were embroidering?" he demanded suddenly, whirling upon Gwendolyn.

Gwendolyn, still beautiful despite the tears which had washed away some of the expensive complexion with which her wealthy father indulged her girlish fancy, made a convulsive movement toward her pocket then checked herself.

"It is no use, Gwen," said the detective. "Your powder puff is gone."

"But that does not prove that Percival stole it," she objected.

"Ah, but the ground was strewn with peanut shells, and Percival is a peanut fiend."

"You cannot prove it," the miserable youth groaned, while Banker Corncob drew back a step.

"A peanut fiend," he gasped.

"Yes," pursued the relentless sleuth, "he must be. How can you account for the way he acts if he is not? Follow my reasoning. He must have stolen the powder puff because he stole the powder puff. He must be a peanut fiend because none other would steal a powder puff. The thing proves itself."

"To think that I trusted him and would have had him for a son-in-law, some day to take over the bank.

"What kind of a banker would you make," he demanded, turning upon Percival, "to go and get caught like this, you stupid bungler?

"How did you learn this method of deductive detecting?" asked Banker Corncob.

"I took lessons from Mr. Suburban Holmes," replied Spuds Gimlet, with just a trace of pardonable pride.

"Mr. Suburban Holmes," cried Gwendolyn. "I'll save you, Percival."

With these words she leaped into a passing taxicab and was whirled away.

Almost before Spuds Gimlet had finished deducting for Banker Corncob what Gwendolyn probably was up to, the taxi whirled back and Gwendolyn alighted, followed by a cadaverous man who devoured narcotics by the handful and paused at every other step to stab himself with poisoned needles.

"Mr. Suburban Holmes himself," cried Banker Corncob in awe.

"Slowly, slowly, Spuds," cautioned Mr. Suburban Holmes. "You know, haste never was a part of my methods."

Spuds leaned back against the stone lion

that guarded the Corncob mansion. It may be mentioned in passing that Banker Corncob chose this guardian in preference to a watchdog, because stone lions do not eat meat. It isn't the original cost, but the upkeep that counts, was one of Banker Corncob's mottoes.

At any rate, Spuds leaned against the lion, which did not seem to mind being leaned upon by the rising young detective.

"This is one time the pupil has outdone the master," he said. "Mr. Suburban Holmes, you have been a great man in your day, but now you look to me like a bungalow, a nickel down and a nickel a minute for life."

Mr. Suburban Holmes, with a commanding gesture which they could not resist obeying, led the way to Golden Gate Park. The park is some four miles from Nob Hill, but for the sake of getting on with our story we will make it considerably less than that.

On the grass plot where Gwendolyn Corncob first missed her powder puff the great deductive detective paused, took a microscope from his pocket and on all four ran nimbly over the grass, pausing now and then to investigate something which excited his interest.

Then, without turning he sprang up, seized the branch of a tree overhead, swung himself up and peered into a hole in the tree.

"The mystery is solved," Mr. Suburban Holmes shouted, just as Spuds Gimlet, who had been searching Percival, took a powder puff from our hero's breast pocket.

Then Mr. Suburban Holmes released his grasp on the branches and dropped.

Spuds Gimlet seemed utterly crushed.

It was upon Spuds that Mr. Suburban Holmes alighted in his drop from the tree.

"I knew from the first that Spuds was wrong about Percival," said Mr. Suburban Holmes. "I saw butter upon Percival's fingers, proving that he had been eating popcorn. No popcorn eater would waste his time upon peanuts. The peanut shells must have come from another source. Also, on the ground, mingled with the peanut shells, I found bits of fur. What kind of an animal in the park has fur and eats peanuts?"

"Squirrels," cried Gwendolyn.

"You are a clever girl," said the great deducter, with an admiration he seldom bestowed upon any female of the human species.

"Why should there be bits of squirrel fur on the ground, when this is not the squirrel flea season? Evidently they were

clawed off. Probably by Mrs. Squirrel, angry because her mate stayed out all night. You can see the scratches on the trunk of this tree, where his feet slipped on his unsteady return to his home after nocturnal peanut orgies.

"In the squirrel's nest I found this bit of a Sunday magazine page. I show it to you. It is an article on how to be beautiful. You may say that lady squirrels do not read Sunday magazines, but I ask you, what else would she be doing with it?

"Here we find ladies advised to make themselves beautiful if they would keep their husbands at home. What more likely than that Mrs. Squirrel should seek to emulate her human sisters and should desire a powder puff? We know that she has had time to meditate, for here upon the grass are bits of blue silk floss. The ends are not snipped off as they would have been had they been used by Gwendolyn, but are nipped off, as my microscope shows, by sharp teeth like those of the squirrel. In the tree trunk residence of the family I saw Mrs. Squirrel carefully tending a baby squirrel. No doubt these bits of silk show that she was embroidering a layette for the little one.

"Given all this time to think, what more natural than for the lady squirrel to swipe Gwendolyn's powder puff?"

"Admirable," cried Banker Corncob. "Your logic is unassailable. Now I will have to take Percival for my son-in-law and pay him $10,000 a year to run the bank. That is absolutely necessary, according to the standard fiction plot."

"But what about the powder puff I found in Percival's pocket?" demanded Spuds Gimlet, who was becoming conscious again.

"You had better keep that to take the shine off your nose and polish your police star," replied Mr. Suburban Holmes, and Banker Corncob nodded his approval of the great deducter's sarcasm.

"How can I reward you for saving me?" cried Percival Giglamps, making as though to throw himself upon Mr. Suburban Holmes and embrace him.

"Promise me never to eat pie with a knife," responded Mr. Suburban Holmes.

Two "Suburban Holmes" stories were published in the San Francisco Chronicle, on October 9 and 16, 1921. Apparently staff-written, the stories were illustrated by staff artist Jim Albright. This one, the first, and better, story, has a pseudonymous author: "Slippery Elm."

The Gubb Diamond Robbery

By Rhoda Montade

"IN the immortal phrase of Benjamin Franklin—'Yes!'"
It was Spiffany, the famous jeweler, who spoke.

Mortimer Mudge, the great detective, had just asked him if he would pay $10,000 for the capture of the thief who had stolen the magnificent Gubb diamond, the historic gem that was the pride of the Spiffany collection.

Mudge had just asked him, and Spiffany had said yes. Nothing had been said about the recovery of the diamond.

"It is the principle of the thing," said Spiffany. "I don't mind losing the diamond nearly so much as I do the thought that anybody could be so mean as to walk into my store and take something that my little boy Otto was so fond of. You can't imagine how crazy that boy was about the Gubb diamond. It was his favorite plaything. The paste diamond that the thief substituted doesn't fool him. Of course, it was valuable—worth a million or two, I fancy. And it had a lot of sentiment connected with it—one of Noah's sons—Percy, I believe it was, bought it for a chorus girl in the Ararat Follies, it is said. But it isn't the money that bothers me; it's the principle of the thing. I don't know what the world is coming to. Do you?"

Mudge said no, just to please the old man. Then he asked to be shown the diamond department.

The diamond department was a hollow square of glass showcases set on mahogany counters. Mudge stared at the showcases for perhaps a minute.

"Where was the Gubb diamond kept?"

Spiffany showed him the spot.

"When did you miss it?"

"This morning, when little Otto wanted to take it to school to show the teacher."

"Are you sure Otto didn't swallow it?"

"Yes, I had him X-rayed immediately. We found several smaller gems and a gold ring or two, but not the Gubb."

"Um."

When Mudge said "Um" I knew he was thinking. He leaned against the showcase at the spot where Spiffany had said the Gubb diamond was kept. "This will be a job for you, Snoggs," he said.

We turned to go. Just as we did so a young woman reached the spot where Mudge had stood. She, too, leaned over the showcase, examining the gems beneath the glass. Then she appeared to grow faint, swayed weakly for a second, and just as we were about to go to her assistance hurried out.

"Poor girl," said Mudge, "they made her dizzy."

"Never saw that happen to a woman before," said the jeweler. "It's generally the men who get dizzy."

We bade him farewell. "Don't worry," said Mudge, "I'll get him before long."

"Hope you do," replied Spiffany earnestly. "Can I take little Otto to see the trial?"

Mudge was silent until we reached his office. There he bade me be seated and pay close attention.

"Snoggs," he said, "this is a job for you. Here is what I have already deduced: In the first place, that diamond was stolen by a heartless person, one who doesn't like children. That means a young person. In the second place, it was stolen by a gum chewer."

He put his hand in his coat pocket and turned his back to me. When he faced about again he held something toward me.

It was a wad of chewing gum!

"Carefully! Don't squeeze it. See the teeth marks? That's what will enable us to identify the crook. From the size of the wad and the fact that they are marks of the jaw teeth I should say a woman had chewed it, and that she was a gum addict. That's very important, Snoggs—in fact, if that were not the case we might never find the thief."

"How do you know it was an addict's gum?"

"Snoggs, you ought to know that much! The continuous gum chewer, the person who has 'gotta have it,' chews with his back teeth; the person who can take it or leave it alone just nibbles with his front teeth. Now, here's where you come in.

"If my deductions are correct this person, a confirmed gum chewer, pretended to examine the Gubb diamond, switched the paste gem to the jewelry clerks, rolled the real gem in this wad of gum, stuck the gum under the counter and left the store. After the excitement of discovering the theft had died down the thief intended to come back, pick up the gum and walk out. An old dodge, but a good one"—

"Well," I cried, "how do you know the thief wouldn't come back now? Are you sure the diamond isn't in the gum now?" And I started to tear open the gum to see.

"Stop!" The great detective's voice compelled obedience. "Don't interrupt," he continued. "I am sure—mark these words, Snoggs—I am sure the diamond is not in that wad of gum! Besides, if you blur the teeth marks how can we find the thief?"

"Yes, how can we, teeth marks or not?" I asked.

"Snoggs, you must do it. You must capture the thief, and claim the reward yourself—paying your own expenses, of course. You must set a trap into which a confirmed gum chewer would walk."

"What would that be?"

"Simple, Snoggs, simple. You must start a service station on lower Broadway, where more than half the gum east of the Mississippi is chewed, including the Scandinavian. This will be called Snoggs Service Station; Gum Re-flavored. You can have various advertisements in the papers and on the billboards:

" 'Have your favorite reflavored.'

" 'Wads rebuilt in all styles and tastes.'

" 'Eventually—why not Snoggs?'

" 'Don't chew mud; take it to Snoggs—he satisfies.'

" 'Let Snoggs handle your gum. By day, week or month.'

"Then you must examine carefully all the gum brought in. When you find a wad with teeth marks in it to match these—that will be the thief. Get me?"

I said I did. I started the service station. I coined money. A year later an old man brought in a quid that matched the gum from Spiffany's. I shoved him down the cellar steps and telephoned Mudge.

"An old man?" he said. "That's not the thief. It was a woman who stole the Gubb diamond."

"But the teeth marks match," I protested.

"Slap the old man in the jaw," he directed. "His teeth will fall out. They are false. Make him tell you where he got them, trace them back to the original owner. That will be a woman—the woman who stole the Gubb diamond. Don't have her arrested—hold her."

I slapped the old man. The teeth fell out. I bribed him with an offer of six months reflavoring service—mint, peppermint, tutti-frutti, spinach, tomato, any flavor he liked—if he would tell me where he got his false teeth.

That brought me to a pawnshop. By a like offer to the pawnbroker I found the person who had pawned the teeth.

And that person, as Mudge had predicted, was a woman.

She was the woman who had nearly fainted at Spiffany's the day Mudge got the jeweler to promise $10,000 for capturing the thief!

In triumph I sent for Mudge. He had a talk in private with the woman. Then he had a private talk with me.

"Snoggs," he said, "would you mind very much if I gave you $10,000 for capturing this woman and say nothing to Spiffany about it?"

I said it would be all right with me if I got the $10,000. I got it.

"But why?" I asked. "Isn't she the person who took the diamond?"

"One of them," he replied.

"Did she get the diamond the day she fainted in the store? Who has it now? Where is it?" I asked, bewildered.

"Simple, Snoggs, simple. But I'd rather not discuss that part of it now. If you didn't mind I just as soon you forgot all about this incident. Keep away from Spiffany, please, and never speak of this to any living soul."

So I never have.

"The Gubb Diamond Robbery" appeared in the Wisconsin News *for February 22, 1922. The individual behind its author, "Rhoda Montade," is unidentifiable and may be male or female.*

Gene Fowler's "Arson Clews"

THE SYLVAN PUZZLE

DANCING was a favorite pastime with Professor Arson Clews during those sullen winter months when his country place was a rendezvous for his society friends. The great detective was never so much at home as when he glided with the commanding grace of a dyspeptic hippopotamus over the waxed floors and mustaches of the ballroom.

One blustery night in January—unless it was in July—I recall that Clews was dancing with Mrs. Evergreen Shrubb, wife of the wealthy but honest shoe-tree manufacturer.

"Professor," I heard her groan on his shoulder, "I understand that you invented some dance steps yourself."

"True, indeed, madam," replied the master sleuth. "I perfected the now popular lock-step while I was attending classes at Sing Sing. Are you enjoying yourself, Mrs. Shrubb?"

"I just love football," I thought the lady answered.

Clews was rapidly becoming fascinated with his brutal amusement as the door bell sputtered. It turned out that the summons came from Evergreen Shrubb's chauffeur, so Clews put aside the disguise he had donned so hastily in the belief it was the sheriff.

* * *

"Boobson," Clews said to me as we waited on the gouty Evergreen Shrubb in the luxurious butler's pantry in his 185-room cottage at the foot of Doughgetter's Hill. "Boobson," he repeated, "we have work to do."

"I knew I never should have left my father," I rejoined, "for he was making enough to support me in my thirst for knowledge."

"It was not the least spectacular of your thirsts," and Clews naively had his little jest. "But Evergreen Shrubb tells me the amazing news that at least forty-three of his rare hardwood trees, the Flintbarkus Adamantus, have been snapped off mysterious and taken away."

* * *

Painstaking and thorough in everything except paying his bills, Professor Clews, spyglass in hand, was counting splinters at the scene of the crime. He was stooped over the stumps of the missing trees. He rose at length. Then, stubbing his toe on an empty bottle, he fell at length.

"Boobson," he explained, "we must look for someone who has three splinters in his head, for there are three missing. Search all the hospitals and other places of amusement at once."

* * *

With customary success, Clews was unable to find the culprit in any of the hospitals. He was glad to dispense with a hasty search of those places, anyway, as the patients were laughing uproariously over their trivial operations and didn't take life seriously enough to suit Clews. Rather, he pointed out, he preferred the company of some of the surgeons, who took life seriously and often.

By chance Clews stumbled on the solution of the crime although I fear he was over modest in saying that his skill led to the denouement. For he ushered me to the home of Cuttlefish Dolphin, father of Klug Dolphin, the champion dunce of six counties. In fact, Klug was so dense, his tutors claimed, that he mistook the Bok Peace Plan for a recipe for beer.

"Boobson," and Clews looked at me as though he suspected I had been mixed up in an oil scandal, "the solution is simple. There is a hill above the cozy cottage of Evergreen Shrubb, as you know. It develops that young Klug Dolphin went coasting there on his new sled."

"I think that all sleds should be equipped with rum runners," I interjected.

"Young Klug," continued the greatest detective of all generations, "crashed into those rare trees on the Shrubb estate and, his head being so hard, no other wood could withstand the shock. The rest is simple. Old man Dolphin removed

Famed as the author of Timberline, Skyline, The Great Mouthpiece, *and—more well known—*Good Night, Sweet Prince, *Gene Fowler wrote the long series of Professor Arson Clews narratives for the Hearst papers between 1923 and 1925. Fowler was also at one time managing editor of the paper in which these pieces appeared first, the New York* American. *The three reprinted here (from March 6, April 13, and June 22, 1924) offer a fair sample of the full run. Curiously, considering the great amount of comic artist talent on the Hearst staffs, the Clews stories were never illustrated.*

the trees. He will cut them up for fire-
wood."

THE PLATE MYSTERY

PROF. ARSON CLEWS and his
Bleecker Street Apartment were both
lit up when I arrived there at 9 o'clock
p.m. one night last week. He had been
working on a very difficult case. It took
an hour's labor with an ax before Clews
could open it. Perspiring effusively, the
Professor disappeared upstairs to change
his spectacles, but soon rejoined me.

Sliding down the staircase, as befitted
a former ski-jumping champion, the
master detective said in that heavy voice,
common to those who are light in the head:

"Ah, my dear Boobson, I have some
grave tidings for you."

"Who is dead?" I inquired.

"I have just heard from that head-
quarters man, Shade Tree," Clews
replied. "I employ him, as you know,
to shadow various suspects. I have found
that the international turf crook, Pancakes Prendergast, is now in New York
and has taken rooms at the Aquarium."

The telephone rang. Clews drew his
automatic pistol and covered the receiver.

"You answer the phone, Boobson,"
hissed Clews, "and if it's an enemy, cut
the wire."

* * *

Professor Clews and I were invited by
telephone to attend a banquet given by
the noted turfman, Andy Kapp. Furthermore or less, Clews was retained by international interests to find why it is that
the Prince of Wales refuses to remain
seated while on horseback. The famous
Russian jockey, Serge Onanoff, was also
to be a guest.

"Shall I hire a dress suit for the festivities?" I asked my illustrious friend.

"Yes, Boobson," replied the Professor,
"go over to Hoboken and rent a room.
Have the suits sent there and be sure to
use an alias."

"Why all this trouble, Professor?"

"Because," replied Clews, "if we like
the suits, it would be unethical to return
them."

* * *

Standing in the trophy room of the
great turfman, Andy Kapp, Professor
Clews and I were studying the form sheets
that were draped about a plaster replica
of the Venus de Milo, Diana, and other
Egyptian actresses. Clews, suddenly
clutching my trachea, motioned me to be
silent. Pancakes Prendergast, disguised

as a bus boy and wearing a Kentucky
Derby, entered the room. The Professor
and I watched.

Prendergast placed a powder in Andy
Kapp's glass. The noted sportsman, top-
pling to the floor, howled to Clews:

"Watch my plate, Professor."

Serge Onanoff remarked, while the turf
king was slipping from his chair:

"He looks natural under the table, eh,
wotsky?"

* * *

"You goofy saphead!" thundered Andy
Kapp to Clews, as the racing magnate
began to revive, "Why didn't you watch
my plate?"

"Your plate is quite safe, I believe,"
Clews smiled, and pointed to the elegant
silver service on the table.

"Dinner plate, yes," returned Mr.
Kapp, "but that's not the plate I meant.
The plate I'm interested in is my false
teeth. They are set in platinum and inlaid
with diamonds. The plate is gone, and now
I must speak in a falsetto voice."

"Hoodwinked!" the Professor said.
"Come, Boobson, we failed to protect the
plate, but," and he turned to the gathering
of turfmen and jockeys and said to both
of them: "I know why the Prince keeps
falling off his mounts."

"Why?" the crowd of two persons
inquired.

"Because," Clews replied, "he rides
when a great many women are among the
spectators, and, as His Royal Highness
is most polite, he does not think it fit to
remain seated in the presence of the
ladies."

THE VAULT MYSTERY

PROF. ARSON CLEWS dreamily
closed his volume of Swinburne's
poems. I thought he had been reading the
Garden of Proserpine. I used to sigh
over the verse:

"I am tired of tears and laughter."

I said to Clews, the master criminologist, who seemed enraptured by the
flights of the poet:

"He flips a snappy quill, eh, Professor?"

"Yes, indeed, my good Boobson," he
replied, "Godfrey Craxley certainly can
write."

"But, Professor," I interjected, "you
were reading Swinburne, I take it?"

"You are always taking things,
Boobson," my mentor rejoined. "You
deduced erroneously that I was reading
from the printed pages of this book—

whatever it is—and as usual you are as
wrong as a knife in a dish of peas."

"What, if I may ask, Professor, were
you reading then?"

"Boobson," and Professor Clews re-
adjusted the hypodermic needle that serves
him as a scarf pin, "Boobson, I was
reading the combination of the safe of
the Celery Growers' International Bank.
Craxley, as you know—"

"Is going to pull another one of his
spectacular robberies," I supplied.

* * *

Disguised as a night watchman, Clews
was sleeping serenely in the office of the
president of the Celery Growers' Bank.

At this moment in stepped the president
of the bank, a high-celeried man as befits
such a growing institution as the Celery
International. He began to reprimand
Clews for seeming inactivity in uncover-
ing the plot to rob the bank, and said
that if something were not done soon,
he would rob it himself.

Clews, although only partially under
the influence of spirits, drew himself up
to his full height, and said:

"Mr. President, the man you want is
your receiving teller, Howard Piazza. I
have found evidence that he has made
plans to leave for Nakazooki, Korea."

The president was aghast. Piazza had
been engaged to marry one or two of the
nieces of a member of the board of
directors.

"But, Professor—"

"Enough," Clews interrupted. "When
I heard that Piazza was about to be
married, my suspicions were aroused. I
always suspect persons who are going to
get married. That's why I kept such a
strict watch on my wife."

"But, surely, professor—if you are
a professor—"

"Piazza is the man, I tell you," Clews
rasped. "Open your vault and you will
see what I say is all too true."

"I can't open the vault," the president
claimed, "because it has a time lock."

"Well," meditated Clews, "it ought to
open easily enough, for Piazza, and not
the renowned Craxley, will be doing time
for this soon enough. We will wait."

* * *

"Boobson," Clews said, while we were
mourning with Godfrey Craxley over his
having been too late on the job, "I deduced
that the villain, Piazza, was hatching
something besides chickens when I heard
that he had been vaccinated.

"He used serums to thwart smallpox.
Now, the smallpox exists today in alarm-

ing proportions in Nakazooki, Korea. Piecing this evidence together, I followed Piazza, knowing that he was going to abscond."

"And, Professor," I said, "when the vault was opened, the president found Piazza?"

"No, Boobson," replied the Professor, "he found the night watchman, who was reading that same volume of Swinburne that I had the other day."

"What was he doing in the vault?" I asked.

"I just told you, my dear Boobson, that he was reading. He was asked to explain further, and he told the president that he was forced to retire to the vault so as not to be interrupted in his literary pursuits by a lot of common, vulgar bandits. They are always intruding in the banks."

FITCH'S LINES

THE MODERN SHERLOCK
One Baffling Mystery by Carlton Fitchett.
Five Deductions by Alton McConkey.

The city gasped in deep dismay; a daring thief and reckless, had broken in and made away with Mrs. Gotrock's necklace. And so she called on "Old Cap Jones," a sleuth with years grown hoary, and choking back her anguished moans, she told the whole sad story.

"Be calm, dear madam!" he replied in tones of vibrant power. "I'll have your jewels back inside of less than half an hour! Now, let us see the jewel case from which the rocks were lifted." He took a look, across his face a look of triumph drifted.

"Call all the servants in!" he cried. His keenness was exquisite. He called a serving maid aside and chirped: "Confess! Where is it?" A look of guilt swept o'er her face, and she with fear was reeling, but led him to the hiding place, the stolen gems revealing.

"You're marvelous!" the mistress gushed, and showed a cultured dimple. "'Twas nothing!" said Old Cap, and blushed. "'Twas really very simple." He named his price—a ten case note—much less than she expected, then told her, having cleared his throat, how he the thief detected.

"The culprit wasn't very slick," he said in manner breezy. "A hairpin was employed to pick the lock—the rest was easy. Your serving maid has not bobbed hair; with pins she has to dress it. So I accused her then and there and caused her to confess it."

A curious admixture of the dime novels' Old Cap Collier and Sherlock Holmes appeared in this short jape, "Fitch's Lines," from the Seattle Post-Intelligencer for November 6, 1924. The art is by Paul Fung, who later drew Dumb Dora *and other comic strips.*

LORD CAMEMBERT SMUDGED?

✦★✦   ✦★✦   ✦★✦   ✦★✦

Holmes Deduces Spirit Pictures

✦★✦   ✦★✦   ✦★✦   ✦★✦

EVERYTHING IS DISPROVED!

LONDON, April 30.—A. A. Campbell Swinton, a consulting engineer and scientist, who is a nephew of Lord Combermere, says he has inspected the photograph exhibited by Sir Arthur Conan Doyle, England's most prominent spiritualist, and which purports to be a spirit picture of the late Lord Combermere, and charges it to be a fraud.

"What is supposed to be a spirit," said Swinton, "looks more like a smudge. To say it bears any likeness to Lord Combermere is ridiculous."

By Doctor Watson
(Alias Earle Ennis)

As usual I found Sherlock Holmes sitting cross-legged on the floor of his Baker Street lodgings entirely surrounded by ciphers, cryptograms, navy shag and cross-word puzzles. He was smoking violently and playing Rubenheimer's "Melody in Q" with one finger on a ukulele. His greeting was characteristic.

"Ha! Watson," he exclaimed. "You have been playing polo, your grandmother was a Beauchamp, and the price of eggs has gone up. What do you know about smudges?"

I was amazed, even though I was used to his remarkable powers.

"Nothing," I confessed, knowing that was what he wanted me to say so he could explain himself.

All Smudged Up, as It Were

"Ah!" he said, rubbing his hands. "I thought so."

He jumped to his feet and took a photographic plate from a drawer and handed it to me.

"What do you see on it?" he demanded.

"A smudge," I said promptly.

"What kind of a smudge?" asked Holmes, his eyes gleaming.

"It looks like a giraffe or a necklace," I said, "or a big cheese."

Holmes closed the door and locked it. Then he pulled down the shades. As I watched, he got down on all fours and crawled over to me and whispered in my ear.

"Watson," he said. "That is the picture of a soul!"

I was dumbfounded.

"Whose?" I asked.

Mar-r-rvelous! But Whose Soul Is It?

"That," said Holmes mysteriously, "is what I have been hired to find out."

"But you have a theory," I said. "Whose soul is it that looks like a big cheese?"

He nodded violently and filled three of his pipes simultaneously.

"Lord Camembert," he said softly and twiddled his fingers.

It was inconceivable. I said so.

"Look again," said Holmes.

I did. This time the smudge resembled a growing tree or a dried abalone in winter.

"It has changed," I said. "It seems longer."

Holmes chuckled with diabolical glee.

Quick—The Needle! It's Peggy Joyce

"Quite a likeness, eh?" he laughed.

"Wonderful," I said. "But who is it?"

"Peggy Joyce,"* he replied. "The woman of mystery."

"But she is not dead," I protested. "How can you have a picture of her soul?"

Holmes laughed so loudly the ormolu clock fell off on its face and positively refused to tick.

"That's what the Duncan Sisters* wanted to know, but I wouldn't tell 'em."

"Marvelous," I exclaimed. "How were these spirit photographs taken?"

*Better known as Peggy Hopkins Joyce: a wealthy New York socialite. The Duncan Sisters were musical comedy stars.—B.B.

Holmes showed me. He took a piece of paper. In the exact center he made a pinhole. Then he handed me the paper.

"Look through the hole and tell me what you see," he commanded. I did so.

"Nothing!" I said, after a moment.

"Ah," said Holmes. "That it is. That is exactly it. Wonderful, isn't it?" I admitted that it was.

Yea, Truly, the Boy Is Clever

Borrowing my cocaine needle he cleaned his pipestem thoughtfully.

"You know, Watson," he said, "some folks do not believe in smudges. For myself—I agree with Bud Corrigan. You can't tell a soul by the company it keeps. The little affair of the czar's taxicab taught me that. This is simple. I have here the soul of Peggy Joyce on a plate. Therefore . . ."

"She is soulless?" I suggested.

"Capital, Watson, capital," said Holmes, slapping me on the back.

"But Lord Camembert—is he also . . . ?"

Holmes shook his head and threw the canary out of the window to note the time it took for it to hit the ground in comparison with the strokes of Big Ben's clapper.

"No," he said, and to this day I believe he meant it.

Before my eyes he smashed the plate. He must have seen my surprise.

"I have saved two souls," he said.

Nor would he ever tell me what it was all about. But always afterward when he saw a smudge his spirits rose.

Earle Ennis, a staffer on the San Francisco Call, *managed to get a Holmes burlesque on the front page of his paper for Friday, April 30, 1926. The piece, reprinted above, ran on the far left-hand side of the page under a banner headline reading: "Girl Bride, 17, Beaten, Blames Father, Brother" and beside another that read: "Gold Strike on Mt. Davidson." The illustrator is Jimmy Hatlo, of later* They'll Do It Every Time *fame.*

The Great Goofus Mystery
(Selected by the Crime of the Week Club)

Chapter 1

"Who killed the Goofus Robin?"
The Great Detective cried,
"There's nary a finger print to show
Or weapon by his side.

Chapter 2

"No motive for his violent death
No trouble in his life,
No gangster put him on the spot,
He didn't have a wife.

Chapter 3

"But I must find a murderer,"
Went on the Great Detective,
"So I'll confess the crime myself
Though it makes the plot defective!'

This "Goofus Animals" rhyme by Herbert Kirk, with art by Nate Collier, anticipates a later section of our book by its focus on the comics and cartoons, but it is placed here because of the syndicated series' obvious bias toward the verse content over its art.

A VARIETY OF
SHERLOCKIAN COMMENTARY

The more serious-voiced American Sherlockiana comprises widely differing topics, and does not exclude poetry, book reviews, or even the short story. Reprinted in this section will be: (1) little-known and/or obscurely printed articles about the Doyle Holmes works, (2) well-known items that are nevertheless hard to come by and are seldom seen in their original layouts, and (3) certain interesting curiosities of Sherlockiana that fit well here. The first, indeed, is one such oddment: an unsigned book review of May 8, 1915, from the Philadelphia Evening Ledger, clumsily written as Holmesian parody to puff an Arthur B. Reeve "Craig Kennedy" detective novel of the period. The second selection, on the following pages, is again a book review—the moving and memorable review of Doyle's collection His Last Bow by the late and eminent Sherlockian Vincent Starrett. Originally published in a St. Louis–area magazine called Reedy's Mirror, on February 22, 1918, it has only been reprinted once, in an issue of the Baker Street Journal for March 1968—itself now a collector's item.

Bottom of this page: a sampling of the dozens of Sherlockian journals. Published quarterly by the Sciolist Press, Chicago, Baker Street Miscellanea at upper left has, though many years younger than The Baker Street Journal, nearly as superb a reputation as the older magazine's. Feathers from the Nest, below it, is published by the Noble and Most Singular Order of the Blue Carbuncle, Portland, Oregon. The Commonplace Book (named after Holmes's scrapbook) is edited and published by Andrew Jay Peck, New York City; it reprints, more than do other journals, articles about Holmes found in the national and international press, both newspapers and magazines. At upper right is shown the Spring 1980 issue of The Serpentine Muse, published quarterly by the Adventuresses of Sherlock Holmes, New York City. Reproduced below it is the cover of the March 1968 issue of The Baker Street Journal, which saw the first reprinting of Vincent Starrett's 1918 "In Praise of Sherlock Holmes," opposite; the Journal, subtitled "An Irregular Quarterly of Sherlockiana," is published by the Baker Street Irregulars, New York City. For more about the Irregulars, and the Adventuresses, see, respectively, pages 143–47 and 67 (caption).

SHERLOCK HOLMES SOLVES A PROBLEM IN PUBLISHING

"NO, MY dear Watson," said Sherlock Holmes, as his aquiline fingers spun the pages of "The War Terror" and his still more aquiline nose dipped into the book which I had just handed him, "no, your literary training has misled you. The threads are not all in my hands now. But before you complete your account of this, my latest exploit, I think I shall be able to show that this is not a novel."

With his accustomed abandon when on the trail of a mystery, my friend threw himself absorbedly into the reading of "The War Terror," which professional courtesy prompts me to say is published by Hearst's International Library Company, New York. No tinge of professional jealousy blighted his enthusiasm as he raced through the adventures of Craig Kennedy as Mr. Reeve has recorded them. An hour by the clock and shag by the pound were scarcely consumed before Holmes had reached his decision.

"Just as I thought," he broke out abruptly, as he sawed on his old violin, "36 chapters divided by three equals 12 short stories. Twelve stories cut up into three parts, the incisions carefully glued and sandpapered, make 36 chapters. A most simple prob-lem. Except that "The War Terror" exhausts the war after three chapters and—as I said—is no novel, your rival's narrative lives up to the implication of its publishers," concluded the great detective with blighting irony.

I wondered if my friend would drop Inspector Lestrange [*sic*] of Scotland Yard a word to institute proceedings. But, with his characteristic discretion, Holmes said nothing of the matter. It was only ten days later, and quite by accident, that I learned his decision. As I entered his study one afternoon, I heard the hurried snap of a closed book, and thought I detected a faint color on Holmes' cheek. Upon his desk lay a well-thumbed copy of "The War Terror," together with some notes of which I could read such fragments as "electro-magnetic gun . . . buy one triple mirror . . . spinthariscope, selenium cells . . . microphone . . . electrolytic murder . . . read Freud on psychoanalysis."

I have read "The War Terror." I appreciate Holmes' interest. In fact, I may go so far as to say I regret that Craig Kennedy has only a reporter to depend upon as assistant and narrator, instead of a trained man of science.

IN PRAISE OF SHERLOCK HOLMES

By Vincent Starrett

OMES to us after a long silence another and final—perhaps one should say "another final"—volume of reminiscences from the pen of John H. Watson, M. D., chronicler of the little problems of Mr. Sherlock Holmes, consulting expert in crime. There is a pang in the staring black letters, on the réd cover (red and black—violent contrast—sinister suggestion!), that seem to spell finality: *His Last Bow* (G. H. Doran, New York).

Is it his last bow? Once before, years ago, Dr. Doyle—he was not then Sir Arthur—had the temerity to dispose of his popular hero. He killed him with a completeness that was appalling. Do you remember that last tale in *The Memoirs of Sherlock Holmes*? —the struggle with the hideous Professor Moriarty on the cliff?—the boiling cauldron beneath, into which friend and foe, hunter and hunted, detective and detected, were hurled, locked each in the other's relentless arms?

Surely there was no chance here for a resurrection. Sherlock Holmes was dead; as dead as the proverbial doornail; as dead as Pontius Pilate; as dead as yesterday's newspaper.

Of course, there was a great to-do about it. Men groaned and cursed and wished the good right hand of Dr. Doyle had withered ere it had penned those final pages. Women wrote reams of copy to the harassed author, beginning their letters with the greeting, "You Brute!" "You Beast!"

But Sherlock Holmes was dead; that Dr. Doyle was convinced of it (whether or not he regretted his hasty action, later) was evidenced by his first surrender to public clamor. He wrote *The Hound of the Baskervilles*, one of the greatest of all the Holmes adventures, but it was a "reminiscence of Sherlock Holmes"; Watson, good fellow, was digging up an earlier tale from his portfolio; Holmes was still unequivocally dead.

What induced Dr. Doyle to bring his immortal sleuth back to life, I don't know. Possibly the incessant demand of the public for more stories; possibly a tardy regret of his own. In point of fact, I don't care, and this reckless emotion is shared by several million readers in all parts of the world. It was sufficient that he did bring him back—and it must be admitted that, while he was at it, he did an artistic job. What could be simpler? What more natural? "My dear fellow . . . about that chasm. I had no serious difficulty in getting out of it, for the very simple reason that I never was in it."

He had not fallen over at all! Professor Moriarty, alone, had taken the plunge! Well, well, that is all over now—but I still get the old thrill when I read again the first extraordinary narrative in *The Return of Sherlock Holmes*. Don't you?

And now Mr. Sherlock Holmes is making "his last bow." Again! Really, I can't help saying that, because I can't help hoping that it isn't really his last bow. Deep down, inside of me, I have a feeling that it is, but I shall not give up my hope, entirely, until I read—and may the day be far distant!—that Sir Arthur Conan Doyle, himself, has made his last bow.

Let me quote the preface to this new—this last—volume. It is signed by Dr. Watson, not by Dr. Doyle; a splendid notion that helps me fortify myself in the pleasant delusion that both the great detective and the excellent doctor did live—that they still do live.

The friends of Mr. Sherlock Holmes will be glad to learn that he is still alive and well, though somewhat crippled by occasional attacks of rheumatism. He has, for some years, lived in a small farm upon the downs five miles from Eastbourne, where his time is divided between philosophy and agriculture. During this period of rest he has refused the most princely offers to take up various cases, having determined that his retirement was a permanent one. The approach of the German war caused him, however, to lay his remarkable combination of intellectual and practical activity at the disposal of the government, with historical results which are recounted in *His Last Bow*. Several previous experiences which have lain long in my portfolio have been added to *His Last Bow* so as to complete the volume.

JOHN H. WATSON, M. D.

How much better that is, if this is indeed the last we are to hear of him, than to think of him as dead at the bottom of the Reichenbach Fall! And, too, there is always a chance, now—just a chance—that Sir Arthur may again relent. The way is open; he has left himself a loophole.

Let us suppose, however, that Holmes's retirement is permanent; that the little adventure of the German master spy, which closes the present volume, is his last contribution to the records of the profession he has so long adorned. Need Sir Arthur quit on that account? Not at all! We have still Dr. Watson's portfolio! How many more cases may not be stored away in that astonishing receptacle, in the form of notes! Old cases—some of those old cases hinted at in so many of the earlier tales.

In this matter, Sir Arthur had laid himself wide open and distinctly "liable." In those glad old days of the first and second series of tales, running in the old *Strand* magazine, with Sidney Paget's illustrations, never an adventure did he chronicle that he did not mention at least one other, the time for the disclosure of which was not yet ripe. We have never had those tales! Someone —I think Mr. Arthur Bartlett Maurice—figured out some years ago that there were dozens, or, at the very least, a dozen, which, he insisted, entitled us, certainly, to one more volume.

I have been at some pains in this matter, myself, and beg to insert here the result of my explorations. I have been through the Holmes reminiscences from *A Study in Scarlet* to *His Last Bow*, and a delightful time I have had. Here then are the stories yet untold, complete notes for each of which are in the possession of Dr. Watson:

The Case of Mrs. Cecil Forrester

The Bishopgate Jewel Case (Inspector Athelney Jones will never forget how Holmes lectured the force upon it!)

The Trepoff Murder Case

The Singular Tragedy of the Atkinson Brothers at Trincomalee

The Dundas Separation Case

The Adventure of the Paradol Chamber

The Adventure of the Amateur Mendicant Society (who held a luxurious club in the lower vault of a furniture warehouse)

The Loss of the British Bark *Sophy Anderson*

The Singular Adventures of the Grice Patersons in the Island of Uffa

The Camberwell Poisoning Case

The Tankerville Club Scandal

The Case of Mrs. Farintosh (which had to do with an opal tiara)
Colonel Warburton's Madness
The Little Problem of the Grosvenor Square Furniture Van
The Tarleton Murders
The Case of Vamberry, the Wine Merchant
The Adventure of the Old Russian Woman
The Singular Affair of the Aluminum Crutch
The Adventure of Ricoletti of the Club-Foot and His Abominable Wife
The Question of the Netherlands-Sumatra Company
The Colossal Schemes of Baron Maupertuis
The Manor House Case
The Adventure of the Tired Captain
The Atrocious Conduct of Colonel Upwood (in connection with the famous card scandal of the Nonpareil Club)
The Case of Mme. Montpensier
The Papers of Ex-President Murillo
The Shocking Affair of the Dutch Steamship *Friesland*
The Peculiar Persecution of John Vincent Harden
The Sudden Death of Cardinal Tosca (an investigation carried out at the personal request of His Holiness, the Pope)
The Case of Wilson, the Notorious Canary-Trainer
The Dreadful Business of the Abernetty Family
The Conk-Singleton Forgery Case
The Repulsive Story of the Red Leech
The Terrible Death of Crosby, the Banker
The Addleton Tragedy (and the singular contents of the ancient British barrow!)
The Smith-Mortimer Succession Case
The Adventure of the Boulevard Assassin
The Case of Mr. Fairdale Hobbs
The Dramatic Adventure of Dr. Moore Agar

And these are only a few, for time and again we have hints of astonishing adventures to which no name is given, as that extremely delicate matter which Holmes arranged for the reigning family of Holland. There are several references to that, and I must insist on having it, as well as the adventures of the Paradol Chamber, the Amateur Mendicant Society, Ricoletti of the club-foot (not forgetting his abominable wife), the Tired Captain, and the Notorious Canary-Trainer. These, at least, I submit, it is unfair to name, if we are not to have the delight of reading them.

And there is another side to this matter that I have not seen mentioned. As a book-lover and -collector, I am eager to possess the collected works of Mr. Sherlock Holmes. In my library, beside the de luxe *Manon Lescaut* and the historical writings of George Alfred Henty, I want to place those little brochures on crime to which Holmes refers so carelessly, yet so often.

In *The Sign of the Four*—quite the best of the list—we read that François le Villard, the French *maître*, "is translating my small works into French. . . . I have been guilty of several monographs. They are all upon technical subjects. Here, for example is one 'Upon the Distinction between the Ashes of the Various Tobaccos.' In it I enumerate one hundred and forty forms of cigar, cigarette, and pipe tobacco, with coloured plates illustrating the differences in the ash. . . . Here is my monograph upon the tracing of footsteps, with some remarks upon the uses of plaster of Paris as a preserver of impresses. Here, too, is a curious little work upon the influence of a trade upon the hand, with lithotypes of the hands of slaters, sailors, cork-cutters, compositors, weavers and diamond-polishers."

Completing the bibliography are the following, mentioned elsewhere in the eight volumes of tales:

"The Book of Life." (A magazine article bearing upon observation and deduction therefrom.)
A "contribution to the literature of tattooing."
Monograph on the subject of old documents and the fixing of their dates.
"Trifling monograph upon the subject of secret writings, in which I analyze one hundred and sixty separate cyphers."
Two short monographs on the subject of the human ear. (In the *Anthropological Journal*.)
Monographs on the music of the Middle Ages.
Monograph on the Polyphonic Motets of Lassus. ("Which has . . . been printed for private circulation, and is said by experts to be the last word upon the subject.")
Thesis on the Cornish language, showing it to be akin to the Chaldean, and largely derived from the Phoenician traders in tin.
Practical Handbook of Bee Culture, with Some Observations upon the Segregation of the Queen.

And again we have hints of other works, either completed or in process of manufacture, including a "monograph on the typewriter and its relation to crime," another on the seventy-five varieties of perfume and the necessity for distinguishing between each, and a "text book which shall focus the whole art of detection into one volume," to which Holmes intends to devote his declining years.

Possibly he is now at work on this latter volume; meanwhile, where are the others? The booksellers do not know them, and there is no record in *Book Prices Current* of a single sale!

Seriously, it is to be hoped that a handsome library edition of the eight volumes of Sherlock Holmes stories will not be long on the way. And while he is about it, will not Sir Arthur just be a little careful in his revision? Inspector Jones must not be Athelney in one tale and Peter in another, and Holmes must not profess ignorance of Carlyle on one day and quote him the next. Nor must Dr. Watson ever be James, although this error in one tale may be typographical.

I think, too, that Watson could be made somewhat less of a lackey and still be preserved as the necessary foil. My rereading has convinced me that he is never quite so much an ass as in *The Adventure of the Dancing Men* and *The Valley of Fear*. Little emendation is required; a few strokes of the Doyle pen, and the thing is done.

The advent of a Sherlock Holmes book is a distinct literary event. Heaven alone knows how many millions of people from China to Peru breathe a delighted sigh at the word and hasten off to purchase the volume. It is very probable that Sherlock Holmes is the most popular single character in contemporary fiction; certainly he is the only one who has passed into the language, as it were; whose name has become a symbol by which all of his type and tribe are known.

Captain Kettle was a popular hero, and so was Mulvaney, but we do not think of calling a man "a Captain Kettle" or "a Mulvaney." But an amateur detective, an unofficial detective, even an official detective—so tenacious is the phrase—is "a Sherlock Holmes." Perhaps I must make an exception in the case of the excellent Raffles; he is indeed in a fair way to becoming a part of our sweet English tongue. But Raffles is young yet, and certainly he has not the popularity of Holmes; the hunter of the criminals is still more idolized than the criminal, however picturesque and fascinating the latter may be. There is something of the burglar in all of us, and something of the sleuth, and I believe, all things being equal, we lean toward the law rather than away from it.

Also, we have really had only one genuinely artistic burglar—this same Raffles individual—while we have had so many hundreds of fictional detectives that a statistician is needed to record them all. We have had Martin Hewitt, a clever fellow, and Luther Trant, an exceedingly clever fellow, and Hamilton Cleek, a burglar turned detective, and Chester Kent and Fleming Stone and Addington Peace—all interesting chaps for an evening's recreation, but all distinctly reminiscent (to put it mildly!) of their greater brethren. But there has been only one Sherlock Holmes; there can be no other.

He is the transcendental detective *par excellence;* an authentic figure in the world's literature; a genuine and artistic creation.

It is doubtless true that many of the later stories—the present volume is the eighth of the Holmes group—are somewhat apocryphal; that they do not quite come up to those earlier tales, such as *The Adventure of the Speckled Band,* which thrilled readers more than a score of years ago. But lovers of Sherlock Holmes are not too particular, and it must be admitted that in many cases Sir Arthur has more than paralleled his earlier yarns. In *His Last Bow,* two or three of the eight adventures—notably *The Adventure of the Bruce-Partington Plans*—are fully the equal of any he has ever done.

Years ago, when the second series of adventures was running in the *Strand,* there was one entitled *The Adventure of the Cardboard Box.* When the tales were gathered into that second surprising collection, *The Memoirs of Sherlock Holmes,* the story was omitted and has not been reprinted since. The reason is said to have been Dr. Doyle's regret that he had, for the first and last time, written a story involving a woman's good name with a bad odor, and his determination to suppress the narrative so far as possible. I know nothing about this, but so I have heard or read. At any rate, that story is included in *His Last Bow,* and now, so far as is known, all the Sherlock Holmes stories that Sir Arthur has written have been published between covers.

Let us hope there will be more, some day; but, if not, let us be grateful that we have had as many as we have, and that Sherlock Holmes is "still alive and well, though somewhat crippled by occasional attacks of rheumatism."

And, too, we have still with us Mr. William Gillette, who does not only play Sherlock Holmes, but is Sherlock Holmes. Physically, intellectually, spiritually, he is the immortal detective himself, and the drama, *Sherlock Holmes,* is in effect a new and diverting adventure, for all that it is made up of half a dozen of the old ones, and for all that its final curtain catches Holmes in the incredible act of laying a woman's head upon his shirt-front.

Mr. Gillette, too, has paid the penalty of popularity, and he, too, has vowed that Sherlock Holmes has permanently retired. But in this connection, also, there is a grain of comfort for the myriad admirers of the celebrated sleuth. Mr. Gillette has been "movie-ized" in the part, and now we are assured that, with the fascinating volumes of Dr. Doyle, posterity will have also the remarkable portrayal of the living detective by America's best-loved actor.

Expert Assistance

By James J. Montague

IN CONAN DOYLE'S creative youth
  He gave the world an able sleuth
Who brought to light the hidden truth
  Concerning craft and crime.
No mystery was too profound
For this lean-visaged human hound,
By mental synthesis, to sound
  In half a fortnight's time.

WHEN gems were lost, or men were slain.
  Sometimes for spite, sometimes for gain,
In good King Edward Seventh's reign,
  And dread spread far and near,
The baffled coppers scratched their domes,
And called in Mr. Sherlock Holmes,
Who read a few old tattered tomes
  And made the whole thing clear.

BUT now, when spooks and spirits foil
  The wit of even Dr. Doyle;
When, as he burns his midnight oil,
  He sees them near and far;
When through his country home they stray,
Half-formless shapes of foggy gray,
He owns he really cannot say
  Just who and what they are.

I WISH the doc would resurrect
  That keen deducing intellect,
And have those spirits tagged and checked,
  And either jailed or short.
For I am sure that in three shakes,
And with no guesswork or mistakes,
He would turn them up as fakes,
  If Dr. Doyle cannot!

The readers always craved more Holmes stories. Nine years after the Starrett article, Doyle brought out The Case Book of Sherlock Holmes, *the fifth and final collection. On January 29, 1929 (not two years later), a poem, "Expert Assistance," printed in the Seattle* Post-Intelligencer *bemoaned the fact that Doyle by his spiritualist activities was neglecting Holmes.*

SHERLOCK HOLMES IN PICTURES

By Frederic Dorr Steele

SHERLOCK HOLMES is fifty years old. William Gillette is dead. Neither fact is quite credible.

This is written by the illustrator who, since "The Return of Sherlock Holmes" in 1903, has made pictures for nearly all the tales. Oddly enough, I do not care for detective stories, and never have had any desire to curl up with a good one. But thanks to my long association with the Emperor of Detectives, I have found myself looked upon as an expert in crime. My plight is a little like that of Mr. Reginald Birch, who drew pictures for "Little Lord Fauntleroy" in 1885 and has carried that golden-curled, velvet-suited incubus on the back of his neck ever since.

Let us consider the pictures of Sherlock, beginning with those drawn long before my time. You know my methods, Watson. We must have facts; it is a capital mistake to theorize before one has data.

Sidney Paget was not the earliest illustrator of Sherlock Holmes (the first was D. H. Friston, who illustrated "A Study in Scarlet" in 1887), but it was Paget who imposed his conception on the English mind. Beginning with the "Adventures" in 1891 in the *Strand Magazine,* he continued through a second series of them; then followed with "The Hound of the Baskervilles" and "The Return." He died, prematurely, a few years later. Sir Arthur writes of "poor Sidney Paget," and of the younger brother who posed for him and made Sherlock handsomer than the author intended. Paget's pictures improved as he went along; if the earlier ones seem imperfect to our eyes, it is partly because of the crude woodcut reproduction. Scenes of gloom and terror were likely to appear faintly comic. Few American readers saw these English illustrations, and for some the first Sherlock was the plump and dapper blade portrayed by W. H. Hyde when a few of the tales were printed in *Harper's Weekly* during 1893. This series ended with the death of Holmes in "The Final Problem."

For most Americans, the image of our hero was created by the actor William Gillette, who wrote the absurd and delightful melodrama entitled "Sherlock Holmes," which reached the New York stage in November, 1899, ran two seasons in America and a season in London. Mr. Gillette was blessed by nature with the lean, sinewy figure and keen visage required, and his quiet but incisive histrionic method exactly fitted such a part as Sherlock. I can think of no more perfect realization of a fictional character on the stage.

In 1903, just ten years after Doyle had killed Sherlock, he brought him back to life. His series entitled "The Return of Sherlock Holmes" began publication at the end of that year, in the *Strand Magazine* with illustrations by Paget, and simultaneously in *Collier's Weekly* with pictures by myself. For the first story, "The Empty House," I made six illustrations, and by a curious coincidence, Paget, who also made six, chose four of the same subjects. That date, 1903, corrects, of course, the faulty chronology of those who have vaguely supposed that my drawings preceded the play.

I did not need to be told to make my Sherlock look like Gillette. The thing was inevitable. I kept him in mind and even copied or adapted parts of a few of the stage photographs. At that time I never had seen the play, and it was not until 1929 that Mr. Gillette actually became my model in the flesh. Lured from retirement for a farewell tour by the artful George C. Tyler, cornered in the Biltmore by the hounds of publicity, he seated himself—with the air of one taking the electric chair—and for the duration of three cigarettes talked to Mr. H. I. Brock of the *Times* and exhibited his famous profile for my first drawing of it from life.

My original model for Sherlock Holmes was an Englishman named Robert King, who posed as him throughout the thirteen tales of "The Return." The drawings for the first story were made in Deerfield, Massachusetts, and Mr. King journeyed there to help me. He was a sensitive, fine fellow; his nose was not hawklike, but he had cavernous eyes—and he owned a frock coat. When later stories came along, about 1908, King, to my regret, had swum out of my ken, and I fell back on that standby of the studios, Frank B. Wilson. Irish by ancestry (his real name was Wall), he had gone on the stage as a youth and had been for some years actor and stage manager in the company of Sir Henry Irving. After a breakdown of health, he

For Sherlockians, easily the best-known New Yorker article of all time is artist Frederic Dorr Steele's "Sherlock Holmes in Pictures," which ran in the magazine's May 22, 1937, issue—one of the very few New Yorker articles ever to carry text illustrations of any kind. Unprinted since, save in Vincent Starrett's 221B: Studies in Sherlock Holmes of 1940 (New York: Macmillan), in which the New Yorker illustrations were omitted, it is reproduced on this and the following pages. Of the three story illustrations included here, the first two are by British, not American, artists; they appear here in an order more logical than were their positions in the original New Yorker article, but with the material of their original captions. A fourth illustration used by The New Yorker—"My Collection of M's Is a Fine One"—is identical to our Steele drawing on page 19; in it, The New Yorker advised, Watson was being shown the dossier on Colonel Sebastian Moran, "the second most dangerous man in London."

set his face resolutely toward a new job. He became a model, kept an amazing store of costumes and other equipment stowed away in odd places, and for thirty years or more was the most resourceful, faithful, and competent man in that stop-gap profession. About 1926, while the later stories were appearing in *Liberty*, two of Wilson's tall sons followed in their father's footsteps; but most of the Sherlocks in this series were drawn from the fine frame and crag-like head of a model called S. B. Doughty.

Mr. Vincent Starrett in "The Private Life of Sherlock Holmes" lists twelve Englishmen and six Americans who have illustrated the text, and even that list is incomplete. Mr. Edmund Pearson, the eminent criminalographer, wrote an admirable paper, "Sherlock Holmes Among the Illustrators," for the *Bookman* for August, 1932. Speaking of Arthur I. Keller, one of the Americans, who had taken a fling at Sherlock in "The Valley of Fear," he says it was he who "dealt the cruelest blow at Watson. From merely the innocent Johnny of Mr. Steele's drawings, Watson emerges in Mr. Keller's pictures as *boobus Britannicus*." ... Mr. Keller himself spoke some memorable words to me on the subject of models: "Oh yes, I probably used Wilson, but it didn't matter who it was. I only use models for construction anyway." The individuality in his figures was supplied from his own head; he never could have been accused of "type casting."

Readers of the early tales have remarked a rapid change in Sherlock. The thinking machine who rigidly excluded from his mental storehouse any knowledge not useful for his immediate purpose soon became a walking encyclopedia. But physically Sherlock needed no change or development; Dr. Doyle from the outset knew what his hero looked like. It is odd that the "great hawk's bill of a nose" so explicitly described was ignored by the English draughtsmen for many years. Not until the "Return" series was well under way did one see in Paget's noses a suggestion of aquilinity. Was it the Gillette influence? Such considerations bring up old questions: Do illustrators ever read the text? And the corollary: Should all illustrators die at dawn, and all books come out with their text undefiled? Shall we make exceptions in the rare instances in which author and artist are one, as in Thackeray, du Maurier, Pyle? What would Doyle's own pictures have been like? Did he like Paget best?

Here I can tell what Sir Arthur said to me on the one occasion when I met him. It was at a luncheon given for him in New York by Mark Sullivan, of *Collier's*, some time during the second term of Theodore Roosevelt. The President could not come, but his daughter Ethel and one or two Cabinet members and their wives were there. A weighty occasion. I was somewhat palpitant when my turn came to talk with the great man. Would he be kind to me? Would he commend my earnest efforts? I must be self-effacing, I thought; I will ask him about Paget first. "Young man," he began briskly, "do you know who did the best illustrations ever made for

FIRST PICTURE OF HOLMES

Sherlock tells Lestrade and Gregson what "Rache" really means. The vacant face on the left belongs to Dr. Watson. From D. H. Friston's frontispiece to "A Study in Scarlet," 1887.

me? Cyrus Cuneo!" He began to tell me why; something interrupted; the interview ended. I had not needed to be self-effacing. Sir Arthur effaced me. I can make no explanation of his preference. Mr. Cuneo was notorious for committing the illustrator's deadliest sin, giving the plot away. If he had done the drawings for Watson's tales, I felt sure no cunningly hidden solution, no trick ending was safe. Later I found out that he had illustrated many of Doyle's other novels but never a Sherlock.

Evidences have come to me in the mail of a vast invisible army of Sherlock Holmes idolaters—bits of curious information, inquiries for the "old originals," now and then a request for "data to help me on a monograph I desire to write on Sherlock Holmes." Perhaps the most extraordinary of these communications came to me from Dr. Gray Chandler Briggs of St. Louis, a devoted collector of Sherlockiana, who wrote me that he had spent a summer vacation in London, mapped Baker Street with care, located the lodgings at the present No. 111 Baker Street, and submitted his findings to the author. He sent me the map, descriptions, and photographs, and they were published later in the Gillette souvenir program. His theory about the location of the house thus attracted much attention. It has been approved by Vincent Starrett, disapproved by H. W. Bell (author of an amazing Holmes-Watson chronology), and, we must add, blandly dismissed by Doyle himself. Whether we can accept the Briggs theory or not, it is a most ingenious addition to the lore of the subject. On a visit to London in May, 1931, I spent a pleasant evening following the ardent Doctor's footsteps, and can report that, save for a new arc light near the "kerb," the premises remained as he described them.

The matter of the original drawings also involves Dr. Briggs. He had seen one at the Louisiana Purchase Exposition in his own city in 1904, and were there any left, and could he get them? Artists are disorderly beings, but something must necessarily be done with studio accumulations. In my own case these were kept in a packing box, the object of frequent profane revilings. My fellow-craftsmen will agree, I am sure, that the joy of creation is exceeded only by the joy of destruction. Hence during the agony of moving, or cleaning, the box was dragged out and the less fit were slaughtered. So some years ago the number had been reduced to perhaps a score, and Dr. Briggs has them all.

The late Ralph Barton cheered one Christmas for me with what is now a valued souvenir. He had redrawn one of my cover designs of long ago, a profile of Sherlock in a dressing gown, with a bloody handprint on the wall. The hawklike beak was undisturbed but the chin had disappeared beneath a Santa Claus beard, complete with string.

"But how did you remember that design so clearly?" I wrote in my letter of thanks.

"Because," he replied, "it was pasted on the ceiling over my bed."

After three years I am still pleasantly embarrassed by the outrageous overpraise accorded my drawings by Mr. Starrett in

"PIPES ARE OCCASIONALLY OF EXTRAORDINARY INTEREST."

"The Private Life of Sherlock Holmes." "No happier association of author and artist can be imagined; one thinks of Tenniel and his Alice." You may take even giddier flights in the chapter called "The Evolution of a Profile." "Sixty tales, in all, comprise the saga of Sherlock Holmes; and Steele has illustrated twenty-nine. While he yet lives and loves, and lifts his pencil, will he not do the other thirty-one?" Meantime my own favorite edition remains the one-volume "Complete Sherlock Holmes," with no cuts—in either sense of the word.

In writing of stage Sherlocks, Mr. Pearson makes a shrewd guess: "The Steele pictures had in their turn an influence on the stage or upon the screen for it seems probable that the enormous number of properties assembled for the Baker Street scene in John Barrymore's film play (1922) originated in Mr. Steele's fascinating pictures of Holmes's rooms." I can testify to the accuracy of that chance shot. I happened to meet Jack Barrymore, just off the train from Hollywood. "There's a film I want you to see," he said. "Just finished it. 'Sherlock Holmes.' I dug up an old German named Von Seyffertitz for Moriarty. Had a lot of fun. Think you'll be interested."

"Indeed I will," I said, hoping the old drawings were remembered. "I used to make pictures of Sherlock."

His eyebrows twisted with the Barry-more grin. "Why, hell, we had all your old pictures out on the lot. You're more to blame than Gillette."

On a murky winter evening two years ago, the Baker Street Irregulars, a little group of Sherlock devotees, met in a coffee-house in the Forties for votive rites in honor of their patron saint. After some tramping in the slush I found the un-marked door and was ushered into a warm, smoky room. Long train of tables, Italian wines, savory odors. Just such a room as one might look for in Soho, perhaps. What were these strange words floating in the smoke? Gasogenes, Trichinopoly cigars, orange pips? Christopher Morley greeted me kindly. He, it seemed, was a gasogene. No, he was *the* Gasogene. The other officers were the Tantalus and the Com-missar, and let no true Sherlockian ask why. "That is your drink, right there by the Blue Carbuncle."

"Fine. It was all perfectly obvious from the first, my dear Watson."

I had been a little cold. If I could catch up in my drinking, would I understand a little better what they were talking about? If someone asked me for the papers, would I know enough to say they were on the sundial? If one muffed the answer to such a challenge, the next round was on him, I was told. Surely this was a dangerous place. Another drink? Well, they all looked friendly enough. Increasingly so. But how did they all know so much? Could I re-member Enoch J. Drebber's address? Another drink, perhaps? Well, why argue? One must not be quarrelsome. On my left sat the Gasogene, on my right Gene Tunney. No, I would not be quarrelsome. Time for the first toast. "There are only three standard toasts, gentlemen, three obligatory toasts. We will rise for the first one, gentlemen. I give you THE Woman!" *The* Woman? Could it be Irene Adler? I was beginning to get the hang of it. Elementary. Alexander Woollcott, who had insisted on coming in a hansom, still wore a hideous red fore-and-aft cap. The second toast was Mrs. Hudson. The third, Dr. Watson's Second Wife. Time for a pipe. Pipes are occasionally of ex-traordinary interest, Watson. But where is Gillette? Afraid he's not coming; it's half past eight. Patience, my dear Watson. If I am not mistaken, I hear his step even now upon the stair.

A commotion at the entrance. Yes, it was he. We saw the tall, fragile figure, the pale, smiling face above the concave dress shirt. "Splendid, Mr. Gillette. We'd given you up. It was good of you to leave your other party to join us."

"Other party? Certainly not. I've been four hours on the way from Hadlyme, Connecticut, and I'm damned hungry."

After he had been fed, he told us that it was Charles Frohman who had suggested his play, that it had been concocted in a few weeks, and—even more incredible—

that before that time he never had read a Sherlock Holmes story. The unquenchable Woollcott reported this incident later in *The New Yorker*. A certain artist, he wrote, wept softly into his soufflé at the sight of his most famous model. Mr. Woollcott must stand corrected. I am sure it was not a soufflé we wept in, but a *compote Lestrade*.

CONAN DOYLE never quite forgave the reading public for preferring "these lighter sketches," nor could he quite forgive his own Sherlock Holmes, who "may perhaps have stood a little in the way of my more serious literary work." But what man can control the lightning of his own fame? Today his brain child, so often disparaged by its father, unquestionably is known to more people living on this oblate spheroid than any other character in secular fiction. Why do these uncounted millions love the tales and, forsaking all others, return to them with deep satisfaction and a sense of personal attachment? In mere ingenuity of structure they are no better than those of the present-day artificers. Not all the tales observe the strict rules of the game—the game between writer and reader. In some, accident rather than deduction plays a part in the solution. Sometimes there is no solution at all. But what do these lapses weigh against the gift of the priceless Watson, against the wealth of color, atmosphere, and racy, humorous character? To read the tales is to take the perfect anodyne, to be carried back gently across fifty years to a dim, gas-lit London, with the four-wheeler coming up out of the yellow fog, bearing our client—and a little problem which may present some points of interest.

My First Meeting with Sherlock Holmes

The letter which accounts for this "First Meeting" was addressed to Allen Robertson of the Six Napoleons of Baltimore in response to an inquiry Mr. Robertson had made as to the handprint on the wall in the likeness Mr. Steele had done of the master for the Collier's cover of October 31, 1903. The historical data provided are important, and the JOURNAL *welcomes the opportunity to reproduce this letter from a man who meant so much to Sherlock Holmes.*

226 W. 13th St., N. Y.
March 3, 1940.

Dear Mr. Robertson:

I'll try to answer your question, tho' I fear the "solution" is a commonplace one, not to say elementary. I am hampered by the fact that the only Sherlock book I own is the one-volume Complete Edition. So I don't know what you mean by the "sketch of six clues" in your copy of the *Return*. I can guess, however, that the publisher may have cooked up a display ad and used the handprint as one of the "clues." My handprint was drawn in the background of the *Collier's* cover, *Oct. 31, '03*, accompanying *The Adventure of the Norwood Builder* which was *No. 2* of the *Return* series. The print had nothing to do with McFarlane's thumb, or with that story, or any other, as I remember it: I put it in merely as a suggestion of what might be seen on the walls of the Baker Street rooms.

As a Sherlockian, you may be interested in the fact that this drawing was sent down to *Collier's* as a rough sketch, from Deerfield, Mass., after I had made it before breakfast, to catch the morning mail. After a few days they wrote me that they were reproducing the sketch as it was, since they thought I couldn't do better if I worked a month on it. This was the first instance in which I used a Gillette photo. (The *first* cover—the one for *The Adventure of the Empty House*—was the "Exit, Moriarty," reproduced in the program.)

Also in the program, by the way, was a transcription of that Christmas card by Barton, in which he reversed the design and put the cap and beard on. A drawing similar to the *No. 2* cover was also made for the play ads and program.

I don't know why the McClure Phillips Co. got that newspaper cartoonist McCauley to make new illustrations for the book. Possibly they may have disagreed with *Collier's* about payment for the use of my drawings—I never heard about that.

Does this answer your questions? In any event, there can be no question of "effrontery" between Sherlock Holmes enthusiasts. I like to include myself among these, altho I have frankly confessed that I am most un-erudite, and most forgetful even about stories I myself illustrated. The fourth dinner of the Baker Street Irregulars took place on the evening of January 30th (at the old Murray Hill Hotel, the perfect spot). It was the best one since the December '36 dinner which I described in the *New Yorker* (and in *221B*). Chris Morley was once more the Gasogene, and I made for him a little sketch for the menu card: Sherlock examining the food and analyzing the wines, and taking no chances. Under this was the caption "We cannot be too careful, Watson." The seriousness of these devotees is shown by the fact that five different men came up to my chair and asked me practically the same question —"Pardon me, Mr. Steele, I can't seem to identify this quotation: will you tell me what story it was taken from?"

I first met Sherlock Holmes in Brooklyn in 1891 or 1892, at the home of a boyhood friend, Alfred E. Heinrichs (a lawyer, now retired). He asked if I ever read detective stories, and I said no. But he said there was a new collection of them called *The Adventures of Sherlock Holmes,* and he'd like to try them on me. He read aloud *The Red-Headed League* and two others—that was enough to attach me to Sherlock and the good Doctor for life.

Very sincerely yours,
FREDERIC DORR STEELE.

Another rarity from the pen of Steele is this memorable letter to Allen Robertson (of the Six Napoleons Irregular group in Baltimore), written in 1940 and printed in the last issue of the old-style Baker Street Journal *(Vol. IV, No. 1 [1949]).*

ACT I. SHERLOCK HOLMES'S FIRST MEETING WITH MISS ALICE FAULKNER.
From a Photo. by Byron, New York.

MR. WILLIAM GILLETTE.
From a Photo. by Sarony, New York.

**ACT II. SHERLOCK HOLMES IN HIS ROOMS
AT BAKER STREET.**
From a Photo. by Sarony, New York.

**ACT III. THE TURNING-POINT IN THE
PLAY—HERE SHERLOCK HOLMES ACCUSES
LARRABEE OF ROBBERY.**
From a Photo. by Byron, New York.

Mr. William Gillette
as
Sherlock Holmes

By Harold J. Shepstone

IT was in the manager's room at the Lyceum Theatre that I first had the pleasure of meeting the famous stage detective, Mr. William Gillette. I have seen him since, both on and off the stage, and have had many pleasant little chats with him. His tall, alert figure, clear-cut features, deep-set eyes, and cool bearing make him an interesting and at the same time a decidedly mysterious personality; interesting because of his individuality and mysterious because of his wonderful versatility. As a stage detective he is a marvel of vividness, of directness, of economy of effort, of dramatic force, of perfect self-poise, of instant command of resources, of unescapable convictions.

But it is of Gillette the man that I wish to speak first. His individuality is remarkable. His very presence impresses you; his manner, his actions, and movements bespeak a personality that is no mere surface cloak that can be removed and explained at leisure. It is an individuality that is bred in the bone; it is a part of the fibre of character and completely beyond analysis. You can tell what a person is, but you cannot say why he is. Forcible and striking as Mr. Gillette's individuality undoubtedly is, he possesses a wonderful versatility in character delineation— a strange and inexplicable histrionic quality that enables him constantly to maintain an insistent, strikingly unique and seemingly fixed personality, and at the same time project an impersonation that is unmistakably individualized. Were it otherwise, Gillette the actor would not have impersonated Dr. Conan Doyle's wonderful creation with such marvellous success.

His tall, slender figure and natural composure enable him to incarnate with astonishing faithfulness the Sherlock Holmes of fiction. Indeed, this personal likeness to the great literary hero has led to some curious incidents. When Mr. Gillette arrived on the *Celtic* in Liverpool, in August last, Mr. Pendleton, of the London and North-Western Railway, had a letter to deliver to him. He went on board and asked one of the passengers if he knew Mr. Gillette. The man replied:—

"Do you know Sherlock Holmes?"

The visitor was rather taken aback, and said: "I have read the stories in THE STRAND MAGAZINE."

"That's all you need know," said the passenger. "Just look around till you see a man who fits your idea of what Sherlock Holmes ought to be, and that's he."

Mr. Pendleton went away, with a laugh. As he was going up the companion-way he collided with a gentleman, and as he looked up to apologize the passenger's advice occurred to him, and he said, "Are you Mr. Gillette?"

"I was, before you ran into me," was the reply.

"Here's a letter for you."

Although Mr. Gillette has been before the public as a popular and successful actor for many years, few know anything of his private life. Even his most intimate friends would never dream of asking him. Extremely modest and unassuming, Mr. Gillette abhors talking of himself.

Those who knew him as a boy describe him as "a precocious youth fond of spouting Webster's speeches." He gave early evidence of theatrical inclinations, and at the age of ten astonished his family by constructing a miniature theatre, fitted with grooves, scenery, foot and border lights, the puppets of which were worked from above with black thread. The next step came a year later, when the juvenile stage-manager organized in the garret a complete high-class stock company. From the attic it descended to the drawing-room, which became an extemporized temple of the drama, to the dubious edification of the Gillette household.

One of Master Gillette's playfellows was Professor Burton, who has very kindly recollections of the pleasant evenings he passed as a boy with his young friend. "When I played as a boy with Gillette," he said, "in Hartford, he was just enough the elder to make patronage and bullying the order, but he never exercised those juvenile rights, and it was typical of him, lad and man. In school his tastes were for science, oratory, and history. When he came on the platform, at the Hartford High School, to deliver a graduation oration, the applause plainly bespoke his popularity amongst his schoolfellows." Throughout his teens he still kept up his determination to know all that he could about stagecraft. When he first walked across the boards he investigated everything connected with the stage and its mechanical operations.

To follow Mr. Gillette's career is unnecessary here, interesting as it undoubtedly is. In 1875, when only eighteen years of age, we find him playing minor rôles; while only six years later, to be exact, in 1881, he was playing in his own dramas. It was at New Orleans that he first made his appearance on the stage. It was during one of his long vacations, for he is a graduate of Yale College. Anxious to obtain actual stage experience he joined a stock company in the famous cotton city, giving his services free and furnishing his own wardrobe. One night he made a decided hit in the part which he played, and next morning sought the manager and hinted that a small salary would be appreciated. The manager evidently thought otherwise, for he there and then dismissed him. Such an action was sufficient to discourage any ambitious youth, but young Gillette was by no means despondent. Indeed, he spent the remainder of his vacation in studying characters for the stage in a decidedly curious way. Desiring to make some special studies among those who imagined themselves ill, he hung out a doctor's

Above and on following pages is reprinted one of the earliest, and certainly one of the most important, of the many studies of William Gillette and his famous play. By Harold J. Shepstone, it was written for **The Strand's** *December 1901 issue. Included on pages 136 and 139 are all the original photographs; only the detailed description of the Holmes play's plot and a bit of biographical detail have been omitted.*

sign in a small Ohio town. In a short time he had many patients. Everything went on satisfactorily for some weeks, when the authorities, doubting his being old enough to have a diploma, asked to see that necessary document, whereupon he had to confess. He convinced the officials, however, that he had wrought some wondrous cures with very simple means, and was allowed to depart.

It was in 1875 that Mr. Gillette made his first appearance on the stage as Guzman, in "Faint Heart Never Won Fair Lady," at the Globe Theatre, Boston. His theatrical godfather was Mark Twain, who was a great friend of his father. Through the humorist's influence he obtained a position in the Boston Stock Company, which, at that time, was one of the most famous companies in America. Mark Twain has declared that he did not think Mr. Gillette was serious, and that when he got him his position he really thought he was having a huge joke with the management. "I do not know," said Mark Twain, "which I like best—having Gillette make a tremendous success, or seeing one of my jokes go wrong. It is the only joke I ever perpetrated that so completely miscarried."

How "Sherlock Holmes" came to be written for the stage is an interesting story. Curiously enough, it was not at the suggestion of Dr. Conan Doyle, Mr. William Gillette, or Mr. Charles Frohman, who is Mr. Gillette's manager, but through the inventive genius of an American reporter. This enterprising individual wrote a paragraph to the effect that Conan Doyle had stated that should anyone ever dramatize Sherlock Holmes it would be William Gillette. The doctor had said nothing of the kind, and at that time had not even met Mr. Gillette or had any correspondence with him. Mr. Charles Frohman came across the paragraph, which was printed in an obscure newspaper, published in the Western States of America, while he was in London. He cut it out and showed it to Mr. Gillette.

To tell the honest truth, Mr. Gillette smiled as he read it. Up to that moment he had voted the stories as almost too impossible for dramatization, and he laughed at the idea of his ever appearing on the stage as the great detective of fiction. He went so far as to suggest to Mr. Frohman, however, that it might probably be a good thing to secure the title of "Sherlock Holmes" for dramatic use, and on this suggestion Mr. Frohman negotiated with the doctor on a royalty basis for the use of the name, regardless of what it might be put to in the future. There the matter ended until two years ago, when Mr. Frohman wrote to Mr. Gillette, who was then on his farewell tour in "Secret Service" in California, asking him to prepare a stage version of the hero detective.

The first thing Mr. Gillette did was to write to Dr. Conan Doyle asking to what extent he might take liberties, if he so desired, with the literary character. The actor speaks in the highest praise of the courteous communications he received from the doctor, who said that he might marry the detective, or murder him, or do anything he pleased with him, preferring to leave a stage detective entirely in the hands of a master actor. Before commencing his task Mr. Gillette made himself thoroughly acquainted with the stories. In four weeks the play was finished, and as Mr. Frohman had given him six weeks' leave of absence from the cast of "Secret Service" for the task, he went to San Francisco to spend the remaining two at his ease.

Here an accident occurred which would spell discouragement to any man not possessed of Mr. Gillette's forceful and resourceful nature. The manuscript was in the possession of his secretary, who was staying at the Baldwin Hotel. As many may remember, this hotel, which adjoins the theatre, was burned and many lives were lost. There was no time to save anything, and the secretary barely escaped with his life, leaving the manuscript in the burning building. The moment he realized what had happened he rushed to the Palace Hotel, where Mr. Gillette was stopping. It was nearly three o'clock in the morning when he gained admission to the playwright's apartments and excitedly told him that the result of their hard work was in ashes. The great stage detective looked up from his pillows in his quiet way and characteristically asked: "Is *this* hotel on fire?" "No, indeed!" said the secretary. "Well, come and tell me all about it in the morning," responded the actor.

Mr. Gillette has not written "Sherlock Holmes" by merely stringing together a number of incidents from the adventurous career of the detective. It is an original play, in the title-rôle of which Mr. Gillette has adopted the methods of Conan Doyle's world-famous creation. It is nothing less than an interesting episode in the career of the great detective, wonderfully conceived and cleverly acted. In the space of three and a half hours' acting, with some 10,000 words, Mr. Gillette and his company present an adventure of the indomitable Sherlock Holmes that would require at least 80,000 words in cold type to relate. . . .

All through the play there are innumerable instances of the marvellous reasoning powers of the great detective. Even now, after the play has had a run of two years, Mr. Gillette receives an extraordinary number of letters asking him how Holmes knew this and that, and why he does certain things. But it is not difficult to see that there is not a part in the whole piece that is not absolutely reasonable, if you once admit that a man like Holmes, with an extraordinary faculty for observing details and reasoning quickly from them, exists, and they certainly do, as we have such men in real life, to a greater or lesser extent. Once admitting that, there is not an unreasonable or improbable speech or situation in the play. There is no time to explain, in every instance, exactly how Holmes arrives at his conclusions, but the explanation is there, and is as simple and easy as those that are shown.

When Mr. Gillette took the play to St. Louis, where the critical fraternity seems to be impressed with the idea that it is paid to kill off anything that is brought to that charming town, the following of Holmes's cigar in the dark was anathematized as unworthy of presentation on the American stage because of its absurdity. They finally sent the chief detective of St. Louis, undoubtedly one of the cleverest detectives in the United States, to see the piece and to tear it to pieces—particularly with reference to this cigar episode.

Next morning the officer wrote a lengthy description of the play, which appeared in the St. Louis *Star,* in which he said that the great cigar-scene, at the end of the third act, where Holmes, after he has extinguished the light, put his cigar in a crevice by the window to fool his would-be captors while he makes his escape, so far from being impossible, as the critics there declared, had a parallel in his own experience. In speaking of the incident he says: "Holmes does a very neat trick in the Stepney gas-chamber scene, where, after smashing the lamp, he sticks his lighted cigar on the window-ledge. The thieves who have him trapped make a rush for the cigar, thinking thus to locate him. When a light is struck Holmes is going out of the door. To show how near fiction is to reality I will relate an actual experience in which a lighted cigar played a prominent part. During the big street-car strike some fifteen years ago, when I was a detective, we received a tip that the leader of the dynamiters, who were doing so much destruction, was in East St. Louis. I got a stool-pigeon, or snitch as they are called. He knew the fellow we suspected, and agreed

ACT III. THE MOST THRILLING INCIDENT IN THE DRAMA—SHERLOCK HOLMES ESCAPES
FROM THE STEPNEY GAS-CHAMBER BY SMASHING THE LAMP AND EVADING
HIS WOULD-BE CAPTORS IN THE DARKNESS.

From a Photo. by Byron, New York.

From a]   MR. WILLIAM GILLETTE'S YACHT, "AUNT POLLY."   *[Photo.*

From a]   THE CABIN ON THE "AUNT POLLY."   *[Photo.*

MR. WILLIAM GILLETTE'S RESIDENCE
AT HARTFORD, CONN., U.S.A.

From a Photo.

to help us. This fellow, myself, and another detective went over to East St. Louis one miserable night, when the rain was coming down in torrents. The snitch told us that the leader and some of the gang were going to a house where the dynamite was stored. He was to go with the dynamiters, we to follow until we located the place. East St. Louis was not then what it is now. There were few pavements and no lights to speak of. So I made a plan by which we could keep our quarry in sight. I provided the snitch with half-a-dozen cigars and told him to keep one constantly lighted. Well, the snitch met the gang and they started out. We couldn't see a figure ten feet in front of us, so we followed the lighted cigar. All we could see, about two blocks ahead, was the little red point, the smoker holding the cigar turned backwards in his hand frequently so we would be sure not to miss it. When about to turn a corner he struck a match, as if to get a better light. In this way we followed our game for several miles through the slush and rain and darkness.

"When they reached the house our confederate lighted two matches. We knew what it meant. In a few minutes he came to the doorway and struck three matches in succession, which was the signal that all was ready for the arrest. We rushed in with levelled revolvers and made the gang throw up their arms. We landed them in the East St. Louis police-station, and searching the house found the dynamite stored away. So you see this little incident in the play had almost a parallel in actual experience."

What surprised the American critics most was the almost perfect personification of the literary hero. That is evidenced by comparing our photographs of the great actor with the well-known drawings of the literary detective by Mr. Sidney Paget. There is the tall, slender figure, the sallow, unhealthy face, and the eternal pipe or cigar. Mr. Gillette loves his smoke on the stage. Indeed, he seldom takes a part in a play where he cannot smoke. He is one of the very few actors who can portray different expressions and emotions in smoke. In "Sherlock Holmes" he is seen smoking a pipe, cigar, and cigarette, but they all serve some purpose.

Not a single item in the production of the famous play has escaped Mr. Gillette's personal attention, from the arrangement of the scenery to the smallest piece of furniture. The novel light effects, by which changes of scene and act are not effected by the familiar rising and descent of the curtain, but by a sort of photographic process, as if the shutter of a camera were opened and closed by the pressure of a button, deserve a passing reference. Suddenly the whole theatre is plunged in darkness, and suddenly the stage is illuminated, and, presto, the scene has entirely changed. The company have their own electric switchboard and carry their own foot and border lights; the former instrument weighs one ton. By it the electrician controls 300 incandescent lights. In the change of scenes some very rapid work is accomplished. In the second act, for instance, the change from the underground office to the apartment in Baker Street occupies some fifty seconds; yet every piece of furniture has to be removed, including the ceiling. I have witnessed some very quick changes on the stage, but never such a smart piece of work as this. With only a pilot light to guide them thirty-five men remove one scene and introduce another boasting of a number of pieces of furniture in the short space of forty-eight seconds. On inquiry I was told that at a theatre in New York the same scene was shifted in thirty-five seconds.

Off the stage Mr. Gillette leads a very simple life. His dislike for society, with its affectations, makes him all the more inter-

esting when one recalls the same point in the character of the detective of fiction. If Mr. Gillette has any recreation at all it is yachting. His yacht is as interesting as her owner. She is what the Americans call a yacht-thouseboat, and rejoices in the name of *Aunt Polly*. . . .

When not fulfilling engagements Mr. Gillette is either yachting or living a very lonely life in his bungalow in the South Carolina Mountains. This retreat of the playwright is at a place called The Thousand Pines, in the very heart of the "Great Smoky" range. His bungalow is deep in the woods, about two miles from the village of Tryon. Not a tree, twig, or leaf was disturbed more than was necessary for the laying of the foundation, and so careful is Mr. Gillette to make his approaches and departure by different ways that not even a path leads through the forest to the doorway. There it is, deep among the rhododendrons and honeysuckle, with the tall pines standing sentinel and the rugged sides of the great mountains hemming it off from the world. This is the spot that the living Sherlock Holmes has selected for his habitation after his contracts with theatrical managers have been fulfilled.

Mr. Gillette does not keep himself absolutely secluded in his bungalow; he often appears at the village in his long, light coat and rough cap, and there is no more approachable man than he at that time. Everyone in Tryon knows him and everyone loves him. Not as Gillette the famous actor and playwright, but as Gillette the man, the kind, good-natured funny gentleman who always has the right thing to say to the children, and gives everyone a word that makes the day seem brighter just for his passing. . . .

South Carolina is a curious retreat for a busy and successful dramatist to select. But, as in most things, there was a reason for such a choice. It was to regain his lost health after a very sad and painful event, and one which threatened to end his career, the death of his wife. At first he occupied a cottage adjoining the one in which Sidney Lanier, the famous poet-musician, lived just prior to his death. Tourists to Tryon are always welcomed at The Thousand Pines, for Mr. Gillette is the essence of courtesy. . . .

I could write much of Mr. Gillette's courteous and practical sympathy with his fellow-actors. Always ready to lend a helping hand to a struggling colleague and to relieve distress, he has gained the respect, nay love, of those who have come in contact with him. Ask those who have acted with him, year in and year out, of Gillette—the man—and you will hear many a touching little story of a great actor who has gone out of his way to render assistance to a less fortunate individual.

Mr. Gillette is a native of Hartford, Connecticut, U.S.A. While appreciating the beauties and advantages of other countries, he nevertheless considers himself fortunate in having been born an American. Although he is over the average height, standing about 6 ft. 1 in., his grace and ease and utter carelessness of effect make him appear considerably less.

His father was a United States Senator, a relative of the late Henry Ward Beecher and of Harriet Beecher-Stowe, the authoress of "Uncle Tom's Cabin."

Mr. Gillette has already played the part of Sherlock Holmes over 600 times. The play was first produced in New York, where it had a run of an entire season. It then went on tour for another theatrical season through the States. From the Lyceum it is expected to go back to New York, and from there to Australia, in which case "Sherlock Holmes" will have had an unprecedented run of over four years.

Conan Doyle as a real "Sherlock Holmes"

How he cleared the reputation of a man unjustly convicted and imprisoned for crime he did not commit

William Gillette in stage conception of "Sherlock Holmes"

Herbert Gladstone, British Home Secretary with whom Sir Arthur Conan Doyle battled to obtain vindication from state for Edalji.

Sir Arthur Conan Doyle, who created "Sherlock Holmes", and proved himself the great detective's peer in Edalji case

George Edalji, hero of the remarkable case in which A. Conan Doyle proved himself the real "Sherlock Holmes"

View of picturesque Wolverhampton, one of the scenes in Edalji drama (FROM A PAINTING BY CULLEY)

SIR ARTHUR CONAN DOYLE created "Sherlock Holmes," prince of modern detectives, and thrilled the fiction-reading and excitement-loving world.

"What an ingenious imagination!" was the exclamation of the millions who had followed the adventures of the masterful sleuth.

"What a fund of fancy, but how thoroughly logical withal!" they cried.

Now, "Sherlock Holmes" is no longer a creature built of the stuff "that dreams are made of." He is no longer merely the stage conception of his dramatic friend, William Gillette. He is a real, live man.

And his name is Sir Arthur Conan Doyle. Thereby hangs a story that has stirred all England and sent its echoes far across the distant seas.

Even as his own hero worked many times in fiction just for the glory of clearing a man's name of dishonor and righting the wrongs of the oppressed, so Sir Arthur has labored in the interests of justice, without reward save the knowledge that his deed was good, and he has triumphed in two particulars.

He has cleared a man unjustly accused—cleared him at least in the eyes of the world, if not completely in the legal sense, and he has gained, through his efforts, the right to be called the original "Mr. Sherlock Holmes, of Baker street."

Tardily enough, but none the less emphatically, hard-headed British justice has indorsed his work, for within a few days the authorities with whom the author worked for years to clear his much-wronged client, have consented to arrest another man accused of the crime, and have admitted that they blundered badly in the first instance. This is how it all came about:

IN THE early part of 1903, all England was startled by a series of fiendish crimes in the country about Great Wyrley, district of Staffordshire. Cattle and horses belonging to farmers and country gentlemen living in that picturesque part of the island, were found by their owners shockingly maimed. Horses, cows and sheep were slashed with knives or stabbed and left lying in field or stable. Many of the beasts were not fatally hurt, indicating that the "slasher's" sole desire was to inflict painful wounds on the dumb brutes. He would visit one or two farm houses in one locality on the same evening, and the next time he would be heard from many miles away from the scene of the previous outrage.

To many it seemed like the work of a lunatic, but the stolid unimaginative land owners decided that it was some one trying to wreak vengeance for a fancied wrong. But so silently and so swiftly did the fiend work that the local police could find no clue to his identity.

Finally anonymous letters began to arrive at houses in Great Wyrley—letters threatening fresh outrages, and the cattle slashing was repeated. Many of the land owners got these letters and turned them over to the police, but still the authorities could find no clew.

AMONG the persons who received letters at this time and turned them over to the police, was George Edalji, son of a church of England clergyman, who was vicar of Great Wyrley. The elder Edalji was a Parsee, who had been educated in England and had become Christianized. The son was a studious youth, who had studied law after a university course, and had obtained admission to the Bar.

Either because of racial prejudice against him, or because the police in their feverish desire to run down the criminal grasped at any straw, the authorities determined to arrest George Edalji, because they fancied they detected a resemblance between his handwriting and that of the anonymous letter writer. They asserted that he had maimed his neighbors' cattle because of fancied insults, and that he had written the anonymous letters and had included himself in the list of those threatened to avert suspicion.

In vain the young man protested his innocence, and in vain his father, the vicar, swore that his son was in his own home on the nights when the outrages were committed. Public sentiment was against Edalji; he was convicted and sentenced to seven years in prison.

Meanwhile there were many who believed that Edalji was the victim of a miscarriage of justice, and among these was Sir Arthur Conan Doyle. The more he thought of the peculiar circumstances, the more he felt convinced that Edalji was not the real culprit. One day he made up his mind to go to Wolverhampton, where the young man was imprisoned, and like his hero, Holmes, he acted on the spur of the moment, hurried to an express, and was soon on the scene of action.

Bringing to bear the famous "Holmes system of deduction," Sir Arthur went to work on the case with an energy that would have thrilled his hero's Boswell, "Dr. Watson." It wasn't long before he had something to work on, and presently he knew that Edalji could not have committed the crimes with which he was charged. It was a perfectly simple, yet apparently conclusive point.

At his first meeting with Edalji the latter peered at him steadfastly, as though trying to see through a fog, and when Sir Arthur extended his hand the young man groped for a moment in the air before he could grip the novelist's fingers.

"NEAR-SIGHTED," said the real "Sherlock Holmes"; "almost blind."

And such was the case. Edalji had been a close student all his days, and he did not realize that his eyes, never naturally strong, were growing weaker and weaker. Sir Arthur, himself a physician, ordered spectacles for his protege. Then, as he thought it over, he realized what his discovery meant.

How could a man who was almost sightless, to whom the world appeared as in a mist, steal across moor, bog and field on the darkest nights, creep up upon horses in the pasture, or find his way into a stable, slash the animals after the manner of the Great Wyrley fiend, and then steal noiselessly away into the dark? How could such a man find his way over streams and ditches without a slip or a false step to betray him?

If Sir Arthur had any doubt of his client's innocence, this development removed the last trace of it.

Then began the battle between the real "Sherlock Holmes" and his theories, and the stern law which called for facts as loudly and as insistently as ever did Mr. Gradgrind. There were sneers for Sir Arthur; he was called "dreamer," "idle theorist," and even "crank." The Secretary of State for Home Affairs, before whom he carried the case, snubbed the author-detective, and other government officials followed suit.

But Sir Arthur had much of the public with him, and so great became the popular clamor that after Edalji had served three years, the Home Secretary, Mr. Herbert Gladstone, announced that the crown would "pardon" the young man. So Edalji got out of prison with a pardon, but not a vindication; he was free,

but he could obtain no satisfaction for the years he had spent in jail.

Edalji, with Sir Arthur's aid, then began a fight to clear his name and recover damages for false imprisonment. But the government was obdurate. A "pardon" was all Edalji could get.

THEN like a thunderbolt from a clear sky came the news that the Great Wyrley "slasher" was at work again. And this time Edalji was a hundred miles away at the hour the outrages were committed. Sir Arthur had prophesied when he was arguing with the government that the "slasher" would return, and that Edalji would then have an absolute alibi. Time had vindicated his client.

At last the officials made an arrest of a suspect at Wolverhampton. There wasn't anything very important about this arrest itself, for the prisoner is not supposed to be the man wanted, and Sir Arthur has a theory that points a vastly different way. But it did show absolutely that the police were ready to admit that Edalji had been wrongfully accused, and that Sir Arthur was right in his protestations of his client's innocence.

That Edalji will get the compensation he seeks for false imprisonment and full restoration of his rights, no one doubts. Meanwhile Sir Arthur may prevail upon his friend, Dr. Watson, to tell another story of the real "Sherlock Holmes."

In an interview the other day on the Edalji case, Sir Arthur said:

"There is no doubt in my mind that the crimes of 1903 and 1907 were committed by the same man. When at Great Wyrley, where, by the way, nobody knew me, I traced back the history of the whole miserable business to personal vengeance. For reasons which I need not go into there were two brothers who hated Edalji like poison. One of them is now dead; the other, who is still alive, appears to me, speaking as a medical man, to be a type of the malignant degenerate.

"He undoubtedly is a madman. His particular mania might be called cruelty to animals. It is a sort of blood lust, and well known to students of the psychology of crime. It can be seen frequently in children who do fiendish things to animals and birds."

SHOULD the Wolverhampton suspect prove his innocence, it is quite likely that the police, now thoroughly humbled, will seek out Sir Arthur and take up his once despised theory of the madman, even as they indorsed his efforts by deciding to make the first arrest.

They are telling stories now in England about Sir Arthur's early ability as a detective. Long before he brought out "Sherlock Holmes" he met a man at his tailor's who was buying a suit of clothes, and seemed to have a strong objection to any material with a stripe in it.

Sir Arthur at once set the man down as an ex-criminal, and, to satisfy himself as to how far his deduction was correct, he determined to try to trace the man's history. This was by no means an easy matter, but some months afterward, chancing to visit a convict prison, he saw the man's portrait in the rogues' gallery.

The preceding article, from the Sunday Portland Oregonian, *September 29, 1907, is typical of many from that early period when Doyle was frequently portrayed as, himself, a Sherlock Holmes. The facts of the story are, of course, true. Touches of art are by H. W. Armstrong.*

Through "The Bowling Green," his long-lived Saturday Review of Literature *column of the 1930s, novelist and critic Christopher Morley managed to bring into being, and then publicize, the American body of Sherlockian activists known as the Baker Street Irregulars. Having occasionally termed by that name those correspondent-contributors to his magazine column who shared his enthusiasm for Holmesian matters, Morley was delighted to preside "in print" over the first formal meeting in Manhattan of the Irregulars (January 1934), and his column brought the news of the organization to the nation. This now-classic body of reportage, sandwiched in among Sherlockian discussions typical of those to be found in "The Bowling Green" over the years, follows on this and the next two pages, with magazine dates given.*

January 6, 1934

Sherlock Holmes and Cocktails

SIR:—Last year—on what evidence I cannot guess—you announced that January 6 was the date of Sherlock Holmes's birthday, and 1853 the probable year. That seemed to be about right: I remember that the beautiful Irene Adler, "*the* woman," the only one toward whom Sherlock might conceivably have felt an impulse of sentiment, was born ("in New Jersey") in 1858. (Where in New Jersey, I wonder?)

Anyhow, every year about Christmas time I get out my Conan Doyle and read Sherlock again. And your comment lately about cocktails having gone back to 25 cents reminded me that Holmes considered even that price a trifle high. In the *Adventure of the Noble Bachelor,* you remember, he examines a hotel bill in which a cocktail costs a shilling and a glass of sherry 8d. He deduces that the bill was from "one of the most expensive hotels."

Will not the Hotel Duane on Madison Avenue, which you say is frequented by Sherlock Holmes's publishers, invent a Sherlock Holmes cocktail in honor of the birthday? I will offer the 2-volume edition of the Complete Stories as a prize for the most appropriate formula.—Of course there should really be two; the *Sherlock* and the *Mycroft.* What subtle and softly influential philtre the *Mycroft* would have to be!

Another thought: what evidence can you give of Sherlock's religious feelings, if any?

CHARING CROSS.
St. George, Staten Island.

* * *

I like Mr. Cross's suggestion about the cocktail, and will be pleased to forward for his judgment any suggested formulae. In regard to Irene Adler ("a face that a man might die for" was Holmes's astonishing description) I have always maintained that she was born in Hoboken.

Of Holmes's religious feelings: I've always supposed that the beginning of his atheistic tendency was the fact that if he hadn't been on his way to the college chapel he wouldn't have been bitten by Trevor's bull terrier. (See the story of the *Gloria Scott.*) It must have been a bad bite; he was laid up for ten days. But he was a student of the Bible (see *The Crooked Man*).

CHRISTOPHER MORLEY.

January 20, 1934

The Baker Street Irregulars

SIR:—Since you have resumed the annual *escarmouche* about Sherlock Holmes, may I point out that Mr. Vincent Starrett, in his recent agreeable memoir, is surely in error in saying, "It was in 1902 that Conan Doyle received his knighthood from a grateful Queen." The Queen died in January, 1901.

Whatever beverage your Holmes-and-Watson club chooses for its ceremonial luncheon, it had better not be the wine of Beaune. For the good Doctor told us (*The Sign of Four,* chapter I) that Beaune at lunch made him irritable.

GASOGENE.

January 27, 1934

* * *

E. R. (Kalamazoo, Michigan), who has been reading *Jack Robinson* by George Beaton, writes: "That man Beaton can make the wettest rain I ever read in a book, it made me worry all afternoon because the cistern hadn't been cleaned."

She adds a tribute to Sherlock Holmes which will please the Baker Street Irregulars:—

Probably no character in fiction was ever loved or so universally known as Sherlock, and probably no other one character ever gave quite so much—courage and tolerance and joy. When everything else has gone stale and I have reached "the last ditch"—and it seems as if I must plunge out of my slough of desperation and futility, I can talk it out with Holmes and Dr. Watson in Baker St.—and go away laughing at my folly and weakness.

* * *

W. S. H., secretary of the Baker Street Irregulars, has allowed us to look over the minutes of the first meeting of the club. Among other business it appears that the matter of an official toast was discussed. It was agreed that the first health must always be drunk to "*The* Woman." Suggestions for succeeding sentiments, which will have their own overtones for all genuine Holmesians, were:—"Mrs. Hudson," "Mycroft," "The Second Mrs. Watson," "The game is afoot!" and "The second most dangerous man in London."

Also agreed that the club rooms must be exactly seventeen steps up, and the first furnishings to be a gasogene and a tantalus.

CHRISTOPHER MORLEY.

February 3, 1934

The Baker Street Irregulars

SIR:—"Charing Cross" mentions a Mycroft Holmes cocktail in a recent number of the *Saturday Review of Literature.* I can name one ingredient of such a cocktail. It is "pollinaris water." If "Charing Cross" recalls O. Henry's *Lost Blend,* he will remember the futile experiments of Riley and McQuirk, and the inspiration of the "pollinaris water." O. Henry's lost blend, and the subtle, elusive Mycroft cocktail must surely be identical. As an award for naming one essential of this elusive philtre, I claim one of the two volumes promised.

It has always seemed peculiar that the two cases in which Mycroft appears, should be, in my opinion, the best and the worst of the saga. *The Bruce-Partington Plans* is not surpassed by any tale in the series. One must agree with Watson that never had Holmes risen to greater heights. Here we get a pleasing picture of Mycroft. We see him as a man of vigor and keenness, despite his lethargic bulk. He springs from his chair. Even allowing for the exigencies of the situation, and the "representations from the highest quarter," we still picture him as alert and alive.

In *The Greek Interpreter* we have a disappointing contrast. The situation is weak, and Sherlock really solves nothing. The author even belittles our hero by having him admit that "again and again" he has taken his problems to Mycroft. We like to have Sherlock handle his problems himself. In no other case is our confidence in the detective so sadly shaken. Mycroft is somewhat disappointing. He appears as an inert hulk, incapable of exciting our enthusiasm. Even his eyes are light watery gray, in contrast to their alert steel gray in *The Bruce-Partington Plans.* (Perhaps during the elapsed time between the two adventures he was treated by Dr. Doyle, who effected the marked improvement in the appearance of the eyes.)

One often thinks that Conan Doyle missed a wonderful opportunity. He did not create quite the perfect Holmes story. Why did he never have Sherlock and Mycroft collaborate on a case? Such a tale, with tireless Sherlock doing the field work, and Mycroft digesting data and notes in the depths of his Diogenes club armchair, would surely have deserved the creation of a subtle ambrosial cocktail.

H. R. STAHL.

Desloge, Missouri.

February 17, 1934

The Two Moriarties

SIR:—"Gasogene" is right—damn him! —about the date of Queen Victoria's death. I had hoped that the error (discovered in the publishers' office just too late to correct) would escape public notice. It is being corrected in the second edition, now printing; and the London edition (Nicholson & Watson) will not carry it—I have attended to that.

Before Miss Priscilla Anderson (of Smith College) writes to the Baker Street Irregulars about me, I hasten to expose another error, and present a very curious problem. Miss Anderson points out, in a charming letter, that on page 141 of *The Private Life of Sherlock Holmes,* I assert that neither Holmes nor Watson knew that Moriarty's name was Robert—the name given him by William Gillette in the stage play, *Sherlock Holmes.* Whereas, Miss Anderson reminds me, both Holmes and Watson knew the professor's name very well indeed; it was James, as recorded in the *Adventure of the Empty House,* along toward the end of which

episode Holmes remarks that "Professor James Moriarty . . . had one of the great brains of the century."

The communication upset me more than, in my reply, I allowed Miss Anderson to suspect. But tracing back the source of my error, and finding it, I have come upon the curious problem referred to. My error arose from a line in the first paragraph of *The Final Problem,* in which it is set forth by Watson that his hand has been forced . . . "by the recent letters in which Colonel James Moriarty defends the memory of his brother."

We have then the unique problem of the Moriarty brothers, James and James, both clearly of record.

When was the Doctor right—when he wrote that line in *The Final Problem* or when he quoted Holmes in *The Empty House?* It may be argued that Watson, at the time of the earlier episode, was distraught; writing, as he was, of his friend's death (as he supposed) in Switzerland: yet at such a time would he not have been particularly careful? And it is to be remembered that he was also distraught at the time of the *Adventure of the Empty House:* he had just received his friend back from the dead!

Which occasion would be more likely to plunge him into error—death or resurrection?

Or were there really two brothers Moriarty, each of them named James?

VINCENT STARRETT.

Chicago.

February 17, 1934

The Baker Street Irregulars

Of course it is for the study of just such savory problems that the BAKER STREET IRREGULARS propose to meet together. One of the most soundly documented Holmesians now comes forward with a suggested Constitution for the club. It runs as follows:—

ARTICLE I

The name of this society shall be the Baker Street Irregulars.

ARTICLE II

Its purpose shall be the study of the Sacred Writings.

ARTICLE III

All persons shall be eligible for membership who pass an examination in the Sacred Writings set by officers of the society, and who are considered otherwise suitable.

ARTICLE IV

The officers shall be: a Gasogene, a Tantalus, and a Commissionaire.

The duties of the Gasogene shall be those commonly performed by a President.

The duties of the Tantalus shall be those commonly performed by a Secretary.

The duties of the Commissionaire shall be to telephone down for ice, White Rock, and whatever else may be required and available; to conduct all negotiations with waiters; and to assess the members pro rata for the cost of same.

BUY LAWS*

(1) An annual meeting shall be held on January 6th, at which those toasts shall be drunk which were published in the SATURDAY REVIEW of January 27th, 1934; after which the members shall drink at will.

(2) The current round shall be bought by any member who fails to identify, by title of story and context, any quotation from the Sacred Writings submitted by any other member.

Qualification A.—If two or more members fail so to identify, a round shall be bought by each of those so failing.

Qualification B.—If the submitter of the quotation, upon challenge, fails to identify it correctly, he shall buy the round.

(3) Special meetings may be called at any time or any place by any one of three members, two of whom shall constitute a quorum.

Qualification A.—If said two are of opposite sexes, they shall use care in selecting the place of meeting, to avoid misinterpretation (or interpretation either, for that matter).

Qualification B.—If such two persons of opposite sexes be clients of the Personal Column of the SATURDAY REVIEW, the foregoing does not apply; such persons being presumed to let their consciences be their guides.

(4) All other business shall be left for the monthly meeting.

(5) There shall be no monthly meeting.

ELMER DAVIS.

March 3, 1934

Two Suppressed Holmes Episodes

The number of allusions to Conan Doyle lately seems to me symptomatic of a widespread revival of interest in that admirable writer. A healthy sign, indeed; personally I confess a deliberated assurance that more intellectual vitamin, and even more sound bourgeois sociology, is to be found in Doyle than in a large number of Key-

---

* The misspelling is, of course, a famed pun.—B.B.

serlings and Spenglers. Good old Sir Arthur! is it not odd how poor a judge he was of his own work? He singled out as his favorites those obviously third-rate *Tales of Long Ago*, sentimental *gouache* (or do I mean goulash?) of Roman legionaries and Christian martyrs, etc. . . .

But to the point. If Mr. Vincent Starrett or other Baker Street Irregulars wish the Sherlock Holmes codex to be complete they must look at two stories in which Holmes is not mentioned by name but where he is certainly present by allusion. The episodes were probably suppressed by Watson because Holmes guessed wrong both times. The stories are *The Lost Special* and *The Man with the Watches*, both mystery tales laid in railway trains; and Holmes's interest in railroad romance is of course familiar to all. In *The Lost Special*, dealing with the complete disappearance between Liverpool and Manchester

of a special train on June 3, 1890, you will find Holmes referred to as "an amateur reasoner of some celebrity at that date." He wrote a letter to the London *Times* of July 3, 1890, in which the familiar Sherlockian principle was stated: "When the impossible has been eliminated the residuum, *however improbable*, must contain the truth."

In the case of *The Man with the Watches*, which "filled many columns of the daily press in the spring of the year 1892," again we learn that "a well-known criminal investigator" wrote at length to the *Daily Gazette* giving his own reconstruction of the mystery. The letter has all the internal evidences of Holmes's style, though not at his best reasoning power; but it is the more interesting because this was during the time when Holmes—supposed by Watson to be dead—was travelling in Tibet. Even at

that distance this remarkable man kept in touch with outrages in Britain. His special interest in this case was undoubtedly the fact that the persons involved were Americans. The number of American malefactors in Holmes's career has often been noted. Does not the typical Sherlockian touch appear in this remark about the unfortunate young man with the watches—"He was probably an American, and also probably a man of weak intellect."

You will find these two stories in the excellent omnibus volume *The Conan Doyle Stories* (John Murray, London, 1200 pp. for 7/6) which reprints all the doctor's short stories other than the Holmes episodes. It has been circulating in England for nearly five years. Among the many mysteries associated with Doyle none is more odd than the enigma of no publisher having issued it here.

CHRISTOPHER MORLEY.

THE CURIOUS INCIDENT OF THE DOGS IN THE NIGHT~TIME

By Wolcott Gibbs

"THIS is a nice place, Freddy," said Harrington, looking around the noisy, crowded room. "You come here often?"

"I used to," said Goetz. "A few years ago, before I got married. Not any more. Ellen claimed it made her head hurt."

"Oh," said Harrington. "That's quite a thing, you getting married," he said after a pause. "That's certainly one nobody ever figured on. What's she like?"

"Ellen?" said Goetz. "She's a wonderful girl, Tom. I want you to meet her."

"Swell," said Harrington. "We'll have to get together sometime. I'll get Jane."

"Who?" said Goetz.

"Jane Inman," said Harrington. "But on second thought I guess not. She's no girl if your head happens to hurt."

The two men had been standing at the bar for about half an hour. When they came in, at seven-thirty, there had been no tables vacant, and the captain had suggested they have a drink while they were waiting.

"Why don't you gentlemen just stand right up here to the bar," he had said. "I'll let you know the first moment there is anything free."

They were on their fourth Martini now,

and in the silence following Harrington's last remark they were both suddenly conscious of the passage of time.

"Listen," said Goetz. "We ought to be sitting down pretty soon. Where the hell is that waiter?"

"Over there," said Harrington. "Leaning up against some damn thing. Hey, captain."

The captain moved slowly toward them. He had a pale, impassive face and an air of having formed a rather low opinion of his surroundings.

"Gentlemen?"

"How about that table?" said Goetz.

"Yeah," said Harrington. "How about us sitting down one of these days?"

The captain looked around the room, tapping his fingers on the menu card in his hand.

"I'm sorry, gentlemen," he said. "I still got nothing free. I'll let you know."

"You said that before," said Harrington.

"You gentlemen get the first table that's free."

"All right, see that we do," said Harrington.

"Yes, sir," said the captain contemptuously, and moved away.

"Now you got him sore," said Goetz.

"Good," said Harrington. "I'm sore, too. How about another drink?" He tapped on the bar. "Hey, a couple more Martinis here."

"This is the one I don't need," said Goetz when the drink came.

"What do you mean you don't need?"

"The one that gets me drunk," said Goetz.

"What's the matter with that? What are you saving yourself for, Freddy? You planning a career or something?"

"Career, hell. I got to get up in the morning. I *work*."

"No. You're saving yourself. I know you married bastards. You plan ahead."

"That's right, Tom," said Goetz pacifically. "I'm planning a career. I want to be a waiter."

"You're too old," said Harrington. "You got to start young in that business. You got to be born in a linen closet or some damn place. All the really great waiters have been born in linen closets. It's like those trunks in vaudeville."

He was interrupted by the return of the captain, who gave them what he conceivably regarded as a smile.

"I got that table now, gentlemen," he said.

"Thank you," said Goetz, finishing his drink. "All right, Tom, let's go."

"Just a minute," said Harrington. "I wonder if I could put a question."

"Yes, sir?"

"This gentleman and I were having a little argument. I wonder if you'd mind telling us if you happened to be born in a closet."

"Sir?" said the captain, looking at him sharply.

"Never mind, captain," said Goetz. "You just show us that table."

"All right, you drunken half-wits," said the captain's expression quite plainly, but aloud he only said, "This way, gentlemen," and led them to the table, which was off in one corner of the room. At his signal, a waiter came up and handed them both a menu.

"We better have another drink first," said Harrington. "Bring us a couple of Martinis. No, you better make that double Martinis. Two *double* Martinis."

"Two double Martinis," said the waiter, and left them.

"That's a good man," said Harrington. "Knows how to take an order."

"Listen, Tom, how about taking it easy? You're getting pretty soused."

"You don't know what soused *is*," said Harrington. He concentrated on the menu, shutting one eye. "Say, what *is* all this stuff? What nationality?"

"Italian," said Goetz.

"Well, it's a terrible language," said Harrington. "You know what I want? Just some eggs. Some scrambled eggs."

"I'm going to have the *cacciatore*. They do that pretty well here."

"They do, do they?" said Harrington. "You know something about you, Freddy? You talk like a God-damn tourist."

The drinks came and they gave their order.

"Some pretty interesting people used to come here, Tom," said Goetz. "The Baker Street Irregulars."

"Who?" asked Harrington.

"The Baker Street Irregulars. The Sherlock Holmes experts. *You* know."

"Oh," said Harrington. "Yeah, I guess I read about them. Woollcott or somebody. This where they met, eh?"

"They did when I used to come here. Here or someplace very much *like* here. Maybe they still do. Woollcott, Morley, Tunney, Elmer Davis, some guy called Starrett—oh, a lot of 'em."

"That's a lovely bunch of boys," said Harrington. "What did they do? All I remember is they wore funny hats."

"They used to ask each other questions," said Goetz. "You know, about the stories. Like the name of the dog in 'The Sign of the Four.'"

"Toby," said Harrington promptly. "A lurcher, whatever the hell that is. And it's 'The Sign of Four.' No second 'the.'"

"The hell it is," said Goetz.

"All right," said Harrington. "Look it up. 'The Sign of Four.' I got five bucks says no second 'the.'"

"I'll take your word for it."

"You better. All right, ask me another. Ask me anything. Any of the stories. No, I'll ask *you*. What's a Penang lawyer?"

"Cane," said Goetz. "Dr. Mortimer carried it in 'The Hound of the Baskervilles.' Dr. James Mortimer, M.R.C.S."

"All right," said Harrington. "How many orange pips? How many Napoleons."

"Five and six," said Goetz. "In that order. For God's sake, is that the best you can do? How about three stories with 'three' in the title?"

"Well, there's one with a funny word in it," said Harrington. "Garribeds'? No, 'Garridebs.' 'The Adventure of the Three Garridebs.'"

"That's one."

There was a long silence while Harrington stared at the tablecloth.

"O.K., Freddy," he said finally. "You win on that one. I give up."

"'The Three Students' and 'The Three Gables,'" said Goetz. "You're a hell of an expert if you don't know that."

The two friends went on like that for some time. Goetz horrified Harrington by not remembering that the villain of "The Speckled Band" was called Dr. *Grimesby* Roylott, and somehow or other Harrington missed on the last name of Jefferson Hope's fiancée, which, of course, was Ferrier, but on the whole they did remarkably well. Time passed, and though the eggs and the *cacciatore* remained substantially untouched on their plates, the double Martinis continued to arrive and vanish.

"Listen," said Goetz suddenly at ten o'clock, "maybe they *still* come here."

"Who?" said Harrington.

"The Baker Street Irregulars," said Goetz, managing so many consonants very successfully, all things considered. "Maybe they're here right now."

"Those sons of bitches," said Harrington. "A lot they know about it."

"Sure they do," said Goetz. "They

write articles."

"Not Tunney," said Harrington. "He's no writer. He just *reads*. Mostly Shakespeare."

"Well, all the rest, then."

They considered this briefly, and Harrington snapped his fingers. "Test 'em," he said.

"What?"

"We go up and test 'em."

"Find out they here first," said Goetz.

"Sure," said Harrington. "Find out. Ask *him*. Hey, waiter."

The waiter came over reluctantly, for he had been instructed to serve no more double Martinis and he saw trouble ahead.

"Sir?"

"You got a meeting here tonight, waiter?" said Goetz.

"Meeting?"

For a moment, the name of the Holmes admirers escaped Harrington. "Bunch of boys with funny hats," he said. "Ask each other questions."

"There's some fellas upstairs," said the waiter. "Some society. I don't know about the rest of it."

"Called Baker Street Irregulars," said Goetz. By this time, however, the Martinis had got in their work and his speech was somewhat blurred.

"Some name like that," agreed the waiter. "Some society."

"Whereabouts?" said Harrington. "What floor?"

"Right up at the head of the stairs," said the waiter, and then, belatedly grasping their intention, "It's a private party though, sir."

"It's all right," said Harrington, getting to his feet. "We're friends."

"Old friends," said Goetz, also rising. "Fellow-members."

"Well . . ." said the waiter doubtfully.

"Old, *old* friends. Don't give it a second thought," said Harrington. "Dismiss it from your mind. Here, let's have the check."

The waiter produced the check from somewhere inside his coat and added it rapidly. The total came to twenty-three dollars and twenty cents, and Harrington gave him three tens.

"O.K.," he said. "You keep that."

"Thank you, sir," said the waiter. There was still a doubtful expression on his face as his customers started across the room but he made no effort to detain them or to communicate with the captain, who would certainly have been opposed to the project they had in mind.

GOETZ and Harrington turned to the right when they left the dining room and started up the stairs.

"Listen," said Goetz when they were halfway up. "Who you going to be?"

"Be?"

"Yes. I just remembered they all pretend to be somebody. Some character in the stories."

"All right," said Harrington. "I'm Holmes. You're Watson."

"Too obvious," said Goetz. "Anyway, they must *have* a Holmes and Watson. Probably the president and vice-president."

"All right," said Harrington. "*Mrs. Watson. Mrs. Watson and Mrs. Hudson.*"

"No," said Goetz. "It isn't that kind of kidding. You got to stick to the right sex."

"Mycroft and Pycroft," said Harrington. "Addison and Steele. Gallagher and Shean." He laughed immoderately, holding onto the railing along the wall, but Goetz was not amused.

"No, the hell with that kind of stuff, Tom," he said. "Listen, how about Gregson and Lestrade?"

"Those dumb bastards," said Harrington. "No. I tell you—Moriarty and Moran. First and second most dangerous men in London."

"Good," said Goetz. "Which one you want? First or second most dangerous?"

"Moriarty," said Harrington. "First most dangerous. Naturally."

Since one of the two doors at the top of the stairs was labelled "Men," they turned to the other.

"After you, Professor," said Goetz.

"Thank you, Colonel," said Harrington, and flung open the door.

There were perhaps twenty men in the small room. They were sitting at a long table and they appeared to be engaged in some general and earnest discussion. They wore no hats. Except for the table and the chairs, there was nothing in the room but a small piano, off in one corner.

"Gentlemen," said Harrington. "The chase is on!"

A silence fell on the room, and then a small, red-faced man got up from the table and approached Goetz and Harrington. He had on a rather jocular suit, but his manner was formal. "Some mistake, fellows, I think," he said.

"Not at all," said Harrington. He waved his hand at Goetz. "Like you to meet Colonel Sebastian Moran, late of the 1st

Bangalore Pioneers. I'm Professor Moriarty."

"Of Reichenbach Falls," said Goetz. "Who are you supposed to be?"

The red-faced man cleared his throat. "Well, I'm Ed Tracy, of Denver," he said, "but—"

Goetz looked inquiringly at Harrington. "How about it?" he said. "You know that one?"

Harrington shook his head. "Might be 'A Study in Scarlet,'" he said doubtfully. "One of the Mormons. I don't remember him, though."

"I told you these boys made it tough," said Goetz. "All right," he said to the red-faced man, who had begun to wear a hunted look. "We give up. What story?"

"I don't know what you fellows are talking about," said the man helplessly. "This is a private party."

"I know," said Goetz. "We just thought we'd drop in. Great admirers."

"Disciples," said Harrington. He spoke thickly, and Goetz was surprised to see that his face was pale and beaded with perspiration.

"You O.K., Professor?" he asked.

"No," said Harrington simply. "Better sit down a minute. Better *lie* down."

He swayed visibly as he spoke, and Goetz caught his arm.

"You going to be *sick*?" he demanded.

Harrington shook his head and then rose to a kind of heroism in his extremity. "No," he muttered. "Just a touch of enteric. Old trouble of mine. Ever since Ladysmith."

His appearance actually was alarming, and between them Goetz and the red-faced man got him to a chair at the table. The other guests looked at him with a mixture of apprehension and respect.

"What's the matter with him?" said one of them. "What'd he say he got?"

"Enteric," said Goetz. "The curse of our Indian possessions."

"Yeah? What does he do for it?"

"Whiskey," said Harrington in a much stronger voice. "Only known cure for enteric. The Fuzzies live on it."

A bottle and a glass stood on the table near him, and without waiting for an invitation he poured himself a rather staggering drink. After a moment's hesitation, Goetz did likewise. Then, suddenly and simultaneously inspired, they raised their glasses in the air.

"To the Woman," said Harrington

solemnly.

"To the Woman," repeated Goetz. "To Irene Adler."

The two emptied their glasses and, still in unison, they sent them both crashing to the floor.

"Listen, fellows," said the red-faced man. "*Please.*"

AFTERWARD, Goetz had no very clear memory of the rest of the evening. Sometimes, in the tormented and fragmentary glimpses he got, he seemed to be shouting at a table of men who retreated from him, gradually and indignantly, until he was left alone at one end with Harrington, who sometimes shouted, too, and sometimes just slept. Sometimes he must have realized that these were not Sherlock Holmes experts, as the waiter and his own romantic heart had somehow led him to believe, but instead simply the innocent conclave of roofing experts from the West that their appearance and conversation indicated that they were. If he did occasionally recognize this for the discouraging truth, however, he never did so for long, and there were considerable periods when, noisily abetted by Harrington, he tried to force them into the shape of the Baker Street Irregulars, harassing them with unanswerable questions about the second Mrs. Watson and the Diogenes Club and whether Holmes went to Oxford or Cambridge. Once, he recalled, a waiter had been summoned and there had been some talk about putting them out, but that mysteriously had passed and there had been an interlude of great good will, when scrawled cards and promises of future gaiety were exchanged.

Goetz's only exact picture, as a matter of fact, was of the end of the evening. Harrington, somehow miraculously resuscitated, was seated at the piano and they were both singing, and it was his impression that they had been doing so for some time. He had looked up suddenly —this vision was as sharp as a photograph—and seen, to his perplexity, a line of figures, led by the red-faced man, tiptoeing from the room. After that, there was only the empty room and Harrington shouting and banging on the piano. Roofers or Baker Street Irregulars, the guests had gone, and they were all alone. His memory stopped there.

Surprisingly little known, even to those Sherlockians who take part in the activities of the Baker Street Irregulars, is this short story from drama critic Wolcott Gibbs's More in Sorrow *(New York: Henry Holt, 1958); it originally appeared in* The New Yorker *for September 18, 1948.*

Was Sherlock Holmes an American?

By Christopher Morley

"I think the fellow is really an American, but he has worn his accent smooth with years of London."

—The Three Garridebs

A CAPRICIOUS secrecy was always characteristic of Holmes. He concealed from Watson his American connection. And though Watson must finally have divined it, he also was uncandid with us. The Doctor was a sturdy British patriot: the fact of Holmes's French grandmother was disconcerting, and to add to this his friend's American association and sympathy would have been painful. But the theory is too tempting to be lightly dismissed. Not less than fifteen of the published cases (including three of the four chosen for full-length treatment) involve American characters or scenes. Watson earnestly strove to minimize the appeal of United States landscapes of which Holmes must have told him. The great plains of the West were "an arid and repulsive desert."[1] Vermissa Valley (in Pennsylvania, I suppose?) was "a gloomy land of black crag and tangled forest . . . not a cheering prospect."[2] Watson's quotation from the child Lucy,[1]—"Say, did God make this country?"—was a humorous riposte to Holmes, spoofing the familiar phrase Watson had heard too often in their fireside talks. There is even a possible suggestion of Yankee timbre in the Doctor's occasional descriptions of the "well-remembered voice." The argument of rival patriotisms was a favorite topic between them. Watson never quite forgave Holmes's ironical jape when after some specially naive Victorian imperialism by the Doctor (perhaps at the time of the '87 Jubilee) Sherlock decorated the wall with the royal V. R. in bullet-pocks. (Or did the Doctor misread as V. R. what was jocularly meant to be V. H.—because Watson too insistently suggested a sentimental interest in Miss Violet Hunter of the Copper Beeches? An H. in bullet-pocks, if the marksman's aim was shaken by a heavy dray in the street, or by the

SHERLOCK HOLMES—WITH CAMBRIDGE HATBAND.
The Strand *Magazine, 1893.*

neighboring Underground Railway, might well look like an R.)

Why, again, does Watson write "It was upon the 4th of March, as I have good reason to remember," that the adventure of the Study in Scarlet began? And why was Holmes still at the breakfast table? It was the 4th of March, 1881, and Holmes was absorbed in reading the news dispatches about the inauguration, to take place that day, of President Garfield.

Was Holmes actually of American birth? It would explain much. The jealousy of Scotland Yard, the refusal of knighthood, the expert use of Western argot, the offhand behavior to aristocratic clients, the easy camaraderie with working people of all sorts, the always travelling First Class in trains. How significant is Holmes's "Hum!" when he notes that Irene was born in New Jersey.[3] And Watson's careful insertion of "U.S.A." after every American address, which always irritates us, was probably a twit to tease his principal. True,

as Inspector MacDonald once said,[4] "You don't need to import an American from outside in order to account for American doings." But let us light the cherry-wood pipe and examine the data more systematically.

H OLMES'S grandmother was "the sister of Vernet, the French artist."[5] This of course was Horace Vernet (1789–1863), the third of the famous line of painters in that family. Horace Vernet's father (who had been decorated by Napoleon for his *Battle of Marengo* and *Morning of Austerlitz*) came from Bordeaux and Horace's grandfather, the marine painter, from Avignon. Here we have an association with the South of France which Holmes acknowledges by his interest in Montpellier[6] where he probably had French kindred. Like Sir Kenelm Digby, who delivered there the famous discourse on

---

1. *A Study in Scarlet.*
2. *The Valley of Fear.*

3. *A Scandal in Bohemia.*

4. *The Valley of Fear.*
5. *The Greek Interpreter.*
6. *The Empty House.* Cf also *The Disappearance of Lady Frances Carfax.*

A little later in the seminal Irregulars year of 1934, Christopher Morley wrote what many regard as his finest piece for "The Bowling Green." "Was Sherlock Holmes an American?" appeared in the Saturday Review issues for July 21 and 28. (The artwork is slightly rearranged.)

the Powder of Sympathy,[7] Holmes knew Montpellier as an important center of scientific studies. (See *The Empty House.*) It is deplorable that our Holmes researchers have done so little to trace his French relationship. It is significant that though he declined a knighthood in Britain he was willing to accept the Legion of Honor in France.[8]

Much might be said of Sherlock's presumable artistic and political inheritance from the Vernets. His great-uncle's studio in Paris was "a rendezvous of Liberals."[9] Surely the untidiness which bothered Watson at 221B is akin to the description of Horace Vernet "painting tranquilly, whilst boxing, fencing, drum and horn playing were going on, in the midst of a medley of visitors, horses, dogs and models."[10] Holmes's grandmother, one of this radical and bohemian and wide-travelling family, brought up among the harrowing scenes of the French Revolution and the Napoleonic wars, may quite possibly have emigrated to America.[11] It is not inconceivable then that at least one of Holmes's parents was an American. My own conjecture is that there was some distant connection with the famous Holmes household of Cambridge (Mass.). Every reader has noticed Holmes's passionate interest in breakfasts: does this not suggest the Autocrat of the Breakfast Table?

I WILL not cloud the issue with futile speculation, though certainly it is of more importance than many of the controversies (such as, was Holmes's dressing gown blue, purple, or mouse-colored?).[12] But before proceeding to recount some specific passages which prove our hero's exceptional interest in America let me add one more suggestion. The hopeless muddle of any chronology based on *The Gloria Scott* and [*The*] *Musgrave Ritual* is familiar to all students; Miss Dorothy Sayers has done her brilliant best to harmonize the anomalies. But all have wondered just what Holmes was doing between the time he left the university and his taking rooms in Montague Street. My own thought is that the opening of the Johns Hopkins University in Baltimore in 1876, and the extraordinary and informal opportunities offered there for graduate study, tempted him across the water. He was certainly familiar with papers in the chemical journals written by Ira Remsen, the brilliant young professor who took charge of the new laboratories in Baltimore. Probably in Baltimore he acquired his taste for oysters[13] and on a hot summer day noted the depth to which the parsley had sunk into the butter.[14] In that devoted group of young scholars and scientists, and in the musical circles of that hospitable city he must have been supremely happy. His American-born mother (or father) had often told him of the untrammeled possibilities of American life. The great Centennial Exposition in Philadelphia (1876) was surely worth visit; there he observed the mark of the Pennsylvania Small Arms Company.[15] During his year or so in the States he travelled widely. He met Wilson Hargreave (who later became important in the New York Police Department[16]) perhaps in connection with the case of *Vanderbilt and the Yeggman*, a record of which he kept in his scrapbook.[17] He went to Chicago, where he made his first acquaintance with organized gangsterism.[18] I suggest that he perhaps visited his kinsmen the Sherlocks in Iowa—e.g. in Des Moines, where a younger member of that family, Mr. C. C. Sherlock, has since written so ably on rural topics.[19] He must have gone to Topeka;[20] and of course he made pilgrimage to Cambridge, Mass., to pay respect to the great doctor, poet and essayist. From Oliver Wendell Holmes, Jr., then a rising lawyer in Boston, he heard first-hand stories of the Civil War, which fired his interest in "that gallant struggle." Indeed he spoke to Watson so often about the Civil War that Watson repeated in the story of *The Resident Patient* the episode of the Henry Ward Beecher portrait which he had already told in *The Cardboard Box*.[21] It is interesting to note, in passing, that when Holmes spoke in that episode of having written two monographs on Ears in the *Anthropological Journal*, the alert editor of The Strand at once took the hint. A few months later, in October and November 1893, The Strand printed "A Chapter on Ears," with photos of the ears of famous people—including an ear of Dr. Oliver Wendell Holmes. Surely, from so retiring a philosopher, then 84 years old, this intimate permission could not have been had without the privileged intervention of Sherlock.

Speaking of The Strand Magazine, it is odd that our researchers do not more often turn back to those original issues which solve many problems. The much belabored matter of Holmes's university, for instance. There was never any question about it, for in Sidney Paget's illustrations Holmes is clearly shown sitting in Trevor's garden wearing a straw hat with a *Light Blue* ribbon.[22] (He was, of course, a boxing Blue.) Why has such inadequate honor been paid to those admirable drawings by Paget?—Oxford was unthinkable to Holmes; with what pleasure he noted that Colonel Moran[23] and John Clay[24] were both "Eton and Oxford."

II.

IN *The Bruce-Partington Plans* one of our most suggestive passages occurs. "You have never had so great a chance of serving your country," cries Mycroft. But is Holmes moved by this appeal? "Well, well!" he said "shrugging his shoulders." All emotions, we know, were abhorrent to that cold, precise mind,[25] and certainly militant patriotism among them; at any rate until many years later when bees, flowers, Sussex, and long association with the more sentimental Watson had softened him to the strange outburst about "God's own wind" on the terrible night of August

7. Anne Macdonell: *The Closet of Sir Kenelm Digby* (1910) p. xxxi.

8. *The Golden Pince-Nez.*

9. Encyclopaedia Britannica, article *Vernet.*

10. Ibid. Perhaps Sherlock as a child got his first interest in boxing and fencing from great-uncle Horace.

11. Turning to the telephone book, as Dr. Watson did for Garrideb, I find that several of the Vernet (Verner) family came to the U.S. There are 2 Vernets in Brooklyn, 3 Verners in Manhattan, 1 Verner in Floral Park, L.I.

12. Elementary. This particular gown was blue when new. (*The Twisted Lip.*) It had gone purple by the time of the *Blue Carbuncle.* During the long absence 1891-94, when Mrs. Hudson faithfully aired and sunned it in the back yard, it faded to mouse (*The Empty House*).

13. *The Sign of Four.*

14. I forget the locus of this allusion. Please will someone else look it up? Holmes's interest in the butter-dish is shown in *The Musgrave Ritual.*

15. *The Valley of Fear.*

16. *The Dancing Men.*

17. *The Sussex Vampire.*

18. "My knowledge of the crooks of Chicago," v. *The Dancing Men.* Cf also allusions in *The Valley of Fear* and *The Three Garridebs.*

19. C. C. Sherlock: *Care and Management of Rabbits* (1920); *The Modern Hen* (1922); *Bulb Gardening* (1922), etc.; v. *Who's Who in America.* Iowa is a great apiarian State; undoubtedly from the Sherlock side came the interest in roses, bee-keeping, etc.

20. Otherwise how could he know that there was no such person as Dr. Lysander Starr? (*The Three Garridebs.*)

21. There was no duplication in the stories as first printed: *The Cardboard Box* in The Strand Magazine of January 1893, *The Resident Patient* in August of the same year. In the latter story as it absurdly appears in the collected editions the description of the "blazing hot day in August" is repeated for "a close rainy day in October." The explanation is that Dr. Watson withheld *The Cardboard Box* from book publication for 24 years; perhaps because it revealed some anti-American bias in his never having had the portrait of Beecher framed. But the Beecher incident showed Holmes's keen observation, and in compiling the *Memoirs* Watson carelessly spliced or trepanned it into *The Resident Patient.* Then, when he republished *The Cardboard Box* in *His Last Bow* (1917), he forgot this.

22. Strand Magazine, Vol. V, p. 398. While speaking of the *Gloria Scott,* has it been pointed out that Holmes never admitted to Watson why he chose Mrs. Hudson's lodgings? She was the widow of the ruffian Hudson who blackmailed old Mr. Trevor—and so more than ever "a long-suffering woman." And of course the rapid disappearance of Watson's bull-pup was because Holmes had been bitten by one in college days.

23. *The Empty House.*

24. *The Red-Headed League.*

25. *A Scandal in Bohemia.*

2nd, 1914.[26]—Plainly he resented Mycroft's assumption that England was his only country. Mycroft, seven years older, had earlier outgrown the Franco-American tradition of the family. If Mycroft had ever been in the States he had striven to forget it; indeed no one can think of Mycroft without being reminded (in more respects than one) of the great expatriate Henry James.[27]

That Holmes had a very special affection and interest in regard to the United States is beyond question. He had much reason to be grateful to American criminals, who often relieved him from the ennui of London's dearth of outrage. The very first case recorded by Watson was the murder of Enoch J. Drebber, the ex-Mormon from Cleveland. Irene Adler, *the* woman, was a native of New Jersey. In *The Red-Headed League* the ingenious John Clay represented the League as having been founded by the eccentric millionaire Ezekiah Hopkins of Lebanon, Pa., "U.S.A." In *The [Five] Orange Pips*, Elias Openshaw emigrated to Florida, rose to be a Colonel in the C.S.A. and made a fortune. Although Watson tries to prejudice the reader by painful allusions to the habits of these people, there is plentiful evidence that Holmes considered America the land of opportunity. (Watson preferred Australia.) Both Aloysius Doran[28] and John Douglas[29] had struck it rich in California. Senator Neil Gibson,[30] "iron of nerve and leathery of conscience," had also made his pile in gold mines. Hilton Cubitt, the Norfolk squire, had married a lovely American woman;[31] and Holmes was glad to be able to save Miss Hatty Doran from Lord St. Simon who was not worthy of her.[32] He yawns sardonically at the *Morning Post*'s social item which implies that Miss Doran will gain by becoming the wife of a peer. That case is a high point in Holmes's transatlantic sympathy. He praises American slang, quotes Thoreau, shows his knowledge of the price of cocktails, and utters the famous sentiment:—

"It is always a joy to meet an American, for I am one of those who believe that the folly of a monarch and the blundering of a minister in far-gone years will not prevent our children from being some day citizens of the same world-wide country under a flag which shall be a quartering of the Union Jack with the Stars and Stripes."

Which reminds one obviously of the fact that when Holmes disguised himself as Mr. Altamont of Chicago, the Irish-American agitator, to deceive Von Bork, he greatly resembled the familiar cartoons of Uncle Sam.[33] He visited Chicago again in 1912–13 to prepare himself for this role; I wish Mr. Vincent Starrett would look up the details.

MYCROFT HOLMES
Drawing from The Strand *Magazine.*

HOLMES'S fondness for America did not prevent him from seeing the comic side of a nation that lends itself to broad satiric treatment. In *The Man with the Watches,* one of the two stories outside the canon,[34] Holmes remarks of the victim "He was probably an American, and also probably a man of weak intellect." (This rhetorical device for humorous purposes was a family trait: we find it in Mycroft's description of the senior clerk at the Woolwich Arsenal—"He is a man of forty, married, with five children. He is a silent, morose man.")[35] After his long use of American cant for Von Bork's benefit Sherlock says "My well of English seems to be permanently defiled."[36] But these japes are plainly on the principle "On se moque de ce qu'on aime." He kept informed of American manners and events: when he met Mr. Leverton of Pinkerton's he said "Pleased to meet you" and alluded to "the Long Island cave mystery."[37] He knew "the American business principle" of paying well for brains.[38] He did not hesitate to outwit a rascal by inventing an imaginary mayor of Topeka—recalling for the purpose the name of the counterfeiter of Reading years before.[39] (Those who escaped him were not forgotten.) But nothing shows more convincingly his passionate interest in all cases concerning Americans than his letter about the matter of the Man with the Watches, alluded to above. Even in Tibet, where he was then travelling as "a Norwegian named Sigerson,"[40] he had kept up with the news. This was in the spring of '92; how Watson, after reading the letter in the newspaper, can have supposed his friend was really dead passes belief. There are frequent humorous allusions to American accent,[41] the shape of American shoes,[42] American spelling.[43] I suspect that Holmes's travels in these States never took him to the South or Southwest;[44] for he shows a curious ignorance of Southern susceptibilities in the matter of race,[45] and in spite of his American Encyclopaedia[46] he did not know which was the Lone Star State. Let it be noted that the part of London where he first took rooms (Montague Street, alongside the British Museum) is the region frequented more than any other by American students and tourists.

That Holmes was reared in the States, or had some schooling here before going up to Cambridge, seems then at least arguable. His complete silence (or Watson's) on the subject of his parents suggests that they were deceased or not in England. A foreign schooling, added to his own individual temperament, would easily explain his solitary habits at college.[47] If he had gone to almost any English school the rugger jargon of Cyril Overton would have been comprehensible to him[48] or he might have picked it up from Watson, who played for Blackheath.[49] Watson, moreover, if he knew more about Holmes's family, may have been moved by jealousy to keep silent. Already he had suffered by the contrast

26. *His Last Bow.*
27. It is possible that Mycroft's experience had been in Canada, not the U.S. Sherlock says Mycroft was known at the Foreign Office as an expert on Canada (*The Bruce-Partington Plans*).
28. *The Noble Bachelor.*
29. *The Valley of Fear.*
30. *Thor Bridge.*
31. *The Dancing Men.*
32. *The Noble Bachelor.*

33. *His Last Bow.*
34. The other is *The Lost Special;* both are to be found in *The Conan Doyle Stories,* London (John Murray), 1929. Holmes appears in both these stories by obvious allusion, but Watson suppressed them, probably because Holmes's deductions were wrong in both cases.
35. *The Bruce-Partington Plans.*
36. *His Last Bow.*

37. *The Red Circle.* The mystery, on true Sherlockian principles, is that there are no caves on Long Island.
38. *The Valley of Fear.*
39. *The Three Garridebs, The Engineer's Thumb.*
40. *The Empty House.*
41. *The Hound of the Baskervilles.*
42. *The Dancing Men, The Valley of Fear.*
43. *The Three Garridebs.*
44. The "remarkable case" of the venomous gila lizard (v. *The Sussex Vampire*) need not suggest Arizona. It probably came from Number 3, Pinchin Lane (*The Sign of Four*).
45. *The Yellow Face.*
46. *The Five Orange Pips.*
47. *The Gloria Scott.*
48. *The Missing Three Quarter.*
49. *The Sussex Vampire.*

between the corpulent Mycroft and his own older brother, the crapulent H. W.[50] Or his neglect to inform us may just have been the absent-mindedness and inaccuracy which we have learned to expect from good old Watson—and which were even acquired by his wife, who went so far as to forget her husband's first name and call him "James" in front of a visitor.[51] The Doctor has hopelessly confused us on

50. *The Sign of Four.*

51. *The Man with the Twisted Lip.* This was probably the cause of the first rupture between Dr. and Mrs. Watson. Has it been pointed out, by the way, that there is premonitory allusion to a second Mrs. Watson in *The Disappearance of Lady Frances Carfax,* where Watson evades Holmes's question, as to who was his companion in the hansom? Also the Doctor had been bucking himself up with a Turkish bath.

FROM THE LIBRARY OF VINCENT STARRETT

even more important matters—that both Moriarty brothers were called James, for instance. Considering the evidence without prejudice, the idea that Holmes was at any rate partly American is enticing.

As Jefferson Hope said,[52] "I guessed what puzzled the New Yorkers would puzzle the Londoners." So I leave it as a puzzle, not as a proven case, for more accomplished students to re-examine. But the master's own dictum[53] is apposite:— "When once your point of view is changed, the very thing which was so damning becomes a clue to the truth."

52. *A Study in Scarlet.*

53. *Thor Bridge.*

The Creator of "Sherlock Holmes"

SHERLOCK HOLMES is immortal.

But his creator, Sir Arthur Conan Doyle, is said to have wished that he be remembered for his works on spiritism.

"It was probably a vain wish," thinks the New York *Evening Post.*

He may have thought he "called spirits from the vasty deep"; but the world admits that when he called the great detective from his inner consciousness, there came a spirit as real as any wearing a corporeal shape.

He even deceived many into thinking that here was one who had once lived on the earth. The Boston *Transcript* puts Doyle, in this respect, into exalted company:

Shakespeare had done that with *Hamlet,* Cervantes with *Don Quixote,* Defoe with *Robinson Crusoe,* Dickens with *David Copperfield,* but in our own time few if any others had been so successful. And the strange part of it is that not a single work from Conan Doyle's pen is a great story, as are the stories of those others. As literature they seem destined to pass into limbo. But *Sherlock Holmes* himself seems destined to live forever, as if he were once flesh and blood, and not a creature of the imagination of a single man.

A few years ago Sir Arthur Conan Doyle wrote "Memories and Adventures" (Little, Brown & Company), and in telling the story of his life he shows us how, to some extent, *Sherlock* was a real person, his prototype being a school-teacher:

Gaboriau had rather attracted me by the neat dovetailing of his plots, and Poe's masterful detective, *M. Dupin,* had from boyhood been one of my heroes.

But could I bring an addition of my own?

I thought of my old teacher, Joe Bell,* of his eagle face, of his curious ways, of his eerie trick of spotting details. If he were a detective, he would surely reduce this fascinating but unorganized business to

something nearer to an exact science.

I would try if I could get this effect.

It was surely possible in real life, so why should I not make it plausible in fiction? It is all very well to say that a man is clever, but the reader wants to see examples of it—such examples as Bell gave us every day in the wards. The idea amused me. What should I call the fellow? I still possess the leaf of a notebook with various alternative names.

One rebelled against the elementary art which gives some inkling of character in the name, and creates *Mr. Sharps,* or *Mr. Ferrets.* First it was *Sherringford Holmes;* then it was *Sherlock Holmes.* He could not tell his own exploits, so he must have a commonplace comrade

"A. CONAN DOYLE DIES AT 71".
— NEWS ITEM

*The Chicago *Tribune,* on May 23, 1930, quoted Doyle: "[There] was an Edinburgh physician named Dr. Bell, under whom I studied," he said. "He had an almost uncanny gift of drawing large inferences from small observations. When I tried to draw a detective, I naturally thought of Dr. Bell and his methods; and what he applied to diagnosis of disease I applied to the diagnosis of crime. Dr. Watson was just an ordinary man."—B.B.

Arthur Conan Doyle died on July 7, 1930. In its issue of July 26, The Literary Digest *published the above article, an interesting and thought-provoking explication of Doyle's creation of his detective as well as a tribute to the author. The illustration is by Will B. Johnstone; captioned "His Greatest Adventure," it also appeared in the New York* World.

as a foil—an educated man of action who could both join in the exploits and narrate them. And so I had my puppets and wrote my "Study in Scarlet."

Sir Arthur adds a comment that explains, perhaps, why he killed off *Sherlock Holmes,* and was forced by public sentiment to resuscitate him:

I do not wish to be ungrateful to *Holmes,* who has been a good friend to me in many ways.

If I have sometimes been inclined to weary of him, it is because his character admits of no light or shade. He is a calculating-machine, and anything you add to that simply weakens the effect.

Thus the variety of the stories must depend upon the romance and compact handling of the plots. I would say a word for *Watson* also, who in the course of seven volumes never shows one gleam of humor or makes one single joke. To make a real character one must sacrifice everything to consistency, and remember Goldsmith's criticism of Johnson that "he would make the little fishes talk like whales."

I do not think that I ever realized what a living actual personality *Holmes* has become to the more guileless readers, until I heard of the very pleasing story of the char-à-bancs of French schoolboys who, when asked what they wanted to see first in London, replied unanimously that they wanted to see *Mr. Holmes's* lodgings, in Baker Street. Many have asked me which house it is, but that is a point which, for excellent reasons, I will not decide.

Harry Hansen of the New York *World* confesses to the same interest as possess the French schoolboys in the locale of *Holmes's* life:

Sherlock Holmes lived on Baker Street, you will recall, hard by what is now Waterloo Station of the Underground, in that district of Georgian houses, with colorless brick fronts, little windows, iron hand-rails at the doors, and chimney-pots. And Baker Street is not very far from Piccadilly, the Strand, Trafalgar Square, and Whitehall, where the trade and politics of the seven seas were somehow unraveled and routed throughout the later nineteenth century.

I myself have stood in Baker Street and surveyed a supposititious upper story, wondering whether *Sherlock Holmes* was standing beside the dark hangings of the windows, looking up and down for a hansom-cab with a suspicious driver. I have wondered just how *Moriarty* went about it to "make the place safe," as he called it, and pictured the streets bare of traffic and pedestrians, pervaded with a feeling of imminent danger.

Stepney I have never seen, but every "gas-house" that I viewed from the windows of the London and Chatham filled me with a queer dread. All the time I knew that this was fiction, and that I was merely indulging in an imaginative intoxication.

But that, particularly, was Conan Doyle's long suit—the ability to make things plausible and real. And he did so by being superficial to a degree, giving the reader's mind a chance to catch up with him and elaborate the pattern.

Great fiction is that which betrays a great mind behind it—of such is Dostoyefsky, Tolstoy. But popular fiction gives the reader a chance, and the mind that writes it best is the mind only a step above the average.

Had Conan Doyle been a thoroughgoing scientist, he would never have created *Sherlock Holmes;* had he been a seer, he would never have retained his interest in the vain traffics of this generation.

Conan Doyle died on July 7, and the newspapers devote unusual space to him and his work, but always *Sherlock Holmes* seems to be present. *The World* sums him up:

The death of Sir Arthur Conan Doyle leaves a gap in the ranks of British men of letters. He ranged in many fields. He was a war historian. In such studies as "The White Company" and "Micah Clarke" he showed a mastery of the well-documented historical novel. In "The Lost World" and "The Valley of Fear" he trenched upon an early field of H. G. Wells's, that of scientific extravaganza. He showed the reformer's social instinct in "The Case of Oscar Slater," an English parallel of the Mooney case, here.

But incomparably his greatest work was that which Doyle himself valued least.

Some hold it curious, remarks Heywood Broun in the New York *Telegram,* "that the creator of the agnostic *Holmes* should himself turn ardent spiritualist." But—

In this I see no lack of logic. Indeed, it was an inevitable development. Any one who had given over his thoughts to the solution of mysteries must necessarily have tackled, sooner or later, the major problem. And Conan Doyle undertook to explore territory where even *Holmes* was of no use to him. This was not a case to be solved by a rare tobacco ash, a curious Indian poison, or any sort of footsteps.

221 B

By Vincent Starrett

Here dwell together still two men of note
Who never lived and so can never die:
How very near they seem, yet how remote
That age before the world went all awry.
But still the game's afoot for those with ears
Attuned to catch the distant view-halloo:
England is England yet, for all our fears—
Only those things the heart *believes* are true.

A yellow fog swirls past the window-pane
As night descends upon this fabled street:
A lonely hansom splashes through the rain,
The ghostly gas lamps fail at twenty feet.
Here, though the world explode, these two survive,
And it is always eighteen ninety-five.

As a fitting close to this section on serious Sherlockiana, here is Vincent Starrett's classic and sentimental Holmesian poem, "221 B," from Two Sonnets, *a very hard-to-find pamphlet published by Edwin B. Hill in 1942.*

Opposite page: detail of a fine drawing by Lee Conrey that accompanied a 1928 article, "Hist! Be Your Own Detective!" in a supplement feature distributed that year by the Philadelphia Ledger *syndicate.*

COMIC STRIPS AND CARTOONS

American use of the Sherlock Holmes image—in close semblance to his description by Doyle and depiction by Paget and Steele, or, far more often, in comic and even grotesque adaptation—found comic strips and cartoons an exceedingly rich field. One of the very earliest uses of Holmes's image in a comic strip occurred in an occasional daily feature by H. A. MacGill drawn in 1904 for the editorial pages of Hearst afternoon papers. Basically filler, the Padlock Bones strip did show a bit of wit at times, notably evidenced here in the Boston episode. But the strip did not catch on; it "died" after seven episodes published over some three weeks.

PADLOCK BONES, THE DEAD-SURE DETECTIVE.

PADLOCK BONES, THE DEAD SURE DETECTIVE.

Padlock Bones, the Dead Sure Detective.

GURLOCK HOLMES JOINS IN HUNT FOR BUNK--BY TAD.

Latest Details of Sausage-Teddy Bear Murder.

BUNK NOT FOUND!

By Tad

THE great Sausage–Teddy Bear murder is still unsolved. The police of New York and Sherlock Holmes are scouting all over for Bunk, the suspect, and have run down many false clews.

Paul Fedink, the great sleuth who came over from Paris to join the hunt, is all in from want of sleep. Oswald Schmalz, the star witness, who saw Bunk on the night of the murder, is still missing. Maudie Frankfurter (Countess de Coney), who came from Chicago to aid searchers, is distracted; has not left her apartments since her arrival. Says she will spend her last bean in prosecution.

The District Attorney has Flossie Giggle, the ballet dancer, in the Tombs and is trying to find out how much money Bunk blew in. She was put through the third degree, but they couldn't get a word out of her. Says she will croak before she squeals on her old pal Bunk.

Mrs. Bunk is sure her son is innocent. She says she will hear from him soon, and that he will come back and face the charges. Had always been a model son and never could commit such crimes. Harlem greatly excited over report that Bunk was seen running down Amsterdam avenue with loaded revolver.

Police find that Jeremiah Bunk, great-granduncle of Bunk, who died in the bughouse, went nutty from too much oil of joy. Had been a fierce booze fighter, and they think Bunk may have been soused when these deeds were done.

Dear Tad:
　Will some one please find little Bunk,
　　I miss his funny face.
　Some say he fled the sporting page—
　　Is hiding in disgrace
　For having slain a frankfurter,
　　The rarest of its kind.
　'Tis false, I'm sure. Bring back our Bunk,
　　Relieve my troubled mind.

　　　　　Yours in distress,
　　　　　MRS. D. A. NUNNELLY.

New York City.

The origin of the "Curlock Holmes" name used by Wex Jones in his aforementioned (but weak) "Foiled in Washington" burlesque is to be found in Tad Dorgan's then-unnamed daily sports-page comic-strip continuity for the Hearst New York Evening Journal of January 22, 1907, reproduced above with the "news story" that accompanied the first installment of the comic. Drawn as a parody of the prolonged and highly sensational Harry Thaw trial of the time, Dorgan's frankfurter- and dog-populated strip quickly developed a pace and comic excitement of its own, turning casual Journal readers into daily regulars while Dorgan kept the madcap antics of his canine and sausage characters rolling.

Having gotten his chief character, a dog named Bunk, accused of the frankfurter murder, Dorgan felt called upon to introduce some sleuths to sic on his trail. First and foremost among these, needless to say, was the English bulldog named Curlock Holmes, who quickly became a regular character of the Dorgan strip. (Some years later, when the ubiquitous Doyle representatives seem to have noticed Curlock, his name was quietly changed to Curlock Bones—actually a more appropriate and intrinsically funnier name.) Dorgan's strip, which never had a permanent name itself (the longest-running and best-known story title was "Silk-Hat Harry's Divorce Suit"), is represented on the next two pages by further episodes involving Curlock Holmes/Bones. The dates are, in order: January 23, 1907; January 29, 1907; March 8, 1907; March 19, 1907; and April 1, 1907.

A final small Curlock Bones cartoon on page 157 shows that he had become much less canine with the years; the cartoon is dated March 26, 1921, and is reproduced as it appeared in the San Francisco Call and Post.

HOLMES' GOAT GONE!!

GREAT LONDON WIZARD SEEMS TO BE UP AGAINST IT.

SPENDS TWO NIGHTS WITHOUT SLEEP ON SAUSAGE MYSTERY

FEDINK SAYS HOLMES IS A LEMON AND HAS MUDDLED UP THE CASE

BUNK STILL AT LARGE.

CURLOCK HOLMES IN HIS DEN. FIRST PHOTO SHOWING WORLD FAMOUS SLEUTH.

GREAT LONDON SLEUTH CAPTURES BUNK IN MONKEY HOUSE—DRAWN BY TAD.

BUNK ARRAIGNED AND LONG-DELAYED HEARING IN FAMOUS FRANKFURTER MURDER CASE OPENED AT LAST

SCHMALZ SWIMS AWAY FROM SLEUTHS UNDER FROZEN RIVER. MOST IMPORTANT WITNESS FOR THE PROSECUTION STILL AT LARGE. OLD CAD COLLIER OFFERS AID.

ALOYSIUS BUNK BROTHER OF DEFENDANT REFUSES TO BE QUOTED. TELLS MISS WRIGGLE OF THE BUGVILLE BANNER THAT PAPERS ARE LYING ABOUT HIS FAMILY.

FIRST PICTURE OF DELPHIN MICHAEL SASSAFRAS BUNK'S LAWYER.

BUNK CHLOROFORMS GUARD; ESCAPES FROM JAIL AND MEETS OSWALD SCHMALZ.---DRAWN BY CARTOONIST TAD

BUNK CHLOROFORMS THE JAILER AND MAKES HIS GETAWAY

BUNK MEETS OSWALD SCHMALZ AS HE IS HEADED TOWARDS THE PINK LINE STEAMERS

WORLD'S GREATEST MAN HUNTERS ON THE JOB!

AT LAST-T-! NOW-FOR SOME FOREIGN CLIME

BUNK'S THRILLING ESCAPE FROM THE SIDE WINDOW----

CURLOCK HOLMES NOTED DETECTIVE WHO HAS MORE CLUES THAN A PIPE HAS PUFFS.

PRIDE OF SCOTLAND YARD. DECLARES THAT OTHER SLEUTHS IN BIG CASE ARE A BUNCH OF DUMB BELLS. SAYS THEY SHOULD WEAR BLACK HATS BEING DEAD FROM THEIR JAW BONES UP.

'Tis Our Old College Chum—*Sherlock Guck, the Eskimo Detective!*

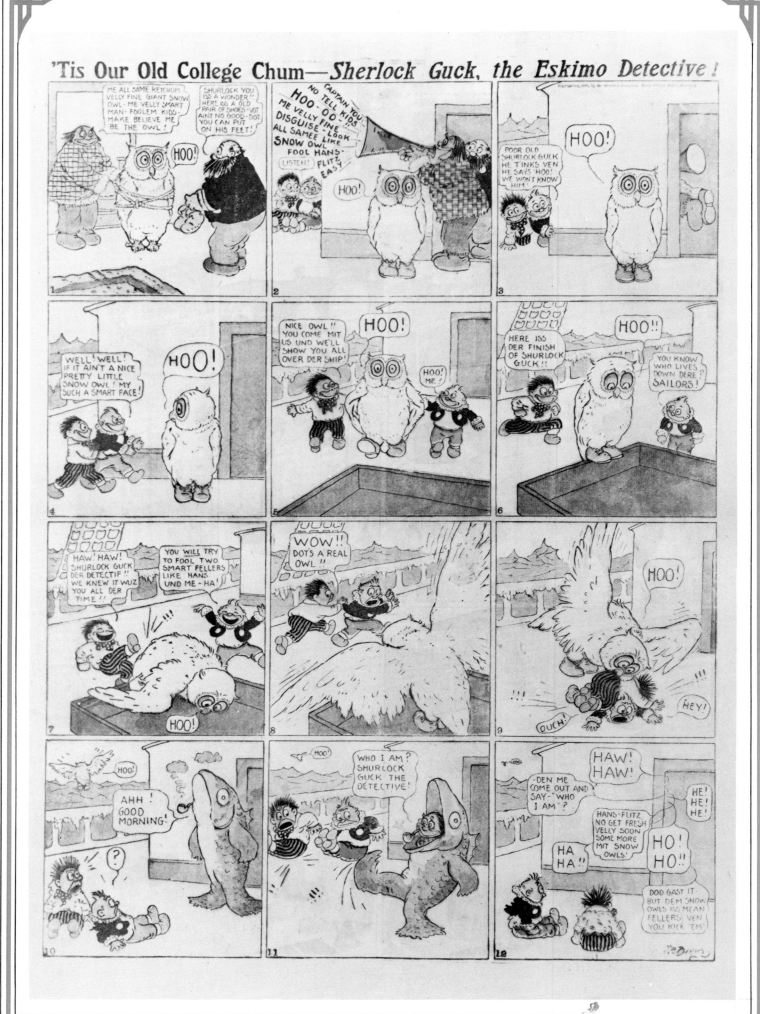

Buck Nix Has an Experience
in London with Sherlock Holmes

By Sidney Smith

Sidney Smith, who later created Sherlock Holmes Jr. *and* The Gumps, *drew his earliest Sherlockian strip image in this* Buck Nix *episode for April 28, 1911, which appeared in the* New York American *and other morning Hearst papers. (Buck has, incidentally, just arrived in London from the United States when this sequence opens.)*

Opposite page: Sherlockian tomfoolery has been incorporated by artist Rudolph Dirks into this early example of his Katzenjammer Kids. *The strip, reprinted here in black-and-white, is from June 9, 1907; another example with "Sherlock Guck" in the strip is to be found at the start of the color comics section.*

Charles W. Kahles, one of the most indefatigably dedicated of all comic-strip artists, introduced two Sherlockian caricatures into his famed Hairbreadth Harry strip: Silk Sock Sam, in the Sunday half-pages above and below, for October 15 and December 1, 1911, and Sniffen Snoop, opposite, in the full-page strip for September 27, 1924. Sniffen Snoop became a regular character in Kahles's daily strip, as well as in his successor, F. O. Alexander's. A final two episodes (page 162, top), from March 9, 1929, and February 4, 1933, are typical—but Snoop occasionally triumphs over Harry, even if only briefly.

HAIRBREADTH HARRY
BY C.W. KAHLES

THE CLANGOROUS TRAIL

HAIRBREADTH HARRY—A Detective Story
By C. W. Kahles

Registered U. S. Patent Office

OUR READERS WOULD BE INTERESTED IN KNOWING JUST HOW YOU GO ABOUT SOLVING YOUR GREAT CRIME MYSTERIES

QUITE SIMPLE. MERELY BY A PROCESS OF ELIMINATION, DEDUCTION AND KEEN OBSERVATION

FOR INSTANCE, THIS IS THE ANNIVERSARY OF THE GREAT BLIZZARD OF 1888 AND IF YOU WILL STEP TO THE WINDOW I WILL ILLUSTRATE TO YOU WHAT I MEAN

YOU WILL NOTE THAT THE SKY IS DARKLY OVERCAST, LIKE AN OPAQUE, DRAB SMUDGE, AND I DEDUCE FROM THAT CIRCUMSTANCE, LOGICALLY, THAT WE ARE IN FOR ANOTHER GREAT BLIZZARD

BUT, SNIFFEN—

— QUITE THE CONTRARY; THE SUN IS SHINING BRIGHTLY, AND I DEDUCE FROM THAT CIRCUMSTANCE THAT YOUR WINDOW NEEDS WASHING BADLY.

BAH!

THE CUB REPORTER INTERVIEWS SNIFFEN SNOOP, THE GREAT DETECTIVE

Copyright, 1929, by Public Ledger

HAIRBREATH HARRY
Greetings Between Sleuths!
By F. O. ALEXANDER

THIS IS THE ENTRANCE TO THE VILAS VENTNOR ESTATE, SIR......

SUPPOSE WE GET OUT HERE THEN, INSPECTOR.

MR. VENTNOR'S ORDERS TO STOP EVERYONE, SIR!

VERY GOOD ORDERS TOO, MY FRIEND! I AM INSPECTOR NEWBERGH AND MY COMPANION IS MR. HOLLINGSWORTH, A PRIVATE DETECTIVE!

I SEE ANOTHER PROFESSIONAL SLEUTH IS ON THE JOB....

THOSE ARE YOUR OWN FOOTPRINTS YOU ARE EXAMINING, YOU KNOW, SNIFFEN! I SHOULD KNOW THEM ANYWHERE!

Four early examples of Gus Mager's amusing forerunner to his classic and long-lived Hawkshaw the Detective *follow, below and on the opposite page. It was called* Sherlocko the Monk, *in faint echo of the animal-character strip from which it evolved. The single panel below, seen in the New York Evening Journal on Saturday, January 20, 1912, promoted Mager's "Monkey Joke Book." The Sherlocko strip at page bottom is an episode of February 18, 1912, which ran in most Hearst evening newspapers. The two episodes opposite are from March 10 and November 28, 1911.*

Sherlocko the Monk Does Some Deducing---By Gus Mager

I DEDUCE FROM THIS BANANA PEEL, WATSO, THAT YOU DID NOT DO THAT SOMERSAULT INTENTIONALLY!

Sherlocko the Monk
The Exasperating Adventure of the Blundering Assistant
Copyright, 1912, by the National News Association
By Gus Mager

WATSO, I HAVE GAINED THE CONFIDENCE OF BLACK PETE'S GANG. WE ARE TO ROB MORGO'S HOUSE TO-NIGHT. YOU CONCEAL YOURSELF THERE AND SPRING OUT WHEN YOU HEAR ME SAY "PLENTY OF SWAG"!

COME ON PALS, I SWIPED THE KEYS OF MORGO'S HOUSE!

GOOD FOR YOU, SKINNY, THAT MAKES IT AN EASY JOB!

PLENTY OF SWAG!

PRETTY SOFT!

A RICH HAUL!

PLENTY OF SWAG! PLENTY OF SWAG! PLENTY OF SWAG!

COME ON SKINNY, SKIP!

WATSO, HOW LONG DID YOU WANT ME TO SHOUT "PLENTY OF SWAG"? HADN'T YOU BRAINS ENOUGH TO RESPOND TO THE SIGNAL BEFORE OUR BIRDS HAD FLOWN?

GEE, I COULDN'T REMEMBER THE SIGNAL. I THOUGHT IT WAS "PUT IT IN THE BAG!"

Sherlocko the Monk

The Strange Case of the Missing Horse

Copyright, 1911, by the National News Association

Sherlocko the Monk ❧ ❧ By Gus Mager

Here and on four additional pages following the color comics section are several gems of early Hawkshaw by Gus Mager—full-page Sunday episodes printed in the New York World and centering on the 1913–14 pursuit of the "Great Bulbul Ruby." Dates for the episodes are: December 7, 1913; January 17, 1914; February 1, 1914; March 22, 1914; and April 26, 1914. One further "Ruby" episode is included in the color comics section; its date is January 11, 1914. (For more details about the extraordinary Hawkshaw strip, see Sherlocko the Monk *[Westport, Conn.: Hyperion Press, 1977].)*

Rudolph Dirks contributed one of the most bizarre Sherlockian spoofs in comic strips in his Katzenjammer Kids *Sunday page for June 2, 1907. A second "Sherlock Guck" story in the* Katzenjammer Kids *appears in the black-and-white comics section.*

On this and the next three pages are included eight Sunday-page examples of Gus Mager's memorable Hawkshaw the Detective *strip. The dates, in the order of the strip episodes, are: August 24, 1913; January 11, 1914; December 27, 1931; February 21, 1932; April 17, 1932; December 4, 1932; February 26, 1933; and August 13, 1933. (The last three episodes shown here were drawn by Bernard Dibble, working from Mager material.)*

Hawkshaw the Detective in England With the Bulbul Ruby

Among the comics illustrations shown in black-and-white only are several more episodes of the long-running "Bulbul Ruby" tale above, as well as three strips of Sherlocko the Monk, Gus Mager's forerunner to Hawkshaw.

CLASSIC COMICS

NO. 33

FEATURING STORIES BY THE WORLD'S GREATEST AUTHORS

The ADVENTURES of

SHERLOCK HOLMES

10¢
PDC.

15¢ IN CANADA

by
Sir ARTHUR
Conan DOYLE

RACHE

H.C.KIEFER

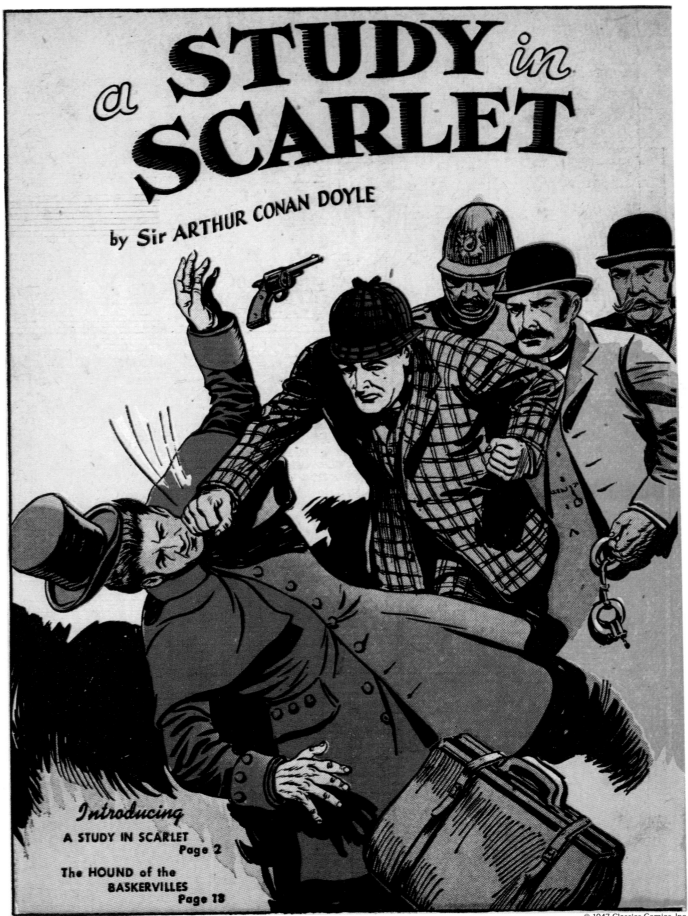

a STUDY in SCARLET

by Sir ARTHUR CONAN DOYLE

Introducing
A STUDY IN SCARLET
Page 2

The HOUND of the
BASKERVILLES
Page 13

© 1947 Classics Comics, Inc.

Not surprisingly, the Classic Comics comic book series of the 1940s seized on the Sherlock Holmes stories in public domain, producing some pungent art in the process. Two examples of this appear on this page and the page opposite, from the cover and inside first page of Classic Comics number 33, the art by H. C. Kiefer.

H. H. Knerr, who drew the nation's second Katzenjammer family strip for the Hearst papers, also drew (above) Dinglehoofer and His Dog Adolph. *In this April 8, 1928, strip Knerr introduced a "Holmesian" type—complete with a "Watson." Some strip artists used Sherlockian trappings for humorous head panels, rather than in the actual content of their strips; in mid-page are four such uses, two in Sunday-page logo panels from Harold Gray's* Little Orphan Annie *(August 6, 1927, and June 24, 1928) and two from Clare Briggs's* Mr. and Mrs. *(December 7, 1930, and May 5, 1935). At page bottom: a Mickey Mouse half-page for December 10, 1939, in which Goofy plays "Sherlock," as he had done before in the strip.*

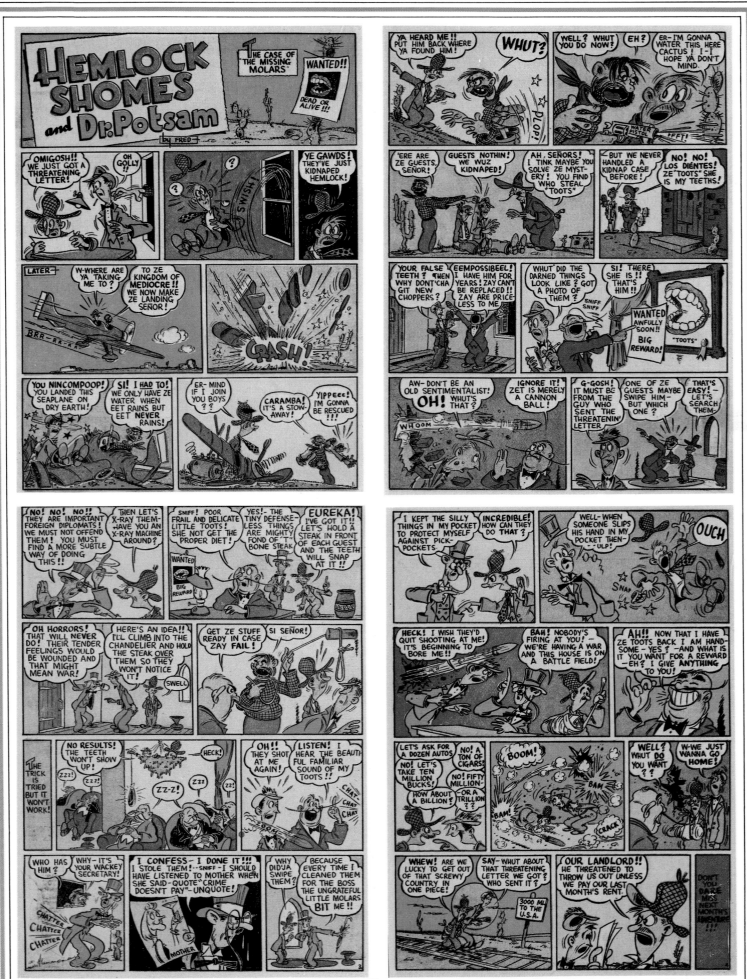

The superhero comic books of the 1930s and 1940s often used humorous filler strips. Among these were some Sherlockian burlesques, notably Hemlock Shomes and Dr. Potsam *by Fred Filchock in* Mystery Men Comics, *and* Padlock Homes *by Ed Wheelan in* Champ Comics *and other magazines. Above is a* Hemlock Shomes *story from* Mystery Men Comics, *number 3, October 1939, followed on the next three pages by two* Padlock Homes *episodes—from* Champ Comics, *number 22, September 1942, and* Speed Comics, *number 29, November 1943.*

Sidney Smith's very remarkable Sherlock Holmes Jr. appeared in the Chicago Tribune just prior to World War I, at about the same time Mager's Sunday Hawkshaw page was getting under way. A very funny half-page gag strip, the Smith comic was striking in its cavalier dismissal of the standard Sherlockian graphic trappings. Smith's hero deigned to smoke a pipe (though not a calabash) and wear a cap (but not a deerstalker)— but only in very early episodes of the strip. Later, even these elements were dropped, and the hero looked quite ordinary, indeed, for anyone calling himself Sherlock Holmes, even in a junior version. (Buster Keaton's film Sherlock Jr., of 1924, may possibly have derived its title from Smith's strip; like Smith's hero, Keaton scorned the popular Sherlockian regalia in his title role.) The Doyle representatives, active as ever, seem to have ferreted out the Tribune strip in their slow but exceedingly fine grind, for after a year or so of publication its title was abruptly changed to Pussyfoot Sam on January 15, 1914; it expired shortly thereafter. The episodes here date from April 21, 1913; May 4 and 25, 1913; June 8 and 29, 1913; and July 27, 1913.

SHERLOCK HOLMES JR. TRIES A NEW TRICK

SHERLOCK HOLMES JR. GETS COLD FEET.

SHERLOCK HOLMES JR. DISGUISE EXPERT.

SHERLOCK HOLMES JR. MAKES A GENUINE HAUL

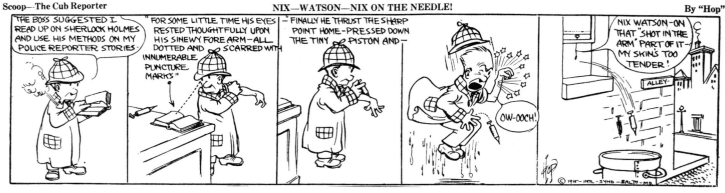

NEITHER OF THE TWO GENTLEMEN CAN TOUCH THE CHIEF   By "Hop"

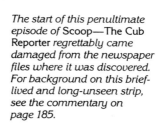

The start of this penultimate episode of Scoop—The Cub Reporter regrettably came damaged from the newspaper files where it was discovered. For background on this brief-lived and long-unseen strip, see the commentary on page 185.

C. A. Voight's *Petey*, above, did an amusing week-long turn based on the theft of a potato; the four panels reproduced are the only episode involving "the detective," rather Sherlockian-garbed (May 5, 1917).

Opposite page: Long forgotten (except by Senator Henry "Scoop" Jackson, who received his nickname from the strip), this amusing comic of small, largely Southern newspaper circulation was uncovered in a file of the Birmingham Age-Herald by the San Francisco Academy of Comic Art—at which time the Sherlockian sequences here (from April 26 to 30, 1915) were brought to light. The number and variety of Sherlockian clichés burlesqued in these five episodes very likely surpass the record of any other comic-strip satire published over so short a span of time.

Bud Fisher's *Mutt and Jeff*, in the March 24, 1919, episode below, showed Jeff in Holmesian gear. On the following page, a lengthier strip, from February 4, 1928, has Mutt as the detective.
  At the top of page 187 may be seen a segment of Jerry Costello's today-little-known Sunday page, *Cosmo*, which often had Sherlockian content along the lines shown in the first three panels of an episode for March 8, 1921.

MUTT AND JEFF—Jeff's More Like Sherlock Holmes Than Holmes Is Himself ∴ *By Bud Fisher*

MUTT AND JEFF   :-:   Mutt a la Sherlock Holmes   :-:   By BUD FISHER

COSMO
HE'S A WONDER!
by Jerry Costello

The Sensational Episode of the Wooden Leg

Below, and on the following page, it may be seen that Elzie Crisler Segar, creator of one of the great popular images of our time—Popeye the Sailor—was obsessed with the endless comic possibilities of Sherlockian caricature. Into his Thimble Theater *strip he frequently introduced Holmesian burlesque, from its inception in 1919 to its effective end with his death in 1938. The* Thimble Theater *episodes reproduced here, from eleven consecutive years, are only representative; they do not exhaust Segar's Holmes burlesques. The dates of the episodes are: November 28 and 29, 1922; August 5, 1927; August 24 and 25, 1932; and February 3 and 4, 1933.*

THE THIMBLE THEATER
"More Than Two Faced"
Registered U. S. Patent Office

© 1922 King Features Syndicate

THE THIMBLE THEATER
Take 'Em Off; We Know You
Registered U. S. Patent Office

© 1922 King Features Syndicate

THIMBLE THEATER
Copyright, 1927, by King Feature Syndicate
Registered at U. S. Patent Office

ALL SAP ISN'T IN TREES

© 1927 King Features Syndicate

187

From *Hotfoot the Detective*, through *Gimlet the Detective* and *Merlock Jones* to *Hancock Homes*, Segar remained original and inimitable in his effects (no one else, anywhere, ever, thought of a Holmes drinking through his pipe), although at points he seems to have based his comic detectives on Thomas W. Hanshew's 1912–19 novel-series hero, Cleek, the Man of the Forty Faces, as much as on Holmes.

THIMBLE THEATRE—Featuring POPEYE—Where There's Smoke There's Fire : : *By E. C. Segar*

THIMBLE THEATRE—Featuring POPEYE—Local Talent : : *By E. C. Segar*

THE GREAT DIAMOND MYSTERY!

A WORLD SERIAL — GALE - CAMERAMAN — BILL HENRY - SCENARIO ED.

SHERLOCK HOLMES GIANTS WHOSE MASSIVE BRAWN IS AT WORK ON THE MYSTERY.

INSPECTOR STRONGARM YANKS WHO IS ALSO TRYING TO SOLVE THE GREAT MYSTERY — WATCH HIM TRY TO GIVE THEM THE THIRD DEGREE! WHO?

THE GELL. DOES HE LOVE HER FOR HERSELF ALONE? AH! THAT'S PART OF THE GREAT DIAMOND MYSTERY!

THE VILLYUN, JASPER JINX ERRORS CU-HEARSE HIM! HE OUT AFTER EVERYBODY!!

KID DOPE, THE MYSTERIOUS STRANGER NEXT RELEASE TOMORROW! DON'T MISS IT!!!

OUR HEROES, SHERLOCK HOLMES GIANTS AND INSPECTOR STRONGARM YANKS HAVE LOCATED THE GAL AND NOW ALL THEY HAVE TO DO IS SAVE HER. FOR WHOM? AH! THAT'S WHERE THE PLOT BEGINS TO THICKEN! — SUBTITLE — TUBE READ TO YOURSELF!

— NEXT EPISODE TOMORROW! IN THIS THEATRE.

OUT IN THE GREAT OPEN SPACES WHERE MEN ARE MEN AND SNAKES ARE REPTILES THE VILLYUN, JASPER JINX ERRORS, DOES HIS STUFF! (SOB TITLE)

"CLOSE" UP OF BABE RUTH

AND THE TWO KIND GENTLEMEN WHO DIDN'T THINK HE HAD ANY TEETH AFTER HIS SHOWING IN THE FIRST GAME!

MEANWHILE OUR HEROES, SHERLOCK HOLMES GIANTS AND INSPECTOR STRONGARM YANKS ARE STILL TRYING TO UNRAVEL THE GREAT MYSTERY. THEY'RE RUNNING NECK AND NECK NOW!

NEXT RELEASE TOMORROW! — GOOD NIGHT!

THAT BUNCH OF GOTHAM GORILLAS SHERLOCK HOLMES STUMBLED INTO FRIDAY SEEM TO BE HITTING THEIR STRIDE AND IT LOOKS LIKE A TOUGH WINTER FOR SHERLOCK — WITH NOTHING IN SIGHT BUT THIS POOR OLD CRIPPLED GENT!

BUT HOLD —
HOLD EVERYTHING!! 'TIS OLD CASEYATTHE BAT STENGEL, THE GORILLA TAMER, HIMSELF! SUB-SUBTITLE — "AND WHAT KELLOGG'S IS TO ANTS, CASEY'S PASTE IS TO YANKS!"

AND SO, ONCE MORE, IS INSPECTOR STRONGARM'S DAY UTTERLY ROONED! "THE BRAIN IS MIGHTIER THAN THE BICEP!"

DON'T MISS THE NEXT EPISODE, TOMORROW!!! GALE

The Los Angeles Times's *Floyd Gale* engaged in continuity-strip narrative run over several days to introduce a Holmesian burlesque in a baseball context, the best episodes of which appear above. They appeared October 10–13, 1923.

Below: Canadian strip artist Arch Dale's fanciful hero, Nicholas Nutt, does a brief Holmesian turn in this March 14, 1923, episode of The Doo Dads.

THE DOO DADS—Nicholas Gets a New Kind of Job   By Arch Dale

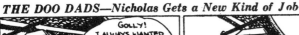

THE GUMPS—The Great Detective

Full Page of The Gumps in Colors in The Sunday Age-Herald

© 1924 Chicago Tribune—New York News Syndicate

BARNEY GOOGLE AND SPARK PLUG—They Thicken the Plot

Registered U. S. Patent Office — By Debeck

BARNEY GOOGLE AND SPARK PLUG—On the Scent at Last

Registered U. S. Patent Office — By Debeck

© 1926 King Features Syndicate

MICKEY MOUSE

By WALT DISNEY

© 1930 Walt Disney Productions

© 1933 Walt Disney Productions

Top of page: The donning of Sherlockian gear by a comic's principal character was, as has been seen, not uncommon. The cap, pipe, and lens do the trick in Sol Hess's The Nebb's *(March 31, 1929). (The seventh, eighth, and ninth panels have been excerpted here from an episode of twelve.)*

In Floyd Gottfredson's daily Mickey Mouse strip (published as by Walt Disney) Sherlockian characters have appeared, and standard characters have donned Sherlockian apparel and gear. The first two panels are from a November 12, 1930, episode; the third panel is from one of October 17, 1933. A full episode, again with Goofy as "Sherlock," may be found in the color comics section.

Opposite, top of page: Creator of Dick Tracy *Chester Gould's first Sherlockian character (and first comic-strip detective!) was in his early Hearst strip,* Fillum Fables. *The episode is for June 17, 1925. Notice how the deerstalker alone works to project the desired Holmesian image.*

Opposite, mid-page: Andy Gump goes maladroitly Sherlockian in an August 22, 1924, episode of Sidney Smith's popular satiric soap-opera comic strip The Gumps—*a disguise dropped immediately after this installment.*

Opposite, bottom of page: Billy Debeck, creator of the most widely acclaimed ne'er-do-well in comics, introduced a lovely Sherlockian caricature in two 1926 (August 26 and 27) daily episodes: a shabby sleuth hot on the trail of the vanished Barney.

The remarkable set of drawings—"comic stamps," as it were—below, by the famed creator of Dick Tracy, *Chester Gould, have never before been noted or reproduced. They originally appeared as tailpieces to three roughly sequential Sunday-page episodes (May 22, June 26, and July 2, 1932) of Gould's short-lived* Cigarette Sadie.

Polly and Her Pals

Above: In the first three panels of this Polly and Her Pals *episode for April 9, 1933, Cliff Sterrett has garbed Ashur Earl Perkins in Inverness cape and deerstalker. Ma and Pa Perkins's trouble-making son not only smokes a calabash but tries out Holmes's violin. Left: A half-page Sunday example of Doc Winner's* Alexander Smart, Esq. *introduced an interesting Sherlockian variation on March 15, 1936.*

Opposite page: The only other full-scale comic-strip burlesque of Holmes before or after Gus Mager's Sherlocko/Hawkshaw *epics was Jim Wallace's* Dinky Dinkerton—Secret Agent 6⅞, *obscurely distributed by a little-known syndicate. Wallace's use of the Holmesian image was nevertheless potent enough to get his work into a number of subscribing newspapers in the late 1930s and early 1940s. Vulgar and obvious, Dinkerton held the reader's attention through his long series of daily mystery-adventures. The five short episodes (beginning and final episodes are shown) are part of a lengthy mystery—a good satire of the 1930s mystery buffs' fascination with "oriental menaces"—that ran from November 6 to December 3, 1939.*

Grace Drayton's Pussycat Princess *Sunday page for August 28, 1935, featured a charming Sherlockian feline who was a recurrent character in the strip at this time. (Only three panels of the episode are shown here.) Below: another cat—more well known to comics readers today. A brief Sherlockian bow is made by an intense aquiline figure in this* Felix the Cat *episode of October 14, 1936—as drawn by Otto Messmer, ghosting for Pat Sullivan.*

© 1949 New York Herald Tribune

A typical comic-strip use of Holmes imagery is seen above in noted Danish cartoonist Mik's Ferd'nand *half-page for May 15, 1949. Below: One of the most amusing latter-day uses of the Sherlockian type in comics is in this Sunday episode of Russ Myers's* Broom Hilda *(December 6, 1971).*

© 1971 Chicago Tribune—New York News Syndicate

FUNKY WINKERBEAN
Opens the Book
On Sherlock Holmes'
Secret Cases

The great Sherlock Holmes is on the sleuth again—this time in the comics pages. And FUNKY WINKERBEAN is the chap who's putting Sherlock on the funny side of Baker Street.

In six special Funky episodes starting Monday, March 13, you'll find Holmes and Dr. Watson solving cases that are more hilarious than hair-raising.

Watch Sherlock Holmes cut a comic caper with FUNKY WINKERBEAN.
Starting Monday in the

CHICAGO
Sun-Times

A special week-long set of Monday–Saturday, March 13–18, 1978, short daily episodes of Tom Batiuk's Funky Winkerbean *represented one of the most novel uses of Holmesian burlesque in comic-strip history: The strip's feature character is effectively dropped to make way for the burlesque content.*

FUNKY WINKERBEAN　　　　　　**Tom Batiuk**

FUNKY WINKERBEAN　　　　　　**Tom Batiuk**

FUNKY WINKERBEAN　　　　　　**Tom Batiuk**

FUNKY WINKERBEAN　　　　　　**Tom Batiuk**

FUNKY WINKERBEAN　　　　　　**Tom Batiuk**

FUNKY WINKERBEAN　　　　　　**Tom Batiuk**

© 1978 Field Enterprises, Inc. Courtesy of Field Newspaper Syndicate

The famed Fred Opper, creator of Happy Hooligan, was at the peak of his talents when the above, his Hearst editorial-page cartoon of November 24, 1909, was drawn and nationally distributed. Opper drew the wryly comic "Honest Man" political-cartoon series for some time, but his personable Holmes and Watson appeared only this one time.

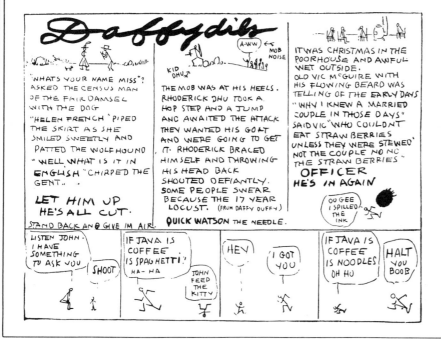

Left: an example of Tad Dorgan's sprightly sports-page prose-and-cartoon feature, Daffydils. The feature was Dorgan's outlet for the verbal humor that animated much of his imagination—and for the wide popularizing of the "Quick, Watson, the needle!" that recurred in innumerable avatars over the years in the Dorgan feature, as exemplified here. The Daffydils at left, with its spoofing of the "dancing men," dates from August 19, 1910; the cartoon above, from September 9 of that year.

DAVID TOBASCO

ANNOUNCES THE APPEARANCE
OF JAMES M. JAMS —
(KNOWN AMONG HIS MANY
FRIENDS AS JIM JAMS)
IN FERDINAND YEGG'S
NEW DETECTIVE DRAMA,
" THE EDUCATED PEANUT "
THE PLAY IS SURE TO HAVE
A LONG RUN BECAUSE
IT HAS NO PLOT AND THERE
IS NO SENSE TO
THE DIALOGUE.

This wonderfully grungy caricaturing of show-man-playwright David Belasco as Holmes was done by Rube Goldberg as part of his daily third-of-a-page graphic feature (it had no name) for the San Francisco Call's *"Page of Sports" for August 26, 1910.*

In political cartooning, "Holmes" (and "Watson") fig-ures were widespread, as can be seen on this and many of the following pages. These two are from a satirical news story in the San Francisco Examiner *for April 4, 1911, and are by artist C. Farr. Farr, a political cartoonist, overlooked the article's continued Nick Carter references in favor of a Sherlockian caricature.*

NICK CARTER, YOU'RE WANTED
❖❖❖   ❖❖❖   ❖❖❖   ❖❖❖
SANTA ROSA SLEUTH HAS CLEW

PLUMBLINE HELPS DETECTIVE TO FIND MISSING GROCERIES

Roy Beide, 18, is a defendant in a case to be tried before Justice of the Peace William Brown, wherein he is charged with the theft of groceries from Auerbach Bros., his former employers. His detection and arrest read like a chapter from the detective classics.

According to Aaron Goldsmith, head of the Goldsmith Detective agency, Beide was employed as driver by the grocers and about a year ago it was observed that goods were disappearing. Suspicion fell upon the young man and soon afterward he disappeared. Goldsmith decided to search the house at 1580 E. 93rd-st, where Beide had resided.

Accordingly he and some of his men went to the place. Goldsmith was convinced that the property was concealed in the house but a search of the residence disclosed nothing. Undaunted Goldsmith sent out for a couple of hammers and some long needles. Then all the walls, floors and ceilings were pounded to find a "hidden chamber" as it were. But to no purpose.

Then Goldsmith got a plumb line and "sinker" and after measuring the distance from the top of the chimney to the base-ment, he borrowed a ladder and went up on the roof. Then he dropped the line down the chimney. To his surprise it didn't go down all the distance.

Investigation showed that the chimney place had been boarded up and that it was filled for some distance with canned milk, cans of tomatoes, corn, peaches, tins of soup and numerous other things. Goldsmith says there was almost a wagon load.

Beide returned to the city recently and was arrested.

William M. Doheny, noted staff artist for the Cleveland Plain Dealer, illustrated the above news item in that paper on February 3, 1912, and produced a charming Holmes with a few swift lines (his Watson is equally interesting).

When We Have Women Detectives—

By T. E. Powers, the Famous Cartoonist

Commissioner Waldo of New York Has Just Appointed a Woman to the Detective Force. Wouldn't an All-Female Force Be Nice!

These four cartoons by T. E. Powers of women in Sherlockian or Hawkshavian guise are among several that (preceded by the sexist heading at page top, slightly rearranged here to fit) accompanied a satire, "Tribes of North America—The Suffragettes," in most Hearst Sunday papers, March 17, 1912. Said Lewis Allen, the article's author: "A woman joins the tribe of suffragettes for only one reason. She wants something she hasn't got. She thinks it is a vote....Men have for ages been treating women as their superiors. Some day they will be egged on until they admit women are only their equal. Then—Weeping suffragettes!"

What Burns Might Have Done

Chuck Harris of the Hearst Chicago American *taunts a city police lieutenant for bungling an arrest (front-page cartoon for September 20, 1912), touching delightfully on a full half-dozen renowned fictional sleuths of the time.*

The use of Sherlockian imagery in sports-page comics was perhaps not as widespread as in political cartoons, but it was by no means infrequent. Here we see a remarkably elongated Holmes, excerpted from a huge, multi-figured football cartoon by Wallace Goldsmith in the Boston Globe *for November 21, 1912.*

The Thrill That Comes Once in a Lifetime. —By Webster

THE DEATH OF
SHERLOCK HOLMES

Copyright, 1921, H. T. Webster

The Thrill That Comes Once in a Lifetime - - By H. T. Webster

PST! A DE-TEC-TUFF!
LOOK! SEE HIS
STAR? GOLLY!
HE DON'T WEAR TH'
SAME KINDA FUNNY
HAT SHERLOCK HOLMES
WEARS. WONDER WHO
HE'S A SHADOWIN'

THE FIRST PEEP AT A
REAL, LIVE DETECTIVE

H. T. Webster, one of the best known of that elite group of syndicated cartoonists who drew daily panels of light social commentary in the first half of the century, was also a founding father of Philadelphia's noted Sherlockian group, the Sons of the Copper Beeches. A lifelong fan of the Doyle canon, Webster devoted at least the eight panels on this and the following page to a central or peripheral concern with Holmes. Few, if any, have ever been reprinted before. The dates of appearance are: top of page, April 25, 1921, and February 11, 1928; bottom of page, April 28, 1928, and March 5, 1929; top of following page, November 23, 1929, and March 21, 1933; bottom of following page, April 16, 1938, and March 11, 1939.

The Thrill That Comes Once in a Lifetime - - By H. T. Webster

THE HOUND OF
THE
BASKERVILLES

The Thrill That Comes Once in a Lifetime --By Webster

IT'S A TRICHINOPOLY
CIGAR ASH, WATSON,
OR MY NAME AIN'T
SHERLOCK HOLMES
YOU MAY RECALL
TH' MONOGRAPH
I WROTE ON CIGAR
ASHES SOME YEARS
AGO

MARVELOUS!

SHERLOCK HOLMES STRIKES
A HOT SCENT —

The Thrill That Comes Once in a Lifetime—By H. W. Webster

SEVERAL YEARS AFTER SHERLOCK HOLMES HAD FOUGHT THE PROFESSOR AND FALLEN OVER A PRECIPICE TO AN UNTIMELY DEATH AND YOU WERE STILL MOURNING YOUR LOSS A MAGAZINE COMES OUT WITH A NEW SHERLOCK HOLMES STORY AND TELLS ALL ABOUT HIS RETURN FROM THE GRAVE

Life's Darkest Moment - - - - - By H. T. Webster

WHY, ALL THOSE PEOPLE ARE JUST FICTITIOUS CHARACTERS, THE AUTHORS INVENTED THEM—MADE THEM ENTIRELY OUT OF THEIR IMAGINATIONS. NOT ANY OF THEM EVER LIVED. I THOUGHT YOU KNEW THAT

WHEN YOU LEARNED THAT CAPTAIN JOHN SILVER, SHERLOCK HOLMES AND HUCK FINN NEVER EXISTED

Life's Darkest Moment

OW-00-0-0-0-0-00H!

THE HOUND OF THE BASKERVILLES

Thrill That Comes Once in a Lifetime

IN THE THIRD WEEK OF NOVEMBER, IN THE YEAR 1895, A DENSE YELLOW FOG SETTLED DOWN UPON LONDON. FROM THE MONDAY TO THE THURSDAY I DOUBT WHETHER IT WAS EVER POSSIBLE FROM OUR WINDOWS IN BAKER STREET TO SEE THE LOOM OF THE OPPOSITE HOUSES. THE FIRST DAY HOLMES SPENT IN CROSS-INDEXING HIS HUGE BOOK OF REFERENCES. THE SECOND AND THIRD HAD BEEN PATIENTLY OCCUPIED UPON A SUBJECT WHICH HE HAD RECENTLY MADE HIS HOBBY—THE MUSIC OF THE MIDDLE AGES. BUT WHEN, FOR THE FOURTH TIME, AFTER PUSHING BACK OUR CHAIRS FROM BREAKFAST WE SAW THE GREASY, HEAVY BROWN SWIRL STILL DRIFTING PAST US AND CONDENSING IN OILY DROPS UPON THE WINDOW-PANES, MY COMRADE'S IMPATIENT AND ACTIVE NATURE COULD ENDURE THIS DRAB EXISTENCE NO LONGER.

SETTING THE STAGE FOR AN EXCITING SHERLOCK HOLMES ADVENTURE

THE DISCREET CONGRESSMAN NOW FILLS HIS CAR WITH HOODS SASAPARILLA ~

In this political cartoon that appeared on the front page of the Los Angeles Record *for June 10, 1924, George Storm, of* Bobby Thatcher *fame, drew an engaging group of Holmeses.*

Above right and below: Hearst newspapers artist Billy Cam is represented here by two of his Holmes caricatures. They are from the Sunday feature sections for September 1, 1929, and February 16, 1930, and illustrate non-Holmesian pieces by Montague Glass and Damon Runyon, respectively.

Quick, Watson, the Stature-Enlarger!

BUSY DAYS FOR SHERLOCK

Above, left and right: two political cartoons. Dorman H. Smith ignores the non-image of Nick Carter to dwell on that of Holmes in the San Francisco Examiner *for January 10, 1930. A caption under the cartoon commented: "The influence of Sherlock Holmes and Nick Carter continues to flourish. Their latest disciple is a former Governor of California, Friend W. Richardson, who is now engaged in prowling about the State armed with political ambition and a dark lantern 'solving' the William Desmond Taylor murder mystery. Cartoonist Smith today shows Big Sleuth Richardson in full regalia." In the second cartoon, of more worldwide focus (as were many of Rube Goldberg's), well-known political cartoonist Vaughn Shoemaker of the* Chicago Daily News *drew a friendly, pipe-puffing Sherlock for the paper's May 11, 1931, edition.*

Below, left: Jimmy Hatlo, later noted for his They'll Do It Every Time *strip and panel, rendered an amusing "Watson and Holmes" cartoon—a Standard Oil advertisement, no less—for the San Francisco* Call and Post *of March 15, 1934. Below, right: For a January 24, 1937, Sunday page, Mush Stebbins—of comic-strip artist Ad Carter's* Just Kids—*does a sprightly Sherlockian turn in the cartoon "Dream Land."*

LOOK BEHIND YOU, SHERLOCK!   By Rube Goldberg.

EVEN THE OLD BOY IS STUMPED.   By Rube Goldberg.

The two Rube Goldberg renderings of Sherlock Holmes above appeared in the New York Sun on, respectively, November 24, 1939, and December 14, 1944.

Below, left: A Consolidated News syndicated Charles Kessler panel cartoon for March 14, 1942, reflected the common recourse of the time to a Holmes story title as the ideal pleasure reading desired by boys. Below, right: This Herblock (Herbert Block) political cartoon from the Washington Post for January 26, 1947, dealt with "un-American" sleuthing in the Senate at that period. It is as witty and memorable as one would expect from a master among American political cartoonists.

SEEMS LIKE YESTERDAY - By C. Kessler

© 1947 Washington Post

"Extraordinary thing, Watson—the clues indicate the killer to have been a man of your exact build and appearance!"

"Perhaps we'd best wait for Inspector Lestrade."

"That's hardly necessary!"

Three of Gahan Wilson's deservedly famous Sherlockian-gag cartoons from Playboy's Gahan Wilson *special issue, 1973 (Chicago, Playboy Press), conclude the cartoons.*

Opposite page: Not story illustrations (as earlier) but stories-in-illustration complete the "Comic Strips and Cartoons" section of the book. The first four, across, are episodes pulled from daily graphic narratives, now little-remembered but once remarkably effective, that were based on the Doyle stories and copyrighted by Doyle himself. They ran in a few American newspapers in 1930—with striking panel art by Leo E. O'Mealia. The stories are undated since the feature was sold in story units, to be published at any time by a given newspaper; these are from the Boston Globe. *In the episodes reprinted here, from stories out of Doyle's* The Memoirs of Sherlock Holmes, *of 1894, it will be seen that O'Mealia has produced a delightfully smiling Holmes in "Silver Blaze" and has depicted Holmes's little-known brother, Mycroft, in "The Greek Interpreter."*

SHERLOCK HOLMES—Silver Blaze—The Lame Sheep—By Sir Arthur Conan Doyle

Silas Brown surlily accompanied Holmes through the gate of the Mapleton stables. Whatever Holmes had whispered to the old horse trainer when the latter had retorted "Lie!", he followed my friend's suggestion that they discuss the matter in Brown's parlor. "I shall only be a few minutes, Watson," Holmes said.

It was twenty minutes before Holmes and the trainer reappeared. Never have I seen such a change in a man as had been brought about in Silas Brown. His bullying manner was all gone, and he cringed along at Holmes' side like a dog with its master. "Your instructions shall be done. It shall all be done," he whined.

"There must be no mistake," said Holmes, and the other winced as he saw the menace in his eyes. "Oh no, it shall be there. Shall I change it first, or not?" Holmes thought a little and burst out laughing. "No, don't," he replied. "I'll write you. No tricks, now...."

On the way to the house Holmes stopped by the paddock where there were a few sheep. He asked a stable-boy: "Have you noticed anything amiss with your sheep of late?" "Only that three of them have gone lame, sir." "A long shot, Watson!" Holmes exclaimed gleefully. "I shall call the Inspector's attention to the singular epidemic among the sheep."

SHERLOCK HOLMES—The Stock Broker's Clerk—A Two-Point Puzzle—By Sir Arthur Conan Doyle

Sherlock Holmes stood by the table with his hands deep in his pockets and his chin upon his breast, regarding the man on the floor, who was beginning to breathe naturally again. "I suppose we ought to call the police now," he said, "but I'd like to give them a complete case when they come."

Hall Pycroft scratched his head. "It's a blessed mystery to me," he declared. "Whatever they wanted to bring me to Birmingham for, and then that?"

"Pooh! All that's clear enough," Holmes returned impatiently. "It's this last sudden move..."

"What do you say, Watson?" Holmes asked me.

"I confess I am out of my depth," I replied. "Oh, surely, if you consider the earlier events in London they can point to only one conclusion," he insisted.

"Well, the whole thing hinges upon just two points," Holmes explained. "The first is the making of Pycroft write a declaration by which he entered the employ of this preposterous company. Do you not see how suggestive that is?"

SHERLOCK HOLMES—The Musgrave Ritual—A New Adventure—By Sir Arthur Conan Doyle

As told by Dr. Watson:
Sherlock Holmes was the most methodical of men, yet the untidiest one that ever drove a fellow-lodger to distraction. His unanswered correspondence was transfixed with a jack-knife into the center of the wooden mantelpiece. He kept his cigars in the coal scuttle and his tobacco in the end of a Persian slipper.

To my mind pistol-practice is an outdoor pastime. Yet Holmes, in one of his strange moods, would sit in the armchair with his hair-trigger, and adorn the opposite wall with a patriotic V R in bullet-pocks. But his papers were my greatest cross. He had a horror of destroying documents, yet he seldom mustered energy to arrange them.

One Winter's night as we sat together by the fire, I ventured to suggest to him that he spend the next two hours in making our room a little more habitable. For his papers had accumulated until every corner was stacked with bundles of manuscript.

"Very well, Watson," Holmes sighed with a rueful face. He went off into his bedroom and in a few moments returned pulling a large tin box. Squatting upon a stool in front of it, he threw back the lid. The box was already a third full of bundles of paper tied with red tape into separate packages.

SHERLOCK HOLMES—The Greek Interpreter—Watson Meets Holmes' Brother—By Sir Arthur Conan Doyle

"My brother Mycroft possesses the powers of deduction to a greater degree than I do, Watson," Sherlock Holmes said to me one evening. I had suggested that my friend's remarkable abilities were due to systematic training rather than heredity. Holmes' mention of his brother surprised me, as he had never spoken of him before.

We set out almost at once for the Diogenes Club, for I had fallen in promptly with Holmes' invitation to meet Mycroft. My companion talked of his brother. "If the art of the detective began and ended in an easy chair," Holmes observed, "Mycroft would be the greatest criminal agent that ever lived. But he is utterly incapable of working out the practical points of a case."

Holmes brought Mycroft to me in the Strangers' Room of the Club. He was a much larger, stouter and older man than Sherlock, but his face had something of the sharpness of expression so characteristic in his brother. We sat down at the window, and the brothers matched wits in some astonishing deductions about the passersby.

"By the way, Sherlock," said Mycroft after awhile, "I have had something quite after your own heart—a most singular problem—submitted to me." He scribbled a note on a leaf of his notebook, and gave it to a waiter. "I have asked Mr. Melas to step over," he explained.

SHERLOCK HOLMES

BASED UPON THE WORKS OF SIR ARTHUR CONAN DOYLE

ILLUSTRATED by FRANK GIACOIA

Reprinted here is a week's daily continuity of The Hound of the Baskervilles *from the Edith Meiser and Frank Giacoia* Sherlock Holmes *strip of the early 1950s—these from September 1955, as can be seen in various panels. Authorized by the Doyle Estate and broadly supervised by contingents of the American Sherlockian body known as the Baker Street Irregulars, this painstakingly accurate and lovingly done strip represents the high point in Holmesian adaptation within the strip medium. A timeless work, and one too swiftly interred by its syndicate, the Meiser and Giacoia* Sherlock Holmes *should be revived for contemporary newspaper publication.*

© 1955 New York Herald Tribune

MR. HOLMES OF BAKER STREET

by William Barry

SIR HENRY TOLD SHERLOCK HOLMES OF HIS LATEST ROBBERY.

BASED ON STORIES OF A Conan Doyle

©1976 William H. Barry
distributed by Adventure Feature Syndicate

"LAST NIGHT THEY TOOK ONE OF MY NEW BOOTS AND TODAY THEY HAVE SNEAKED ONE OF THE OLD ONES."

"WHAT DO YOU MAKE OF IT, MR. HOLMES?"

4/16

"WE ARE DEALING WITH A CLEVER MAN, SIR HENRY. I DON'T PROFESS TO UNDERSTAND IT, YET WE HOLD SEVERAL THREADS IN OUR HANDS."

HOLMES AND WATSON DINED WITH SIR HENRY BASKERVILLE.

BASED ON STORIES OF A Conan Doyle

"YOU DID NOT KNOW, DR. MORTIMER, THAT YOU WERE FOLLOWED THIS MORNING?"

4/17

©1976 William H. Barry distributed by Adventure Feature Syndicate

"I THINK, SIR HENRY," SAID HOLMES, "THAT YOUR DECISION TO LEAVE FOR BASKERVILLE HALL IS A GOOD ONE."

"FOLLOWED! FOLLOWED BY WHOM?"

SHERLOCK HOLMES ADVISED HIS NEW CLIENT.

"SIR HENRY, YOU MUST TAKE DR. WATSON WITH YOU TO DEVONSHIRE. HE MUST BE ALWAYS BY YOUR SIDE."
©1976 William H. Barry
distributed by Adventure Feature Syndicate

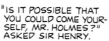

"IS IT POSSIBLE THAT YOU COULD COME YOURSELF, MR. HOLMES?" ASKED SIR HENRY.

"NO, IT IS IMPOSSIBLE FOR ME TO BE ABSENT FROM LONDON AT THIS TIME..."

4/19

BASED ON STORIES OF A Conan Doyle

SUDDENLY THERE WAS A KNOCK AT THE DOOR!

©1976 William H. Barry
distributed by Adventure Feature Syndicate

THE SUMMONED CABBY ENTERED THE HOTEL ROOM.

4/20

"MY NAME IS JOHN CLAYTON. MY CAB IS NUMBER 2704 OUT OF SHIPLEY'S YARD, NEAR WATERLOO STATION."

"VERY GOOD OF YOU TO COME SO QUICKLY, MR. CLAYTON."

BASED ON STORIES OF A Conan Doyle

"NOW, CLAYTON, TELL ME ALL ABOUT THE FARE WHO FOLLOWED THE TWO GENTLEMEN DOWN REGENT STREET THIS MORNING."

© 1976 Adventure Feature Syndicate

Mr. Holmes of Baker Street, drawn and written by William Barry, is the most recent of the Holmes comic-strip adaptations. Introduced to a largely disinterested American press in 1976, the feature was not long-lived, but has already become—due to its very limited circulation—a major collector's item in Sherlockiana. These four April episodes are, again, of The Hound. Note the very dapper Watson.

PSEUDO-SHERLOCKIAN STORIES AND BURLESQUES: II

John Kendrick Bangs, certainly the most prolific of the better authors of Holmes burlesque, turned out so much Sherlockian spoofery that the amusing example which begins this section went unnoted in even Ronald Burt De Waal's World Bibliography of Sherlock Holmes and Dr. Watson *(Greenwich, Conn.: New York Graphics Society, Ltd., 1974); in fact, Bangs's* Over the Plum-Pudding *(New York: Harper & Bros., 1901) and its Holmesian japery in the book's introduction is still known to only a handful of Sherlockians. The excerpts below, which comprise the Sherlockian content of* Over the Plum-Pudding, *are all from its introduction. (The indicated omissions involve Bangs's burlesques on writers other than Doyle.) The nominal "author" of the text, Horace Wilkinson, is—needless to say—merely a comic invention by Bangs.*

Opposite: Not as little known as Bangs's Over the Plum-Pudding *sketch, but nevertheless a work seldom seen, is Oswald Crawfurd's curious American detective novel,* The Revelations of Inspector Morgan *(New York: Dodd, Mead, 1907), in which one Purlock Hone makes prominent entrance in one of the "Revelations," reprinted here with the book's Introduction. Generally a writer of light romance, Crawfurd embarked on some remarkable fantasies in this episodic book—including one of the few involvements of the scandalous Victorian penny-dreadful hero, Spring-Heeled Jack, in respectable prose.*

Over the Plum-Pudding

By John Kendrick Bangs

I

 HAVE been asked so often and by so many persons known and unknown to me why it was that a Christmas book that was to have been issued some years ago under my editorial supervision never appeared, although announced as ready for immediate publication, that I feel that I should make some statement in explanation of the seeming deception. The matter was very annoying, both to my publishers and to myself at the time it happened, and while I was anxious then to make public a full and candid statement of the facts as they occurred, Messrs. Hawkins, Wilkes & Speedway deemed it the wiser course to let the affair rest for a year or two anyhow.... I must give in brief outline some idea of the contents of the book. It was to be called "Over the Plum-Pudding; or, Tales Told Under the Mistletoe, by Sundry Tattlers. Edited by Horace Wilkinson"—in fact, I hold a copyright at this moment upon this alluring title. Furthermore, it was to be unique among modern publications in that, while professing to be a Christmas book, the tales were to be full of Christmas spirit. The idea struck me as a very original one. I had observed that Fourth-of-July issues of periodicals were differentiated from the Christmas numbers only in the superabundance of advertisements in the latter, and it occurred to me that a Christmas publication containing some reference to the Christmas season would strike the public as novel—and, in spite of the unfortunate overturning of my schemes, I still think so. Messrs. Hawkins, Wilkes & Speedway thought so, too, and gave me *carte blanche* to go ahead, stipulating only that I should spare no expense, and that the stories should be paid for on publication. I was also to enlist the services of the best persons in letters only.

Taking this last stipulation as the basis of my editorial operations, it is not a far cry to the conclusion that I sought to get stories from such eminent writers as Mr. Hall Caine, Dr. Doyle, Mr. Kipling, Richard Harding Davis, Andrew Lang, George Meredith, and myself. There were a few others, but these were people whose light shone forth suddenly and brilliantly, and then went out. I shall have no occasion to mention their names. It is enough to call attention to the fact that ultimately they were all I had left.

* * *

V

IT WAS my pleasure next to have a Sherlock Holmes story from Dr. Doyle, wherein the great detective is once more restored to life, and through an ingenious complication discovers himself. His sudden disappearance, which was never fully explained, did not really result in his death, but in a concussion of the brain in his fall over the precipice which drove all consciousness of his real self from his mind. Found in an unconscious condition by a band of yodelers, he is carried by them into the Tyrolese Alps, where, after a prolonged illness, he regains his health, but all his past life is a blank to him. How he sets about ferreting out the mystery of his identity is the burden of the story, and how he ultimately discovers that he is none other than Sherlock Holmes by finding a diamond brooch in the gizzard of a Christmas turkey at Nice, where he is stopping under the name of Higgins is vividly set forth:

" 'And you have never really ascertained, Mr. Higgins, who you are?' asked Lady Blenkinsop, as they sat down at Mrs. Wilbraham's gorgeous table on Christmas night.

" 'No, madame,' he replied, sadly, 'but I shall ultimately triumph. My taste in cigars is a peculiar one, and no one else that I have ever met can smoke with real enjoyment the kind of a cigar that I like. I am searching, step by step, in every city for a cigar dealer who makes a specialty of that brand who has recently lost a customer. Ultimately I shall find one, and then the chain of evidence will be near to its ultimate link, for it may be that I shall turn out to be that man.' "

Thus the story runs on, and the pseudo-Higgins delights his fellow-guests with the brilliance of his conversation. He eats lightly, when suddenly a flash of triumph comes into his deep-set eyes, for on cutting open the turkey gizzard the diamond brooch is disclosed. He seems about to faint, but with a strong effort of the will he regains his strength and arises.

" 'Mrs. Wilbraham,' he said, quietly and simply—'ladies and gentle-men, I must leave you. I take the 9.10 train for London. May I be excused?'

"The eyes of the company opened wide.

" 'Why—must you really go, Mr. Higgins?' Mrs. Wilbraham queried.

" 'It is imperative,' said he. 'I am going to have myself identified. The finding of this diamond brooch in a turkey gizzard convinces me that I am Sherlock Holmes. Such a thing could happen to no other, yet I may be mistaken. I shall call at once upon a certain Dr. Watson, of London, a friend of Holmes's, who will answer the question definitely.'

"And with a courteous bow to the company he left the room, his usually pale features aglow with unwonted color."

Of course, the surmise proves to be correct, and the great detective once more rejoins his former companions, restored not only to them, but to himself. It was one of the most keenly interesting studies of detective life that Dr. Doyle or any one else has ever given us, and my regret that the story is lost to the world amounts almost to a positive grief.

—Horace Wilkinson

The Revelations of Inspector Morgan

By Oswald Crawfurd

Introduction

THIS collection of stories is an attempt to establish the professional detective police of my own country in that position of superiority to the mere amateur and outsider from which he has been ousted in contemporary fiction.

What I have alleged, with knowledge, of the British detective, I allege on good authority of the American detective. Crime detection is, as no one needs to be told, as international a business, nearly, as diplomacy. The wary criminal sins against his fellow-man and his nation's laws in one country and hides from the Law's vengeance and justice in another. Hence extraditionary pursuit across neighbouring frontiers and over-seas, and the guardian officers of the law, in full chase of the criminal, make friendly inquisition abroad in the interest of justice and order. It is thus that our British officers have come to know and assess the foreign and the American police officer. I betray no official secret when I say that he has not that respect for the foreign detective police that he has for his English-speaking colleague across the Atlantic.

I make claim to represent the methods and opinions of the British detective in the following pages. They are, in point of fact, the biography of a member of our British force, and in drawing up this biography I have unconsciously—for in composing this book I had no thought of addressing an American public—testified in more passages than one to the good opinion which Scotland Yard entertains for the American detective.

To go back for a moment to my original proposition that the professional is a better man than the amateur detective, I stoutly maintain that to think otherwise is a pestilent heresy. Let us not forget, however, to say that this heresy took its rise in the United States. The first preacher of any heresy has always been a man of magnetic and inspiring genius, for without magnetism, inspiration and genius men can no more be led into error than they can be led into the paths of right reason, and the beginner of this particular heresy was that extraordinary genius, your great prose writer and poet, Edgar Allan Poe. No detective stories before or since Poe's time have come anywhere near "The Purloined Letter," "The Gold Bug," and "The Murders of the Rue Morgue." Poe set the fashion in a quite new and interesting branch of literature, and he has had a host of imitators, some of them men of high literary talent, but no one since has struck so true, so human and so thrilling a note as Poe. No one of his successors has come anywhere near to Edgar Allan Poe in the matter of literary style. It must be remembered in favour of Poe's patriotism and good sense that he never disparaged the detective of his own race. His detective amateur, Monsieur Dupin, was a French analytical philosopher, and Dupin's triumph was over the officers of the Parisian police. Poe's successors have neither been so patriotic nor so wise, and the victims of the triumph of the English analytical amateur have invariably been our native detectives.

I confess that the injustice and unfairness in this statement of the facts filled me with indignation long before it occurred to me that a set of fortuitous circumstances had put it in my power to confute this disparagement of a set of men, my own countrymen, whom I knew to be deserving of all praise.

Hence this book, which contains four tales that are, in fact, four indictments and refutations of the prevailing heresy that the amateur is a better detective than the professional.

I ascribe the remarkable popularity and wide circulation which the "Revelations of Inspector Morgan" has attained entirely to the fact that my own feelings of indignation against the injustice so long done—in literature and journalism—to the Professional Detective is shared by a vast number of my countrymen.

I was about to proceed to work my point further, in this introduction and dedication of my work to the American public, when it struck me that the business of a novelist is not to argue and to reason, and that he does wrong to encroach upon the province either of the preacher or the politician. If he have a point to make or doctrine to put forth, let him not depart from his own fictional modes of expression. In other words, if he has anything to say to the public let him not dully "point a moral." Let him tell it in a story.

That is sound sense enough, and as I really have something more to say in disfavour of the ways of the amateur detective I propose to tell it in fiction form. Here is my story. It is told in the character of a worthy gentleman of the medical profession, by name Jobson.

Our Mr. Smith

After a hard day's professional work I was sitting in my little room in Baker Street, deeply meditating on a subject never very long absent from my thoughts. Reader, you can guess what that subject is. I was considering the marvellous analytical faculty of my friend Purlock Hone, when the door opened and Purlock Hone himself appeared on the threshold. In my accustomed impulsive and ecstatic way, not unmingled with that humour which I am proud to say tempers the veneration I feel for that colossal intellect, I was beginning with the trivial phrase, "Talk of the—!" when my friend cut me short, with "Sh," and put his finger on his lips.

He sat down by the fire without a word, deposited his hat, gloves and handkerchief in the coal scuttle (I have before referred to my friend's untidy habits) and reached to the mantlepiece for my favourite meerschaum. He filled the pipe with long cut Cavendish, and, sitting with knotted brows, smoked it to the end before he spoke a word. Then he said:

"Humph!" It was little enough perhaps, but from Purlock Hone it meant volumes.

"Well?" I said. "Go on."

He did. He filled the pipe anew, and, for a second time, smoked it to the bitter end.

"Your pipe, Jobson, wants cleaning!" and he gently threw it upon the fire, from which I rescued it before the flames had done it much injury. From any one else this action had seemed hasty, if not inconsiderate; in this gifted and marvellous being it betokened a profound train of abstract and analytical meditation. I waited patiently for some revelation of the subject of his thoughts.

I need not remind the reader that in the spring of this year the world of international politics was gravely agitated. Menacing rumours were about everywhere, the international atmosphere was electrical and mutterings of the tempest were to be heard on every side, but no one could divine where and when the storm would burst—on whom the bolt would fall.

Mysterious messages were daily passing between the Dowager Empress of China and Kaiser William; what did they portend? President Castro of Venezuela was known to be in secret communication with the Dalai Lama. Our eminent statesman, Mr. Keir Hardie, was said to have despatched an ultimatum to the Emperor of Japan and an identical document to President Roosevelt. The aged wife of the 2d Commissionaire at the

Foreign Office (Irish by birth and of convivial habits) had made certain compromising revelations of the policy of the government in a tavern in Charles Street, Westminster, and the Cabinet of St. James' was already tottering to its fall!

I eagerly recapitulated to my friend these various sources of disquietude to the nation, to Europe and the World, and urged him eagerly to enlighten me as to which of these great world problems he was preparing to solve. His answer was characteristic of this remarkable man, characteristic at once of his geniality, his simplicity, his wonderful self-control, his modesty, and at the same time of his refusal, even to me, to commit himself to an avowal.

"Any one of them, or none—or all; I cannot guess," said Purlock Hone.

My friend could not guess! I forbore from speech, but I smiled when I reflected that I was in the presence of the man who had more than once interposed to save a British Ministry from defeat, who had maintained the balance of power in Europe by discovering a stolen naval treaty, nay, of the man who had restored the jewelled crown of England when it had been lost for nearly three hundred years!

"A penny for your thoughts," said Purlock Hone gaily. "Or, come, you shall hear them from me for nothing."

"I defy you to know what I was thinking of," I said impulsively, but a moment later that defiance seemed to me rash, as in truth it proved to be.

"My dear Jobson," said this greatest of clairvoyants, "if you wanted me not to guess your thoughts you should not have smiled and looked towards the portrait of the late Premier. That told me, as clearly as if you had spoken, that you were recalling my little service to the late Unionist Government. I suppose you are unconscious of the fact, but you distinctly hitched the belt of your trousers as you crossed the room, with a sailorlike roll in your walk; what more was needed to tell me your thoughts were of my modest success in the matter of the lost naval treaty?"

"Amazing! And the recovery of the Crown of England?"

"You have tell-tale eyes, Jobson, and you rolled them regally as you directed them to the print of His Gracious Majesty over the mantlepiece."

"Wonderful man! Stupendous perspicacity!" I muttered.

Purlock Hone filled my rescued pipe for the third time and resumed his smoking. As in most other things, so in his taste for tobacco he resembles no other human being. I happened to know that he had not touched a pipe, a cigar, or a cigarette for a month before.

"Smoking, Jobson, is one of the world's follies. No ordinary man needs tobacco. It is poison!"

"Yet *you* smoke, Hone, even to excess at times," I said.

"I said no *ordinary* man, Jobson," retorted my friend.

I quailed under the justice of the reproof. Any other man would have pressed his victory. He generously forbore.

"I smoke only when some very heavy work is before me," he went on; "not otherwise."

Then I had guessed aright! He had some great work in hand. Never before had I seen so deep a frown between those sagacious eyes, never had the thoughtful face been so pale, the whole physiognomy so enigmatic. Never had so thick a cloud of tobacco smoke issued from between those oracular lips.

"I expect a visitor," he observed presently, between two puffs of tobacco smoke.

"Where?" I asked.

"Here," said Hone simply. "I left word at home that any

one who called at my place was to come on here. Read this!" He tossed a letter across the table. I read aloud:

" 'DEAR SIR: I will do myself the pleasure of waiting upon you between 5 and 6 to-day.

" 'Yours faithfully,
" 'JOHN SMITH.' "

"A pregnant communication, Jobson, eh?"

"I dare say, but I confess I don't see anything peculiar about it." I looked again at the letter. It seemed to me as plain an epistle as any man could write. A dunning tradesman might have written it—a tax collector might have subscribed it.

"What do you make of those *t's*, Jobson? Does the spacing of the words tell you anything? Are those *w's* and *l's* there for nothing?"

"To me, Hone, they are there for nothing, but then—I am not a Purlock Hone."

He smiled as he regarded me with pity, and cocked his left eye, using one of those fascinating and favourite actions of his that bring him down to the level of our common humanity.

"It is a disguised hand, Jobson, and do you observe the absence of an address?"

The lucid and enlightened explanation that I expected was cut short by a ring at the door bell. Immediately afterwards the maid announced Mr. Smith. A little man with grey side whiskers, a neat black frock coat and carrying a somewhat dampish silk umbrella, entered the room.

"Be seated, Mr.—Smith." The slight pause between the last two words of Hone's sentence was eloquent.

"Which of you two gentlemen is Purlock Hone, Esq.?" The accent on which "Mr. Smith" spoke was cockney and the tone deprecating.

I looked to Hone to answer. He smiled upon the stranger. It was a smile of complete approval.

"Admirable!" said my friend. "Pray go on, sir."

The visitor was visibly taken aback.

"I asks a plain question, gentlemen, and I looks to get a plain answer."

"It does you the greatest credit, my dear sir," said Hone. "It would pass almost anywhere."

The little gentleman with grey side whiskers got red in the face and his eyes grew round. He was obviously angry, or was he only acting anger?

My friend Purlock Hone, as I think I have observed before in the course of these memoirs, often smiles, but seldom condescends to laugh.

Our visitor coloured violently and struck the end of his umbrella on the floor. "Look here," he said, "play acting is play acting, but I comes here on business; my name is John Smith, and I don't want none of your chaff."

"Capital! Capital! Go on, Mr.—Smith!"

"I will do so, sir, if *you* please!" The little gentleman put his hand in the inner breast pocket of his coat and produced therefrom a blue envelope; a quick glance at the superscription showed me that it was addressed to my friend and was written in that bold, regular, cursive hand which is characteristic of the man engaged in commercial pursuits. My interest was now strongly roused. I waited eagerly for developments.

The mysterious visitor looked from one to the other of us. "As you two gentlemen refuse to say which of you is Hone, Esq., I'll make so bold as to read this communication to the two of you."

"You may do so with perfect safety, Mr.—Smith. My friend is in my confidence."

The little gentleman cast a puzzled look at us both and read as follows: " 'To Purlock Hone, Esq., Dear Sir—Our Mr. Smith will wait on you in respect of our little account already rendered and which you have no doubt overlooked. Early attention to the same will oblige.' "

The reader paused and looked at my friend. I, too, looked. His face was inscrutable, his lips were grimly closed. My curiosity—shall I say my indiscretion?—got the better of me.

"And whose Mr. Smith may you be, sir?" I asked.

The little man glibly read out the conclusion of the letter; " 'Yours obediently, Dear Sir, Jones and Sons; Hatters; Oxford Street.' And here is the bill, gentlemen. 'To one fancy broad brimmed silk hat; cathedral style;—To one clerical soft felt bowler;—To one slouched Spanish Sombrero;—To one . . .' "

Purlock Hone raised his hand, as if deprecating a list of further items, and Mr. Smith stopped and stared at him.

"What!" I thought. "Is it a real account for hats—after all!" For I remembered all these unusual forms of head-covering having formed parts of the various disguises in which my friend had walked the streets of London, incognito. No! there must be some deep diplomatic secret behind the seemingly simple transaction!

"What is the total amount, Mr. Smith?" asked my friend in muffled tones.

"Nine, eleven, four, sir."

Without another word Hone walked across to my writing table, took his cheque book from his pocket, sat down, and wrote and signed a cheque for nine pounds eleven shillings and fourpence.

"There you are, Mr. Smith. No—don't trouble to give me a receipt. The cheque is to order and Jones & Sons' endorsement will be as good as a receipt."

"Mr. Smith" rose quickly as my friend pronounced these, no doubt, pregnant words, bowed, and took his departure with "I wish you good-morning, gentlemen." He preserved the deprecating attitude and the cockney accent of the small tradesman to the very last.

Purlock Hone preserved a pregnant silence. He slowly filled my pipe for the fourth time with strong Cavendish tobacco. I struck a match and handed it to him. It was my tacit tribute of admiration to the skill with which this mysterious scene, of evidently the highest diplomatic tension, had been played through without a hitch by the two great actors concerned. Words would have failed me—had I attempted to use them. My friend held my wrist while he lit his pipe at my match. His hand did not tremble more than mine—indeed not so much.

"Purlock Hone!" I cried with rising enthusiasm, "if I did not know that a great thing had passed and that Mr. Smith was the emissary of some great European Power and the bearer of some deep international secret, and that you have conveyed a secret reply to some European potentate under the pretence of writing a cheque on your banker, I could have sworn that Mr. Smith was a dunning hatter's assistant, and that you had paid an over-due bill!"

"Jobson, you know I make a rule never to take you in—every one else, but not you. Mr. Smith *was* in point of fact an emissary, but only from Jones & Sons of Oxford Street, and I have paid their bill."

Purlock Hone is one of the few men who can afford to tell the plain truth when it is against him. He is great even in defeat!

The Detective

I WANT to be a plain-clothes man,
　Fierce criminals to trace,
All made up in a deep disguise
　With whiskers on my face.

When I should catch a crafty crook,
　By "make-up" most effective,
I'd snatch my whiskers off, and say:
　"I'm Hawkshaw, the Detective."

Like Sherlock Holmes, one finger-mark
　Would be quite all I'd need
To trace and catch the villain
　Who did the gruesome deed.

When I should catch a crafty crook,
　By "make-up" most effective,
I'd snatch my whiskers off, and say:
　I'm Hawkshaw, the Detective.

All robbers bold would quake with fear,
　So great would be my fame,
They'd pack up and get out of town
　At mention of my name.

I would be known by many names
　In countries far and near;
But "Ole Sleuth" is the one I think
　Would fill 'em full o' fear.

If need be I would trail my man,
　And it would be my pride
To follow him for years—until
　I caught him or he died.

W. W. Denslow, first limner of Frank Baum's Scarecrow, Tin Woodman, Wizard, and other characters in the 1900 classic The Wonderful Wizard of Oz, *drew his only known Sherlockian caricature to illustrate his verses in "The Detective," as published in* When I Grow Up *(New York: Century Co., 1909). Originally tinted in color, the only printed version of the Denslow portrait of Holmes is this one, in black-and-white.*

Sherlock Holmes

Solves the

Mystery of Edwin Drood

THE FAMOUS DETECTIVE APPLIES HIS CRITICAL METHOD
TO THE MOST FASCINATING OF ALL LITERARY PUZZLES

By Harry B. Smith
Author of "Robin Hood," "The Spring Maid," etc.

I—The Mystery of Charles Dickens's Last Novel

IN the novel which he did not live to finish, Dickens had planned a story in which the plot should be the all-important thing, critics having found his other works lacking in plot interest. He determined to construct a novel in the style of his friend Wilkie Collins, with a plot that would keep the reader guessing. He succeeded so well that "The Mystery of Edwin Drood" has been a mystery for more than fifty years.

The following is a brief outline of the story as we have it:

Young *Edwin Drood* and *Rosa Bud* were betrothed in infancy by their parents. They are good friends, but do not love each other. *Drood* has an uncle, *John Jasper*, a musician and a drug addict, who becomes infatuated with *Rosa*. To prevent the pre-arranged marriage, he plans to murder *Drood*.

Jasper cultivates the acquaintance of a stone mason, *Durdles*, his intention being to conceal *Drood's* body in a tomb, to which *Durdles* has the key, and to destroy the body with quicklime. He also creates a feud between *Drood* and a young fellow named *Landless*, on whom he means to cast suspicion of the murder.

Drood disappears, and *Jasper* charges *Landless* with murder; but no body is found, and there has been much talk of *Drood's* going to Egypt to work as a civil engineer. Then, in a very dramatic scene, *Jasper* learns from *Grewgious*, a lawyer, that his supposed motive for the crime did not exist, *Edwin* and *Rosa* having broken off their engagement.

The first problem is—was *Drood* murdered? *Jasper* undoubtedly believes that he killed his nephew; but he is a drug addict, subject to delusions.

Six months later, one *Datchery*, who has evidently disguised himself, takes lodgings near *Jasper*, to watch him and bring him to justice. The second problem in the novel is—who is *Datchery*? He might possibly be any one of six characters in the story, including *Drood* himself.

There are other mysteries, less conspicuous, but more fascinating to the reader; and the plot is perhaps the most interesting in all fiction, because it remains a riddle without an answer—unless, indeed, Mr. Sherlock Holmes's solution proves to be correct.

II—Sherlock Holmes Solves the Mystery

PROVIDENT people whose arrangements for the future include plans for being shipwrecked on a desert island naturally give careful consideration to the selection of books that are to be the companions of their solitude. After making their lists of the volumes that no shipwrecked gentleman's library should be without, they frequently communicate their decisions to the press, giving the benefit of their judgment to others who contemplate oceanic disaster and isolation.

It seems to be a fixed condition precedent that the literary *Crusoe* is to be restricted to ten books—about as many as a sole survivor could be expected to tuck under his arms when a giant wave swamps the life raft. Or perhaps it is assumed that the waves cannot be relied upon to wash ashore more than ten volumes when the good ship goes to pieces on the rocks. Presumably, in the latter case, the castaway recovers consciousness, and, with sinking heart, realizes the sadness of his plight. He

Perhaps the most interesting (and certainly the best organized) of the generally abortive attempts to involve Sherlock Holmes in a "solution" to Dickens's famous unfinished crime novel, The Mystery of Edwin Drood, *is Harry B. Smith's rarely encountered lead story for the Christmas issue of* Munsey *magazine, 1924: "Sherlock Holmes Solves the Mystery of Edwin Drood." Only once reprinted—in a very limited edition in 1934 by Walter Klinefelter of Glen Rock, Pennsylvania—Smith's intriguing novelette does not really necessitate a reader's knowledge of the Dickens text (although it would be a rare reader who would not be inclined to take up the partly completed novel after reading Smith), and holds up well in casual reading today. The* Munsey *color cover is reproduced in black-and-white on page 216. No credit is given in the magazine to the photographer who made the cover shot, or to his slightly effete and puffy-eyed Sherlockian model.*

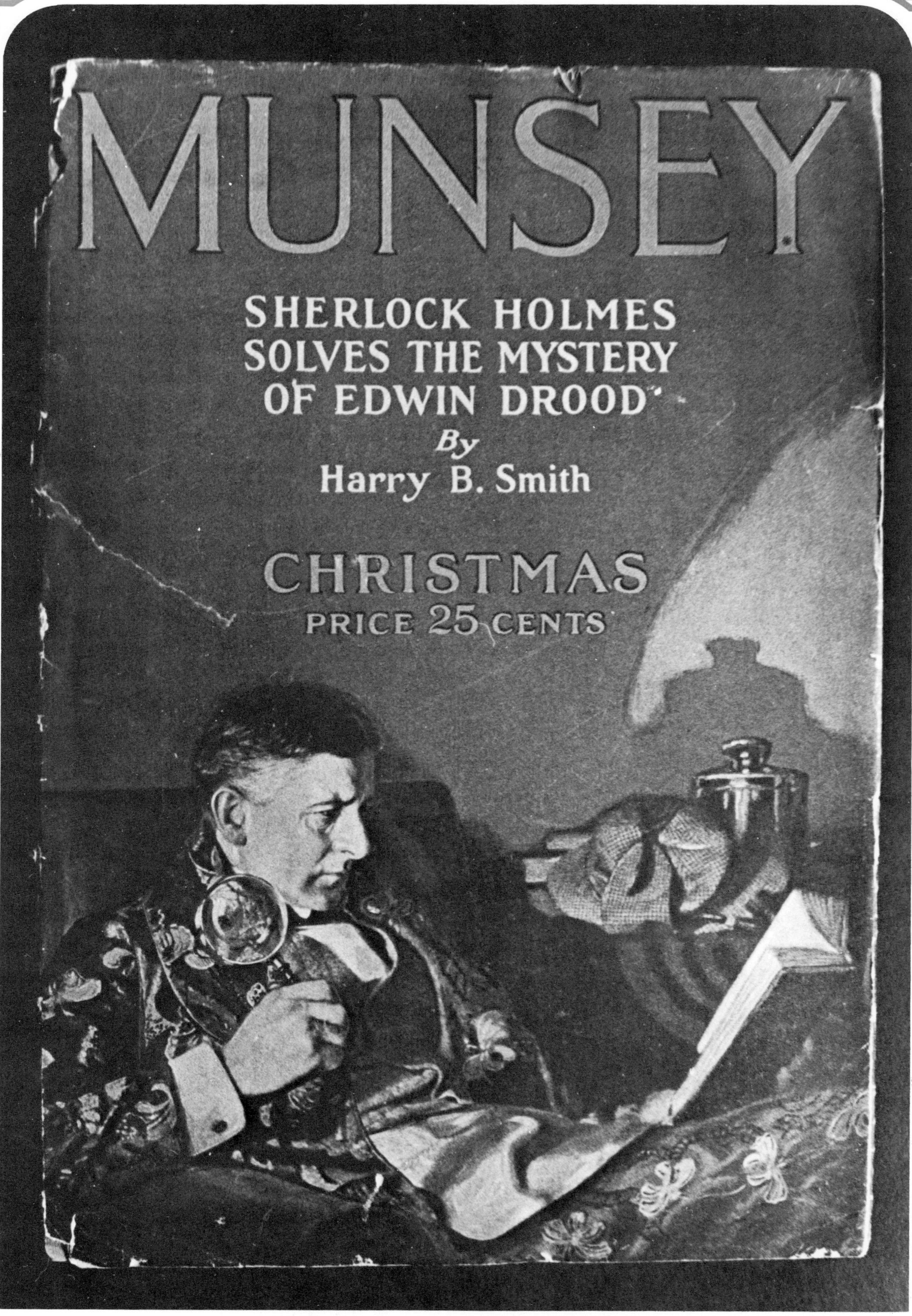

MUNSEY
SHERLOCK HOLMES
SOLVES THE MYSTERY
OF EDWIN DROOD
By
Harry B. Smith
CHRISTMAS
PRICE 25 CENTS

From the collection of Jerry Margolin; photo courtesy April DeSalvo

bewails his loneliness, with no companions to make up a quartet at bridge. Then, suddenly, he finds among the wreckage on the beach the ten volumes of his choice.

"What luck!" he exclaims. "Here is 'The Sheik'!"

Or, if he be more seriously inclined:

"Well, there's always a silver lining. One can never be poor with Adam Smith's 'Wealth of Nations,' nor need one revert to savagery with Buckle's 'History of Civilization.' "

It may be taken for granted that, if books are salvaged, a portion of the ship's stores may be tossed up by the surf. Personally, I do not propose to be shipwrecked without food; and this condition *sine qua non* being admitted in the hypothesis, the first volume of my selection shall be a cookery book. The chapters on "One Hundred Ways of Preparing Hardtack" and "What a Good Housekeeper Can Do with Tinned Corned Beef" would provide both mental relaxation and variety of diet. With an optimistic imagination, reading the recipes for the more delicate and complicated dishes might take the place of desserts; though, on the other hand, it might be conducive to discontent and homesickness.

After this first choice, which differs from the leading item in any list that I have seen, I should conform to tradition, selecting the Bible and Shakespeare, as the best substitutes for those necessary institutions, church and stage. The fourth book on my list would be a novel, and I would choose "The Mystery of Edwin Drood," as the only work of fiction known to the deponent the interest in which increases with every reading.

Several eminent writers, in their enthusiasm over "A Christmas Carol," have boasted—or confessed—that they read it once a year; but there are Dickensians far gone in Droodism who spend most of their leisure time in reading Dickens's last book. This novel becomes an obsession. It has fascinated minds as different as those of Andrew Lang and Richard Anthony Proctor, the astronomer. Both of these men wrote books and magazine articles about it.

A few years ago, a number of distinguished English authors held a mock trial of *John Jasper* for the murder of *Edwin Drood,* Judge G. K. Chesterton presiding, and George Bernard Shaw acting as foreman of the jury. Sir W. Robertson Nicoll has contributed a book to the discussion; and the literature that has been inspired by the puzzle of Dickens's last plot would require for its accommodation at least two of the widely advertised five-foot shelves.

Somewhat curiously, although the mystery has fascinated many men of letters, no professional detective has ever been consulted in the case; yet there are several well known investigators to whom it would be a simple one, compared to the baffling problems which they are sometimes called upon to solve. That the matter should be referred to an expert in criminology is no new idea of the present writer's. It was several months before the last of Sherlock Holmes's lamented deaths, as chronicled by his biographer, that I first thought of applying to that wizard of criminal investigation.

Unfortunately I had no acquaintance with Mr. Holmes, and I was deterred by the thought that he might resent the presentation to his attention of a case which existed only in the imagination of a novelist. Holmes's admiring satellite, Dr. Watson, I knew well—so well, indeed, that I had shunned his services as a physician. When I learned recently that the famous detective had survived the last apparently successful attempt to end his career, my first step was to enlist the interest of the excellent Watson; and this I accomplished by loaning him the novel and

a number of the books and magazine articles containing the theories of writers who have attempted to elucidate the mystery.

The result was precisely what I had anticipated. Dr. Watson became infatuated with the story. Indeed, he devoted so much of his time to it that he neglected his professional duties, with the consequence that the decreasing death rate in his residential section was mentioned in the reports of the Board of Health.

One morning Watson called upon me, looking so pale and haggard that I advised him to consult a competent physician; but he assured me that his condition was due merely to loss of sleep. Having puzzled vainly over the *Drood* enigma, he said, and having now despaired of a solution, he would soon recuperate.

"There is a man to whom I should like to refer this case," said Watson. "I am sure it would interest my friend Holmes, and he is quite likely to succeed, even where so many have failed."

Naturally I agreed with a plan so completely in accord with my own aim and object; but I suggested that Watson should present the case to Holmes as one of actual occurrence. In that way it would be more likely to appeal to him as worthy of his skill as a detective and of his extraordinary ingenuity in deductive reasoning. Watson considered this to be good diplomacy. As he claimed to have the case "at his fingers' ends," as he expressed it, he insisted upon going at once to interview his friend, who still occupied lodgings in Baker Street.

Dr. Watson Interviews Holmes

On the following day the doctor called again, and reported to me that he had found Holmes in excellent health. It appeared that the rumor of his death had been instigated by himself, in order to avoid the too frequent visits of a friend of his—whom he did not name to Watson, but who had become a bore through excess of vacuous admiration.

"After congratulating him on his survival," said the doctor, "I informed him that I had lately become interested in a very puzzling case, which I mentioned to him with a certain diffidence, because another detective was engaged upon it."

Holmes had received this information with a smile of gentle sarcasm, and with his usual comment upon the singular incompetency of the regular force. The interview, according to the résumé of it made for my benefit, proceeded thus:

"The investigator is not connected with Scotland Yard," said Watson. "I have reason to believe that he has a personal motive in exculpating one who is suspected, and a personal interest in bringing the real culprit to justice."

"Ha!" exclaimed Holmes. "Do you happen to know the young man's name?"

Watson looked at him with the blank expression that his friend knew so well.

"How do you know that this investigator is a *young* man?" he asked.

"He is either a young man with no particular business of his own, or he is a middle-aged man who has retired from active business," replied Holmes. "To devote much time to amateur detective work, one must have abundant leisure."

"Upon my word, Holmes!" Watson exclaimed, aghast as usual. "You are absolutely uncanny! As a matter of fact, this person might be either. He has a heavy shock of white hair, black eyebrows, and a habit of carrying his hat in his hand much of the time; but he is believed to be in disguise."

"If this white-wigged person is on the scent, why come to me?" Holmes asked. "Perhaps, in spite of his disguising himself in a way that would certainly attract attention and would not delude a child, he may be equal to an ordinary case."

"As far as I know," said the doctor, "he has done very little, aside from learning that the suspect has an enemy—an old woman who has reasons for hating him. This the investigator, whoever he may be, thought so important that he recorded it in chalk marks on a door."

"Chalk marks on a door! Extraordinary, indeed!" Holmes commented. "A man in disguise is investigating a murder, and records the information that he obtains by making chalk marks on a door! What door?"

"His own, I suppose," Watson answered.

"But why?"

"He himself explains it by saying that he 'likes the old tavern way of keeping scores.' He makes a long mark for anything important that he discovers, and a short mark for matters of less consequence. I don't know just what the system is, but he indicates his discoveries in this way."

"For whose information?" inquired the detective.

"His own, I suppose."

"Doesn't he know what they are without making chalk marks on a door? Watson, I don't think I should care to take the case. It is no pleasure to me to coöperate with the simpletons of the regular force, but this white-wigged amateur of yours insults my intelligence. Good God, Watson, I should think he would almost insult yours! Let us forget this queer case. Kreisler plays at Albert Hall this afternoon, and I am curious to learn in what manner his interpretation of the Bruch Concerto differs from my own."

"But, my dear Holmes," Watson protested, "you have heard nothing about the case!"

"I trust it is as remarkable as the so-called detective," returned Holmes. "Suppose you give me, in as few words as possible, the salient features of the affair."

"Briefly, then," Watson began, "the supposed murdered man was a young fellow, *Edwin Drood* by name. He was betrothed to a *Miss Rosa Bud*. His uncle, *John Jasper,* a few years older than himself, conceived a violent passion for the young lady, and is thought to have committed the murder in order to prevent the marriage."

"In what manner was the murder committed?" Holmes inquired.

"That is not positively known."

"But surely," Holmes insisted, "there has been an inquest? The body must have shown some evidence of the manner of death."

"No body has been found."

Holmes uttered an exclamation of impatience, and reached for his hat and topcoat.

"My good Watson," he said, "why be so certain that there has been a murder, if no body has been found?"

"*Drood* has unaccountably disappeared."

"Surely, Watson, you must know that every day men disappear unaccountably, yet no one imagines that they have been murdered. This young *Drood* was to have been married, you say?"

"He and his *fiancée* had agreed to break off the engagement," Watson answered.

Holmes smoked meditatively for several minutes before asking:

"Do you happen to know whether he has contemplated foreign travel? You will observe that I do not use the past tense, for I always assume that a man is alive until his body has been found."

"Now that you mention it," replied Watson, "I remember that it was all settled that he was to go to Egypt, to enter upon a business career."

"And has it not occurred to his family—to his former sweetheart, say—that the young man may have gone about his business—in Egypt—without consulting his relatives?"

"As far as we know, he had no relatives," answered the doctor, "except the uncle, *John Jasper,* who insists that *Drood* was murdered."

"The uncle who is under suspicion?"

"By certain persons *Jasper* is suspected; but he is doing his utmost to establish the guilt of a young fellow, *Landless* by name, who recently came to England from Ceylon, with his twin sister."

"Twins!" exclaimed Holmes, with renewed interest. "The brother and sister resemble each other, I suppose, as twins usually do?"

"They are very much alike."

"Where twins are involved in a case," remarked the great detective, "they introduce an element of particular interest. I have in mind the Halberg tragedy in Copenhagen and the Sadler affair in Cincinnati. In both the resemblance of twin brothers gave rise to extraordinary complications. To return to this case of yours, Watson—its most peculiar feature is that the uncle, who is suspected, seems to be the one who most strongly insists that a murder was committed."

"And vows to devote his life to bringing the assassin to justice," said Watson. "This *Jasper* is a somewhat eccentric person. He is an opium addict."

Holmes gave a start of surprise, and, with a subconscious association of ideas, thrust his hand into the coat pocket wherein he habitually kept his favorite surgical instrument.

"My dear Watson," he remarked, "you now interest me strangely. The element of opium in a criminal case is particularly fascinating to me, as from the time of my earliest appearances before the public I have experimented with hypnotic and narcotic drugs of every description."

The eminent investigator reclined in his armchair, and for some time remained lost in meditation.

"Watson," he said at last, "this affair, as you describe it, has many absurdities, but it presents certain aspects that appeal to my curiosity. A case in which opium is a factor is likely to develop some vagary of abnormal psychology. Such problems differ from all others, and one's deductions are materially affected. In fact, Watson, I need not tell you, a medico, that in such cases, after deducing from the facts, a certain allowance must be made for mental conditions artificially stimulated or depressed. Both the immediate influences of a drug and its after effects have to be carefully considered."

With the promptitude that is customary when his interest is aroused, Holmes slipped a microscope and an automatic pistol into his pockets, and suggested going at once to the scene of the crime. In the circumstances, however, the doctor was obliged to temporize.

"If you don't mind, Holmes," he observed, "I think that in this particular case it might be well for you to vary your usual routine of investigation. This is an affair with many remarkable features, and before you visit the localities and interview the persons concerned I shall place in your hands certain documentary evidence. It is possible that after you have examined these papers you may be able to evolve a theory upon which definite action may be taken.”

Holmes protested that he could not alter his methods in any case, however out of the ordinary; but upon Watson's threatening to deliver then and there one of his familiar private lectures on the evils of the cocaine habit, the great detective reluctantly consented to meet the doctor's wishes. That same evening Watson sent to Holmes a copy of “The Mystery of Edwin Drood,” together with a number of monographs and magazine articles, the contributions of various writers who have minutely studied this strangest problem in the annals of imaginary crime and have arrived at widely different conclusions.

A week or more passed before I heard anything further from Watson. As the worthy doctor afterward informed me, he had had a patient suffering from that rare and insidious malady, coryza,* which had worried him greatly, his professional reputation being at stake. As soon as this invalid passed over to the great majority—of Watson's patients, the doctor communicated with Holmes by telephone, and immediately afterward called upon me.

“Holmes is enormously interested,” he reported. “I expected that he would reproach me for wasting his time on a case that exists only in a novel; but if I myself had been murdered he could not have displayed greater enthusiasm. I have an appointment to call upon him, and I asked permission to bring a friend who is familiar with all the details of the affair.”

I Meet the Famous Detective

I gladly welcomed an opportunity to meet the eminent criminologist, and after a hasty luncheon we proceeded by motor bus to his rooms in Baker Street. As we ascended the stairs, I heard the weird violin gymnastics of Paganini's “Witches' Dance,” and I felt intuitively that the Italian master was turning over in his grave.

Sherlock Holmes welcomed us with old-world courtesy.

“I am delighted to meet any friend of Dr. Watson's,” he said, rolling down his sleeve over a sinewy forearm, which bore the marks of innumerable punctures by his trusty needle. “I do not ask you to take any refreshment, as I perceive that you have had luncheon—eggs, if I am not mistaken. I also observe, doctor, that when coming here in a public conveyance you sat next to a blond-haired lady. It is well, perhaps, that you came here before going home, as Mrs. Watson, I know, is a brunette.”

Watson laughed at my amazement at these deductions, which, however, were extremely simple when Holmes explained them.

“My good friend, the doctor,” he said, “has brought to my attention a fantastic affair which is quite as complicated as any actual crime of recent occurrence. For once, fiction has approximated the interest of fact.”

“And what is your theory?” I asked, eager to hear the opinion of an acknowledged authority.

“If I were talking to any of the characters in that admirable novel,” answered Holmes, “I would say: ‘My dear sir, or madam, your young friend *Edwin Drood* may turn up at any moment. He is no more a murdered man than *I* am.’ ”

“You are not alone in your opinion that *Drood* was not murdered,” I ventured to say.

“I quite realize that,” Holmes agreed. “As I have read all the documentary evidence that Watson kindly provided, I know

there is no novelty in the theory that *Drood* survived; but I believe that my reasons for certainty on that point are based upon scientific deductions which in this instance, singularly enough, are not inconsistent with common sense. Let us consider the affair as if it were an actual case, which I am employed to investigate in the usual course of business. If a young man has parted finally from his *fiancée,* has no particular object in remaining in England, has long contemplated a career in a foreign country—if such a young man suddenly disappears, and no trace of him is found, is it not reasonable to infer that circumstances have arisen which determined him to carry out his plan to go to that foreign country?”

“By Heaven, Holmes,” exclaimed Watson, “your powers of deduction are a source of constant amazement to me!”

“I am not amazed at your amazement, my good Watson,” returned Holmes, with his gentle and almost feminine smile; “but in reality it is quite simple. If *Drood* was not to go to Egypt, why did the author, Mr. Dickens, make such a point of his intention to go? The young man has a long talk with *Miss Bud,* in which she expresses her distaste for sharing his life in that country, declaring that she has no interest in sphinxes and pyramids. You may say that the author's intention in this insistence was to make readers, like ourselves, believe that *Drood* had gone to Egypt, whereas he was really murdered. If I had no further evidence of *Drood's* survival, I would agree that all this talk about Egypt might be an author's false clew, intended to delude his readers; but I think I shall be able to convince you that *Drood* did go to Egypt.”

“In that case,” said Watson, “you are inclined to agree with Andrew Lang, Richard Proctor, and others, who maintain that *Datchery,* the investigator in Cloisterham, is *Drood* in disguise.”

Holmes's celebrated enigmatic smile became frankly ironic as he replied:

“My good Watson, I regard the theory that *Datchery* is *Drood* in disguise as wholly untenable. *Datchery* has an interview with *John Jasper.* If he were *Drood* in disguise, it is preposterous to suppose that *Jasper* would not recognize him, the disguise being, we are told, a white wig, black eyebrows, and a tightish blue surtout. *Jasper* was *Drood's* uncle, and presumably had known the young man all his life. In his hatred of his nephew, *Jasper* had studied him, knew his every gesture, and every inflection of his voice, knew his eyes—which, by the way, are the most difficult feature to disguise. *Drood* could not have spoken three words without *Jasper's* recognizing his voice. As a musician, a singing teacher, *Jasper* would have an especially keen ear for the detection of voices. Dickens was writing a novel, but a writer of fiction with a modern, or even a mid-Victorian period, must keep within the bounds of probability. If *Datchery* is *Drood* in disguise, Dickens asks his readers to believe the impossible. In fact, *Jasper,* shrewd and suspicious, would have recognized any one with whom he was even slightly acquainted, in such an obvious disguise. Perhaps, Watson, with the alert perceptions for which you are justly famous, you can tell me why *Drood* should be pottering around as *Datchery,* knowing that his friends believe him to be murdered, and that an innocent man, *Neville Landless,* is under suspicion?”

Watson and I agreed that such conduct on the part of *Drood* would be both heartless and brainless.

“As I have often told you, doctor,” Holmes resumed, “one must begin an analysis by eliminating impossibilities. There are other indications that *Datchery* is not *Drood. Datchery*—with no suggestion that any one is watching him—cannot find his way to the cathedral precincts, where *Tope* and *Jasper* live. He asks the vagabond boy, *Deputy,* to direct him, whereas *Drood* is familiar with Cloisterham topography."

"It has been suggested," I said, "that *Datchery,* if *Drood* or any one else acquainted in Cloisterham, might have pretended that he did not know his way about and might have asked *Deputy* for effect."

"If so," Holmes replied, "I must say that *Datchery* is carrying realistic acting very far when he tries to impress a vagrant street boy. Why, gentlemen, the book itself contains proof that *Datchery* is not *Drood*. In Chapter XIV *Drood* meets the opium woman.

" 'Do you eat opium?' is one of the questions he puts to her.

" 'Smokes it,' is her reply.

"In Chapter XXIII *Datchery* meets the opium woman, and when she begs him for money to buy 'a medicine as does her good,' he asks:

" 'What's the medicine?'

" 'It's opium,' says the woman, and '*Mr. Datchery,* with a sudden change of countenance, gives her a sudden look.'

"Now, if *Drood* be *Datchery,* why the 'sudden change of countenance' and the 'sudden look,' for the opium woman was only telling *Datchery* exactly what she had told *Drood?*"

Watson turned to me with a triumphant smile, taking a vicarious pride in the acumen of his great friend.

"That seems strong evidence that *Drood* is not *Datchery,*" he said; "but if *Drood* is alive, why has he not communicated with his friends and told them not to worry about him, as he is doing very nicely in Egypt as an engineer?"

"Your question is a pertinent one, doctor," replied Holmes. "Like all your questions, it would occur to any one of ordinary intelligence. According to my theory, *Drood* was on his way to Egypt before there had been any suggestion that he had been murdered. In fact, the young man might have disappeared as he did, and there would have been no suspicion of foul play, had not *Jasper* himself raised the hue and cry. Would not his friends have said, quite naturally:

" 'The boy had a disappointment in love, and has gone to Egypt to follow his career, as he had been planning to do.'

"But Jasper startles them all by charging that his nephew has been murdered. This, I believe, is one of the elements of strength and originality in Dickens's plot. The criminal sounds the alarm and starts in motion the machinery that finally convicts—himself."

"But of what crime, since you assert that *Drood* is alive?" I ventured to inquire.

"We shall come to that presently," said Holmes. "It is an important part of my theory that *Drood* did communicate certain circumstances to one person before leaving England."

"To whom?" Watson asked, bewildered as usual.

Why Grewgious Visited Jasper

"I feel positive that *Drood* communicated with *Grewgious*. That angular but good-hearted lawyer calls upon *Jasper,* and the latter falls in a fit when he learns that he did not have to kill his nephew to prevent *Edwin's* marriage to *Rosa,* as the two young people had agreed to break off their engagement. *Grewgious's* language, and the manner in which he imparts this information to *Jasper,* prove that he knows something. My deduction is that *Drood* has told *Grewgious* that his uncle made a murderous attack upon him. Let us reconstruct the interview

that I believe took place between *Drood* and the lawyer.

"*Jasper's* attack on *Drood* occurred at about midnight on Christmas Eve. Early on Christmas morning, as early as the young man could get to London from Cloisterham, *Grewgious* is surprised by a visit from *Drood,* who is in a state of extreme agitation. He explains to the lawyer that during the night his uncle made a murderous assault upon him. *Drood's* resistance and *Jasper's* terror on being recognized—his ambush failing—caused the assailant to fall into one of his accustomed fits, super-induced by the opium debauch in which, we are informed, he indulged on the preceding night. *Drood,* horrified, rushed from the scene before *Jasper* recovered consciousness. He can conceive of no reason for the attempted homicide. *Grewgious* would suggest referring the matter to the police. *Drood* would hesitate to make a charge of assault with intent to kill against his uncle, who, he thinks, must have become insane. Clearly the young man has nothing to make him anxious to stay in England. He has parted from his sweetheart; his only known relative has tried to murder him; his career lies in a foreign land. He leaves *Grewgious* to investigate. If *Jasper* is insane, the lawyer will have him placed in an asylum. In the circumstances, *Drood* does not care to meet his uncle again. He decides to go to Egypt as soon as possible."

"It is quite likely that a boat was opportunely sailing," observed Watson.

"As you say, doctor. Boats usually are opportunely sailing in novels. *Grewgious* was probably enjoined to take no action beyond having *Jasper* watched, for the purpose of learning whether his mental condition warranted his being placed under restraint; but after *Drood* has gone on his way, matters take a different turn. *Jasper* declares that his nephew has been murdered, and he tries to inculpate *Neville Landless*. *Grewgious* hears this. He knows that *Jasper* himself was the assailant. The lawyer is perplexed. What kind of a game is the opium-smoking precentor playing? He commits assault with intent to kill, and then charges an innocent man with murder. The legal mind seeks a motive. At this juncture, *Helena Landless* has an interview with *Grewgious*."

I made the suggestion that almost the first words of the lawyer when he visits *Jasper* are:

"I have just left *Miss Landless*."

"Significant words indeed!" said Holmes. "Now let us attempt to reconstruct the interview between *Helena Landless* and *Grewgious*.

" '*Jasper,*' says *Helena,* 'charges that my brother murdered *Drood*. If any one killed *Drood,* it was *Jasper,* whose love for *Rosa* is a mania.'

"*Grewgious* learns from her what *Drood* did not know—that *Jasper* is infatuated with *Rosa,* who fears him, and over whom he has a kind of mesmeric influence. *Grewgious* knows now that *Drood* was wrong in thinking that *Jasper's* attack might be a sudden outbreak of madness. He knows now that it was an attempt to commit murder, with the motive of jealousy. *Jasper* meant to kill his nephew because, as he thought, *Drood* was about to be married to *Rosa*."

Watson gazed at Holmes in blank astonishment. Apparently used to that expression on his friend's face, the great detective continued:

"This new knowledge of *Grewgious's* establishes the reason for the lawyer's otherwise purposeless visit to *Jasper*. The object of the lawyer is to test the truth of his theory that *Jasper* attempted a murder with a motive. The language and manner of *Grewgious* during the whole interview, as described in the novel, prove this. He reasons thus—if *Jasper* planned to kill his nephew to prevent the latter's marriage to *Rosa,* the revelation that there was no necessity for the crime will be a shock to him. *Grewgious,* in a cruelly cold and deliberate manner, tells *Jasper* that *Edwin* and *Rosa* had decided not to marry. He watches the effect. He expects the shock. When *Jasper* shrieks and collapses, 'a heap of torn and miry clothes upon the floor,' *Grewgious,* 'not changing his action even then,' warms his hands at the fire and looks calmly down at the unconscious form of the man he now knows to be a murderer in intention. The sardonic manner of *Grewgious* throughout the interview with *Jasper* is, I believe, proof of the truth of my deductions."

"But surely," Watson commented, "having learned this, *Grewgious* would have been justified in going to the authorities and demanding the arrest of *Jasper,* thus exonerating *Neville?*"

"Not so fast, my good Watson," said Holmes. "Admirable as your capabilities as a physician may be—I speak from hearsay only, as my own health is unimpaired—your knowledge of legal procedure is limited. Matters resting as I have outlined, no indictment could have been found against either *Jasper* or *Neville Landless. Jasper* himself is the only person who insists that there has been a murder. Otherwise, in the minds of friends and of the community in general, the fate of *Drood* is in doubt. He has disappeared. There is no *corpus delicti.* The only evidence even of assault is *Drood's* own story. *Jasper's* conduct and the suspicions of *Helena* and *Grewgious* do not constitute legal evidence; yet *Grewgious* knows that *Jasper* has done his best to commit an atrocious crime, and is now trying to fix the guilt on *Neville.* There is no evidence against *Neville,* but *Jasper's* enmity is a menace. From this time it is *Grewgious's* plan to give *Jasper* plenty of rope and let him hang himself. This is why *Grewgious* declares that he has 'a fancy for keeping *Jasper* under his eye.' It is *Grewgious* who arranges that the so-called *Datchery* shall keep a close watch of Jasper, living as his neighbor. *Grewgious* is playing a deep game. *Jasper* himself has raised the cry of murder, and by leaving him to his own devices, by artful counterplotting, *Grewgious* intends that *Jasper,* instead of incriminating an innocent man, shall convict himself."

"Very cleverly reasoned, Holmes," I said; "but there is a weak link in your chain. You have overlooked the fact that *Jasper* unquestionably believes *Drood* to be dead."

Jasper Thinks Himself a Murderer

"Naturally, for *Jasper* thinks that he himself murdered the young man, and believes him to be safely laid away in quicklime in the *Sapsea* vault."

"But you must admit, my dear Mr. Holmes," I urged, "that it is impossible that a man should not know whether he actually committed a murder, or merely led up to it and failed."

"You might as well assert," added Watson, "that I, a physician, would perform an operation without knowing anything about it."

"I shall not dispute your parallel case, doctor," said Holmes; "but I will ask you a question or two. Why does Dickens make his villain an opium addict? Why is he so particular to establish the fact that *Jasper* has strange fits and weird seizures, in which he 'wanders away in a frightful sort of dream, in which he threatens most'? Why does he speak of having 'gone the journey' —meaning that he has done the deed—'hundreds of thousands of times'? Why does *Jasper* go on an opium spree the night before his attack on *Drood?* Are these things for no purpose? I

am no literary critic, but common sense tells me that an author does not make his villain a morphinomaniac subject to fits in moments of excitement, and does not send him on an opium spree just before he commits a crime, unless that author has a good reason for doing so."

"And what, in your opinion, is this reason?" I asked.

"To me it seems clear enough," answered Holmes. "In his thoughts and his dreams, *Jasper* had contemplated the murder again and again—so the novel assures us. He took a diabolical delight in rehearsing it in his mind. Let us make an attempt to reconstruct the crime. On Christmas Eve, the night of the dinner at *Jasper's,* at about midnight, *Drood* and *Neville Landless* take a walk together. We are informed that *Drood* returns alone to his uncle's rooms. *Jasper* makes a sudden and ferocious attack upon him, and attempts to strangle him with a heavy silk scarf, to which the author has pointedly alluded. Now, unless *Jasper* were a practiced thug, adept in murder by garrote, he was not likely to avoid a struggle. However unexpected the assault, *Drood* would have been able to make some resistance."

"He might have been attacked in his sleep," I suggested.

"In that case," said Holmes, "he would presumably have been murdered. If *Drood* be dead, the story becomes the commonplace one of a man killing a rival and fixing the crime on an innocent person. Before he began writing the novel, Dickens wrote to his friend, John Forster, that he had an idea for his story which he described as 'curious and new,' 'incommunicable, strong, though difficult to work.' If *Drood* was actually murdered, the idea of the novel has none of these qualities, for the story becomes trite and conventional.

"Let us return to my reconstruction of the attack. *Drood* resists sufficiently for him to recognize his assailant. *Jasper,* realizing that he is caught in an attempt to murder, has one of his seizures, and collapses just as he does subsequently in his interview with *Grewgious.* Drood is horrified and bewildered. He cannot imagine any motive for such an attack, for he knows nothing of *Jasper's* mad love for *Rosa.* He thinks the attack must be a maniacal outburst. He has noticed *Jasper's* strange symptoms on other occasions—so the novel tells us. He rushes from the house, leaving *Jasper* in his swoon, and makes his way to London. By the way, I find in the first edition of 'Bradshaw's Railway Guide' that there were trains at five and six o'clock in the morning on English railways as early as 1840, and the period of 'Edwin Drood' is certainly later than that. *Drood* tells *Grewgious* the facts as I have outlined them, and takes his departure for Egypt, as he had planned to do. Why should he remain in England? His career lay elsewhere; he had parted from his betrothed; his only known relative had attempted to kill him."

"By Jove, Holmes," exclaimed Watson, "I believe you are right!"

"Thank you, doctor," said Holmes. "It's very good of you to concur; but nevertheless I believe I am. Now what happens to *Jasper?* He awakens after a repetition of the dream that he has had 'hundreds and thousands of times'; and, as Mr. Lang quotes, he 'thinks it all very capital.' He might have thought that he had only dreamed again of the murder that was his obsession; but there is the evidence of a struggle. There is the scarf. *Jasper* has dreamed of the crime so often that it is all vivid to him, including the long-planned burial of the body in the *Sapsea* vault. This time he believes that he has accomplished his purpose, for *Drood* has disappeared."

"Certain passages in the novel," I suggested, "seem to hint

that *Jasper* intended to kill *Drood* by throwing him from the cathedral tower."

"I regard that as highly improbable," said Holmes. "To throw a man from a church tower would present some difficulty to the average murderer. *Drood* was a confiding youth, but even he might have been suspicious of an uncle who, in a midnight storm, on Christmas Eve, suggests climbing to the top of a cathedral tower. *Jasper* would realize that killing a man by throwing him from a tower would make a sad mess to be cleared up on Christmas morning. If such a crude and primitive method of murder was to be adopted, why was the scarf insisted on? I observe that the artist who illustrated the book affirms that Dickens told him that *Jasper* must wear that scarf, as *Drood* was to be strangled with it."

"Sir Luke Fildes was the artist," I said. "By the way, he used this remark of the author's as an argument to prove that *Drood* was actually murdered."

"It is no argument at all," protested Holmes. "Dickens could not be expected to go into all the intricacies of his plot. He told Fildes that *Jasper* must wear the scarf, as he was to strangle *Drood* with it. One could not expect the novelist to say that 'he tries to strangle *Drood,* but does not succeed,' and then to explain the whole story, opium and all. The author told the artist all that was necessary for his purpose, and no more."

"That seems plausible," said Watson; "but why did *Jasper* make his mysterious trip to the top of the tower, accompanied by *Durdles,* the stone mason?"

"In my opinion," Holmes replied, "he wished to see if it would be safe for him to convey *Drood's* body to the *Sapsea* vault, to which he had obtained a key by drugging *Durdles.* The text says that from the tower *Jasper* contemplates the scene, 'and especially that stillest part of it which the cathedral overshadows.' Reference is made to the moonlight. When *Crisparkle* suggests that *Neville* should meet the uncle and nephew for the purpose of a reconciliation, we are told that *Jasper's* face indicates 'some close internal calculation.' Is it not likely that he was figuring on what night the rise of the moon would be most favorable for his purpose? If I have not accurately reconstructed the crime, give me some good reason for the novelist's making *Jasper* an opium addict. Why is opium in the story at all, if not for some purpose such as I have indicated? To deny that opium is in the novel for a purpose is to assert that Dickens devoted many pages to an irrelevant matter.

"*Jasper's* next move," continued Holmes, "is to declare that his nephew has been murdered, and he tries to fasten the crime upon *Neville Landless.* He has already spread the report of a feud between *Drood* and *Neville,* and he hates the latter for admiring *Rosa. Drood's* watch and pin are accounted for, being discovered by *Crisparkle* in the weir, where they were placed by *Jasper,* probably with the idea of incriminating *Neville,* whose midnight walk with *Drood* was in that vicinity."

"How did the watch and pin get into *Jasper's* possession, if *Drood* was not murdered?" asked Watson.

"The question is an ingenious one, doctor," answered Holmes, "but it concerns an unimportant detail. *Drood* may not have been attacked until he had started to undress. The removal of his collar and necktie would have made the garroting with the scarf an easier matter. *Jasper* was not likely to overlook the fact that gold articles would not be destroyed by quicklime. He would have found some way to get them. It is expressly stated in the book that he knew his nephew wore no other jewelry. Later in the story, deliberately but with an appearance of casualness, *Grew-*

gious lets *Jasper* know that *Drood* had in his pocket a ring of rubies and diamonds, to which the novelist refers as a link of evidence possessing 'invincible force to hold and drag.' *Jasper* concludes that this ring is in the quicklime in the *Sapsea* vault. It is just the evidence that he needs. He decides to recover it, and to dispose of it in such a manner as to incriminate *Neville.* Close watch is kept on *Jasper,* and the time of his visit to the tomb becomes known. A trap is set for him. Somebody is placed in the tomb to confront him. His presence there, opening the door with the key that he had made from *Durdles's* key, proves his belief that *Drood's* body is there and his own guilt of assault with intent to commit murder."

"Evidently," I said, "you have studied the pictorial cover of the monthly parts in which the novel was first published. That is the only authority for believing that there was to be such a scene in the tomb."

"It is the best authority possible," Holmes declared. "Dickens described to the artist just what he wanted on that pictorial cover—some of the striking scenes in the story, as he had it outlined in his mind. The tomb scene, with *Jasper,* lantern in hand, confronting the menacing figure, is the most important feature of the cover design. It was to be the strongest climax in the novel."

"And who is it that *Jasper* sees?" asked Watson eagerly.

"One of two persons," Holmes replied. "It might be *Drood* or it might be *Datchery*—whoever he may be. According to the chronology of the novel, more than six months have passed since *Drood* went to Egypt. *Grewgious* would have written to him, telling him that *Jasper's* attack was not an outbreak of insanity, but a premeditated attempt to murder. *Drood* might have returned. If the man facing *Jasper* in the tomb is *Drood,* Dickens was developing an idea which he briefly suggested in 'Martin Chuzzlewit':

"The dead man might have come out of his grave and not confounded and appalled him so.

"Judged by dramatic values," continued Holmes, "the man who confronts *Jasper* in the tomb should be *Drood.* The would-be murderer and his supposed victim face to face—it is a sensational melodramatic situation. The man in the tomb bears a striking resemblance to *Drood* as he appears in another picture on the same cover. I believe it is *Drood.* Certainly, if it is any one else, the situation is not nearly as strong. There is not much dramatic value in *Jasper's* going to the tomb and finding a detective. The large hat and the overcoat suggest *Datchery,* but the face is not the face of an 'elderly buffer'—it is the face of *Drood.*"

The Problem of Datchery

"And now," said Watson, "we come to the second important problem—who is *Datchery?* He might be *Neville Landless, Tartar,* or *Bazzard,* and Mr. Cuming Walters and Sir W. Robertson Nicoll make out quite a good case for *Helena Landless.*"

Holmes leaned back in his armchair, placed the tips of his long, delicate fingers together and smiled a pitying smile.

"With all due respect to the amateur investigators who fancy that *Datchery* is *Helena,*" he said, "I must exclude that young lady from the calculations. Mr. Walters's argument for *Helena* is based principally upon her brother's story that when they ran away together in their childhood, *Helena* 'dressed as a boy and showed the daring of a man.' Mr. Walters also makes much of the fact that when *Helena* is asked if she would not be afraid of *Jasper* in certain circumstances, she replies, 'Not under any circumstances.' On these passages indicating the girl's courage, and on her having a motive—the exculpation of her brother— Mr. Walters rests his case. He was one of the counsel for the prosecution in the mock trial of *Jasper* in 1914, in which *Helena's* claim that she was *Datchery* was shattered by the cross-examination of Mr. Cecil Chesterton."

"Mr. Andrew Lang," I remarked, "expressed the opinion that 'if *Helena* is *Datchery,* the idea is highly ludicrous.'"

"And so it is," Holmes agreed. "My own opinion is that if Dickens intended to present *Helena* to his readers as an elderly gentleman wearing a white wig and 'buttoned up in a tightish blue surtout,' his sense of humor must have been in abeyance, and he was asking his readers to have the credulity of a child hearing a fairy tale. Here is the novelist's description of *Helena* :

"An unusually handsome, lithe girl, very dark and very rich in color, almost of the gypsy type; slender, supple, quick of eye and limb; half shy, half defiant, fierce of look.

"You may see the lady, with her 'lustrous gypsy face,' in the illustration, which, presumably, was approved by Dickens. Could such a girl masquerade as an elderly man without being detected? Would she, recently arrived from Ceylon, make chalk marks on a door to 'keep score, as they do in taverns'? *Datchery* drinks sherry and beer, eats a hungry man's substantial meal, and 'makes a leg'—which, I believe, is a sort of masculine equivalent of a curtsy. He chaffs *Sapsea* and the boy *Deputy.* He interviews *Jasper,* and becomes his neighbor. Would not *Mrs. Tope* suspect the sex of her lodger? Would the camouflaged *Helena* deceive *Jasper* for a moment?"

"Not unless he were a greater fool than I am," said Watson.

"As I have said, we must eliminate the impossible," Holmes continued. "The girl who defied *Jasper*—a girl of unusual appearance—lodges near him and talks with him. She closely resembles her brother, on whom *Jasper* is trying to fix a crime; yet he, with a supposed murder on his conscience, watchful, suspicious, sees her in a white wig and a 'tightish blue surtout' and does not suspect her identity or her sex. *Jasper* is a singing teacher, with an ear trained to judge the quality of voices; yet he cannot tell a woman's voice from that of an elderly man. A 'tall, lithe girl' with a 'lustrous gypsy face,' white hair 'blowing in the breeze,' 'buttoned up in a tightish blue surtout,' meets and talks to no fewer than six of the leading characters in the story, and none of them suspects that she is a woman."

"You must remember, Holmes," Watson observed, "that Shakespeare frequently disguises female characters as boys or young men, and, as the Americans say, gets away with it."

"Your criticism is sound," Holmes retorted—"sound, if nothing else; but you overlook the fact that Shakespeare is in the realm of romantic drama, where the impossible can happen, and generally does. Mr. Dickens was writing a modern novel, in which the plot, characters; and incidents must approximate real life, must be plausible and convincing. He could hardly ask his readers to believe that all his characters are such imbeciles that they cannot tell a masquerading girl from an elderly man. What is admissible in the Forest of Arden, or any other fairyland of fancy, becomes incredible in everyday life."

"Now that you mention it," remarked Watson, "I have never seen a *Viola* or a *Rosalind* who made me forget for a moment that she was a lady in doublet and hose."

"Which proves your keen powers of observation, doctor," said Holmes. "The characters surrounding these shapely ladies believe that they are young men, because in poetic drama characters may be asked by their creators to believe anything. No writer of a modern novel or play would ask readers or auditors to believe in a *Caliban* or an *Ariel.* Sir James Barrie can play such pranks; so could Lewis Carroll; but they deal in the fantastic. Occasionally, in modern plays, young actresses are cast for boy characters; but such impersonations carry no conviction, even in the theater."

Watson and I mentioned several instances of this in our own experience as theatergoers.

"There is a theatrical tradition," I said, "that Peg Woffington, playing *Sir Harry Wildair,* remarked, 'I believe half the men in the audience think I am a man'—to which Quin, the veteran actor, made the obvious retort, rude but witty. Charlotte Cushman played *Romeo,* but nobody ever believed that she was a man, though Miss Cushman had a voice and a personality that gave an unusual degree of realism to masculine impersonation. Coming nearer to our own time, Sarah Bernhardt's *Hamlet* was a very graceful and charming Princess of Denmark."

"There you are," said Holmes. "If *Helena Landless* be *Datchery,* she is a greater actress than any who has ever appeared on the stage. *Helena,* just arrived from Ceylon, where she had always lived, knew nothing of the art of make-up, one of the technicalities of the profession—one of the most difficult, by the way. Tell me, Watson—if an elderly man in a white wig should suddenly be revealed as 'a tall, lithe girl with a lustrous gypsy face,' would it give you the thrill of a striking dramatic situation?"

"I fancy I should find it more or less laughable," said Watson, after prolonged reflection.

"I am sure you would," agreed Holmes. "The idea is essentially comic. Dickens, we know, took his plot very seriously, and the revelation of *Datchery* was to have been his strongest situation."

"Then, in your opinion, who was *Datchery?*" Watson asked.

"Before answering that question, doctor, I ask you to glance at this book, which has been placed at my disposal by the present owner."

Holmes placed in Watson's hands a small volume, on the flyleaf of which I observed the following inscription:

To Mr. and Mrs. Comyns Carr, from their friend, Kate Perugini.

I recognized the name of the donor as that of Charles Dickens's daughter.

"That book," said Holmes, "was used by Dickens for several years, including the period immediately preceding the writing of 'The Mystery of Edwin Drood.' Let me call your attention to a note in Dickens's autograph, which I think has a decided bearing upon the question you have asked me."

Holmes indicated the paragraph, and I read the following note in the novelist's well known hand:

The two men to be guarded against as to their revenge. One whom I openly hold in some serious animosity, and whom I am at the pains to wound and defy and estimate as worthy of wounding and defying. The other whom I treat as a sort of insect, and contemptuously and pleasantly flick aside with my glove. But it turns out to be the latter who is the really dangerous man, and when I expect the blow from the other, it falls from *him.*

"That note," said Holmes, "is placed among memoranda of material used in the later novels, and in my opinion it refers to the disguised personality of *Datchery.* It is true that Dickens used something like it in 'Hunted Down,' but that was merely a short story written to order. I believe that in depicting the impersonator of *Datchery*, Dickens developed this idea entered in his notebook."

"And who, in reality, is this negligible and insignificant person?"

Is Datchery Bazzard in Disguise?

"Again let me adopt my favorite method of elimination," replied Holmes. "I hope I have convinced you that no woman could successfully impersonate an elderly man. *Datchery* cannot be *Grewgious, Crisparkle, Neville, Tartar, Durdles, Sapsea,* or the dean, because they are all constantly before the reader, playing the rôles provided for them. Not one of them disappears, so that for any considerable period he could be *Datchery.* He would have to be in and out of disguise, running up and down between London and Cloisterham. Aside from *Drood*—who is probably in Egypt, but who may possibly have returned—only one character disappears—*Bazzard.*"

"*Bazzard!*" I exclaimed. "Surely, Holmes, you cannot believe that *Grewgious's* uninteresting clerk can be *Datchery?* The *Datchery-Bazzard* theory was broken down by Sir W. Robertson Nicoll, who brought heavy German guns forward to shatter the claim. He quotes from Dr. Hugo Eick's book, 'On the Psychology of Dissimulation.' The gist of the argument is summed up by another writer, Professor Jackson:

"Capacity can ape incapacity; but incapacity cannot ape capacity."

"I am the last man in the world to dispute scientific theories, however German," said Holmes; "but what has all this about capacity and incapacity to do with *Bazzard?* Who has imputed incapacity to *Bazzard?* He is a lawyer's clerk, and while there are lawyer's clerks who are not intellectual giants, they are not imbeciles as a class. *Bazzard* has written a play. It may not be a good play; but to write even a poor play requires intelligence of a sort—or so I am credibly informed. As *Grewgious* himself says: 'Now, you know, *I* couldn't write a play;' and he makes this admission as if he were intimating that *Bazzard* is not such a nonentity as he seems."

"Now that you mention it," I remarked, "I have often wondered why, when *Rosa* takes refuge with *Grewgious* to avoid *Jasper's* persecution, the lawyer devotes most of his conversation to the subject of his absent clerk, just as he does in an earlier interview with *Drood.*"

"Obviously because *Bazzard* is destined to take some important part in the story," Holmes declared. "Bazzard is invited to have Christmas dinner with his employer. The clerk is rather a surly fellow, soured, perhaps, by the refusal of managers to produce his play. He is associated with a group of amateur playwrights—so we are told. In short, his tastes and affiliations are theatrical. It might have been shown later that he belonged to one of the companies of amateur actors that Dickens was so fond of, both personally and as a writer."

"It does seem rather curious," I suggested, "that *Grewgious* should say to *Rosa,* 'Let's talk,' and then proceed to talk almost exclusively of *Bazzard.*"

"It is for the reason that this is the only chance the novelist left himself to establish *Bazzard* as a character in connection with his appearance as *Datchery.*"

"The principal argument in favor of the *Bazzard-Datchery* theory," said Watson, "has been *Grewgious's* remark that his clerk 'is off duty here, altogether, just at present, and a firm downstairs lent me a substitute.'"

"And the remark is extremely significant," Holmes commented. "Observe, *Grewgious* does not say that *Bazzard* has left him, but that he is 'off duty just for the present'—meaning that he is temporarily engaged on business away from the office. *Grewgious* has borrowed a substitute, which clearly shows that the lawyer expects his clerk to return, and knows why he is away. *Grewgious* might have said that *Bazzard* was taking a vacation, or was away because his play was going to be produced, or otherwise accounted for his absence; but he leaves the reason for the clerk's absence vague and mysterious. *Datchery* appears just as Bazzard is 'off duty' in the novel. All the other characters are in evidence. *Neville Landless* has a room engaged for him, where he is studying law and is visited by *Crisparkle. Helena,* we are told, is to be with him to cheer and encourage him. *Tartar* has his rooms in the same building, and does not disappear from the story. *Bazzard* alone vanishes from the scene after the reader has been told a great deal about him."

"But," I ventured to say, "Dickens often introduces characters for incidental humor, and soon allows them to drop out of the story."

"But *Bazzard* is not one of these transient comedy characters. He is not comic. He is negative, an uninteresting person. In fact, he completely realizes the type of man referred to in Dickens's notebook—'a sort of insect to be brushed aside.'"

"You seem to forget, Mr. Holmes," I reminded him, "that *Helena Landless* is the person who has the strongest motive for proving the guilt of *Jasper*—the establishing of her brother's innocence."

"It is true that *Helena* has a motive; but, in spite of that, the improbability—nay, the impossibility—of a girl's masquerading as an elderly man and deceiving everybody, including the criminal himself, in my opinion, nullifies the claim of the Helenists."

"And what motive could *Bazzard* have?" asked Watson.

"In the first place, the motive of serving his employer, *Grewgious.* Secondly, the motive of doing work congenial to a man of theatrical inclinations. There is also the motive of helping to bring a scoundrel to justice. The only ambition indicated in *Bazzard* is connected with the theater. If *Grewgious* had suggested such a melodramatic mission to the clerk who had written a play, *Bazzard* would probably have jumped at the chance to try his hand at an employment far more congenial than law office routine. It would not be difficult for him to disguise himself as an elderly man. He would need just enough disguise to avoid a chance recognition as *Grewgious's* clerk."

Holmes ceased, and for a few moments seemed to be lost in thought.

"We are still here," Watson reminded him; and he emerged from his cogitations.

Minor Mysteries of the Novel

"To go further into *Bazzard's* motive for the *Datchery* masquerade," he said, "I should have to know secrets that Dickens carried to his grave. I have given you a fair exposition of my argument to show that *Drood* was not killed; and it is possible that I have convinced you, as I have convinced myself, that *Datchery* is *Bazzard.* These are the two leading problems in the novel; but it contains other mysteries—enigmas that will never be satisfactorily solved, and can only be vaguely guessed. For example, why does the opium woman hate *Jasper?* She says she knows him 'better than all the learned parsons put together know him.' Perhaps the fact that *Jasper*, in her presence and under the influence of the drug, has babbled of the crime he contemplated is enough to account for that remark; but would it be enough to take her to Cloisterham, to look, as she says, 'for a needle in a bundle of hay'? She is so poor that she begs three shillings and sixpence on two different occasions, yet she journeys twice to a town twenty-six miles from London to trail and spy upon *Jasper*, whom she often has had at her mercy in her opium den."

"Mr. Cuming Walters," I suggested, "believes that the opium woman is *Jasper's* mother."

"So I have observed," said Holmes. "Mr. Walters also asserts that 'the opium vice is hereditary'—which it is not, as I happen to know. The opium woman speaks the dialect of the lowest slums. *Jasper* is a man of education, a musician. If she is his mother, she must be old *Mrs. Jasper*, *Drood's* maternal grandmother. She says she 'got heavens-hard drunk for sixteen years' before she took to opium. We are told that *Drood's* father was a college man and a prosperous business man. I see nothing in the novel to indicate that he married the daughter of a disreputable old hag. It is probable that the woman was to be a witness at *Jasper's* trial.

"Then," continued the great detective, "there is the impish vagrant boy, *Deputy*. His nocturnal roamings mean something. He and *Jasper* hate each other. He is referred to in Dickens's preliminary notes for the novel—'Remember there is a child,' and 'Keep the boy suspended.' Probably he, too, was to be a witness at the trial. He saw *Jasper* and *Durdles* leave the cathedral after their midnight visit to the crypt and the tower. It is likely that *Datchery* learns a good deal from the boy, with whom he makes friends."

"One of the interesting secondary mysteries," I suggested, "is *Durdles's* story told to *Jasper* during the nocturnal expedition to the cathedral. *Durdles* relates that on the preceding Christmas Eve he was in the crypt, sleeping off a debauch. He was awakened by a 'terrific shriek,' followed by the 'long, dismal, woeful howl of a dog.' *Jasper* is agitated by this information, but there is no further allusion to it in the novel. Several of the writers on the subject think that this incident is a sort of occult premonition—that the shriek is *Jasper's* shriek as he falls, or is thrown, from the tower on the Christmas Eve following the supposed murder of *Drood*."

"According to this theory," answered Holmes, "the shriek and the howl would have been premonitions just two years before their fulfillment. Why should they be heard by *Durdles*, about the last person who could be thought to be psychic or clairvoyant? I fancy that the mason's story is merely a bit of weird detail to add to the suggestion of *Jasper's* sinister motive in visiting the crypt and the tower. If *Jasper* had been up to any mischief in the cathedral on the Christmas Eve preceding the attack on *Drood*—anything to cause a shriek and a howl actually heard—he would have been familiar with the premises, and would not have had to go on the reconnoitering expedition with *Durdles*. *Jasper* becomes nervous when the mason tells the story. Perhaps he, with a murder in contemplation, regards the weird nocturnal noises as ominous."

"There is one more point on which I would like to hear your opinion," said Watson. "In the last chapter written, *Jasper*, under the influence of opium, speaks of 'a hazardous journey, over abysses where a slip would be destruction.' 'Look down, look down!' he says; 'you see what lies at the bottom there?' He

'points as though at some imaginary object far beneath.' 'And yet I never saw *that* before,' he says. '*That* must be real. It's over!' As Mr. Andrew Lang asked, what can all this mean?"

Holmes thought deeply for a moment.

"I'm damned if I know," he finally replied. "And yet the science of deduction is of value even here. The illustrations on the cover are evidently a pictorial summary of the principal incidents in the novel. They cannot be anything else. One of them represents three men rushing up a circular staircase—that of the cathedral tower, of course. The leader points upward. It is *Neville Landless*. The other men are *Crisparkle* and *Tartar*. They are pursuing some one. Who could it be but *Jasper*? The inference is that *Jasper*, discovered in his visit to the tomb, rushes up the tower staircase. The three watchers pursue, *Neville* leading. At the top of the tower he and *Jasper* struggle. *Neville* is thrown from the tower and killed; so there is an actual murder, for which *Jasper* is to pay the penalty. 'Look down! I never saw *that* before. *That* must be real.' These ravings, I believe, are premonitory, and refer to *Neville's* body."

"Your deductions have interested me greatly," I observed, helping myself to the very excellent Irish whisky proffered by our host; "but you have not taken into account the assertion of John Forster, Dickens's biographer, that the novelist told him that *Drood* was to be murdered. The son and the daughter of the author made similar statements."

"I attach no importance whatever to such testimony," said Holmes. "My friend Watson states in one of his stories that I have no knowledge of literature. I don't deny the charge; but I am sure of one thing—no novelist with a complicated plot in his mind is likely to go around telling it to his friends and relatives. Dickens guarded his plot jealously. He expressly told Forster, in a letter, that the plot was 'incommunicable.' I don't believe that he revealed it to anybody. I am by no means certain that if Dickens had lived to complete 'The Mystery of Edwin Drood,' it would not now be considered the best of his novels. An admirable critic, the writer whose *nom de plume* is John o' London, recently said of it:

"It is a novel whose very style, so unusually wrought, poetic and haunting in its movements and cadences, might alone suggest that he had formed a fine design."

"One more question, Holmes," said Watson.

The great detective displayed unmistakable evidence of impatience.

"My good Watson," he said, "I must remind you of the forceful words of old *Father William* in that excellent work, 'Alice in Wonderland':

"' I have answered three questions, and that is enough,'
    Said his father; 'don't give yourself airs!
Do you think I can listen all day to such stuff?
    Be off, or I'll kick you downstairs!'

"While I do not seriously meditate any such breach of hospitality, I must remind you that I have answered many more questions than the three that exhausted the patience of that estimable patriarch."

With this remark, Holmes took up a volume, which I recognized as "The Mystery of Edwin Drood," and immediately became absorbed in it. As he seemed determined to ignore our presence entirely, after some fifteen minutes of silence Watson quietly intimated to me his own deduction that the interview was at an end.

The Great Flea Mystery   By Snowshoe Al

Alaska's Cold Comedian, Bored to Tears by Modern Detective Mystery Plays, Writes One for Himself

"I've got it pretty well figured out, Wilson," said Unlock Homes. . . . "I'm fairly certain that the flea will stroll by here within the next 45 minutes."

ACT I

SCENE: Interior of Unlock Homes' lavishly furnished one-room apartment on Fifth avenue in the quaint old village of New Yawk. Through the front window one can see the famous Waldorf-Astoria Rooming House. Through the side window one can see nothing, due to the fact that the window needs a bath. Through the rear window one can also see nothing. There's no rear window.

Unlock Homes, the great sleuth, is squirming around beneath the davenport trying to find his coat an' vest. His bosom friend an' drinking companion, Dr. Wilson, is crawling around under the carpet trying to find Mr. Homes' pants.

MR. HOMES: "Well, Wilson, I'm afraid I can't recall just where I put my coat an' vest. I give up!"

DR. WILSON: "Yeh, an' I can't locate your pants either! Why ain't you more careful about your clothes when you take 'em off in the evening? Why don'tcha lay 'em over a chair, huh? A swell detective you are, you ! ? ! ? Your brain is smaller than an ant's appendix! You couldn't pick out a giraffe among a flock o' rabbits."

MR. HOMES: "What! You can't find my trousers? I wonder what I did with 'em. Oh, well, let 'em go—I'll wear my long overcoat today. Uh—er—I wonder where my long overcoat is."

DR. WILSON: "I ain't seen it since the day your shirt disappeared."

(At this moment somebody knocks timidly on the door.)

Dr. Wilson opens the door an' admits a tough-looking hombre with a bald head and a red snoot.

MR. HOMES (snatching a blanket from the bed an' wrapping it around himself): "Ah, a customer! Let her in, Wilson. I know it's a lady—"

Dr. Wilson opens the door an' admits a tough looking hombre with a bald head, a crop of whiskers an' a red snoot. The nude knob an' the chin shrubbery are the work of Nature, but the crimson bugle is a work of art.

VISITOR: "Mr. Homes, my name is Black. I want you to handle a matter for me—a matter which will necessitate your going out on the streets an' mingling with the crowds—"

MR. HOMES: "Not a chance! No! Every time I mingle with a crowd, somebody swipes my detective badge."

MR. BLACK: "But, Mr. Homes, you *must* help me! I will pay you well. You see, I am the owner of a highly intelligent troupe of trained fleas, among which is one flea named Galahad. Galahad is a very rare specimen; in fact, his present market value, allowing for depreciation, is at least five hundred shekels. Last night—"

MR. HOMES: "A flea worth half a grand? Baby, he *must* be a rare kid! What kind of a dog did he graduate from?"

MR. BLACK: "Ah, Mr. Sleuth, that's just it! That's why he's so valuable! He came from a specie of canine that isn't supposed to have fleas. Galahad was captured while reposing on a Coney Island frankfurt!

"I WAS putting my troupe through a rehearsal last night when suddenly Galahad started acting queer. He began kicking himself in the face, an' this, as you undoubtedly know, is almost a sure indication of earache, so I thrust him hurriedly into my pocket an' rushed over to the home of a prominent veterinary surgeon on Fifth avenue.

"Gentlemen, you can imagine my horror when, after entering the physician's dwelling, I discovered that Galahad had fallen out of my pocket an' was lost in the darkness somewhere on the sidewalks of New Yawk!

"That's the whole story. An' so, Mr. Homes, I want you to find Galahad. Take your magnifying glass, go out on the street an' study the sidewalk closely. Sooner or later, he will stroll past, headed south! Always remember that a flea, unless mentally unbalanced, will invariably start walking southward!"

MR. HOMES: "How will I know it's him? What does a flea look like?"

MR. BLACK: "A microscopic examination of a flea reveals the fact that its body closely resembles that of a hippopotamus, while its face reminds one of a dinosaur. Anyhow, Galahad is wearing a tiny, red sweater, so you'll have no trouble recognizing him."

MR. HOMES: "I'll take the case! I'll start right now! Wilson, my hat!"

DR. WILSON: "Where is it?"

MR. HOMES: "It's uh—er—I think—never mind, I'll go bare-headed. By the way, Mr. Black, suppose Galahad fools me by discarding his red sweater—is there any other way of knowing him?"

MR. BLACK: "Yes! He's got his hair parted in the middle."

MR. HOMES: "This is a cinch! Wait here for us, Mr. Black. Come with me, Wilson!"

ACT II

TIME: One hour later.

SCENE: Fifth avenue. The great sleuth is standing 30 feet south of the veterinary surgeon's residence an' is studying the sidewalk silently an' closely through a huge magnifying glass. Dr. Wilson is at his side. Hurrying throngs of passersby stare curiously at the pair.

MR. HOMES: "I've got it pretty well figured out, Wilson. Assuming that the flea fell to the sidewalk directly in front of the surgeon's home, an' estimating his walking speed to be about 11 inches per hour, I'm fairly certain that he will stroll by this spot within the next 45 minutes. By the way, the sidewalk seems rather crowded."

DR. WILSON: "Yeh, there's lots o' people starin' at you. Remember, you ain't got nothing on except your shoes, your underwear an' that blanket!"

MR. HOMES: "G'wan! I've also got my detective badge on—it's pinned on my underwear."

An hour rolls slowly by, an' little Galahad has not yet put in his appearance. A beaten look settles upon the great sleuth's face. Sighing heavily, he removes his eyes from the sidewalk an' discovers that a large policeman is standing nearby gazing at him suspiciously.

OFFICER KELLY: "What's the idea o' parading around on Fifth avenue in a blanket? Nobody wears blankets except Indians an' horses. Which do you think you are, huh? What are you advertising?"

MR. HOMES: "Ah, officer, I'm looking for a little, lost flea named Galahad. He wears a red sweater an' has his hair parted in the middle."

OFFICER KELLY (patting Homes' back reassuringly): "Now, don't get all excited, Napoleon, I'm gonna take you to your little padded bungalow! I've picked up a dozen o' youse brain-wrecked boys since the stock market flopped last Wednesday. Come, Prince Charming, I'm gonna lead youse to a fairy castle where you can forget all about Wall Street. Accompany me, Filbert, an' I shall see that no harm befalls thee—"

MR. HOMES (very indignantly): "Sir! I do not care for that 'Filbert' stuff. Your phraseology would seem to indicate that you suspect me of being non compos mentis! I would have you know that I am a private detective of great renown!"

OFFICER KELLY: "Oh, yeh? Where's your clothes?"

MR. HOMES (blushing furiously): "They're somewhere in my apartment but I can't find 'em."

OFFICER KELLY: "I still think my first guess was correct. Come, Filbert—"

DR. WILSON: "Homes, you better show the officer your badge."

MR. HOMES (reaching inside his blanket): "A good idea—a *very* good idea! I shall prove to this policeman that I am—er—uh—" (His face turns pale. Then, slowly an' warily he partly unfolds his blanket an' peers within.) "Yeowww! It's gone—somebody's hooked it! They didn't bother unfastening it—they took my underwear too!"

ACT III

TIME: One hour later.

SCENE: Same as Act I. Mr. Homes is seated at his desk. Dr. Wilson is crawling around under the carpet looking for the sleuth's slippers.

THE FLEA CROUCHED FOR ITS SPRING

MAGNIFIED SEVERAL THOUSAND TIMES

MR. HOMES: "The day has been an awful flop, Wilson. Very annoying—ah, the phone is ringing. Answer the phone, Wilson."

DR. WILSON (in a voice that can be heard for two blocks): "Hello! Who? Oh, hello, Mr. Black, I thought you was gonna wait here until we—what? He *did*? All right, Mr. Black. Goodby."

MR. HOMES: "What happened?"

DR. WILSON: "Well, it seems that, while Mr. Black was sitting here, his assistant trainer rushed in an' informed him that little Galahad had returned home. You see, when he fell to the sidewalk last night he bruised three of his knees an' therefore he couldn't walk at all, the poor little fellow."

"However, a strong gust of wind blew him across the street, so he crawled painfully up the steps of a branch post-office an' sneaked beneath the door. After what must have been a terrible search, he finally found a letter addressed to Mr. Black, so he clung to the stamp with his teeth an' was delivered today on the noon mail!"

MR. HOMES: "Damned clever, these fleas! Hand me my trusty briar pipe, Wilson."

DR. WILSON: "Sa-ay, if you think I'm gonna start lookin' for that!?!? pipe again—"

MR. HOMES (hurriedly): "Gimme a cigaret!"

A last, pseudonymously bylined story closes our Sherlockian burlesques. It appears to have been a syndicated release that ran in the San Francisco Chronicle *for October 2, 1932, but it carries no credit or copyright notice. (Nor did any other "Snowshoe Al" material run in the* Chronicle.) *The art, however, is by the noted cartoonist Don Wootton.*

THE REAL, RIGHT THING

It is difficult to affirm that any particular Sherlock Holmes story by Doyle is more American in its narrative elements than several others with similar American characters, narrative background, or case origins. However, a check with a number of active Sherlockians has produced a consensus of opinion that pointed to "The Adventure of the Noble Bachelor" as their own favorite "American" Holmes story. It has accordingly been selected for reprint here as a fit conclusion to Sherlock Holmes in America. The story was first published in The Strand for April 1892 and became a part of The Adventures of Sherlock Holmes of that same year.

The Adventure of the Noble Bachelor

By Arthur Conan Doyle

THE Lord St. Simon marriage, and its curious termination, have long ceased to be a subject of interest in those exalted circles in which the unfortunate bridegroom moves. Fresh scandals have eclipsed it, and their more piquant details have drawn the gossips away from this four-year-old drama. As I have reason to believe, however, that the full facts have never been revealed to the general public, and as my friend Sherlock Holmes had a considerable share in clearing the matter up, I feel that no memoir of him would be complete without some little sketch of this remarkable episode.

It was a few weeks before my own marriage, during the days when I was still sharing rooms with Holmes in Baker Street, that he came home from an afternoon stroll to find a letter on the table waiting for him. I had remained in-doors all day, for the weather had taken a sudden turn to rain, with high autumnal winds, and the jezail bullet which I had brought back in one of my limbs as a relic of my Afghan campaign, throbbed with dull persistency. With my body in one easy-chair and my legs upon another, I had surrounded myself with a cloud of news-papers, until at last, saturated with the news of the day, I tossed them all aside and lay listless, watching the huge crest and monogram upon the envelope upon the table, and wondering lazily who my friend's noble correspondent could be.

"Here is a very fashionable epistle," I remarked, as he entered. "Your morning letters, if I remember right, were from a fish-monger and a tide-waiter."

"Yes, my correspondence has certainly the charm of variety," he answered, smiling, "and the humbler are usually the more interesting. This looks like one of those unwelcome social sum-monses which call upon a man either to be bored or to lie."

He broke the seal and glanced over the contents.

"Oh, come, it may prove to be something of interest after all."

"Not social, then?"

"No, distinctly professional."

"And from a noble client?"

"One of the highest in England."

"My dear fellow, I congratulate you."

"I assure you, Watson, without affectation, that the status of my client is a matter of less moment to me than the interest of his case. It is just possible, however, that that also may not be wanting in this new investigation. You have been reading the papers diligently of late, have you not?"

"It looks like it," said I, ruefully, pointing to a huge bundle in the corner. "I have had nothing else to do."

"It is fortunate, for you will perhaps be able to post me up. I read nothing except the criminal news and the agony column. The latter is always instructive. But if you have followed recent events so closely you must have read about Lord St. Simon and his wedding?"

"Oh yes, with the deepest interest."

"That is well. The letter which I hold in my hand is from Lord St. Simon. I will read it to you, and in return you must turn over these papers and let me have whatever bears upon the matter. This is what he says:

"'MY DEAR MR. SHERLOCK HOLMES,—Lord Backwater tells me that I may place implicit reliance upon your judgment and discretion. I have determined, therefore, to call upon you, and to consult you in reference to the very painful event which has occurred in connection with my wedding. Mr. Lestrade, of Scotland Yard, is acting already in the matter, but he assures me that he sees no objection to your co-operation, and that he even thinks that it might be of some as-sistance. I will call at four o'clock in the afternoon, and, should you have any other engagement at that time, I hope that you will postpone it, as this matter is of paramount importance.
Yours faithfully,   ST. SIMON.'

"It is dated from Grosvenor Mansions, written with a quill pen, and the noble lord has had the misfortune to get a smear of ink upon the outer side of his right little finger," remarked Holmes, as he folded up the epistle.

"He says four o'clock. It is three now. He will be here in an hour."

"Then I have just time, with your assistance, to get clear upon the subject. Turn over those papers, and arrange the extracts in their order of time, while I take a glance as to who our client is." He picked a red-covered volume from a line of books of reference beside the mantel-piece. "Here he is," said he, sitting down and flattening it out upon his knee. "Lord Robert Walsingham de Vere St. Simon, second son of the Duke of Balmoral—Hum! Arms: Azure, three caltrops in chief over a fess sable. Born in 1846. He's forty-one years of age, which is mature for marriage. Was Under-secretary for the Colonies in a late Administration. The Duke, his father, was at one time Secretary for Foreign Affairs. They inherit Plantagenet blood by direct descent, and Tudor on the distaff side. Ha! Well, there is nothing very instructive in all this. I think that I must turn to you, Watson, for something more solid."

"I have very little difficulty in finding what I want," said I, "for the facts are quite recent, and the matter struck me as remarkable. I feared to refer them to you, however, as I knew that you had an inquiry on hand, and that you disliked the intrusion of other matters."

"Oh, you mean the little problem of the Grosvenor Square furniture van. That is quite cleared up now—though, indeed, it was obvious from the first. Pray give me the results of your newspaper selections."

"Here is the first notice which I can find. It is in the personal column of *The Morning Post,* and dates, as you see, some weeks back. 'A marriage has been arranged,' it says, 'and will, if rumor is correct, very shortly take place, between Lord Robert St. Simon, second son of the Duke of Balmoral, and Miss Hatty Doran, the only daughter of Aloysius Doran, Esq., of San Francisco, Cal., U.S.A.' That is all."

"Terse and to the point," remarked Holmes, stretching his long, thin legs towards the fire.

"There was a paragraph amplifying this in one of the society papers of the same week. Ah, here it is. 'There will soon be a call for protection in the marriage market, for the present free-trade principle appears to tell heavily against our home product. One by one the management of the noble houses of Great Britain is passing into the hands of our fair cousins from across the Atlantic. An important addition has been made during the last week to the list of the prizes which have been borne away by these charming invaders. Lord St. Simon, who has shown himself for over twenty years proof against the little god's arrows, has now definitely announced his approaching marriage with Miss Hatty Doran, the fascinating daughter of a California millionaire. Miss Doran, whose graceful figure and striking face attracted much attention at the Westbury House festivities, is an only child, and it is currently reported that her dowry will run to considerably over the six figures, with expectancies for the future. As it is an open secret that the Duke of Balmoral has been compelled to sell his pictures within the last few years, and as Lord St. Simon has no property of his own, save the small estate of Birchmoor, it is obvious that the Californian heiress is not the only gainer by an alliance which will enable her to make the easy and common transition from a Republican lady to a British peeress.'"

"Anything else?" asked Holmes, yawning.

"Oh yes; plenty. Then there is another note in *The Morning Post* to say that the marriage would be an absolutely quiet one, that it would be at St. George's, Hanover Square, that only half a dozen intimate friends would be invited, and that the party would return to the furnished house at Lancaster Gate which has been taken by Mr. Aloysius Doran. Two days later—that is, on Wednesday last—there is a curt announcement that the wedding had taken place, and that the honey-moon would be passed at Lord Backwater's place, near Petersfield. Those are all the notices which appeared before the disappearance of the bride."

"Before the what?" asked Holmes, with a start.

"The vanishing of the lady."

"When did she vanish, then?"

"At the wedding breakfast."

"Indeed. This is more interesting than it promised to be; quite dramatic, in fact."

"Yes; it struck me as being a little out of the common."

"They often vanish before the ceremony, and occasionally during the honey-moon; but I cannot call to mind anything quite so prompt as this. Pray let me have the details."

"I warn you that they are very incomplete."

"Perhaps we may make them less so."

"Such as they are, they are set forth in a single article of a morning paper of yesterday, which I will read to you. It is headed, 'Singular Occurrence at a Fashionable Wedding':

"'The family of Lord Robert St. Simon has been thrown into the greatest consternation by the strange and painful episodes which have taken place in connection with his wedding. The ceremony, as shortly announced in the papers of yesterday, occurred on the previous morning; but it is only now that it has been possible to confirm the strange rumors which have been so persistently floating about. In spite of the attempts of the friends to hush the matter up, so much public attention has now been drawn to it that no good purpose can be served by affecting to disregard what is a common subject for conversation.

"'The ceremony, which was performed at St. George's, Hanover Square, was a very quiet one, no one being present save the father of the bride, Mr. Aloysius Doran, the Duchess of Balmoral, Lord Backwater, Lord Eustace, and Lady Clara St. Simon (the younger brother and sister of the bridegroom), and Lady Alicia Whittington. The whole party proceeded afterwards to the house of Mr. Aloysius Doran, at Lancaster Gate, where breakfast had been prepared. It appears that some little trouble was caused by a woman, whose name has not been ascertained, who endeavored to force her way into the house after the bridal party, alleging that she had some claim upon Lord St. Simon. It was only after a painful and prolonged scene that she was ejected by the butler and the footman. The bride, who had fortunately entered the house before this unpleasant interruption, had sat down to breakfast with the rest, when she complained of a sudden indisposition, and retired to her room. Her prolonged absence having caused some comment, her father followed her, but learned from her maid that she had only come up to her chamber for an instant, caught up an ulster and bonnet, and hurried down to the passage. One of the footmen declared that he had seen a lady leave the house thus apparelled, but had refused to credit that it was his mistress, believing her to be with the company. On ascertaining that his daughter had disappeared, Mr. Aloysius Doran, in conjunction with the bridegroom, instantly put themselves into communication with the police, and very energetic inquiries are being made, which will probably result in a speedy clearing up of this very singular business. Up to a late hour last night, however, nothing had transpired as to the whereabouts of the missing lady. There are rumors of foul play in the matter, and it is said that the police have caused the arrest of the woman who had caused the original disturbance, in the belief that, from jealousy or some other motive, she may have been concerned in the strange disappearance of the bride.'"

"And is that all?"

"Only one little item in another of the morning papers, but it is a suggestive one."

"And it is—"

"That Miss Flora Millar, the lady who had caused the disturbance, has actually been arrested. It appears that she was formerly a *danseuse* at the 'Allegro,' and that she has known the bridegroom for some years. There are no further particulars, and the whole case is in your hands now—so far as it has been set forth in the public press."

"And an exceedingly interesting case it appears to be. I would not have missed it for worlds. But there is a ring at the bell, Watson, and as the clock makes it a few minutes after four, I have no doubt that this will prove to be our noble client. Do not dream of going, Watson, for I very much prefer having a witness, if only as a check to my own memory."

"Lord Robert St. Simon," announced our page-boy, throwing open the door. A gentleman entered, with a pleasant, cultured face, high-nosed and pale, with something perhaps of petulance about the mouth, and with the steady, well-opened eye of a man whose pleasant lot it had ever been to command and to be obeyed. His manner was brisk, and yet his general appearance gave an undue impression of age, for he had a slight forward stoop and a little bend of the knees as he walked. His hair, too, as he swept off his very curly-brimmed hat, was grizzled round the edges and thin upon the top. As to his dress, it was careful to the verge of foppishness, with high collar, black frock-coat, white waistcoat, yellow gloves, patent-leather shoes, and light-colored gaiters. He advanced slowly into the room, turning his head from left to right, and swinging in his right hand the cord which held his golden eye-glasses.

"Good-day, Lord St. Simon," said Holmes, rising and bowing. "Pray take the basket-chair. This is my friend and colleague, Dr. Watson. Draw up a little to the fire, and we will talk this matter over."

"A most painful matter to me, as you can most readily imagine, Mr. Holmes. I have been cut to the quick. I understand that you have already managed several delicate cases of this sort, sir, though I presume that they were hardly from the same class of society."

"No, I am descending."

"I beg pardon."

"My last client of the sort was a king."

"Oh, really! I had no idea. And which king?"

"The King of Scandinavia."

"What! Had he lost his wife?"

"You can understand," said Holmes, suavely, "that I extend to the affairs of my other clients the same secrecy which I promise to you in yours."

"Of course! Very right! very right! I'm sure I beg pardon. As to my own case, I am ready to give you any information which may assist you in forming an opinion."

"Thank you. I have already learned all that is in the public prints, nothing more. I presume that I may take it as correct—this article, for example, as to the disappearance of the bride."

Lord St. Simon glanced over it. "Yes, it is correct, as far as it goes."

"But it needs a great deal of supplementing before any one could offer an opinion. I think that I may arrive at my facts most directly by questioning you."

"Pray do so."

"When did you first meet Miss Hatty Doran?"

"In San Francisco, a year ago."

"You were travelling in the States?"

"Yes."

"Did you become engaged then?"

"No."

"But you were on a friendly footing?"

"I was amused by her society, and she could see that I was amused."

"Her father is very rich?"

"He is said to be the richest man on the Pacific slope."

"And how did he make his money?"

"In mining. He had nothing a few years ago. Then he struck gold, invested it, and came up by leaps and bounds."

"Now, what is your own impression as to the young lady's—your wife's character?"

The nobleman swung his glasses a little faster and stared down into the fire. "You see, Mr. Holmes," said he, "my wife was twenty before her father became a rich man. During that time she ran free in a mining camp, and wandered through woods or mountains, so that her education has come from Nature rather than from the school-master. She is what we call in England a tomboy, with a strong nature, wild and free, un-fettered by any sort of traditions. She is impetuous—volcanic, I was about to say. She is swift in making up her mind, and fearless in carrying out her resolutions. On the other hand, I would not have given her the name which I have the honor to bear"—he gave a little stately cough—"had not I thought her to be at bottom a noble woman. I believe that she is capable of heroic self-sacrifice, and that anything dishonorable would be repugnant to her."

"Have you her photograph?"

"I brought this with me." He opened a locket, and showed us the full face of a very lovely woman. It was not a photograph, but an ivory miniature, and the artist had brought out the full effect of the lustrous black hair, the large dark eyes, and the exquisite mouth. Holmes gazed long and earnestly at it. Then he closed the locket and handed it back to Lord St. Simon.

"The young lady came to London, then, and you renewed your acquaintance?"

"Yes, her father brought her over for this last London season. I met her several times, became engaged to her, and have now married her."

"She brought, I understand, a considerable dowry?"

"A fair dowry. Not more than is usual in my family."

"And this, of course, remains to you, since the marriage is a *fait accompli?*"

"I really have made no inquiries on the subject."

"Very naturally not. Did you see Miss Doran on the day before the wedding?"

"Yes."

"Was she in good spirits?"

"Never better. She kept talking of what we should do in our future lives."

"Indeed! That is very interesting. And on the morning of the wedding?"

"She was as bright as possible—at least, until after the ceremony."

"And did you observe any change in her then?"

"Well, to tell the truth, I saw then the first signs that I had ever seen that her temper was just a little sharp. The incident, however, was too trivial to relate, and can have no possible bearing upon the case."

"Pray let us have it, for all that."

"Oh, it is childish. She dropped her bouquet as we went towards the vestry. She was passing the front pew at the time, and it fell over into the pew. There was a moment's delay, but the gentleman in the pew handed it up to her again, and it did not appear to be the worse for the fall. Yet, when I spoke to her of the matter, she answered me abruptly; and in the carriage, on our way home, she seemed absurdly agitated over this trifling cause."

"Indeed! You say that there was a gentleman in the pew. Some of the general public were present, then?"

"Oh yes. It is impossible to exclude them when the church is open."

"This gentleman was not one of your wife's friends?"

"No, no; I call him a gentleman by courtesy, but he was quite a common-looking person. I hardly noticed his appearance. But really I think that we are wandering rather far from the point."

"Lady St. Simon, then, returned from the wedding in a less cheerful frame of mind than she had gone to it. What did she do on re-entering her father's house?"

"I saw her in conversation with her maid."

"And who is her maid?"

"Alice is her name. She is an American, and came from California with her."

"A confidential servant?"

"A little too much so. It seemed to me that her mistress allowed her to take great liberties. Still, of course, in America they look upon these things in a different way."

"How long did she speak to this Alice?"

"Oh, a few minutes. I had something else to think of."

"You did not overhear what they said?"

"Lady St. Simon said something about 'jumping a claim.' She was accustomed to use slang of the kind. I have no idea what she meant."

"American slang is very expressive sometimes. And what did your wife do when she finished speaking to her maid?"

"She walked into the breakfast-room."

"On your arm?"

"No, alone. She was very independent in little matters like that. Then, after we had sat down for ten minutes or so, she rose hurriedly, muttered some words of apology, and left the room. She never came back."

"But this maid, Alice, as I understand, deposes that she went to her room, covered her bride's dress with a long ulster, put on a bonnet, and went out."

"Quite so. And she was afterwards seen walking into Hyde Park in company with Flora Millar, a woman who is now in custody, and who had already made a disturbance at Mr. Doran's house that morning."

"Ah, yes. I should like a few particulars as to this young lady, and your relations to her."

Lord St. Simon shrugged his shoulders and raised his eyebrows. "We have been on a friendly footing for some years—I may say on a *very* friendly footing. She used to be at the 'Allegro.' I have not treated her ungenerously, and she has no just cause of complaint against me, but you know what women are, Mr. Holmes. Flora was a dear little thing, but exceedingly hot-headed, and devotedly attached to me. She wrote me dreadful letters when she heard that I was about to be married; and, to tell the truth, the reason why I had the marriage celebrated so quietly was that I feared lest there might be a scandal in the church. She came to Mr. Doran's door just after we returned, and she endeavored to push her way in, uttering very abusive expressions towards my wife, and even threatening her, but I had foreseen the possibility of something of the sort, and I had two police fellows there in private clothes, who soon pushed her out again. She was quiet when she saw that there was no good in making a row."

"Did your wife hear all this?"

"No, thank goodness, she did not."

"And she was seen walking with this very woman afterwards?"

"Yes. That is what Mr. Lestrade, of Scotland Yard, looks upon as so serious. It is thought that Flora decoyed my wife out, and laid some terrible trap for her."

"Well, it is a possible supposition."

"You think so, too?"

"I did not say a probable one. But you do not yourself look upon this as likely?"

"I do not think Flora would hurt a fly."

"Still, jealousy is a strange transformer of characters. Pray what is your own theory as to what took place?"

"Well, really, I came to seek a theory, not to propound one. I have given you all the facts. Since you ask me, however, I may say that it has occurred to me as possible that the excitement of this affair, the consciousness that she had made so immense a social stride, had the effect of causing some little nervous disturbance in my wife."

"In short, that she had become suddenly deranged?"

"Well, really, when I consider that she has turned her back—I will not say upon me, but upon so much that many have aspired to without success—I can hardly explain it in any other fashion."

"Well, certainly that is also a conceivable hypothesis," said Holmes, smiling. "And now, Lord St. Simon, I think that I have nearly all my data. May I ask whether you were seated at the breakfast-table so that you could see out of the window?"

"We could see the other side of the road and the Park."

"Quite so. Then I do not think that I need to detain you longer. I shall communicate with you."

"Should you be fortunate enough to solve this problem," said our client, rising.

"I have solved it."

"Eh? What was that?"

"I say that I have solved it."

"Where, then, is my wife?"

"That is a detail which I shall speedily supply."

Lord St. Simon shook his head. "I am afraid that it will take wiser heads than yours or mine," he remarked, and bowing in a stately, old-fashioned manner, he departed.

"It is very good of Lord St. Simon to honor my head by putting it on a level with his own," said Sherlock Holmes, laughing. "I think that I shall have a whiskey-and-soda and a cigar after all this cross-questioning. I had formed my conclusions as to the case before our client came into the room."

"My dear Holmes!"

"I have notes of several similar cases, though none, as I remarked before, which were quite as prompt. My whole examination served to turn my conjecture into a certainty. Circumstantial evidence is occasionally very convincing, as when you find a trout in the milk, to quote Thoreau's example."

"But I have heard all that you have heard."

"Without, however, the knowledge of pre-existing cases which serves me so well. There was a parallel instance in Aberdeen some years back, and something on very much the same lines at Munich the year after the Franco-Prussian war. It is one of these cases—but, hello, here is Lestrade! Good-afternoon, Lestrade! You will find an extra tumbler upon the sideboard, and there are cigars in the box."

The official detective was attired in a pea-jacket and cravat, which gave him a decidedly nautical appearance, and he carried a black canvas bag in his hand. With a short greeting he seated himself and lit the cigar which had been offered to him.

"What's up, then?" asked Holmes, with a twinkle in his eye. "You look dissatisfied."

"And I feel dissatisfied. It is this infernal St. Simon marriage case. I can make neither head nor tail of the business."

"Really! You surprise me."

"Who ever heard of such a mixed affair? Every clew seems to slip through my fingers. I have been at work upon it all day."

"And very wet it seems to have made you," said Holmes, laying his hand upon the arm of the peajacket.

"Yes, I have been dragging the Serpentine."

"In Heaven's name, what for?"

"In search of the body of Lady St. Simon."

Sherlock Holmes leaned back in his chair and laughed heartily.

"Have you dragged the basin of Trafalgar Square fountain?" he asked.

"Why? What do you mean?"

"Because you have just as good a chance of finding this lady in the one as in the other."

Lestrade shot an angry glance at my companion. "I suppose you know all about it," he snarled.

"Well, I have only just heard the facts, but my mind is made up."

"Oh, indeed! Then you think that the Serpentine plays no part in the matter?"

"I think it very unlikely."

"Then perhaps you will kindly explain how it is that we found this in it?" He opened his bag as he spoke, and tumbled onto the floor a wedding-dress of watered silk, a pair of white satin shoes, and a bride's wreath and veil, all discolored and soaked in water. "There," said he, putting a new wedding-ring upon the top of the pile. "There is a little nut for you to crack, Master Holmes."

"Oh, indeed!" said my friend, blowing blue rings into the air. "You dragged them from the Serpentine?"

"No. They were found floating near the margin by a park-keeper. They have been identified as her clothes, and it seemed to me that if the clothes were there the body would not be far off."

"By the same brilliant reasoning, every man's body is to be found in the neighborhood of his wardrobe. And pray what did you hope to arrive at through this?"

"At some evidence implicating Flora Millar in the disappearance."

"I am afraid that you will find it difficult."

"Are you, indeed, now?" cried Lestrade, with some bitterness. "I am afraid, Holmes, that you are not very practical with your deductions and your inferences. You have made two blunders in as many minutes. This dress does implicate Miss Flora Millar."

"And how?"

"In the dress is a pocket. In the pocket is a card-case. In the card-case is a note. And here is the very note." He slapped it down upon the table in front of him. "Listen to this: 'You will see me when all is ready. Come at once. F. H. M.' Now my theory all along has been that Lady St. Simon was decoyed away by Flora Millar, and that she, with confederates, no doubt, was responsible for her disappearance. Here, signed with her initials, is the very note which was no doubt quietly slipped into her hand at the door, and which lured her within their reach."

"Very good, Lestrade," said Holmes, laughing. "You really are very fine indeed. Let me see it." He took up the paper in a listless way, but his attention instantly became riveted, and he gave a little cry of satisfaction. "This is indeed important," said he.

"Ha! you find it so?"

"Extremely so. I congratulate you warmly."

Lestrade rose in his triumph and bent his head to look. "Why," he shrieked, "you're looking at the wrong side!"

"On the contrary, this is the right side."

"The right side? You're mad! Here is the note written in pencil over here."

"And over here is what appears to be the fragment of a hotel bill, which interests me deeply."

"There's nothing in it. I looked at it before," said Lestrade.

"'Oct. 4th, rooms 8s., breakfast 2s. 6d., cocktail 1s. 6d., lunch 2s. 6d., glass sherry 8d.' I see nothing in that."

"Very likely not. It is most important, all the same. As to the note, it is important also, or at least the initials are, so I congratulate you again."

"I've wasted time enough," said Lestrade, rising. "I believe in hard work, and not in sitting by the fire spinning fine theories. Good-day, Mr. Holmes, and we shall see which gets to the bottom of the matter first." He gathered up the garments, thrust them into the bag, and made for the door.

"Just one hint to you, Lestrade," drawled Holmes, before his rival vanished; "I will tell you the true solution of the matter. Lady St. Simon is a myth. There is not, and there never has been any such person."

Lestrade looked sadly at my companion. Then he turned to me, tapped his forehead three times, shook his head solemnly, and hurried away.

He had hardly shut the door behind him when Holmes rose and put on his overcoat. "There is something in what the fellow says about out-door work," he remarked, "so I think, Watson, that I must leave you to your papers for a little."

It was after five o'clock when Sherlock Holmes left me, but I had no time to be lonely, for within an hour there arrived a confectioner's man with a very large flat box. This he unpacked with the help of a youth whom he had brought with him, and presently, to my very great astonishment, a quite epicurean little cold supper began to be laid out upon our humble lodging-house mahogany. There were a couple of brace of cold woodcock, a pheasant, a *pâté de foie gras* pie, with a group of ancient and cobwebby bottles. Having laid out all these luxuries, my two visitors vanished away, like the genii of the Arabian Nights, with no explanation save that the things had been paid for and were ordered to this address.

Just before nine o'clock Sherlock Holmes stepped briskly into the room. His features were gravely set, but there was a light in his eye which made me think that he had not been disappointed in his conclusions.

"They have laid the supper, then," he said, rubbing his hands.

"You seem to expect company. They have laid for five."

"Yes, I fancy we may have some company dropping in," said he. "I am surprised that Lord St. Simon has not already arrived. Ha! I fancy that I hear his step now upon the stairs."

It was indeed our visitor of the morning who came bustling in, dangling his glasses more vigorously than ever, and with a very perturbed expression upon his aristocratic features.

"My messenger reached you, then?" asked Holmes.

"Yes, and I confess that the contents startled me beyond measure. Have you good authority for what you say?"

"The best possible."

Lord St. Simon sank into a chair and passed his hand over his forehead.

"What will the duke say," he murmured, "when he hears that one of the family has been subjected to such humiliation?"

"It is the purest accident. I cannot allow that there is any humiliation."

"Ah, you look on these things from another standpoint."

"I fail to see that any one is to blame. I can hardly see how the lady could have acted otherwise, though her abrupt method of doing it was undoubtedly to be regretted. Having no mother, she had no one to advise her at such a crisis."

"It was a slight, sir, a public slight," said Lord St. Simon, tapping his fingers upon the table.

"You must make allowance for this poor girl, placed in so unprecedented a position."

"I will make no allowance. I am very angry indeed, and I have been shamefully used."

"I think that I heard a ring," said Holmes. "Yes, there are steps on the landing. If I cannot persuade you to take a lenient view of the matter, Lord St. Simon, I have brought an advocate here who may be more successful." He opened the door and ushered in a lady and gentleman. "Lord St. Simon," said he, "allow me to introduce you to Mr. and Mrs. Francis Hay Moulton. The lady, I think, you have already met."

At the sight of these new-comers our client had sprung from his seat and stood very erect, with his eyes cast down and his hand thrust into the breast of his frock-coat, a picture of offended dignity. The lady had taken a quick step forward and had held out her hand to him, but he still refused to raise his eyes. It was as well for his resolution, perhaps, for her pleading face was one which it was hard to resist.

"You're angry, Robert," said she. "Well, I guess you have every cause to be."

"Pray make no apology to me," said Lord St. Simon bitterly.

"Oh yes, I know that I have treated you real bad, and that I should have spoken to you before I went; but I was kind of rattled, and from the time when I saw Frank here again I just didn't know what I was doing or saying. I only wonder I didn't fall down and do a faint right there before the altar."

"Perhaps, Mrs. Moulton, you would like my friend and me to leave the room while you explain this matter?"

"If I may give an opinion," remarked the strange gentleman, "we've had just a little too much secrecy over this business already. For my part, I should like all Europe and America to hear the rights of it." He was a small, wiry, sunburnt man, clean shaven, with a sharp face and alert manner.

"Then I'll tell our story right away," said the lady. "Frank here and I met in '84, in McQuire's camp, near the Rockies, where pa was working a claim. We were engaged to each other, Frank and I; but then one day father struck a rich pocket and made a pile, while poor Frank here had a claim that petered out and came to nothing. The richer pa grew, the poorer was Frank; so at last pa wouldn't hear of our engagement lasting any longer, and he took me away to 'Frisco. Frank wouldn't throw up his hand, though; so he followed me there, and he saw me without pa knowing anything about it. It would only have made him mad to know, so we just fixed it all up for ourselves. Frank said that he would go and make his pile, too, and never come back to claim me until he had as much as pa. So then I promised to wait for him to the end of time, and pledged myself not to marry any one else while he lived. 'Why shouldn't we be married right away, then,' said he, 'and then I will feel sure of you; and I won't claim to be your husband until I come back?' Well, we talked it over, and he had fixed it all up so nicely, with a clergyman all ready in waiting, that we just did it right there; and then Frank went off to seek his fortune, and I went back to pa.

"The next I heard of Frank was that he was in Montana, and then he went prospecting in Arizona, and then I heard of him from New Mexico. After that came a long newspaper story about how a miners' camp had been attacked by Apache Indians, and there was my Frank's name among the killed. I fainted dead away, and I was very sick for months after. Pa thought I had a decline, and took me to half the doctors in 'Frisco. Not a word of news came for a year and more, so that I never doubted that Frank was really dead. Then Lord St. Simon came to 'Frisco, and we came to London and a wedding was arranged, and pa was very pleased, but I felt all the time that no man on this earth would ever take the place in my heart that had been given to my poor Frank.

"Still, if I had married Lord St. Simon, of course I'd have done my duty by him. We can't command our love, but we can our actions. I went to the altar with him with the intention to make him just as good a wife as it was in me to be. But you may imagine what I felt when, just as I came to the altar rails, I glanced back and saw Frank standing and looking at me out of the first pew. I thought it was his ghost at first; but when I looked again, there he was still, with a kind of question in his eyes as if to ask me whether I were glad or sorry to see him. I wonder I didn't drop. I know that everything was turning round, and the words of the clergyman were just like the buzz of a bee in my ear. I didn't know what to do. Should I stop the service and make a scene in the church? I glanced at him again, and he seemed to know what I was thinking, for he raised his finger to his lips to tell me to be still. Then I saw him scribble on a piece of paper, and I knew that he was writing me a note. As I passed his pew on the way out I dropped my bouquet over to him, and he slipped the note into my hand when he returned me the flowers. It was only a line asking me to join him when he made the sign to me to do so. Of course I never doubted for a moment that my first duty was now to him, and I determined to do just whatever he might direct.

"When I got back I told my maid, who had known him in California, and had always been his friend. I ordered her to say nothing, but to get a few things packed and my ulster ready. I know I ought to have spoken to Lord St. Simon, but it was dreadful hard before his mother and all those great people. I just made up my mind to run away and explain afterwards. I hadn't been at the table ten minutes before I saw Frank out of the window at the other side of the road. He beckoned to me, and then began walking into the Park. I slipped out, put on my things, and followed him. Some woman came talking something or other about Lord St. Simon to me—seemed to me from the little I heard as if he had a little secret of his own before marriage also—but I managed to get away from her, and soon overtook Frank. We got into a cab together, and away we drove to some lodgings he had taken in Gordon Square, and that was my true wedding after all those years of waiting. Frank had been a prisoner among the Apaches, had escaped, came on to 'Frisco, found that I had given him up for dead and had gone to England, followed me there, and had come upon me at last on the very morning of my second wedding."

"I saw it in a paper," explained the American. "It gave the name and the church, but not where the lady lived."

"Then we had a talk as to what we should do, and Frank was all for openness, but I was so ashamed of it all that I felt as if I should like to vanish away and never see any of them again—just sending a line to pa, perhaps, to show him that I was alive. It was awful to me to think of all those lords and ladies sitting round that breakfast-table and waiting for me to come back. So Frank took my wedding-clothes and things and made a bundle of them, so that I should not be traced, and dropped them away somewhere where no one could find them. It is likely that we should have gone on to Paris tomorrow, only that this good gentleman, Mr. Holmes, came round to us this evening, though how he found us is more than I can think, and he showed us very clearly and kindly that I was wrong and that Frank was right, and that we should be putting ourselves in the wrong if we were so secret. Then he offered to give us a chance of talking to Lord St. Simon alone, and so we came right away round to his rooms at once. Now, Robert, you have heard it all, and I am very sorry if I have given you pain and I hope that you do not think very meanly of me."

Lord St. Simon had by no means relaxed his rigid attitude, but had listened with a frowning brow and a compressed lip to this long narrative.

"Excuse me," he said, "but it is not my custom to discuss my most intimate personal affairs in this public manner."

"Then you won't forgive me? You won't shake hands before I go?"

"Oh, certainly, if it would give you any pleasure." He put out his hand and coldly grasped that which she extended to him.

"I had hoped," suggested Holmes, "that you would have joined us in a friendly supper."

"I think that there you ask a little too much," responded his lordship. "I may be forced to acquiesce in these recent developments, but I can hardly be expected to make merry over them. I think that, with your permission, I will now wish you all a very good night." He included us all in a sweeping bow and stalked out of the room.

"Then I trust that you at least will honor me with your company," said Sherlock Holmes. "It is always a joy to meet an American, Mr. Moulton, for I am one of those who believe that the folly of a monarch and the blundering of a minister in far-gone years will not prevent our children from being some day citizens of the same world-wide country under a flag which shall be a quartering of the Union Jack with the Stars and Stripes."

"THE case has been an interesting one," remarked Holmes, when our visitors had left us, "because it serves to show very clearly how simple the explanation may be of an affair which at first sight seems to be almost inexplicable. Nothing could be more natural than the sequence of events as narrated by this lady, and nothing stranger than the result when viewed, for instance, by Mr. Lestrade, of Scotland Yard."

"You were not yourself at fault at all, then?"

"From the first, two facts were very obvious to me, the one that the lady had been quite willing to undergo the wedding ceremony, the other that she had repented of it within a few minutes of returning home. Obviously something had occurred during the morning, then, to cause her to change her mind. What could that something be? She could not have spoken to any one when she was out, for she had been in the company of the bridegroom. Had she seen some one, then? If she had, it must be some one from America, because she had spent so short a

time in this country that she could hardly have allowed any one to acquire so deep an influence over her that the mere sight of him would induce her to change her plans so completely. You see we have already arrived, by a process of exclusion, at the idea that she might have seen an American. Then who could this American be, and why should he possess so much influence over her? It might be a lover; it might be a husband. Her young womanhood had, I knew, been spent in rough scenes and under strange conditions. So far I had got before I ever heard Lord St. Simon's narrative. When he told us of a man in a pew, of the change in the bride's manner, of so transparent a device for obtaining a note as the dropping of a bouquet, of her resort to her confidential maid, and of her very significant allusion to claim-jumping—which in miners' parlance means taking possession of that which another person has a prior claim to—the whole situation became absolutely clear. She had gone off with a man, and the man was either a lover or was a previous husband —the chances being in favor of the latter."

"And how in the world did you find them?"

"It might have been difficult, but friend Lestrade held information in his hands the value of which he did not himself know. The initials were of course of the highest importance, but more valuable still was it to know that within a week he had settled his bill at one of the most select London hotels."

"How did you deduce the select?"

"By the select prices. Eight shillings for a bed and eight-pence for a glass of sherry pointed to one of the most expensive hotels. There are not many in London which charge at that rate. In the second one which I visited in Northumberland Avenue, I learned by an inspection of the book that Francis H. Moulton, an American gentleman, had left only the day before, and on looking over the entries against him, I came upon the very items which I had seen in the duplicate bill. His letters were to be forwarded to 226 Gordon Square; so thither I travelled, and being fortunate enough to find the loving couple at home, I ventured to give them some paternal advice, and to point out to them that it would be better in every way that they should make their position a little clearer both to the general public and to Lord St. Simon in particular. I invited them to meet him here, and, as you see, I made him keep the appointment."

"But with no very good result," I remarked. "His conduct was certainly not very gracious."

"Ah, Watson," said Holmes, smiling, "perhaps you would not be very gracious either, if, after all the trouble of wooing and wedding, you found yourself deprived in an instant of wife and of fortune. I think that we may judge Lord St. Simon very mercifully, and thank our stars that we are never likely to find ourselves in the same position. Draw your chair up and hand me my violin, for the only problem we have still to solve is how to while away these bleak autumnal evenings."

Andrew Jay Peck, editor and publisher of the Sherlockian journal The Commonplace Book, comments: "While 'The Noble Bachelor'—with its references to mining, 'claim-jumping,' Indians and the Wild West—may be the favorite American Holmes story, another, 'His Last Bow' (chronologically the last short story in the Holmes canon), is also replete with American references. Indeed, it is the only recorded proof of Holmes's travels in America. In it, in order to trap the German spy Von Bork (the tale anticipates, by its 1914 setting, World War I), Holmes assumed the guise of Altamont, an Irish American. He reported to Watson: 'When I say that I started my pilgrimage at Chicago, graduated in an Irish secret society at Buffalo, gave serious trouble to the constabulary at Skibbareen and so eventually caught the eye of a subordinate agent of Von Bork, who recommended me as a likely man, you will realize that the matter was complex.'

The inclusion of "The Adventure of the Noble Bachelor" at book's end provides an appropriate and convenient example of the real, right thing against which all the burlesques, parodies, and pastiches in this volume can be readily measured. Hopefully, any person not yet familiar with Doyle's steadfast characters in prose action (if one can conceive of such a phenomenon among the functionally literate in this country), and who does actually encounter them first here, will surely and speedily rectify his or her previous omission by seizing upon the complete sacred works, in a word, instanter.

ENVOI

Again, in yet another book, the door to 221b closes—having this time released the golden lamplight of a host of American Sherlockian fancies unseen and unheard of since their first fleeting appearances over the ninety years since 1891, together with other, long-fabled but seldom accessible Holmesian tributes from a dozen dusty corners of America's publishing past.

In the envoi, that last glimmer between the fore-edge and jamb, however, it is appropriate to mention some small part of the American Sherlockiana which was not included, either for want of space or want of requisite *in*accessibility. Among these unadmitted items, obviously, are such well-known Sherlockian pastiches and burlesques as Mark Twain's "A Double-Barreled Detective Story," 1902; Bret Harte's "The Stolen Cigar Case," in *Condensed Novels: Second Series,* 1902; August Derleth's "Solar Pons" series published by Mycroft & Moran between 1949 and 1975; and others—including, of course, the marvelous multitude of works produced by America's Baker Street Irregulars and their confreres within a long series of books, pamphlets, and periodicals since the mid-1930s. The above-cited titles and much of the other material can readily be found in any well-stocked public library or acquired via interlibrary loan; more ambitious readers can ferret out and buy many of the works themselves through used-book dealers. In a few instances, certain virtually unknown items were regretfully omitted from *Sherlock Holmes in America* despite their famed sources because of the tenuousness of their Sherlockian content. Typical here was a brief Dashiell Hammett article from the *Smart Set* magazine for January 1923 called "The Master Mind," in which Sherlock Holmes was mentioned amusingly, but irrelevantly for the purposes of the present volume.

The final line of light in the door frame, as fine as a hair from the head of Irene Adler, flits out—and the Baker Street demesne is shut. But there is still a bit more to say....

It is unlikely that this work would have existed in anything like its present form had it not been for the literally endless and painstaking winnowing of the millions of thickly printed pages in a hundred bound newspaper runs from 1890 to date by the staff of the indefatigable San Francisco Academy of Comic Art. In the still-ongoing process of culling these ceiling-high stacks of yester-

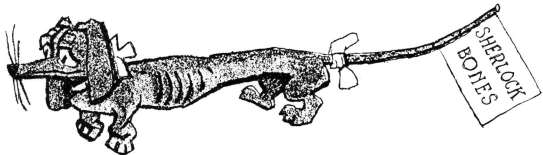

day's newspapers, the academy staff maintains a regularly augmented file of Sherlockiana and Doyleana that has now blossomed to some fifteen fat folders of slippings and photocopies from innumerable other sources as well. The bulk of the preceding pages has been selected from the contents of these

Two early-twentieth-century comics characters: Above, at left, is artist Jacob Myer's Sheerluck Holmes, *excerpted here from a panel in the nationally distributed Keystone Syndicate comic section for July 14, 1907. Following some static from American Doyle representatives, Myer's 1906–7 Sunday half-page strip was renamed* Sheerluck Homes. *The worried-looking dachshund below Sheerluck is a creation of the accomplished German American abstract painter Lyonel Feininger, a noted cartoonist in his youth. Sherlock Bones, a character in the artist's* The Kin-der-Kids, *created for the Sunday Chicago Tribune, is taken here from a large 1906 Feininger illustration presenting the strip's personae.*

ever-filling folders; the remaining items have largely come from books and periodicals in the academy's Sherlockian reference library.

However, much help in rounding off the book's contents and adding to its presentation of Yankee Sherlockiana (particularly with regard to recent items of theatrical and cinematic import) must gratefully be credited to such eminent Sherlockians and bookmen as Dean Dickensheet (whose prefatory essay opens this work in regulation Irregularity), Andrew Jay Peck, Jerry Margolin, Paul Oakley, and Bob De Frantz. Additional thanks (and great credit) are due to Donn Teal, whose literally total devotion to the technical editing of the foregoing mass of highly recalcitrant odds and ends of everything from everywhere has to have been experienced to be fully appreciated, and to the exceptionally gifted Judith Michael, who laid out this jigsaw of art cuts and texts of impossibly variegated sizes and forms over a period of many painstaking months. A final note of thanks is also to be accorded Margaret L. Kaplan, whose editorial acumen and foresight made this book possible from the outset.

© 1932 New York Herald Tribune

This remarkable and solitary limning of Holmes and Watson themselves by H. T. Webster—saved to follow, and top, the cartoonist's eight shown in the "Comic Strips and Cartoons" section of the book—appeared nationally through the auspices of the New York Herald Tribune syndicate on October 24, 1932.

None of the material in the editor's introductory commentary to each section of the book, or in his running-commentary captions throughout, has been included in the following index; nor has material from Dean Dickensheet's foreword or from the editor's introduction or envoi; nor have Arthur Conan Doyle or any of the characters in Doyle's Holmes stories been indexed. A further note: Indexed artwork, or illustration, has not been given an italic page or picture number, but simply a roman page number as with printed textual materials.

Five (hopefully helpful) major entries are included in the index: an "artists" entry and a "writers" entry; a "product advertisements" entry; an "illustrations (story)" entry, locating the illustrative art for the many Sherlock Holmes adventures; and a "surrogate Holmeses" entry, should you wish to locate Sheerluck Holmes or Timelock Foams or any of their cartoon or burlesque confreres by name rather than by author or comic/story title.

PERMISSIONS ACKNOWLEDGMENTS

Permission is gratefully acknowledged for the use of the following materials:

"Bowling Green" column excerpts from *The Saturday Review* for 1934 by Christopher Morley are all copyright © 1934 by Saturday Review. All rights reserved. Reprinted with permission.

"The Curious Incident of the Dogs in the Night-Time," by Wolcott Gibbs, originally published in *The New Yorker* for September 18, 1948. From *More in Sorrow* (Henry Holt); © 1948, 1976 Wolcott Gibbs.

Gahan Wilson's cartoons are reprinted from *Playboy Magazine* and the book *Playboy's Gahan Wilson,* with all copyrights held by Playboy Magazine; and are reprinted here with the permission of Playboy Magazine.

"In Praise of Sherlock Holmes," by Vincent Starrett, from *Reedy's Mirror* for February 22, 1918; reprinted by *The Baker Street Journal* for March 1968. Reprinted here by permission of Michael Murphy for the Starrett estate.

"My First Meeting with Sherlock Holmes," by Frederic Dorr Steele, from *The Baker Street Journal,* vol. 4, no. 1 (1949). Reprinted by permission of The Baker Street Journal.

"Sherlock Holmes in Pictures," by Frederic Dorr Steele, from *The New Yorker* for May 22, 1937. Reprinted by permission; © 1937, 1965 The New Yorker Magazine, Inc.

"221-B," by Vincent Starrett; copyright 1945 by Vincent Starrett. Reprinted by permission of Michael Murphy for the Starrett estate.

Comic-strip and cartoon permissions are individually credited in the captions for each copyrighted example that is reprinted herein; these are reprinted, as acknowledged, by courtesy of: Adventure Feature Syndicate, Chicago Tribune–New York News Syndicate, Classic Comics, Inc., Field Newspaper Syndicate, H. C. Fisher, International Herald Tribune Corporation, King Features Syndicate, The Los Angeles Times, United Features Syndicate, Walt Disney Productions, and The Washington Post.

Note: Every effort has been made to locate copyright holders for material in these pages that was originally published in now long-defunct magazines or distributed by long-dismantled news- or feature-syndicating organizations; author and estate pursuit has also been undertaken. Where no permissions acknowledgment has been given, the material has either been determined to be out of copyright, to have never been copyrighted (as in the case of most newspaper material), or to have proven untraceable to such present holders of copyright as may exist.

© 1964 United Features Syndicate

Charles Schulz's Snoopy—whose name is itself a pejorative for detective work—goes Holmesian in this August 28, 1964, episode of Peanuts. *For this book's last graphic bow (wow), today's comics' foremost dog ponders the classic hound of literature.*